The Violin Lesson

by Simon Fischer

A manual for
teaching and
self-teaching
the violin

LONDON·FRANKFURT·LEIPZIG·NEW YORK

Peters Edition Limited
2–6 Baches Street
London
N1 6DN

First published 2013

© Copyright 2013 by Peters Edition Limited, London

ISMN 979-0-57708-896-9

A catalogue record for this book is available from the British Library

Cover image: Violin and Checkerboard, 1913 (oil on canvas): Juan Gris (1887–1927)

With thanks to Jennifer King, who modelled for the photographs.

Also by Simon Fischer:

EP 7440   Basics
300 exercises and practice routines for the violinist

EP 7578   Practice
250 step-by-step practice methods for the violin

EP 71908   Scales
Scales and scale studies for the violin

Copyright Acknowledgements

Bartók: First Rhapsody

© Copyright 1929 by Hawkes & Son (London) Ltd. Reproduced by permission of Boosey & Hawkes Music Publishers Ltd.

Britten: Simple Symphony

© Copyright 1935 by The Britten Estate Limited. Publishing rights licensed worldwide to Chester Music Limited. All Rights Reserved. International Copyright Secured. Used by permission.

Kabalevsky: Concerto in C

© Copyright 1948 by Boosey & Hawkes Music Publishers Ltd for the United Kingdom and Republic of Ireland. Reproduced by permission of Boosey & Hawkes Music Publishers Ltd.

Kreisler: Praeludium and Allegro

© 1910 Schott Music, Mainz - Germany. © renewed 1938. Reproduced by permission. All rights reserved.

Prokofiev: Sonata no. 2 in D, op. 94

© Copyright by Boosey & Hawkes Music Publishers Ltd for the UK, British Commonwealth (ex Canada), Eire and South Africa. Reproduced by permission of Boosey & Hawkes Music Publishers Ltd.

Provost, Heinz: Intermezzo

© Gehrmans Musikforlag AB. Reproduced by permission.

Schnittke: Suite in the Old Style

© Copyright by Musikverlag Hans Sikorski, Hamburg. Sole publisher for the UK, British Commonwealth (ex Canada), Eire and South Africa: Boosey & Hawkes Music Publishers Ltd. Reproduced by permission of Boosey & Hawkes Music Publishers Ltd.

Sibelius: Concerto in D minor, op. 47

© 1905 by Robert Lienau Publ., Germany. Reproduced by permission.

Tartini-Kreisler: Variations on a theme of Corelli

© 1910 Schott Music, Mainz - Germany. © renewed 1938. Reproduced by permission. All rights reserved.

Contents

lesson 1   The tone production lesson   1

lesson 2   Holding the violin and bow   27

lesson 3 The intonation lesson   55

Lesson 5   Setting up the bow arm   117

lesson 6 Setting up the left hand 133

lesson 7 Avoiding aches and pains   163

lesson 8   Background essentials 2   205

lesson 9   All about changing position   231

lesson 10   The vibrato lesson   249

lesson 11 Improving key bow strokes   261

lesson 12   Background essentials 3   301

Introduction

The idea for *The Violin Lesson* came one Christmas after going to a concert performance of Puccini's *Madame Butterfly* in London. I was sitting quite near to the front and could not help noticing a violinist in the orchestra who was directly in my line of vision, a woman in her early twenties. At first, I thought she was a former student of mine. I later found out that the two women are often mistaken for each other in the London orchestral scene.

I could see in detail how she was playing. The way she was holding the violin, and using the bow, was clearly making things more difficult for her than necessary. I thought of how easy it would be to help her, perhaps because I had seen her 'twin' become a much better player by making the same changes that this woman could make.

It seemed sad that all she needed was one or two lessons in which to learn some simple things that she had missed so far – not the whole story of violin playing, from beginning to end, but a few important points and basic principles that would help her greatly.

It would take only a couple of minutes to explain how everything was a question of getting the right proportions (*The magic word*, page 96), and that she should hold the violin a little more in front of her because of her short arms; or how, if she kept her left fingers closer to the strings her finger action would be easier.

Her bow was constantly too near the fingerboard. I thought of how quickly she could improve her sound and feel for the instrument if she practised the *Five essential tone-production exercises* (page 11). They take only seconds to demonstrate, almost anybody can do them at once whatever their standard, and the improvement in tone is always immediate.

Yet I had no way of helping her; and solving her problems would not help the many other violinists around the world who were in exactly the same position as her – one or two really quite simple steps away from a very different experience of playing the violin.

The answer seemed clear: if she needed to know only a few basic things, and if just a few lessons would be enough, it should be possible to jot the basic ideas down on only a few sheets of paper. Then she would be able to go away and sort it all out for herself in her own time.

The subjects in the first few chapters of the book immediately fell into a logical order. However, what if the same player returned for another series of lessons? What would the typical subjects be then? What if they came for a whole course of 12 lessons?

The division of *The Violin Lesson* into 12 is naturally only a starting-point. Working with an advanced student, and in a session that lasts a couple of hours, it is possible to cover much of the material of each 'lesson' in a single session. Working with less advanced students, a single point from one of the lessons, or from the *Background essentials*, may be all that is covered in one actual violin lesson.

The science of violin playing

To develop technique on the violin you have to learn the Science of Violin Playing. But this must not be confused with studying 'real' sciences like physics, chemistry, biology, DNA and so on. Any field like these is obviously a lifetime's work, and however much you know is only ever a tiny speck compared to the amount you do not know – even if you study all day, every day, for 50 years. In comparison, the entire science of violin playing *is* only the size of a tiny speck.

You cannot study for the rest of your life how to draw a straight bow; or study how to raise and drop the fingers, how to shift, vibrate and so on. There simply isn't that much to learn. You can study *music* for the rest of your life – and after fifty years, the amount you know about music will be only a tiny speck compared to what you do not know – but that is a different matter.

On a practical, physical level of violin technique, there is not so much to know about. There are all the things you have got to learn *to* do; and all the things to learn *not* to do. Yet all this amounts to only a few principles about how to hold the instrument and bow, how to use each hand in all the various ways, and so on. The list of 'things you need to know and do' is not endless, and is not even very long.

The Violin Lesson covers the main areas where you can easily and noticeably make a difference. While not every subject is for everyone, *The Violin Lesson* has something in it for every level and type of player – elementary or advanced, amateur or professional, teacher or student.

Can you improve your playing by reading a book?

No book can replace a teacher or the living, practical experience of playing or listening to music. But gaining information from a book, or gaining that information through having somebody listen to you play and then saying those same things to you, can often be the same thing in the end.

If you want to change the way you play the violin, you have to change the way you *think* about playing the violin. You can do that by practising or by going to a concert, and by many other means; but reading about, say, tone production, can so change your picture of bowing the string that your whole approach changes immediately and dramatically – even before you have actually put the bow on the string and started to try things out.

 But the points in a book can only be general ones. In a lesson the teacher deals with your specific, individual needs.

Everyone has their own unique set of physical, technical and musical characteristics, their own particular gifts, problems, strengths and weaknesses; yet the same technical and musical points tend to appear again and again, and in the same way, in most players.

- Typical technical points in the left arm include freeing the thumb; moving the fingers freely from the base joints, without partly moving them from the hand or forearm; widening the hand at the base joints, rather than contracting; fingers remaining light without over-pressing; co-ordination, and the fundamentals of vibrato, intonation, shifting and so on.

- Typical technical points in the right arm include the basics of how to make a pure and expressive tone; fundamentals of the bow hold; the mechanics of drawing a straight bow; how to improve key strokes like *spiccato* or *martelé*, and so on.

There are actually quite a limited number of technical problems that you can have, and they tend to crop up in the same ways all the time. So the topics and issues that are explored in *The Violin Lesson* may easily be exactly those that you need to explore yourself.

Suppose your left hand does not feel comfortable. You do not necessarily need someone to look at what you, specifically, are doing, and make suggestions that are tailored only to you. The same principles are going to apply to you as to anyone else.

Building a good left hand position, or strengthening intonation, or developing tone or vibrato, or gaining confidence in shifting, is almost entirely the same process whoever you are, and whatever your age or standard.

I'm too old – you can't improve at my age

It used to be said that unless you had fully developed your violin technique by the time you were twenty or so, it would be too late. After that, the entire process of learning becomes slow and difficult, it was thought, and you stand little chance of making further progress.

Johann Quantz expressed this in 1752:

[1] Johann Joachim Quantz: *Essay of a Method for Playing the Transverse Flute* (Berlin 1752; trans. Edward R. Reilly, London, 1966), 24.

> He who wishes to distinguish himself in music must not begin the study of it too late. If he sets about it at an age when his energies are no longer vigorous, or when his throat or fingers are no longer flexible, and thus cannot acquire sufficient facility to perform…the passage-work roundly and distinctly, he will not go very far.[1]

[2] See *The magic word*, page 96

The truth is that you can improve your playing at any age. 'Improving' means changing the way you play Everything in violin technique can be described, and the language used to describe it is all about proportions: how much of this, in proportion to how much of that.[2]

To change the way you play, first you must know what all the different things are that can be measured in proportion to one another. (It is no use knowing only that the recipe for a cake is made up of certain proportions. You need to know what the ingredients are in the first place.)

Then, making every change by altering the proportions of one thing to another, you can build changes into your playing at any age whatsoever.

 Q **What are some examples of changing certain actions, to improve your playing, that you could do if you were, say, fifty?**

To change from banging fingers down onto the string and then pressing the string hard into the fingerboard, and instead to place the fingers gently and to feel the springiness of the string, is something you can introduce into your playing at any age and immediately notice the difference.

- At any age and stage, you can change from playing everything with the bow too near to the fingerboard, to playing a little nearer to the bridge where the string has greater tension

- Or find a new feeling of release and lightness in the left hand by stopping squeezing the neck hard between the fingers and thumb

- Or start to encourage a feeling of forward–forward–forward–forward in the vibrato movement instead of forward–back–forward–back

- Or refine your intonation by tuning all your Gs, Ds, As and Es to the open strings, and by measuring all the sharps from the natural above, and the flats from the natural below

- Or stop extra, unnecessary physical motions that get in the way of everything else; and so on.

All of these changes are perfectly easy to make, and anyone can make them. There is no special aptitude or talent required to feel such things as the difference between the give of the bow at the heel and at the point; or to feel how you can *balance* the bow in your hand (when appropriate) rather than *hold* it; or to experiment with a new arrangement of the fingers on the bow; or to do anything else.

You simply need to know exactly what you are doing; what to do and what *not* to do; make simple changes; and then continue in the new way until the changes become new habits and 'stick' without your having to think about them. In just a few lessons or a few days, an adult violinist – amateur, student or professional – can change their playing as much as an unfocused child may do in months or years.

 Q **But don't children learn much faster than adults?**

Obviously, young children can learn a foreign language without even noticing; their muscles are marvellously soft and responsive; every stage of their learning traces a brand-new path, without conflicts or confusions with previous paths; learning takes place on the deepest level of the psyche, rather than having first to be processed by the intellect.

It is common for a 10-year-old to be able to master difficult virtuosic pieces after playing for five years or less, but not so common for an adult who has taken up the violin at a late age.

Yet in a lot of ways, as an adult, you can learn and improve your playing just as quickly as a child, and in many cases much faster. You are able to measure, which is a skill young children develop only gradually. You have the benefit of the general life experience that the child has not had, so you can make connections that they cannot make; and you have the powers of reason, self-motivation and will.

You can be clear about where you are now, clear about where you want to be in the future, and take steps to move from here to there.

Not just trying harder

Simply trying harder often makes things worse. Everything is a matter of cause and effect, which means that for every specific action there is a specific reaction. If you carry on performing the same actions, you can expect to keep getting the same reactions or results.

In other words, if you carry on doing what you are already doing, you just get more of what you are already getting. Then, if you try harder, you just get even more of what you are already getting. Instead, the answer is always to *change* something. The slightest change in what you are doing, or how you are doing it, will always bring about a completely new result.[1]

[1] Albert Einstein said: "The definition of insanity is to do the same thing in the same way, over and over again, and expect a different result."

A useful catch-phrase commonly used in everything from sport to business: "Do not work harder, work smarter!"

See also
The importance of making mistakes, page 333

[1] See *Which part of the fingertip?*, page 253

For example, the tiniest change in the exact area of the fingertip that contacts the string, changes the character of the vibrato. Instead of continuing to put the finger down on the string on the same part of the fingertip each time, and trying harder to make different colours, all you have to do is put the finger down a little flatter (Fig. 1a), or a little more upright (Fig. 1b).[1]

Fig. 1

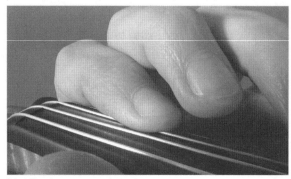 

(a) Vibrating more on the pad   (b) Vibrating more on the tip

Advancing without improving

The danger to avoid is that you play more and more difficult pieces, but the way you play them, or the way you approach the instrument, remains the same.

The path many students follow is like this: at age 11 they are playing elementary or intermediate-level repertoire without good listening, not quite in tune, their fingers moving out to the left instead of hovering above the strings, the bow always too near the fingerboard without producing sonority, and so on.

Over the years they learn pieces of ever-increasing difficulty until they reach age 18 and are now playing advanced repertoire – but still without good listening, not quite in tune, fingers not above the strings, the bow too far from the bridge, and so on. They are playing more advanced pieces but they have not improved.

Finding the single most important next step to take

The three-stage process

- If you are practising, how can you be certain of making the fastest possible progress?

- If you are teaching, how can you be certain of your students making the fastest possible progress?

When someone stands in front of you and plays the violin, a huge amount of information floods towards you: aural, visual, physical, musical, technical, emotional, intellectual, and so on. It is similar when you are practising: there is a lot going on and you are right in the middle of it all.

There is always one question to ask: what is the single most important next step for your student, or yourself, to take? Then, what is the second most important, and so on.

Whether you are teaching or practising, there is a simple three-stage process to follow:

1 The first thing is to notice everything. You have to hear, see, and sense everything that is happening in the playing – every detail of technique, expression, posture and so on – without missing a thing.

2 Then, from the mass of information received, you have to make a list of each musical, technical or other point that could be improved or helped in some way.

3 Then you have to sort that list into the right order of importance. Of all the things that could be improved or helped in some way, what is the most important thing to improve right now? What is the second most important thing to improve right now?

The fastest progress comes when you isolate and improve the most important point, and perhaps also the second and third most important points. Then, once progress has been made in those areas, they fall away and others take their place at the top of the list.

The challenge is to get the list into the right order. If you work hard on what should be steps 8, 9 and 10 because you think they are 1 or 2 or 3, progress may be slower than it could be.

The list may never be absolutely complete; and there is often more than one best possible order, and more than one best way to work. However, the more complete the list, and the better the judgement in deciding what is more important and what is less important, the faster the progress.

Knowing where to put the X

Spotting problems and solutions in violin playing is all about 'knowing where to put the X':

> There was once a nuclear power station that had developed a fault. The power output was slightly below normal but none of the plant's engineers could locate the source of the fault. So they called in a specialist.
>
> The specialist, a man in a white coat with a clipboard, wandered around taking notes. The control room contained a host of dials and meters and readout displays, all connected to equipment located around the plant. After a couple of hours the specialist took a piece of chalk out of his pocket and marked a large 'X' on one of the readout displays.
>
> 'Replace the unit linked to that display,' he told the management, 'and it will fix the problem.'
>
> They did as he suggested, and immediately the power output returned to 100%.
>
> A few days later the manager of the plant received the bill from the specialist, who was asking for a fee of $10,000.
>
> Now although this was a multi-million dollar plant, it was the manager's job to keep down expenses. So he wrote back to the specialist thanking him for his work, but saying that $10,000 seemed a very high amount to charge considering he had been at the plant for only two hours. Would he please itemise his bill?
>
> Some days later a new bill arrived from the specialist, and this time he had broken it into two parts: $100 for time spent on the premises; $9,900 for knowing where to put the X.[1]

Around the time when I first heard this story I was scanning quickly through an article about cello playing in a strings magazine when a particular paragraph caught my eye. The writer said that if you do such-and-such with somebody's technique, you will cause problems which may take years to fix.

It is difficult not to think: yes, if you don't know where to put the 'X', it probably would take years to fix. But if you *do* know where to put the 'X' wouldn't it take weeks, days or even minutes to fix?

Noticing everything: blind spots

If you do not notice details of posture, technique, musicianship and so on, crucial items may not even get on the list, never mind in the right order of importance. If you are not to miss anything, it means you have to be completely free of any type of 'blind spot'.[2]

If you do not know about details of technique or music, important subjects may again be missed off the list entirely. Although the facts are there straight in front of you, you do not perceive them because you do not know what to look for, or what they look like.[3]

One problem is that when we look intently in one direction, it is like using a small flashlight in a dark room. You point it one way, and everything in that area is lit up, but everywhere else is dark. You point the flashlight in another direction. Now the area that you could see a moment ago is dark, and a new area is lit up.

For example, there are two blind spots that often set in at the beginning of learning to play, because of all the attention on keeping the bow straight. At least as important as bowing parallel to the bridge is 1) how far is the bow from the bridge, and 2) pushing the wood of the bow down towards the string, i.e. not playing only horizontally 'along the string'.

Yet having learnt how to move the bow up and down along the string, a player may end up years later playing advanced pieces while still never really ever thinking about these other two factors.

After I had finished studying I sometimes went to New York for a few days to observe Dorothy DeLay teaching at the Juilliard School. In one of the brief chats we would often have between lessons, she asked me what I thought about a fault in the previous student's bow hold. I confessed that I had not particularly noticed the bow hold.

"You didn't notice THAT?!" she said, making her hand into the shape the student's hand had been in.

It was an embarrassing moment. I made a quick mental note at least to *try* never to be caught out like that again.

Aural blind spots

You can also have aural blind spots, or 'deaf spots', where you do not hear sounds that are right next to you and around you. Notes that are out of tune, 'bulge notes' (page 270), scratches and squeaks, acoustic beats (page 57) and lack of colour contrast (page 205) easily go unnoticed.

The American violinist Joseph Silverstein said that much playing and teaching is carried out on a visual rather than an aural basis, and that during lessons even he catches himself watching the hands and the bow, and forgets to hear the sound.

[1] Brian Tracy: *The Power of Clarity* (Illinois 2004).

[2] A formal word meaning 'blind spot' is 'scotoma' [sco-toe-ma]. A dictionary definition might be 'an area within the total field of vision in which your vision is weaker or completely absent'. In psychology it means a mental blind spot, an inability to see or understand certain matters.

[3] Therefore, the first thing is to make sure that there are no blank areas in your knowledge of the subject. Constantly add to your understanding of music and violin playing, in every way you can, by reading about players and teachers, studying technique books by Carl Flesch, Ivan Galamian, Demetrius Dounis *et al*, violin in hand; by going to concerts, listening to recordings, watching videos, and so on.

Sometimes, the more musically talented or inspired a player is, the worse their listening is. There are two clear reasons for this. First, if they experience the music intensely inside themselves, and get lost in their musical imagination, they may forget to 'hang their ears' on the actual sound.

Second, if too much (or any) of the musical expression ends up as expressive physical movements that have no effect on the instrument – for example, head or face movements, or moving the instrument or feet, and so on – the player may be disappointed when they listen to a recording of themselves, since none of these expressive movements are picked up by the microphone.[1]

[1] See *Localizing: the key to mastery*, page 198

The most common technical areas to check

One solution to the problem of blind spots is simply to keep checking everything anyway, just in case you can find something to adjust, even if at first you think that it is okay. You have to keep an eye on everything all at the same time.

Yfrah Neaman used to say that the sweep of your attention should be like radar which scans the entire 360° range without gaps through which an intruder could slip undetected. Your awareness must be in one instant on sound, in the next instant on intonation, in the next on the left hand, right hand, arms, fingers, vibrato, expression, phrasing, and so on, and all this within the space of a single second or less.

One reason why blind spots easily occur is because habits often develop very gradually. Having begun invisibly, by the time something is a constant feature of your playing you may have got used to it. It looks or feels 'normal', or a natural part of your own – or your student's – violinistic character.[2]

[2] A blind spot may also be caused by looking for the wrong thing. For example, you are searching in your house for a book. It has a blue cover, but you are mistakenly imagining a green cover. You look at the book many times when you are searching for it – it is sitting there, in front of your eyes – but it does not register because you have the wrong idea of what you are looking for.

In the same way, you can have an idea of what a bow arm or hand should, or should not, look like – or a concept of vibrato, intonation, projection, the rights or wrongs of posture, and so on – which completely blinds you to what is clearly there in front of your eyes. You do not see or hear what is there, because you are looking for something else.

Here is a list of some of the most common technical areas that should be checked regularly to make sure that they are in good working order. Check and re-check these areas, constantly experimenting with slight, subtle adjustments and noting the different results that you get.

General

- Feet positioned to provide a strong base and balance, with a feeling of the weight of the body going down through the feet into the floor

- Not gripping the violin hard between the chin and the collar bone

- Violin held up so that the strings are close to horizontal – sometimes slightly above, sometimes slightly below the level position

- Scroll pointing more to the left for longer arms; more towards the centre for shorter arms

- Chin more to the left of the tail-piece for longer arms; closer to it (or above it) for shorter arms

- Violin not too tilted

- Keeping the shoulders free

- Lengthening the back

Left hand

- Thumb not squeezing backwards or pressing against the neck

- Finger pressure on the string usually as light as possible

- Using the correct fingertip placement to create a comfortable hand shape

- Fourth finger base joint not sticking out

- Fingers moving from the base joints freely, without partly moving from the hand or forearm

- In low positions, using the side of the first finger to orientate the hand against the neck

- Fingers staying in the same shape, on or off the string, during simple up-and-down movements

- In low positions, the shape of the fingers changing from square to extended

- Wrist not pushing out as the third or fourth fingers descend onto the string

- Hand widening at the base joints, rather than the fingers squeezing sideways together

- Hand often based on an upper finger, the lower fingers reaching back – not always based on the lower finger, the upper ones stretching forwards

- Angle of left knuckle joints neither too parallel to the neck nor too steep

- Fingers staying close enough to the strings

- Perfect co-ordination, the left fingers always leading the bow

- Vibrato not too wide or slow

- Vibrato pitch throbbing up to the in-tune note, not going above it

- Only one active movement in the vibrato: forward, to the in-tune note

- The vibrating finger going slightly more heavily into the string on the forward motion and releasing on the backward motion, rather than having an equal weight forwards and backwards

- Changing fingertip placement for different colours of vibrato

- Vibrato not stopping on random notes

- The elbow always free under the violin

- The development of the trill

- Independence of the hands, so that the actions of the left fingers do not disturb the bow

Right hand

- Understanding the bow hand and bow arm (and left hand) in terms of balances and levers

- The role of each finger on the bow

- The hand soft, with every joint flexible and acting as a 'shock absorber'

- Thumb placed on the tip not on the pad

- Thumb curving out, not bent inwards

- First finger not too close to the second finger

- Knuckles not sticking up

- Second finger positioned opposite the thumb so that when the hand leans into the bow the second finger can exert leverage

- Suitable balances of speed, pressure and distance from the bridge

- Seamless connections between strokes

- For legato string crossing, keeping close to the string you are going to cross before beginning to move.

- Playing down into the springiness of the wood of the bow, not just 'horizontally along the string'

- The feeling of playing into the string at the heel (where the hair gives) in contrast to playing into the string at the point (where the hair is rigid and the wood gives in the middle of the bow)

- Feeling the momentum of the bow, with a sense of the bow leading the right hand rather than the other way round

- Sustaining evenly as you move from one area of the bow to another

- Bowing 'from the lower back' rather than trying just to move the arm

- Including forearm rotation as an intrinsic part of bowing, not just a part of string crossing

- Including making tonal colours from the hand as a normal part of bowing

The higher the standard the less obvious the next step

The higher the standard of playing, the more of a challenge it is to identify the next step. I often think of a concert I went to as a student at the Aspen Music Festival, in which a very good Russian violinist called Mark played the Strauss Sonata. Dorothy DeLay, Mark's teacher, was there too. Afterwards, when I was chatting with her about the concert, she asked:

"What do you think the most important next step is for Mark now, as a musician or as a violinist?"

I did not know what to say. He had a fabulous technique and had given a superb performance: it had been effortless playing, and really without technical blemish. Besides, it was the sort of convincing musical performance where you forget about technique because you are so involved in the music.

What was the next step for him to take? I felt so positive about the performance I could think of nothing whatsoever that could be better. So I felt relieved when Miss DeLay, seeing me pause, said that it had taken her the last three months, hearing Mark regularly each week, to work out what the most important next step was for him to take; but now, she said, finally she was sure that at last she had got it.

What was she going to say? I was fascinated to know what had taken her three whole months to decide. She was just about to continue and tell me, when someone approached us and interrupted the conversation. Unfortunately, the subject never arose again, and I never found out the answer.

How long realistically does it take to improve?

True stories: Jenny (less advanced)

Jenny had been playing the violin since 9, but because she had never thought she could take it up professionally she had not given much priority to it, and had concentrated on academic work instead. She got straight A's at high school, but by the time she left school, and started on her music degree course, she knew little repertoire and had had almost no performance experience.

She had played the elementary Accolay Concerto over and over again for years, using it as an audition piece for youth orchestras, but little else – one or two Kreutzer studies, one or two little pieces. Now 17, she was learning the Kabalevsky Concerto, and brought it to her first lesson:

Kabalevsky: Concerto in C, op. 48, *mov. 1, b. 9*

She did not have a good tone: she was bowing too far from the bridge throughout, and there was no real musical purpose or design in her use of the bow. She did not use much vibrato, and when she did vibrate it seemed mechanical rather than expressive.

__SEG1__

The tempo was too slow; and the rhythms in each phrase had no underlying pulse or musical expressiveness. The intonation was clearly Level 4 (unstructured and with mistakes) throughout.[1] This was the starting level of her playing at the beginning of that first lesson.

[1] *Four levels of intonation,* page 55

The first thing we did was the tone-production exercise described on page 11. We went through it quickly without going into too much detail except for a few fundamentals, e.g. the tension of the string is greater nearer the bridge; the string needs to be able to swing freely from side to side underneath the bow-hair so you must 'stroke' the string (however heavily) rather than 'press'; every sound is the result of different proportions of speed, pressure and soundpoint; high-frequency impurities in the sound (squeaks, harmonics and surface noises) are the result of too little weight; low-frequency impurities (scratching and tearing noises) are the result of too much weight.

Then she learnt how to take one phrase at a time in the Kabalevsky, and to play it first on soundpoint 5, then on 4, 3, 2, and finally – very, very slowly – on soundpoint 1:

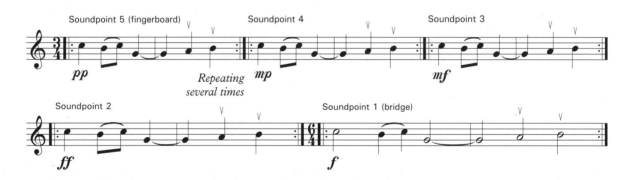

Turning to rhythm, it does not take long to explain that there is a difference between playing the written note-values, and playing with an underlying rhythmic pulse;[2] and she had a first go at playing the opening passage with the metronome at ♩ = 60, then at 70, then 80, and so on.[3]

[2] See *Feeling the pulse,* page 218

[3] See *Speeding up with the metronome,* page 256

Then we went through the few simple principles of intonation: how every note must be related to another; how to tune all the G's, D's, A's and E's to the open strings, so that the open strings vibrate sympathetically (page 60); how to tune the sharps high, close to the natural above, and the flats low, close to the natural below (page 62). There is so little you need to think about, yet once awareness of these points becomes more acute, intonation immediately begins to fall into place like a blurred photograph coming into focus.

[4] To achieve any goal quickly and easily, two things have to be clear. First, the goal itself must be clearly defined; second, a definite time-frame, within which the goal is to be achieved, must also be clearly defined. If you are not clear about what to do or what is important, or if you have only a vague notion that at some point in the future you should have got there, progress will be slower.

At the end of the hour we discussed how long all this work on intonation and sound should take.[4] She agreed that it would be a pity if she had to wait until the end of her four-year course, or halfway through it, before she got her intonation professionally focused and structured. Nor could she afford to wait six months or six weeks.

She was impressed by the idea that in only six weeks she could apparently be playing much more in tune. She had thought that improving intonation was something that happened at the same rate as, say, a tree growing from a seedling.

But you don't really want to wait any longer than six days, I told her. It is perfectly simple and you can do it easily: what you should aim for is to play this movement again in your lesson next week, and to play every note in tune.

Between now and then, test every note one by one, repeating the process several times over the course of the week. Check every G, D, A and E with the open strings. Tune every sharp to the natural above; tune every flat to the natural below. Put a question mark on every note.[1]

As well as doing that, work on the sound. Practise each phrase separately on different soundpoints, so that next week you can play the first movement of the Kabalevsky concerto with 1) every note sounding, and 2) with every note in tune, and 3) with good rhythmic pulse – and at a faster tempo, having cranked it up, bit by bit, with the metronome.

While I was confident that she *could* transform her playing in one week, at the same time I knew it depended on many unknown factors in her circumstances and character as to whether she would.

But the next week her tone was very much fuller and more expressive. This was not surprising, since now the bow was more often playing on soundpoint 3, and at times even approaching soundpoint 2. The intonation was much better as well. Sometimes it was Level 3, but some of the time it was Level 2.

This was a good start, and she carried on from there at the same pace. This rate of progress is not remarkable or unique. Anyone can do it.

True stories: Elaine (advanced)

I had heard Elaine over the years at examinations and in the occasional college competition, but had never worked with her. She had always seemed talented, and had been at a specialist music school as a teenager, so it was not surprising that she was quite an advanced player; and yet there was often something slightly wooden about her bowing. Her bow hold did not look quite right. There was something about it that needed some sort of adjustment, but I could not tell what it was. Then she went abroad to study, and I did not hear of her for a couple of years.

Then one day she telephoned and explained that she was having problems with her use of the bow in general, and changing bow at the heel in particular. I expressed surprise, given how talented and experienced she was, and all the years of professional training she had had. She said that in fact she had always had these problems, since as far back as she could remember.

She came for a lesson and played the first movement of the Beethoven concerto. She played well: she was a serious, committed musician who did not give up easily, and was used to working hard to get the result she was looking for, however long it took.

After she finished playing, I asked her to describe what she was encountering in her bowing. She explained again that playing at the heel often felt awkward. I asked her to show me exactly how she held the bow, now that she was no longer playing. She held her hand up to show me.

"Yes, but hold it as you would hold it to play," I said.

"I am," she replied.

"But put your thumb where it would be if you were playing."

"It is!" she protested.

"But it can't be," I insisted. "The tip is sticking out slightly. That's what little children do!"

"That's how I have always held it," she said.

It did not take long to show her that if you put the tip of the thumb on the bow, the thumb wants to bend outwards and then naturally makes tiny flexing and straightening movements all the time; but if you put more of the pad of the thumb on the bow, the thumb will want to straighten and all flexibility is lost.

It was no wonder she felt awkward in her bow hand if that was what she did with her thumb on the bow. Fig. 2 shows an exaggerated faulty thumb position. Hers was less obvious than this, but it was too much on the pad nevertheless. Of course she understood the point instantly, and fought to contain her frustration that the solution to her problem had been so simple all the time. At her specialist music school, she said, her bow hold was never mentioned.

Fig. 2

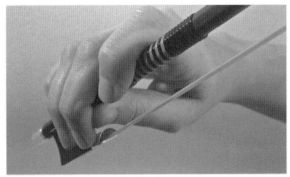

The pad of the thumb is on the bow

Then, at college her teacher had constantly urged her, for four years, to bend her thumb outwards more, but had never commented on its placement on the tip or pad. Then, when she was abroad during her postgraduate study, her teacher had constantly said: "No *legato* at the heel, no *legato* at the heel: it's a pity!" but had left it at that, and offered no solution. Yet all the time it had been such a simple thing to fix.

True stories: Morven (professional)

Morven was a professional violinist who came for a refresher lesson. She did not have the luminous tone production that the *Five essential tone-production exercises* (page 11) would easily give her, but she was a good violinist and she managed the tricky passages of her concerto well. Her phrasing and general use of the bow was what you would expect from an experienced musician. But what seemed to stand out was her intonation, which was a definite Level 3 throughout.

When she had finished, I explained how the job of the teacher or coach is to identify the single most important next step that the student should take. "Before I tell you what I think the most important area is that you should focus on, why don't you tell me what you think it is?" I suggested.

She mentioned one or two things, perhaps phrasing or tone, but she was surprised when I said that I thought the most important thing she needed to improve was her intonation. "Oh, really?" she said, "I've always thought my intonation was okay. I've never really considered it."

We discussed how to relate notes to each other, how to tune the major scale and double stops, how to play closer semitones the faster the passage, and I showed her how to do the *Two essential intonation exercises* (page 73). It took about 10 minutes, by the end of which she could see exactly what I meant about the need to rethink her intonation.

She came back a week later and played the same piece again. When she had finished, and we had begun to work on phrasing, or tone, or whatever the single most important area now seemed to be, she asked if the intonation was better. In fact, the moment she had started to play I had forgotten about intonation, and it had not once occurred to me – such was the improvement she had made in one week.

Building good intonation or tone depends on only a few simple principles. Such fast progress can be repeated any number of times with students at every level.

The tone production lesson

Working on tone production is often a good first step with new students, if they are able to draw the bow sufficiently parallel to the bridge:

- When you play tone exercises, even if they are only long, sustained bows on one note, you have to play that note with feeling and musical imagination for it to be technically successful. This establishes, from the start, the vital principle that when you work on technique you nearly always have to do it *musically* and with inspiration, rather than only with detached mental control.

- Tone exercises have an immediate effect, so working on tone is an encouraging and exciting way to start a new course of study.

- As students focus on the different qualities and components of the sound, their listening is immediately alerted and sharpened. Then, because they are listening better, every aspect of playing naturally improves quickly at the same time.

- Starting with tone follows the principle of always beginning with the result you want, and working your way back from there, rather than 'starting from nowhere'. Always go straight for the tone and the expression, and then find how to do it, rather than the other way round.

- Tone-production exercises are a direct way for the teacher to begin to understand exactly what the pupil is doing with the bow, bow arm, right hand and fingers, and the pupil's entire musical and technical approach to making the instrument sing.

Knowing the instrument

Five soundpoints

The first step is to subdivide the area between the bridge and the fingerboard into 5 'tracks' or 'soundpoints' (Fig. 3). You can then also think of soundpoints 1½, 2½, 3½, 4½, 5½.

The moment you give a name or label to each distance from the bridge you can plan your use of the bow, and explore each soundpoint's ideal balances of bow speed and bow pressure, in an entirely more practical and organised way. Then everything in your use of the bow improves.

Fig. 3

Divide the playing area into 5 'soundpoints'

Understanding what the bow does to the string

Everything in violin playing, as in the rest of Nature, is a simple matter of cause and effect. Every specific cause leads to a specific effect. If you repeat the same cause you get the same effect.

Everything the bow does to the string is a cause, and every sound that comes out of the violin is an effect. And, like the familiar saying 'the customer is always right', the violin is always right: each sound is a perfect representation of what the bow did to the string.

What exactly does the hair of the bow do to the string? This is one of the first questions to ask at the beginning of any first session of working on tone. Most string players, even beginners, will immediately reply that the hair of the bow makes the string 'vibrate'.

The next question is: what does 'make the string vibrate' mean, and how does the bow do it? Not so many will be able to answer this, even advanced players. Often, a new understanding of what is happening underneath the bow-hair completely changes their use of the bow, and does so instantly.

An instrument of friction

Imagine watching the bow moving along the string in ultra-slow-motion, and magnified through such a strong lens that the string and the hairs of the bow are huge. You can see clearly how the friction of the bow causes the string to swing from side to side.[1]

[1] If things had turned out differently, we might today speak of the four sections of the orchestra as the percussion, the wind, the brass, and the frictions.

On the down bow the hair catches the string and pulls it sideways to the right. As it does so the tension of the string increases. This sideways bending of the string can only continue for so long, before the tension is so great that the string springs back in the opposite direction, to the left. It is then caught again by the hair and pulled to the right again, and the next cycle begins.

The reverse happens on the up bow. The bow-hair pushes the string to the left. Therefore the string moves sideways, backwards and forwards. This sideways movement is called the amplitude.

It looks like a blur around the string and is widest at the middle point between the bridge and the nut (or the bridge and the finger). The wider the amplitude, the more carrying the tone.

The pitch of the note remains the same, however, whatever the amplitude. The note A vibrates (i.e. the string swings from side to side) 440 times each second whether it is played *pp* or *ff*, but the distance the string swings from side to side is narrower in the *pp* and wider in the *ff*:

The violin, working by friction, is a sustaining instrument. The piano, basically a percussion instrument, is an instrument of *diminuendo*: after the hammer has hit the string, all that can happen is that the vibrations of the string diminish.

Fig. 4

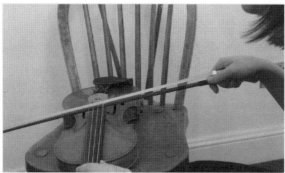
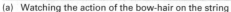
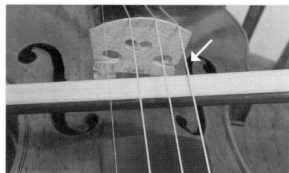

(a) Watching the action of the bow-hair on the string

(b) The string vibrates beyond the bow hair

Looking at the hair-string contact from 'underneath'

What would the hair's action on the string look like if you could see it from underneath the string? A simple way to find out is to place the instrument on a flat surface, insert the bow *under* the strings, and bow upside-down on the G or E string (Fig. 4a).

See how the string swings widely from side to side at the precise contact-point of the hair with the string.

Notice how the string vibrates between the bridge at one end, and the finger or nut at the other. It is not that the string vibrates from the contact-point of the bow with the string, but vibrates *beyond* the contact-point on the bridge side (Fig. 4b).

Find how to make the friction of the bow cause the widest possible amplitude.

Getting more for less: speed not pressure

[2] The beauty of the sound depends upon a regular pressure and movement of the bow. If a really artistic tone is to be produced, it never will be the result of pressing alone, but rather of pulling. All violinists who produce sound more by pressing than by pulling will get an unpleasant rough tone, but never reach truly beautiful and sympathetic strains.
E. Kross, H. Leonard: *La Gymnastische Übungen auf der violine* (Mainz, 1911), 3.

If it is too much, the downward pressure of the bow into the string prevents the string from swinging freely from side to side. Then, although you are pressing hard and it feels as though you should therefore be getting a lot of volume, in fact you get more sound if you release the pressure slightly.[2]

Experiment

1 Play a note in 1st position on the D string. Use quite fast bows, playing midway between the bridge and the fingerboard. See how widely you can make the string vibrate. Watch the string midway between the first finger and the bridge.

2 Now slow the bow a little, and slightly over-press. Notice how the width of the string-vibration becomes narrower as the bow pressure constricts the string. Notice how the tone, which is now slightly squashed and less pure, is actually smaller than it was before.

3 Move the bow a little more quickly and lightly again. Notice how the width of the string vibration increases, as the string is now free again to move lightly and quickly from side to side. Notice how the tone is now purer and sweeter, and seems to travel much further.

When you press too hard it is as though you are trying to drive the sound down in the direction of your feet (Fig. 5a). When instead you lighten the bow, and use speed to create the sound, you *draw* the tone out of the string (Fig. 5b).

Fig. 5

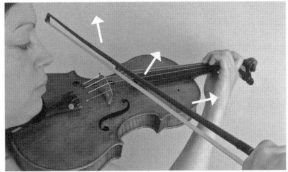

(a) Pressing chokes the string

(b) Lift the sound out of the string, however heavy the downward weight

Q **Doesn't that mean that you end up playing everything too lightly and sweetly?**

You often have to sink the bow into the string as heavily as you can.[1] 'Speed not pressure' simply means that even when the bow is near the bridge, and slow and deep in the string, you still draw out the tone and expression with horizontal movement of bow, rather than pressing it out with downward pressure.

In playing *spiccato* there is a feeling of an upward movement to make each stroke, not a downward one into the string.[2] There is the same feeling of 'up' rather than 'down' when playing sustained strokes.

'Pressure' or 'weight'?

Many players and teachers avoid using the word 'pressure' through fear that it may lead to pressing the bow and squashing the sound, and use the word 'weight' instead, to encourage a feeling of 'sinking the weight of the bow into the string'.

Another view is that 'pressure' indicates focus on one point, and 'weight' expresses more of a spread-out, unfocused feeling of general heaviness. Sometimes one term is appropriate, sometimes either.

If the fingers on the bow are well distributed;[3] if you are sensitive to the balances of speed, pressure and soundpoint; if you let the bow lead the hand;[4] if you have a clear concept of the freely vibrating string, and of the purity and beauty of tone that you require – and then if you listen – there is little chance of playing with a pressed tone whatever words you use.

Visual image

What is the hair of the bow doing to the string? This is the central question to consider during every moment of playing. What is happening there, at the contact-point between hair and string? How are they reacting to each other? What does the friction feel like? What does the give of the string under the bow-hair feel like?

To create an easily-remembered visual image for a young pupil, take a large sheet of paper and fold it in half lengthwise. Tear off a rectangle the size of the playing area.

Place the sheet of paper on top of the violin (Fig. 6). (Obviously the student cannot play at the same time; the point is simply to see it.) Encourage the student to forget everything except this area, to focus on nothing else, to put all of their energy and effort into directing and controlling what is happening *there*.

[1] The great French cellist Pierre Fournier used to say that sometimes, when you are playing deeply into the string, you can have a feeling of moving the bow 'through thick mud'. While cello strings are much thicker than violin strings, violinists can still look for a similar feeling, especially on the G string.

[2] See *Up not down: playing spiccato like a pianist*, page 283

[3] See *Experiment in leverage*, page 40

[4] See *Feeling the momentum of the bow*, page 14

Fig. 6

Focus on this area

Image of the cat

When you stroke a cat, it often arches its back up against your hand so that while you push one way, the cat pushes the other. Unless it does not wish to be stroked, the cat is not passive but takes part actively.

In the same way, do not let the violin or string sit passively and inactively while the bow plays on it. Play with an 'ardent violin' which rises up to meet the contact of the bow. The amount is so slight that it is imperceptible. If you can see it, it is probably too much; but the difference in the sound and the feel of the bow, between an 'active' and a 'passive' violin, is striking.

Understanding resonance

The body of the violin is a 'resonating box'. If it were made of solid wood rather than being hollow, the sound of the bowed string would be small and thin. The bridge transmits the vibrations down into the resonating box where they are amplified.

- Using your knuckles, gently tap the body of the violin. Listen to the sound of each tap resonating through the instrument.

- Using your fingernail, scratch the top of the bridge between the strings very, very lightly. The sound is amplified greatly by the violin. Make the same scratching movement on a solid tabletop, or the wall, and notice the difference.

- Place the palm of your left hand flat against the underside of the violin and feel the vibrations of the back plate as you bow the open strings.

- Then bow a few notes on each string, listening to the amplification and resonance of the violin.

Listening to the background resonance

Play a short note and listen to the ring that continues on after the end of the bow stroke. The question is, what happens to that ring during a longer note. In other words, what happens to the ring if the sound that produced it continues at the same time?

If you listen carefully you can hear two distinct sounds: the sound of the principal note, and at the same time a continuous background ring which is like a distinct note ringing on its own. You have to listen *behind* the sound.

The moment you start to focus on the background ring as well as the 'principal sound', an entirely new quality comes into the playing.

In the following exercise focus on the sound and duration of the background resonance. Afterwards, listen for that resonance as a fundamental part of any note.

- First listen to a stopped G, D, A or E, since these ring more easily than a sharp or flat:

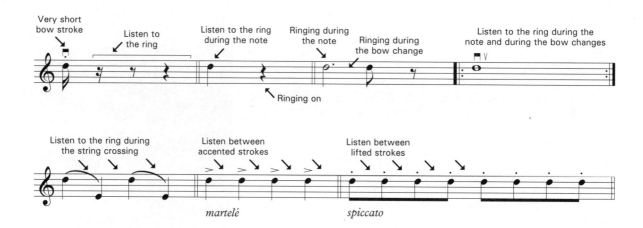

- To produce even more ring, or when teaching young children, play the exercise on the open strings.

Practising in a dry acoustic

Whenever possible, practise in a room that has a dry acoustic: the challenge of playing cleanly and sweetly, and drawing the resonance out of the violin, is far greater than in an acoustic that muddles all the sounds together.

If you can play well in a dry acoustic, you will sound even better in a resonant one. But if you practise in too resonant an acoustic and then play in a dry one, you may find that what had before seemed good is now disappointing.

One way to deaden the sound is to pin some kind of fabric up on the wall. If it is not possible to play in a dry acoustic, sometimes stand in a corner of the room facing inwards to the wall. The sound bouncing straight back to you will be clearer and more truthful than the echoes in the room.

The legendary American violinist Michael Rabin liked to practise while standing facing into the bay windows of his music room: the curved windows threw the sound straight back out at him.

That would not have been to Yehudi Menuhin's taste, however. He recommended using a heavy practice mute during long sessions of practice to avoid deadening the sensitivity of the ears.

Understanding the properties of the string

The feel of the string

Fig. 7

(a) The string feels hard near the bridge

(b) The string feels soft near the fingerboard

The closer a part of the string is to the bridge, the more rigid it is. Using your finger, press at different distances from the bridge to feel the resistance of the string (Fig. 7).

- Since the nearer you play to the bridge the less flexible the string is, you need more bow weight, to catch the string, than when bowing nearer to the fingerboard.

- The bow must also move more slowly when nearer the bridge, otherwise it whistles over the surface of the taut string without catching it – particularly on the thick G string.

- However, the higher the note, i.e. the shorter the string, the less pressure it can take, so you have to play high notes lightly near the bridge.[1]

[1] See *Bow-pressure and pitch*, page 84

The thinner the string, the nearer the bridge

Each string prefers a different soundpoint from the string next to it. Near the bridge the open G string feels too stiff. You need to play faster, longer strokes around soundpoint 4 to make it vibrate the widest.

The open E string is the opposite. To make it vibrate the widest, you need to play around soundpoint 2. It feels too weak and fragile when bowed on soundpoint 4 or 5.

Another approach to take, or to consider as well as the choice of soundpoint, is the length of bow: the thicker (lower) the string, the less bow you must use to avoid having to apply very great pressure:

In chord-playing you can often adjust the soundpoint during the chord:

Bruch: Concerto in G minor, op. 26, *mov. 1, b. 16*

The proportions of other string instruments

The way the strings on the violin get thicker as you descend, so that the E string is the thinnest and the G string the thickest, is mirrored in the string section as a whole, where the violin has the thinnest strings and the double bass the thickest.

The question of proportions of speed, pressure, and soundpoint applies whatever the instrument, from a violin with metal or gut strings to a double bass. A player with a natural feel for bowing can take a piece of ordinary household string, stretch it tightly between two points, and set that string into continuous and regular vibration with a violin bow.

If you can bow a violin string successfully, so that the proportions of speed–pressure–soundpoint are correct and the string vibrates widely and freely, then you can do the same, without practice, on a viola, or even on a cello or double bass.

After all, just in playing the violin you are already playing several 'instruments': there is more difference between playing the E string on the violin and the G string on the violin, than there is between playing the A string on the violin and the A string on the viola.[1]

Point-of-contact: not following the line of least resistance

Water always flows downhill. It can never flow uphill unless another element of force acts upon it, because natural forces always follow the line of least resistance.

One of the most common faults in string playing is that of unknowingly following the line of least resistance and bowing too far from the bridge all the time. There are four main reasons why the player allows the bow to slide over to the fingerboard and stay there:

Fig. 8

1 Unless the violin is held with the scroll up, the strings slope down from the bridge. Following the line of least resistance, the bow slips 'downhill' away from the bridge towards the fingerboard.

2 The nearer the bow is to the bridge, the greater the tension of the string and the 'harder' the string feels under the bow. Playing further from the bridge requires much less weight and energy, so following the line of least resistance the bow drifts to soundpoint 5.

Do not spend all your time playing on the fingerboard

[1] There is also more difference in finger spacing between playing in 1st position and 5th position on the violin, than there is between playing in 1st position on the violin and in 1st position on the viola.

In earlier centuries most violinists would also play the viola. The German musicologist Hans Keller used to point out that if, because of the different sizes of the instruments and therefore the different stops, it is necessary to have a dedicated profession called 'violinist', and another dedicated profession called 'violist', then it should equally be necessary to have a dedicated profession called '1st position violinist', and another called '5th position violinist'.
Hans Keller: *Criticism* (London, 1987), 18.

3 The nearer the bow is to the bridge, the deeper into the string you have to play; but all that the wood of the bow wants to do, once it is pressed down towards the string, is to spring back up again (see Fig. 138a, page 281).

The bow naturally wants to move away from the bridge to a place nearer the fingerboard, where it can play more 'along the surface of the string' rather than playing deep down into the string.

4 The deeper the bow plays into the string, the more the string is 'bent' down. The more bent down the string is, the greater the tension of the string and the more it wants to spring up again. Following the line of least resistance, the bow drifts away from the bridge to an area where it can play 'along the surface of the string'.

To avoid following the line of least resistance, violinists and violists need to spend a lot of time *pulling in* towards the bridge; cellists need to *push out* towards the bridge.

The secret of tone: proportions of speed–pressure–soundpoint

Applying the bow to the string, there are only three things to think about: the speed, the pressure or weight of the bow into the string, and the distance of the bow from the bridge (soundpoint, or point of contact). Every sound that comes out of the violin can be described using only these three factors.

Being able to describe, instantaneously, any sound created by the bow, using only references to speed, pressure, and distance from the bridge, is one of the hallmarks of real mastery of the bow.

Imagine that it is possible to measure speed or pressure exactly, using a scale from 1 to 9:

1 = Very slow bow, or very light

9 = Very fast bow, or very heavy.

Suppose that the 'widest possible vibration' of the string is '10'. On each soundpoint, you could express the ideal balance of speed and pressure as follows:[1]

Soundpoint	5	Speed	9	+	Pressure	1	=	10
Soundpoint	4	Speed	7	+	Pressure	3	=	10
Soundpoint	3	Speed	5	+	Pressure	5	=	10
Soundpoint	2	Speed	3	+	Pressure	7	=	10
Soundpoint	1	Speed	1	+	Pressure	9	=	10

Of course, the widest possible vibration on every note, sometimes called the 'tonus',[2] is not necessarily what you want. Sometimes you want light and airy sounds (i.e. slightly 'too little' weight for the soundpoint, or 'too fast' speed); sometimes you want dark, depressed sounds (i.e. slightly 'too much' weight for the soundpoint, or 'too slow' speed).

Disharmony

When the speed, pressure and soundpoint are not in harmony with each other and in proportions that 'work' or 'add up', there is often a distinct impression of the sound *coming out of the violin*.

Whether you sit twenty metres away from the player or two metres away, it seems as though the sound is *there*, where the player is. The sound comes *from* the instrument, and seems to stay in a small area around the instrument and the player.

Then, when they try to play louder and project the tone further, it may get louder but still appears to be coming out of the violin, and to stay around the violin.

The sense of the proportions not adding up in the tone production is similar to the feeling of conflict in the sound when the violin itself is not set up correctly. If the bridge is not the right thickness, height or design, or the soundpost is not in the right place, or the tail gut not the right length, the instrument may feel as though it is fighting against itself rather than the sound ringing out with freedom.

[1] These numbers illustrate the point, but in reality they do not add up like this. There is little difference between bowing on soundpoint 6 and soundpoint 5; but a huge difference between bowing on soundpoint 2 and soundpoint 1.

When the bow is on soundpoint 6 it is 10 centimetres away from the bridge. On soundpoint 5 it is 9 centimetres away, i.e. a difference of 10%.

When the bow is on soundpoint 2 it is one centimetre away from the bridge. On soundpoint 1½ it is half a centimetre away, i.e. a difference of 50%.

[2] After I had been teaching for a couple of years it occurred to me that no single word existed which meant 'the right balance of speed, pressure and soundpoint so that the string vibrates to its maximum'. I could not say to a student: 'Get the ???? on that note.'

I tried to invent a word and asked friends, colleagues, students and parents of students for suggestions. We played around with various Greek or Latin prefixes with the meaning of 'three'; but every idea seemed clumsy or contrived, and we never arrived at a perfect new word.

Then, years later, I came across a violinist who had studied in Leningrad, Russia (now St. Petersburg). He said that all the focus there was on finding the 'tonus' on every note. Here at last was the word; it already existed.

Magical quality

Instead, when the speed, pressure and distance from the bridge are all perfectly in harmony with each other, and in the right proportions, a magical quality comes in to the sound. In a small room, even when you are sitting only two metres away from the player, there is no sense of the sound coming 'out of the instrument', but a sense of the whole room being full of the sound.

It is the same in a large room or concert hall. The sound seems to come from everywhere all at the same time. The tone of a soloist seems to come from a wide area of the stage, rather than from the place where they are standing; even if they are playing with an orchestra, the tone easily rises above it and carries to the back of the hall, even in quiet passages.

The quality of the sound: upper partials

When you raise or lower the volume control on your television or music player, the quality of the sound does not change. The sound gets louder or softer, but in itself it stays the same.

It is different when you play more loudly or softly on the violin. When you move the bow closer to the bridge or further away, the sound not only gets louder or softer but the quality changes as well:

> …a musical note is not a single note, but a whole series of notes. A number of higher tones are present as well as the prime tone, these being the harmonics…[the natural harmonics obtained by placing a finger lightly on the string at certain points], plus other higher ones.
>
> The associated notes are known as partial tones, and all except the prime tone are described as upper partials. These upper partials are fainter than the prime tone which gives the pitch to the note, but scientists tell us that the quality of the sound is determined by the number and relative intensities of the partials.
>
> Applying the bow too far from the bridge diminishes the number of upper partials; applying it too near adds to the number of very high ones, when in extreme cases only upper partials (or harmonics) are heard.[1]

[1] Percival Hodgson: *Motion Study and Violin Bowing* (London, 1934), 18.

Playing nearer to the bridge produces a tone that has more 'edge', and is brighter and more penetrating, than playing nearer to the fingerboard does. Playing nearer to the fingerboard is similar to playing with a mute on the bridge since both actions reduce the quantity of upper partials in the sound.

The sound under your ear is not the sound the audience hears

What you hear as a player, with the instrument close to your ear, is quite different from the sound that the audience hears from a distance.

This is because the upper partials in the sound are the first to 'drop off', while lower partials travel further. A low note played on a large, booming horn, in a range of hills or mountains, may be heard several miles away, whereas a high note played on a piccolo would be lost after a far shorter distance.

This means that if you play near to the bridge, where more upper partials are produced than when playing nearer the fingerboard, the sound next to your ear may seem edgy; but because those upper partials do not travel as far as the audience, the sound they hear is mellow and sweet.

The danger is that if you try to produce too mellow and sweet a tone directly under your ear (i.e. if the sound you hear is actually the exact sound you want somebody many metres away from you to hear), then the sound that reaches them may end up sounding nothing but too weak.

Of course this does not mean that it is acceptable to play too near to the bridge and to play with a scratchy, impure tone. Even if the audience did not mind, you surely would. You still have to play with a sweet, pure tone near the bridge – but it will have a different quality from the sound produced further away.

Experiment on the piano

You can observe a similar phenomenon (though in this case as much to do with the length of the strings as to do with the shorter life of upper partials), by playing a widely-spaced chord on the piano, striking all the notes at the same time, and holding the keys down without releasing them.

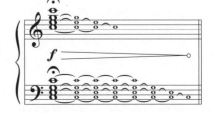

At first, you can hear every note sounding at the same time. Then the top note fades and disappears, and then the next note down from the top fades, and then the next note, and so on. The lowest notes are the last to go.

Closing the top of a grand piano, or playing on a 'half-stick', does not make it 'quieter' but only 'duller', since only the upper partials are affected – and these are the ones with the least carrying power anyway. Closing the lid does little to stop the lower partials from travelling, so the piano continues to sound loud in the lower registers.

Improving listening

There is a four-step process going on in every moment of every note you play:

- **Imagine**

  During every second of practising or performing, the first thing is always to picture the exact sound quality or expression that you want, before going to play it.

- **Listen**

  The next thing is to listen so well that you catch every sound that comes out of the instrument.

- **Describe**

  The next is to know instantly what the factors are that make up each sound as you create it. For example, 'too much pressure too far from the bridge', 'too little pressure for the fast bow speed'.

- **Change**

  Then, whatever technical adjustment is necessary must be made instantly.

 How does the 'imagine–listen–describe–change' process actually work during the practical experience of playing?

Suppose, when you begin a note, you give too little bow-weight and produce a thin or harmonic-like tone; or the note is out of tune or the vibrato too slow, and so on. If you are an excellent listener you hear any of this in the first fraction of a second.

Then, if you are clear about what you are doing, and clear about how it all works (knowing about different proportions of speed–pressure–soundpoint, the different sensations in the bow, and so on), in the next fraction of a second you are able to describe (albeit unconsciously) what is happening.

Then, if your technique is based on natural balance, freedom and ease, in the next fraction of a second your brain is able to make an instinctive correction – all before anyone else even notices that there was something 'wrong' in the first place.[1]

[1] See *The impossibility of playing in tune*, page 89

Clearly, if you begin a note without listening you will not notice any poor or inexpressive tone, and it will continue long enough to be heard; or if you do hear it, but do not know why it sounds like that, and do not know what to do, again it will continue too long; or if you hear it and know what the problem is, but are too tense (or badly set up on the instrument) to be able to correct it, again the poor tone will continue for too long.

Testing the student

Sharpen a student's listening, and their ability to describe the speed–pressure–soundpoint proportions that are behind any particular sound, by playing faulty sounds and asking them to identify them.

To describe the sounds, the student must use only references to speed of bow and pressure, relative to the distance from the bridge, e.g.:

'Too light/too heavy, for the speed of bow at that distance from the bridge'

'Too fast/too slow, for the pressure at that distance from the bridge'

'Too near the bridge/too far from the bridge, for that speed/pressure'

● Make up variations and combinations of the following, using high and low notes on each string. Make the faulty sounds subtly, without exaggeration:

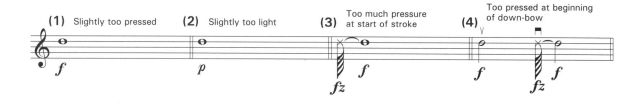

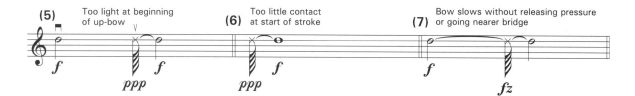

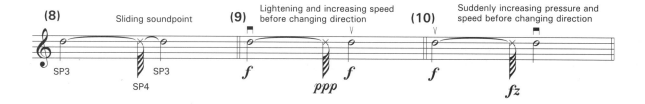

(1) Sustain the bow very slightly too heavily, all the way from heel to point, so that there is a faint quality of the tone being squashed.

(2) Use very slightly too little pressure, so that there is a faint quality of high-frequency edge in the sound.

(3) Scratch by pressing too hard, with the bow too slow, for a fraction of a second at the beginning of the stroke (shown as an x-note). Play in all parts of the bow, beginning down-bow and up-bow.

(4) Begin up-bow in the lower half, and scratch the tone at the beginning of the down-bow by making the bow too slow and heavy.

(5) Sustain the bow well until the point; then 'skim' along the string for a few centimetres at the beginning of the up-bow.

(6) Skim along the string for a few centimetres at the beginning of the stroke, making a high squeaking or whistling sound.

(7) Sustain the note with a good balance of speed/pressure/soundpoint on, say, soundpoint 3 until the middle of the bow; then scratch or squash the sound by keeping the soundpoint and pressure the same but slowing the bow speed; then return to the previous good balance and good sound.

(8) Sustain the note well on, say, soundpoint 3 until the middle of the bow; then squash the tone by 'wandering' over to soundpoint 4 without releasing the pressure, and then correct the tone by moving back to soundpoint 3 again.

(9) Just before changing direction at the point, suddenly lighten the bow and increase the speed at the end of the down-bow.

(10) Just before changing direction at the heel, suddenly scratch with too much pressure at the end of the up-bow.

Learning how to make faulty sounds deliberately

The next step is for students deliberately to make these same faulty sounds themselves. They should alternate between pure and impure, e.g. play (1) with a very slightly pressed tone, down-bow and up-bow; repeat with a pure, resonant tone; repeat with a very slightly over-pressed tone again, and so on.

After focusing on these sounds, describing them and playing them on purpose, it is a simple step for the student to begin to notice the same sounds in their own playing. Instant improvement in tone then naturally follows.

Five essential tone-production exercises

These methods have been used by great players and teachers throughout the ages. They are very simple because everything is stripped down to one issue alone: making the string vibrate freely by finding the best balances of speed and weight at each distance from the bridge.

The exercises focus entirely on sound and the sensations in the bow, without any other factors getting in the way and complicating things – such as intonation, rhythm, shifting, co-ordination, string crossing, interpretation, and so on.

There are five main exercises. By mixing different elements of the five you can create others, but you do not even need to go that far since the five principal ones are so powerful and effective anyway.

Tone-production exercises are 'sensitisation' exercises: they increase your sensitivity to the feel of the bow in the string, and the feeling of the fingers on the bow. They produce immediate and noticeable improvement for any player, however elementary or however advanced. As soon as string players begin to practise them the results are always extraordinary and immediate.

The endless well

The smallest amount of time spent practising these simple exercises can actually save you years, since they quickly propel you on to a professional level of tone production. You can gain today what you would otherwise have had to work hard over many years to achieve, and might never have achieved.

- If you are an advanced player, they are a way to maintain your already high standard in the shortest possible practice time. They also improve your tone production still further. You can liken each of them to a well of endless pure spring water where, however much water you draw up out of the well, there is always more that you can take and use, without ever running out.

- If you are a teacher or parent of a less advanced or elementary player, with these exercises you can enable them to make a deep, rich, soloistic tone within a single coaching session. Then they have to learn how to keep it and carry on by themselves, but it is a short step from there to finding the same 'voice' in pieces.

Be the world's first string-player

Imagine that somebody, far back in time, has just finished making the first bowed string instrument ever. They string it up for the very first time, take the first bow that has ever been made, and play the first notes ever heard on a string instrument.

What is the first thing they are going to do? Surely, they would bow the string at one distance from the bridge to see what it felt like; and then play the same stroke at another distance from the bridge to see what the difference is.

They would also try faster strokes and slower strokes, and heavier and lighter. What could be more natural than that?

Testing the string at different distances from the bridge, while experimenting with different pressures and speeds, is the single most effective way to understand and develop tone production. Transform this original, natural exploration of the string, and the bow, into dedicated 'exercises' and practice routines.

Exercise 1: Whole bows on each soundpoint

This exercise is the starting-point for all work on sound, and all work on the bow in general. Using this exercise even elementary players can begin to produce a fine tone. Professional players equally never fail to benefit from it, and can go on using it for the duration of their careers.

¹ See *True stories: Jane*, page 226

1 Draw continuous whole bows, down-bow and up-bow, on soundpoint 5. Play without vibrato, but play expressively, pretending that the note is part of a phrase in a piece of music.¹

The aim is to find the exact combination of weight and speed, at that distance from the bridge, to make the string vibrate at its widest.

On this soundpoint the bow will have to be very light: you may want to turn it on to the outer edge of the hair and play on 'one hair' of the bow. Experiment with more and less pressure, and faster and slower bow speed, until the string vibrates (swings from side to side) as far as possible.

2 When you are sure the speed and pressure are exactly right, add vibrato.

Do not immediately move away from soundpoint 5. Stay on it, listening to the 'throb' of the vibrato, and continue to adjust the exact weight and speed as you search for the widest, and most even, vibration of the string.

3 Move to soundpoint 4 and start again without vibrato. Find the new balance of speed and pressure that makes the widest string vibration and then add vibrato. Repeat on soundpoints 3, 2 and 1.

Suggested *tempi*: Soundpoint 5 ♩ = 80
Soundpoint 4 ♩ = 75
Soundpoint 3 ♩ = 70
Soundpoint 2 ♩ = 56
Soundpoint 1 ♩ = 40

Do the exercise on all four strings in low, middle and high positions (4 × 3 = 12 basic areas to explore). The sensations of the bow-hair contacting the string are entirely different in each area.

The process of finding the correct balances

In a scientific experiment you have to isolate factors and change things only one at a time. If you change more than one thing you cannot tell what is causing what.

Practising this sound exercise, two of the three elements of soundpoint–pressure–speed are fixed: you have decided that you are playing on a particular soundpoint; you are using whole bows at a particular tempo which decides the speed of bow; which leaves only the weight of the bow: so keeping the soundpoint and speed unchanged, experiment with more weight and less weight until the string is vibrating at its maximum. Then, without changing the speed/pressure/soundpoint balance, add vibrato.

Suppose you are playing whole bows on soundpoint 3. The process of finding the right balances of speed and pressure is like this:

● You note how widely the string is vibrating, and how much ring there is in the tone.

● You try a little more pressure. The string vibrates more widely, and the ring increases. So increasing the pressure is the right direction in which to go.

● So you increase the pressure further. The string vibrates more widely still. So increasing the pressure is still the right direction in which to go.

● You increase the pressure still further. Now the string vibrates slightly less widely, and the ring is slightly diminished. So less pressure is now the right direction in which to go.

● So you decrease the pressure, but only by a fraction: now you are using less pressure than last time, but still more than the time before that. Now the string vibrates more widely. So less pressure is still the right direction in which to go.

● So you decrease the pressure a tiny fraction further. Now the string vibrates less widely again. So less pressure is now the wrong direction.

- So you give the slightest amount more pressure, i.e. not enough to take you back to where you were before, but an infinitesimal amount more than you were using a moment ago.

This is probably the optimum pressure, coupled with that particular bow speed, on that soundpoint, to make the string vibrate the widest.

Giving the student a model

Give pupils a clear picture of what to do without having to use words, by bowing for them while they hold the violin (Fig. 9).

Demonstrate each soundpoint before they play it, so that they can aim for that same combination of speed and weight themselves, and start off much closer to the target.

This is helpful not just for children but for students of any age.

Fig. 9

Giving the student a model

On first playing the exercise

Getting started on soundpoint 5 is often the most challenging for many players, perhaps because of the delicacy required at such a soft part of the string. The weight of the bow alone is enough: you do not have to add extra weight, as you do when playing nearer to the bridge. You may even have to lift some weight out of the strings. Glide the bow across the string with an almost entirely horizontal feel.

At first, because it is resting so lightly on the string, the bow may bounce and seem to have a life of its own that is impossible to control. Keep a feeling of following the bow, so that it leads the hand, rather than 'holding' it and trying to move it. See *Feeling the momentum of the bow*, page 14.

Soundpoint 4 already feels a lot easier than soundpoint 5; and on soundpoint 3 it begins to feel safe to play quite deeply into the string, since the string begins to have enough resistance to take it.

Soundpoint 2 is an area where, even when doing the exercise for the first time, most people feel safe playing deeply into the string; but soundpoint 1 again is a challenge for many players until they discover how extremely slowly and heavily you must play there.

On soundpoint 1 many players misinterpret the feedback the scratches provide. While they think that the scratches are caused by too much pressure, in fact usually they are caused by too little pressure and too fast bow speed.

Key point: High-frequency scratches, full of harmonics, are the result of too little weight, or too fast a bow; low-frequency scratches, where the bow really tears at the string, are the result of too much weight, or too slow a bow.

Four ways to approach the exercise

While playing any tone-production exercise, approach it from four angles at the same time:

1 **Listen**

When playing anything, the first thing (after picturing the sound and expression you want) is to listen so closely that you hear every sound that comes out of the instrument.

2 **Feel**

The second thing is to be sensitive to the feeling of the hair in the string and the fingers on the bow. Connect every sound with a physical sensation; connect every physical sensation with a sound. The sensations of playing are what the sound *feels* like; the sound is what the sensations *sound* like.[1]

[1] See *Uniting technique and music,* page 95

3 **Look**

The third thing is to look at the vibrating string. See how wide you can get it, at the point midway between the bridge and the finger.

Of course you do not look at the strings vibrating when you are in the middle of performing music; but you can look at them when you are experimenting with tone production on one note.

4 Think

The final thing is to understand what is actually happening at the contact-point of the hair with the string. You can describe everything that is happening in the bow and in the sound, and be able to do so instantly, and using few words.

All you need to think is 'less pressure, more pressure; nearer the bridge, further from the bridge; faster bow, slower bow'; and by trying more and less of each, and noting the result, you can find the balances and proportions that make the string vibrate the widest.

Evenness

The most important goal on each soundpoint, after initially finding the combination of speed and pressure that produces the widest string vibration, is to keep it constant so that it is all *even*.

Whether a note or phrase is smooth or accented – or whether it sustains, crescendos or diminuendos, or is joined or separate – the more even it is, the better.

- If you want to create an even tone, the factors that create the tone must be even. In this exercise, the speed must be even, the pressure must be even, and the bow must stay on one soundpoint.

- Keep the bow so steady that the hair stays on a single winding of the string. Imagine a needle on a dial in a recording studio flickering up and down as the volume increases and decreases with changes in speed and pressure. Aim to keep the needle absolutely steady.

Don't speed up when you open your arm at the elbow

A common fault in playing long bows from heel to point is suddenly to increase the bow speed in the middle of the bow. This is the place where the arm opens at the elbow much more quickly than before, making a speed pattern of slow–fast on the down-bow, and fast–slow on the up-bow.

- Playing at the extreme heel there is no opening-and-closing of the arm at the elbow. The movement of the arm is all in the upper arm.

- Playing at the point-of-balance there is a slight degree of movement at the elbow added to the upper arm movement.

- Playing in the middle of the bow there is much more opening-and-closing at the elbow. It is at this place – when the speed of the opening forearm is added to the speed of the upper arm movement – that you have to be careful to maintain the evenness of the bow stroke.

Feeling the momentum of the bow

Although the element that players usually need to work on the most is evenness of speed, pressure and distance from the bridge, it is not so difficult to find.

Does the arm lead the bow or does the bow lead the arm? Most people answer that the arm leads the bow. After all, the bow cannot move itself.

Yet many strokes work much better when there is a sense of the hand *going along with* the bow, of allowing the bow to travel with its own momentum. Then the bow does indeed seem to have its own power to move.

This is one of the things that makes the biggest difference in achieving silky smoothness and evenness of the bow. The sense of the hand *following* the bow is an entirely different feeling from that of *holding* the bow and attempting to guide it by pushing and pulling it yourself.

Imagine that if you took your hand away the bow would simply keep on going, on its own, in the same direction and at the same speed; and that when it reached the point or frog it would not stop there either, but carry on going beyond the violin.[1] A wonderful ease and smoothness then comes into every bow stroke.

[1] A model car, or ball, or anything that will roll before coming to a halt, is useful for explaining the idea of momentum to children. They can easily understand that after the initial push the car carries on going with its own momentum.

Q **Is the feeling of momentum just an image in your mind? Or is it really in the bow?**

The feeling of momentum in the bow is real, like the natural bounce when the bow plays *spiccato*.

If you throw a ball at the wall, the ball 'knows' at what angle to bounce off the wall. You know the angle at which it will bounce off the wall too, and can easily throw a ball so that it bounces off straight towards someone else, wherever they are standing.

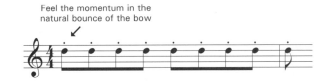

Feel the momentum in the
natural bounce of the bow

Similarly, the bow knows how to bounce out of the string, and it does so with a feeling of natural momentum. To play a really even, controlled *spiccato*, you have to *let* the bow play – going along with the natural momentum of the bow – while at the same time providing just the occasional little bit of guidance so that the bow stays parallel to the bridge or on the same soundpoint and so on.

Variation

If it seems difficult to play the strokes evenly, with even speed and pressure, and with the bow remaining on one soundpoint without drifting, begin with less bow and build up from there:

- The shorter the length of bow, the easier it is to keep the stroke even. So begin on soundpoint 5 as before, but play very short strokes in the middle of the bow.

- Adjust the speed and pressure until the string is vibrating as widely as possible.

- Then gradually lengthen the stroke, adjusting the pressure as necessary to keep the string vibrating at its widest.

- Continue adding more bow, and adjusting the ratio of pressure to speed on that soundpoint, until using whole bows:

Tiny strokes in the
middle of the bow

Gradually using more and more bow...

Whole bows

Repeat several times

The give of the wood and the hair

At the heel, the hair gives and the wood of the bow is rigid; at the point, the wood gives (in the middle of the bow) and the hair is rigid; in the middle of the bow, both the wood and the hair give.

Therefore the feeling of the bow's contact with the string changes, during the journey from the heel to the point, centimetre by centimetre; and each bow stroke feels slightly different, and works differently, depending on where in the bow it is played.

Proportions

Number the give in the wood and the hair from zero to 10: 10 = very soft, yielding; 0 = hard, no give.

- At the heel the hair 'bends' easily; but however hard you press down you cannot change the shape of the wood of the bow. The balance is 10:0 (Fig. 10a).

- At the tip of the bow, however hard you press you cannot bend the hair at its point of contact with the string (Fig. 10b); but the wood of the bow gives completely in the middle of the bow (Fig. 10c). The balance is 0:10.

- At the middle of the bow both wood and hair give equally. The balance is 5:5.

- The proportions of give, during one down-bow sustained f from heel to the point: 10:0 (all hair no wood), 9:1, 8:2, 7:3, 6:4, 5:5, 4:6, 3:7, 2:8, 1:9, 0:10 (all wood no hair).

Fig. 10

(a) The hair gives at the heel

(b) The hair is rigid at the point

(c) The wood gives in the middle of the bow while the hair is rigid at the point

Experiment

Experiment by playing quite short strokes heavily into the string in all parts of the bow:

Curiously few players, even advanced ones playing difficult pieces, seem aware of this aspect of the bow. The subject usually comes up quite early with a student if you work on tone exercises. For example, in this exercise it is obvious in nearly all players, by the time they reach soundpoint 2, that they are *not* playing into the wood of the bow when they are in the upper half.[1]

[1] See *Playing into the wood of the bow at the point*, page 19

The moment a player begins to bow in the new way – so that although they play deeply into the hair in the lower half, they start to play deeply into the wood when playing in the upper half – the difference and the instant improvement is always obvious.

Nor does it matter how good the player already is. As soon as they begin to bow like this, there is always a step up to a new level of sensuality and control, and you can always tell the difference.

How to sound as good as the best violinist in the world

Suppose you are practising long bows on each soundpoint and you are playing on, say, soundpoint 2. If you can do three things:

1 If you can draw the bow parallel to the bridge (which really anyone can learn to do, even if they do not do it automatically at first)

2 If you can balance the speed and pressure on one soundpoint so that you can get the string to vibrate at its widest (which again almost anyone can learn to do)

3 Most importantly, if you can do all this *evenly*

If you can do all three, then you can say that given this violin, with these strings, and given this bow with this bow-hair, you are playing this one note D as well as anybody in the whole world can play it.

After all, what more can anyone else do, sustaining this one note up and down the bow without vibrato? If you gave this violin, with these strings on it – and this bow, with this hair on it and amount of rosin – to Jascha Heifetz or David Oistrakh, what more could they do with it other than to adjust the speed and pressure, and distance from the bridge, until the balances are right?

Of course, if they were to add vibrato or play that same note as part of a musical phrase, other factors would come into it; but here we are looking at the pure mechanics of the bow making the string vibrate.

Making the string vibrate evenly, by adjusting the balances of speed and pressure on any soundpoint, is little to do with being a musician or artist. It is simply a matter of natural human sensitivity of touch. This is one reason why somebody may be a good violinist but not a moving musician.

The next step is to apply the same process to individual phrases or passages in the repertoire.

Applying Exercise 1 to the repertoire

- Take any type of phrase or stroke, and experiment with playing it only on soundpoint 5.

  Adjust the balances of speed and pressure, amount of hair, place in the bow, and tempo, until each note is pure, ringing, and even.

- Then repeat only on soundpoint 4, again only on soundpoint 3, and again only on 2. It may not be possible to play the phrase on soundpoint 1, depending on the string and the position, but it does not matter if you cannot. Simply go as far as you can.

  After making the strokes, phrase or passage work at every distance from the bridge, when you play it again on the correct soundpoints the improvement in the tone, and the increase in the sense of control and security, will be dramatic.

Exercise 2: Fast, short bows on each soundpoint

This exercise is like Exercise 1 but uses very short bows. Like the other tone exercises, you can use it regularly as a simple but super-effective warm-up exercise:

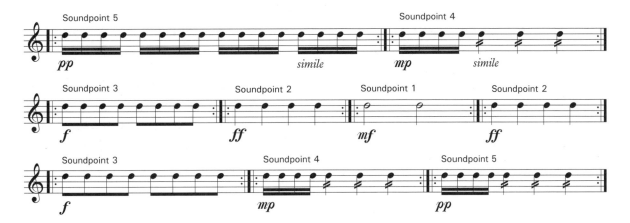

- Do not stop after each soundpoint before moving to the next: play as a continuous sequence.

- As you work your way nearer to the bridge use gradually less and less bow (therefore slower and slower bow speed), and play the strokes at a slower and slower tempo.

On soundpoint 1 play at an extremely slow tempo, use little bow length (perhaps only a few centimetres), and move the bow very slowly.

Suggested *tempi*: Soundpoint 5 ♩ = 80   (A typical range of tempi for this exercise, playing
                   Soundpoint 4 ♩ = 75   third-finger D on the A string)
                   Soundpoint 3 ♩ = 70
                   Soundpoint 2 ♩ = 56
                   Soundpoint 1 ♩ = 40

- Practising this exercise in different parts of the bow is a superb way to improve bow control. Play on each string in low, middle and high positions, at the heel, middle and point. There are 36 possibilities to explore (4 strings × 3 areas of the fingerboard × 3 areas of the bow).

The next step is to apply the same process to phrases and whole passages.

Applying Exercise 2 to the repertoire

Suppose you are playing a passage of sixteenth-notes (semiquavers):

Suppose the bow strokes are uneven, each one different from the last; some strokes too heavy, some too light; the tone is scratchy and whistling, and so on. Improving the tone is a simple process:

- Take certain notes on each string, and perform the soundpoints exercise on those notes:

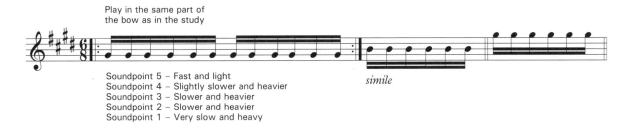

- Then find the same sounds, and the same feeling of the bow in the string, when playing the passage normally.

Exercise 3: The pressure exercise

The pressure exercise, which consists simply of alternating heavy and light bow-pressure within one long bow stroke, is another of the very best in the entire repertoire of technical exercises.

Mozart's father, Leopold, was already teaching it in 1756, the year of Wolfgang's birth. Since Leopold taught Wolfgang the violin, it is likely that Wolfgang himself would have played the pressure exercise:

> This example of…loudness, alternating with softness, can obviously be performed four, five, and six times; yes, often even more in one stroke. One learns through practice of this…to apply strength and weakness in all parts of the bow; consequently it is of great use…By diligent practice of the division of the stroke one becomes dexterous in the control of the bow, and through control one achieves purity of tone.[1]

[1] Leopold Mozart: *A Treatise On The Fundamental Principles Of Violin Playing* (Augsburg, 1756; Eng. Trans. Editha Knocker, Oxford, 1948), 99.

The same exercise was taught at the end of the eighteenth century by Campagnoli, the famous player, composer and teacher. This is how it is represented in the Campagnoli Violin School, circa 1800:

1	2	1	2	1	2	4
weak	*strong*	*weak*	*strong*	*weak*	*strong*	*weak*
p	*f*	*p*	*f*	*p*	*f*	*p*

Violinist Lucien Capet, quartet player and teacher in nineteenth century Paris and an expert on tone production and use of the bow, taught it to Ivan Galamian who in turn taught it to Dorothy DeLay.

Dr D.C. Dounis was another famous teacher who used the pressure exercise, as did the Russian teacher Yuri Yankelevich. So did the Catalan cellist Pablo Casals. He described the pressure exercise as a 'strength-inflection' exercise:

> I believe in daily technical exercise. I practise scales, repeated notes, trills in different rhythms; and as to the bow I use special exercises for the point, frog and middle, as well as exercises in strength-inflection, to accustom the bow-hand to finely marked differences of strength and pressure.[2]

[2] Frederick H. Martens: *String mastery: Talks with master violinists, viola players and violoncellists* (New York, 1923), 233.

The aim of the pressure exercise is to explore how deeply you can sink the bow into the string, and then immediately how lightly you can 'float' the bow along the surface of the string, while keeping the tone absolutely pure, even and unforced.

Leopold Mozart and Campagnoli both start with a 'weak', but with a modern bow and modern strings it makes more sense to begin with the 'strong'. If you begin with the 'weak' there might be a danger of introducing 'bulge notes' into your playing.[3]

[3] See *Avoiding bulges*, page 270

- Begin with one heavy–light on the down-bow, one on the up-bow:

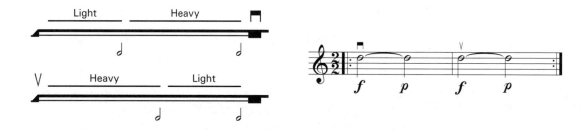

- Then play two heavy–lights on the down-bow, two on the up-bow:

Eight heavy–lights in one bow is often enough for general purposes (and for younger players). The sequence can be represented as follows:

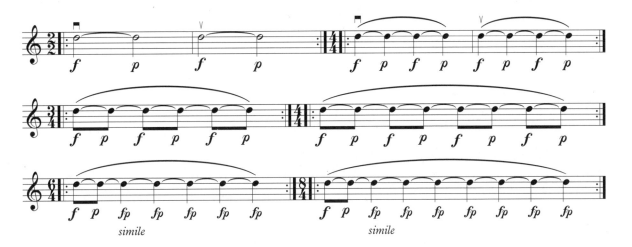

Later take the exercise further than eight groups:

- Play nine heavy–lights in one bow (3×3); twelve (3×4); sixteen (4×4).

- Then five groups of four, six, seven, eight, nine and ten groups of four (i.e. forty heavy–lights in one bow).

 Does the bow speed stay the same during each heavy–light, or is there a fast–slow speed–pattern at the same time?

To maximise the effects of the exercise, do as much as you can with pressure alone. Try to make any changes in the bow speed as slight as possible.

However, if you use no extra speed at all in the heavy part of the stroke it is impossible to play without scratching. Just use as little extra speed as possible, and see how far you can go without the tone breaking, rather than making the exercise 'too easy' by being too free with extra bow speed.

The differences in speed get less and less as you increase the number of patterns in one single bow, since the overall bow speed gets slower and slower.

Bow division

These exercises are naturally good for improving bow division. If you play two heavy–light patterns in one bow, begin the second pattern exactly in the middle of the bow. Playing three patterns, divide the bow into equal thirds; divide into four equal quarters to play four, and so on.[1]

When they do the exercise for the first time, many players make the mistake of using too much bow at the beginning of the bow and not having enough left at the end; it is not so common to see someone use too little bow at the beginning.

Playing into the wood of the bow at the point

The pressure exercise quickly shows whether the player knows the difference between sinking into the hair at the heel, and sinking into the wood (in the middle of the bow) when beginning f at the point.[2]

- Practise playing from the last p at the end of one bow to the f at the start of the next.

- Make both ends of the bow sound identical:

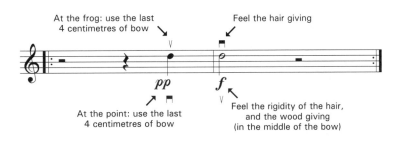

[1] If you ask a young pupil to say which heavy–light pattern begins exactly in the middle of the bow when they play eight patterns, many answer pattern number four – after all, four is half of eight. Of course this is wrong. In playing eight patterns you have four in the lower half and four in the upper half, so five begins exactly in the middle. Playing six patterns, number four begins exactly in the middle.

[2] See *The give of the wood and the hair*, page 15

Practising last *piano* of bow before first *forte* of next bow

The most common mistake in the beginning, one which nearly everybody makes, is to play *f* again just before the change of bow at the heel or at the point. The last pattern in the bow then becomes *fp* – *f* instead of *fp*.

- Practise playing evenly from the last *p* at the end of one bow to the *f* at the start of the next.

- Play subito *f* with strictly no crescendo during the *pp*.

- Aim for absolute evenness and purity of tone in both the *pp* and the *f*.

- Make both ends of the bow sound identical:

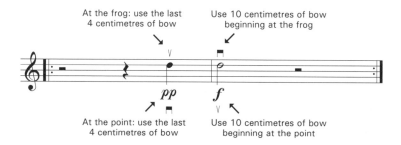

Practising playing *piano* at the point

As you approach the point, playing the last *p* in the last part of the down-bow, draw the bow with absolutely even speed and weight.

- Place the bow on the string near the point, and then take your fingers off and support it with only your thumb, with no other finger touching the bow (Fig. 11a); or lightly secure the bow with the tip of the first or second finger directly opposite the thumb (Fig. 11b).

Fig. 11

(a) Pull the bow, supporting it with only the thumb

(b) The first finger helping to support the bow

- Starting near the point, pull the bow very slowly, evenly and gently, using only your thumb to guide the bow along the string.

- Listen to the evenness of the tone; concentrate on the evenness of the bow speed while letting the bow lead the hand.

- Make sure the fingers that are not touching the bow are relaxed.

Afterwards, find the same feeling of extraordinary smoothness and evenness while playing properly with all the fingers on the bow.

Playing with a soft hand

All the joints in the right hand must be soft and giving, acting like shock absorbers to the ever-changing conditions of the bow on the strings. Flexibility, even if it is so subtle that you cannot see it, is the secret of how to play with a sweet, warm, full, singing tone.

Play a stage of the pressure exercise; briefly do the following simple flexibility exercise; play the next stage of the pressure exercise; repeat the flexibility exercise; and so on.

- Draw continuous whole bows, down-bow and up-bow, at a medium speed.

- Slowly bend and straighten the thumb and fourth finger 10 or 12 times in each bow.

  Feel them moving together. As one bends or straightens, so does the other at the same time.

- As the fingers curve, feel the knuckles flattening.

Then feel an imperceptible degree of the same give, in each joint in the hand, as you play the exercise.

Evenness: sustaining between the stages of the exercise

Sustain long, smooth bows between each stage of the exercise. This instantly produces greater smoothness and evenness when you then continue with the heavy–light patterns.

- As you sustain the long bows, make sure that the overall speed of bow is the same as the speed you will use for the heavy–light patterns that follow:

Variation: using less bow

- As an interesting variation, perform the entire pressure exercise in the lower half only; in the upper half only; and in the middle of the bow only.

Exercise 4: The speed exercise

The speed exercise uses exactly the same divisions as the pressure exercise, but here the bow moves fast–slow instead of heavy–light. The sequence, up to 4 fast–slows in a bow, can be represented as follows:

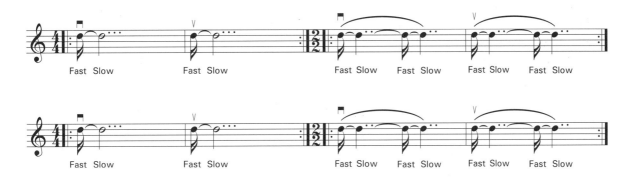

- As in the pressure exercise, continue through 6, 8, 9, 12, 16, 20, 24, 28, 32, 36 and 40 fast–slow divisions in each bow.

Use more bow and very slightly more pressure for the fast part of the stroke; less bow and less pressure for the slow part. Use as little extra pressure as possible during the fast part of the stroke: only as much as necessary to keep in good contact with the string – 'float' the bow along the string horizontally, rather than digging in vertically.

 The speed and pressure exercises sound quite different from each other when you do only a few divisions in each bow; but do they end up sounding the same by the time you are playing 12, 16, 20, and so on?

You can feel and hear the difference throughout both exercises – the difference between bowing 'deep down' into the string in the pressure exercise, and 'fast along' the string in the speed exercise.

In the pressure exercise, when there are few divisions in each bow the feeling of the contact of the hair with the string is: 'deep-down-into-the-string, release', 'deep, release', 'deep, release', etc., and 'deep, deep, deep, deep' when there are many in the bow.

In the speed exercise, when there are few divisions the feeling is: 'fast-along-the-string, slow', 'fast, slow', fast-slow, fast-slow, etc., and 'fast, fast, fast, fast' when there are many in the bow.

Practising last 'slow' of bow and first 'fast' of next bow

As in the pressure exercise, the last past of the bow – before you change from up to down, or down to up – is the place where you have to be extra careful.

The danger is that you move the bow quickly again just before the change of bow at the heel or at the point. The last pattern in the bow then becomes 'fast–slow…fast', instead of fast–slow.

Equally, another danger is that the first group of the bow (down or up) starts by 'creeping in', so the speed pattern then becomes 'slow…fast–slow' instead of fast–slow.

- Practise playing evenly from the last 'slow' at the end of one bow to the 'fast' at the start of the next.

- Slow the bow slightly just before changing direction and playing the fast stroke.

- Aim for absolute evenness and purity of tone in both the slow and the fast.

- Make both ends of the bow sound identical:

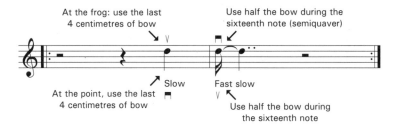

Evenness: sustaining between the stages of the exercise

Sustaining long bows, between the stages of the exercise, instantly produces greater smoothness and evenness, as in the pressure exercise.

- Make sure that the overall speed of bow is the same as the speed you will use for the fast–slow patterns that follow:

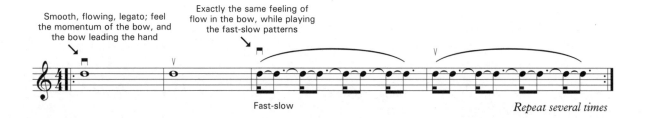

Variation: using less bow

Play the entire exercise in the lower half; in the upper half; and in the middle of the bow.

Exercise 5: Changing soundpoint

All tone exercises require great sensitivity of touch, and springiness, flexibility and responsiveness in every joint; but this exercise is one of the most sensuous of all – perhaps because all three factors of speed, pressure and distance from the bridge change at the same time, or because there is a feeling of breathing about it: the build-up as you breathe in, or more in

- Feel the qualities and tensions of the string while moving the bow towards and away from the bridge:

⑤ ④ ③ ① = Soundpoints

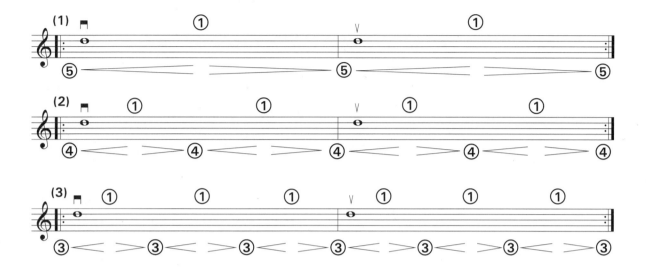

(1) Play whole bows, down-bow and up-bow on one note. Start on soundpoint 5, move to 1 during the lower half, and back to 5 during the upper half. Repeat on the up-bow.

Speed pattern: fast–slow–fast. Pressure pattern: light–heavy–light. Throughout, play with a faster, lighter stroke further from the bridge, slowly and heavily near the bridge.

(2) Move towards and away from the bridge twice in one bow. Start at the heel on 4. Use a quarter of the down-bow to reach the bridge, drift back to 4 by the middle of the bow, and the same in the upper half.

(3) Then move to and from the bridge three times, four times, etc., up to about eight. With each increase in number start nearer the bridge, ending up using only soundpoints 2–1 or 1½–1.

It is virtually impossible to do tone exercises using 'detached mental control'. You have to *feel* the bow in the string, and feel the string 'bending' under the bow, and the increasing 'hardness' of the string as you get nearer to the bridge – meanwhile slowing the bow and playing deeply into the string.

Also do the exercise the other way round, starting at the bridge.

- Focus on changing bow smoothly and seamlessly at each end of the bow. Now the changes of bow are *f*, not *p* as before:

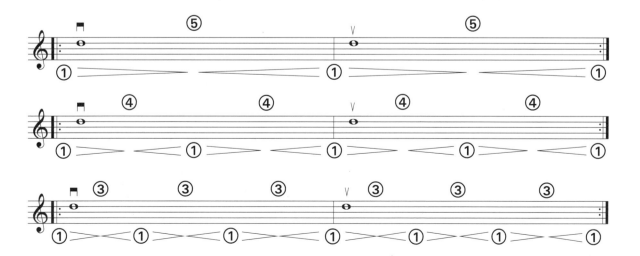

Two ways to do the exercise

There are two ways to approach the exercise: with a straight bow, or by using bow angles.

Doing the exercise for the first time, it is less complicated if you do it with a straight bow. Angling the bow often begins to happen naturally; if not, it is a simple thing to introduce:

- When the bow is angled 'in', so that the point is nearer the fingerboard than the frog (Fig. 12a), the bow naturally wanders towards the fingerboard during the down-bow. During the up-bow the bow naturally wanders towards the bridge.

- When the bow is angled 'out', so that the frog is nearer the fingerboard than the point (Fig. 12b), during the down-bow the bow wanders towards the bridge, and during the up-bow towards the fingerboard.

Key point: The single most important thing if you are angling the bow is to *let* it glide towards, or away from, the fingerboard or bridge; do not try to make it do it.

Fig. 12

(a) The bow moves towards the fingerboard on the down-bow; towards the bridge on the up-bow

(b) The bow moves towards the bridge on the down-bow towards the fingerboard on the up-bow

Get to the bridge before you change the angle

Doing this exercise for the first time, many players angle the bow so that it travels naturally towards the bridge, but then – *before* arriving at the bridge, but still wanting to get there – they change the angle as though they already want to travel towards the fingerboard.

Instead, keep the angle that is making you naturally travel towards the bridge until you arrive at the bridge; then, while sustaining the sound there with a very slow bow, close to the bridge, change the angle to send the bow travelling towards the fingerboard again.

Not increasing energy with the bow speed

When doing this exercise for the first time many players automatically move the bow faster as they pull in to the bridge, instead of slowing into the bridge.

This happens because playing nearer to the bridge requires extra weight, which is an increase in energy; moving the bow faster is also an increase in energy; the one sets off the other.

Instead, you need to slow the bow dramatically as you move into the bridge.

Unintentionally speeding up the bow as it moves nearer to the bridge is like unintentionally pressing the left fingers harder simply because of playing more heavily with the bow; or unintentionally playing an accelerando because of playing a crescendo.[1]

[1] See *One thing triggering another*, page 202

Preparatory exercise no. 1: drifting the bow

Use this as a warm-up exercise for Exercise 5, or as an exercise in its own right.

Place the bow on the A string at the point, on soundpoint 5, and angle the bow inwards (Fig. 12a):

- Beginning there on soundpoint 5, slowly push the bow up-bow a few centimetres. As the bow moves, allow the bow to drift across to soundpoint 2 or 1. Do not *make* the bow change the soundpoint: *let* it drift naturally because of the angle of the bow to the bridge.

- Having arrived at the bridge, stop the bow on the string; do not change anything; then pull the bow down-bow back to where you started. As the bow moves, allow it to drift back towards the fingerboard to soundpoint 5.

- Each group of four tied quarter-notes (crotchets) represents one continual, unbroken whole-note (semibreve). Draw the bow smoothly, without making each quarter-note distinct from the next:

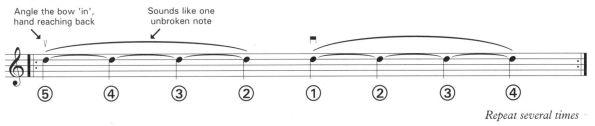

- Repeat at the middle; at the heel.

- Repeat using longer strokes in the lower half; at the middle; in the upper half.

- Repeat using three-quarters of the bow beginning at the heel; beginning at the point-of-balance.

- Repeat using whole bows.

- Then angle the bow outwards (Fig. 12b), and repeat the sequence the other way round:

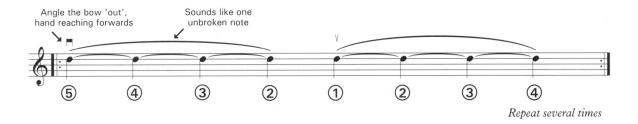

- Repeat on each string in low, middle, and high positions (3 × 4 = 12 possibilities). Also play on double stops, making 24 possibilities to explore in all.

Preparatory exercise no. 2: proportions of 'along' with 'in and out'

This exercise explores the balances of speed and pressure in relation to how fast the bow travels towards or away from the bridge.

Begin with only the movement backwards and forwards across the strings, with no horizontal movement of the bow whatsoever. Naturally this produces no proper tone. Then gradually add the horizontal movement:

- Place the bow on the A string on soundpoint 5.

    Without moving the bow *along* the string, slide the bow across the soundpoints to the bridge, and then back again to soundpoint 5.

    In other words, if the bow is placed on the string on soundpoint 5 at a place exactly 20 centimetres from the frog, it should still be 20 cm from the frog when the bow arrives at the bridge. Naturally this will produce no proper violin tone at all, but only the surface noise of the hair sliding across the string.

- Then add the tiniest amount of horizontal movement – no more than one centimetre – to the forwards-and-backwards movement.

    Again this will not produce a sensible tone because all the proportions are awry.

    Gradually add more horizontal movement – 2 cm, 4, 6, 8, 10 – until the proportions 'add up' and the tone is full, fat and ringing throughout.

This works the same way as the *spiccato* exercise where you begin with only vertical tapping, which similarly produces no proper tone, and then you gradually add the horizontal movement of the bow until the *spiccato* begins to sound.[1]

[1] See *Understanding proportions in spiccato*, page 284

Combining the tone exercises

To take the tone exercises further, mix them together in a variety of different combinations. For example, you can get a very good feel for the string if you play a mixture of the speed and pressure exercises on each soundpoint.

● Take any number of accents you like, and experiment with them on each soundpoint in turn:

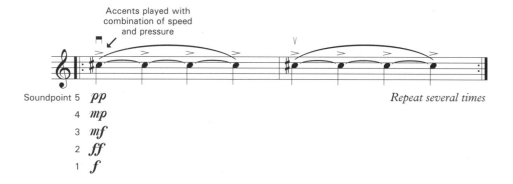

Soundpoint 5 *pp*
          4 *mp*
          3 *mf*
          2 *ff*
          1 *f*

Repeat several times

● On soundpoint 5, play the accents at a faster tempo, or with faster, lighter bow strokes. Playing on soundpoints 4, 3, and 2, play progressively more slowly and heavily, until on soundpoint 1 the accents are extremely slow and heavy.

● Play the whole speed exercise only on soundpoint 5, then only on soundpoints 4, 3 and 2.

● See how far from the bridge you can successfully play the pressure exercise.

Groups or phrases on each soundpoint

Another way to combine the exercises is to play a group of notes on each soundpoint in turn, staying strictly on one soundpoint at a time. This enables you to approach the work musically, as you give shape or expression to the group of notes, and produces excellent results.

● Make up any combination or type of notes you like:

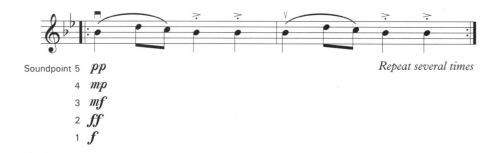

Soundpoint 5 *pp*
          4 *mp*
          3 *mf*
          2 *ff*
          1 *f*

Repeat several times

● Choose an area of the bow, i.e. upper half, lower half or 'middle half', or at the point, in the middle, or at the extreme heel.

● Decide on a length of bow, ranging from very little to as much as possible.

● Begin on soundpoint 5, repeating several times while experimenting with the balances of speed and pressure.

● Once the tone of every note is pure and ringing, move to soundpoint 4, then 3, 2 and 1.

On soundpoint 5, play the phrase at a faster tempo, or with faster, lighter bow strokes. Playing on 4, 3, and 2, play progressively more slowly and heavily. On soundpoint 1 you may have to play extremely slowly and heavily.

Holding the violin and bow

Putting the violin on the shoulder

Using a shoulder rest

The ideal, if your neck is short enough, is to play without a shoulder rest. Then the violin feels more part of you, and you can better feel the vibrations going into your ribcage. Even better would be to be able to play without a chin rest either – at least, if you did not mind spoiling the varnish in that area.[1]

Without a shoulder rest the instrument sits flatter on the collar bone (Fig. 13a), and also sounds better. But if you have a long neck the problem is how to fill the gap between the collar bone and the jaw bone. This space may be 10 or more centimetres, but the violin (with chin rest) may be only half that.

Filling the gap

The instinctive reaction to the gap is to hunch the left shoulder up (Fig. 13b); but this easily creates tension, particularly if the shoulder becomes locked there. If you do not use a shoulder rest, sit the violin on the collarbone and keep the space open (Fig. 13c), or you might use a small pad, either attached to the violin or under the clothing, to fill the space.

One solution to the gap between the collar and jaw bones is to raise the chin rest. They can be custom-made as high as 7 or 8 centimetres; and an ordinary chin-rest can be extended by putting cork between it and the violin. The drawback is that a very high chin-rest can make you feel separate from the instrument, as though 'you' are somewhere in your head – between your ears and behind your eyes – directing what is going on 'down there' where the instrument is.

Another way to fill the gap is to use a very tall shoulder rest. The drawback then is that the strings are on a much higher level than the shoulder (Fig. 13d). This is less comfortable for the bow arm than when the strings are lower, as they are when the violin sits directly on the collar bone (Fig. 13e). The head should not lean to the right, and if it does this is often a tell-tale sign that the shoulder rest is too high. (Fig. 13f).

[1] It was not until the first decade of the nineteenth century that Louis Spohr introduced the chin rest, or 'fiddle-holder' as he called it, which he declared was 'a contrivance of my own invention'.

Many violins from the centuries before the fiddle-holder have areas of discolouration on either side of the tailpiece which were caused by the chins, beards and sweat of those who played them.

Fig. 13

(a) The violin is often flatter without a shoulder rest

(b) Hunching the shoulder to fill the gap causes tension

(c) Do not try to fill the gap by raising the shoulder. Keep the space open.

(d) The level of the strings is much higher than the level of the shoulder

(e) The strings and the shoulder are more on the same level

(f) A too-high shoulder-rest may cause the head to tilt to the right

The subject of trying not to raise the left shoulder is a continual issue for many players, and many teachers are insistent about it. Yet there is another alternative to either raising your shoulders or keeping them down. When the shoulders are free they can take part in the alive, active process of holding the violin.[1] This is entirely different from 'hunching' the shoulder up.

[1] See also *Raising or not raising*, page 178

The best approach for players with long necks is often a combination of all three approaches, i.e. a medium-high shoulder rest with a medium-high chin rest and, whenever necessary, to feel an alive, active engagement by the shoulder.[2]

[2] See also *3. How high or low on the shoulder?*, page 34

The length or shape of the chin is a factor. A long chin effectively shortens the neck, so a long neck and a long chin is less of a disadvantage than a long neck and a short chin.

Further in or out

The left end of a shoulder rest should not sit too close to the edge of the shoulder, since this can cause immobility in the left upper arm (Fig. 14a). Instead, position the rest as close in towards your neck as you can (Fig. 14b):

Fig. 14

(a) The shoulder rest is too close to the edge of the shoulder

(b) Position the rest as far away from the edge of your shoulder as you can

Higher or lower

Players who do not use a shoulder rest are unlikely to position the violin too low on their shoulder, at the top of the chest, since it simply feels too difficult to play like that.

But if you use a shoulder rest you need to make sure that it sits sufficiently high on the shoulder. If it is positioned too low (down towards the top of the chest) it causes the violin to be too tilted.[3] It also causes the shoulders to pull in, and the back to stoop forward (Fig. 15a). A higher placement helps the shoulders to widen and the back to lengthen (Fig. 15b).

[3] See also *4. The tilt of the violin, page 35*

Fig. 15

(a) Positioning the rest too low on the shoulder causes the violin to be too tilted, the shoulders to pull down and in

(b) A higher setting on the shoulder helps the shoulders to widen and the back to lengthen

Raising the violin

Fit the instrument to you, not yourself to the instrument

The first principle of holding the violin is to arrange the instrument, chin rest and shoulder rest to fit and suit you, rather than trying to fit yourself to them.

Similarly, you have to bring the instrument up to you, rather than taking yourself forwards to the instrument. There is a story about the French cellist Paul Tortelier:

> Paul Tortelier was once staying with a friend who was a flautist. One day Tortelier came downstairs and said: 'I've had enough of practising the cello today. Will you show me how to play the flute?'
>
> As Tortelier picked up the flute and began to bring it towards his mouth, he pulled down in his upper chest and bent forwards slightly; thrust his head as far forwards as it could go while sticking his chin out and slightly up; and raised both shoulders as his hands moved upwards.

His friend immediately scolded him. 'Paul!', she said. 'You would never go to play your cello like that. You bring the instrument to you! You don't take yourself to the instrument!' Tortelier pretended to look shamefaced.

Violinists and violists typically pull down and lean forwards as they bring the instrument up to play.

Fig. 16

- Find a posture where you are upright and balanced (standing or sitting). Lengthen your back and raise your chest, and feel your head sitting in a 'forward and up' position on top of your spine.[1]

- Practise raising the violin and bow without moving your back or altering the balance of your head.

Starting from above

A traditional way to get a feeling of the violin being light, rather than it feeling like a heavy weight that you somehow have to keep in the air, is to start with the violin held high above your head (Fig. 16a).

When you then descend from there into playing position, the violin feels light and buoyant.[2]

[1] Continually find a sensation of the back of your head rising while your forehead imperceptively moves forward. Do this not only in relation to playing the violin, but many times each day during ordinary activities as a matter of habit. It can be so subtle that nobody can even see you doing it.

[2] The American teacher Paul Rolland called this the 'Statue of Liberty' pose.

Raising the violin quickly

If you raise the violin to your shoulder quickly, the instrument feels much lighter – once it arrives on your shoulder – than if you raise it slowly.

- Starting with the violin hanging down vertically from your left hand (Fig. 16b), there is a kind of a 'flick' you can do with the left hand that throws the violin up, and into position, in one go.

  It is almost the same movement as when you lift it slowly, except that you make the beginning of the movement very quickly, and then *follow* the violin up into playing position.

  The violin feels light because after the initial lift, or push, you really are not lifting the weight of the violin – it travels under its own momentum – and you really are just lifting your arm into the air.

(a) Descend into playing position from here

Lifting with the right hand

Although you will not do this during the normal course of playing (though you easily can when playing seated), you can get a real feeling of lightness, and of the violin 'floating', if you 'flick' it up into position using the right hand.

The left hand feels light and easy because it has nothing to do with raising the instrument into position.

- Starting in the position shown in Fig. 16c, use the right hand to flick the violin up into position.

  Because the violin travels with its own momentum the left hand merely follows, and there is no sensation of the left hand lifting any weight whatsoever.

(b) 'Throw' the violin onto your shoulder with a flick of the left hand

Putting the chin on the chin rest

Head position

It used to be suggested that the nose should be in line with the strings; also that you should look at the contact-point of the bow with the string, or at a place in the air slightly above and beyond the scroll. But keeping the head rotated in order to look down the strings may easily lead to tension or locking in the neck and shoulders. A position where the strings and the nose form a 'V' shape is often more comfortable. Then the head remains much the same as when you are not playing the violin.

(c) 'Push' the violin onto your shoulder with a flick of the right hand

Since everything should always be free and mobile rather than being 'fixed', you can have a range of head positions: from turning to look down the strings, to facing forwards as normal, to rotating the head to the right while bringing the left ear close to the strings (in order to hear the sound closely).

Which part of the chin touches the chin rest?

The 'chin rest' should really be called a 'jaw bone rest', since that is more the actual contact-point with the lip of the chin rest (Fig. 17a) rather than the point of the jaw which is called the 'chin' (Fig. 17b).

Unless the violin is held pointing straight in front, thinking of the chin as belonging on the chin rest may force the head to stay in too fixed a position.

Some players put their cheek too flatly on the chin rest, making it more a 'cheek rest' (Fig. 17c). This causes an excessive tilt of the head which easily leads to tension in the neck and shoulders.

Keep the head upright, or make the traditional slight tilt to the left. This is good for listening since it makes the violin play more directly into the ear. Leaning the head any degree to the right never seems to work well for any player (Fig. 13f, page 27).

Fig. 17

(a)   Contact with the rest is more with the jaw than with the chin

(b)   You do not have to rest the 'chin' on the 'chin-rest'

(c)   The chin rest has become a 'cheek rest'

Rotate, then drop

There are two things you have to do to place the chin on the chin rest. One is to rotate your head slightly to the left. The second is to lower your head slightly, until your chin contacts the rest.

- The way *not* to put the chin on the chin rest is to do both of these actions at the same time, i.e. moving the head diagonally down. If you rotate and drop at the same time, there is an immediate feeling of tension in the neck and shoulders; and it forces vertebrae in the neck to twist onto each other, which over time may easily cause extremely serious problems. Instead, first rotate and then drop.

- If first you rotate the head and only then drop the chin, there is a feeling of great freedom in the neck and shoulders, and the vertebrae in the neck work together perfectly.

   This is one of the most important of all issues in holding and playing the violin.

Avoiding pressing

Relaxing the weight of the head

Do not clamp the violin hard between chin and shoulder. Simply relax the weight of the head into the chin rest. Most of the time there is no need to press – the head is an extremely heavy object on its own.

You have to hold the violin firmly during certain descending shifts or powerful vibratos, in order to keep the violin or the bow steady; but pressing in a fixed way may quickly create tension which will spread from the neck, upper back and shoulders down into the arms and hands.

- Suppose you hold the violin between two fingers (Fig. 18a). To support the violin, all you need is the finger on top of the chin rest (Fig. 18b). The violin seems to push up against that finger.[1]

Fig. 18

[1] Note the pronounced upward curved lip of the chin rest illustrated in Fig. 18b. Though not every chin rest fits or suits everyone, many players find that a chin rest with a good lip makes holding the violin much easier, as the jawbone can 'hook' against the lip without the need for downward pressure.

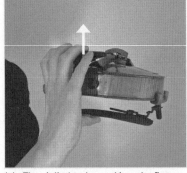  

(a)   The violin 'pushes up' into the first finger

(b)   Note how little you have to do to support the violin

(c)   Eliminate or minimise any bulging out of this tendon

- You can find the same feeling with the violin sitting on your shoulder, but still using the finger to prevent the violin from falling (Fig. 18c). Again, the violin seems to push up against the finger.

- Then, holding the violin normally, use the weight of the head alone to sit the jaw bone on the chin rest and resist the upward direction of the chin rest.

Mind the gap

Do not allow any space between the violin and the neck. If you hold the violin as shown in Fig. 19a, you have to press down hard to hold the violin. There is an immediate feeling of strain and tension in the muscles in the neck and shoulders.[1]

Look out for where the button of the violin (to which the tailpiece is attached) is in relation to your neck. It should usually be more or less in the centre, so you should not be able to see it.

Don't press in

Hold the violin well in to the neck, though without any hint of pressing it in. If you push the violin too hard against the side of the neck, it can easily press on the main artery and lead to breathlessness or worse.

Watch the large veins in the forehead: you can often see that the moment the player puts the violin under the chin and starts to play, these veins immediately swell and stick out – and then immediately recede again the moment the violin is taken away from the neck. The swelling is caused by the restriction of blood flow in the neck.

Make sure you cannot see any light between the violin and the neck

Another effect of pressing the violin against the neck, or of pressing the jaw down hard into the chin rest, is the danger of sores and abscesses developing at the point of contact with the instrument.

[1] The reason for this is another illustration of the principles of pivots and leverage. Think of a nut-cracker, or a pair of scissors: the laws of leverage dictate that the closer in to the centre the two levers connect, the more powerful is the clamping or cutting.

Fig. 19

Adjusting the four planes

Adjust the position of the violin in four ways:

1 Fixed point: chin-rest end of violin

   Moveable point: vertical movement of scroll up or down (Fig. 20a)

2 Fixed point: chin-rest end of violin

   Moveable point: horizontal movement of scroll left or right (Fig. 20b)

3 Fixed point: scroll

   Moveable point: horizontal movement of chin-rest end left or right (Fig. 20c)

4 Fixed points: scroll and chin-rest end of violin

   Moveable point: rotational tilt of violin (Fig. 20d)

(a) Vertical movement at scroll end

(b) Horizontal movement at scroll end

Fig. 20

(Fig. 20)

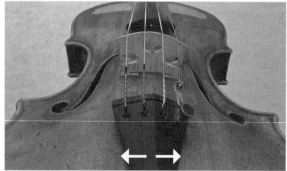

(c) Horizontal movement at chin rest end

(d) Rotational movement, both ends fixed

1. Finding the correct height of the scroll

[1] The Russian violinist Jascha Heifetz said that when you shift up, you should actually be shifting 'down' – because of the downward slope towards the bridge when the scroll is held up.

[2] The necks of earlier violins, in the Baroque and early Classical periods, were joined to the body of the instrument in a straight line. A wedge was inserted between the neck and the fingerboard to raise the fingerboard up at an angle, so that the strings could rise to the bridge.

The problem with this was that the wedge made the neck of the violin much thicker in the hand. Finally the solution was found of doing away with the wedge and instead angling the neck itself downwards.

It is not so usual to see the scroll of the violin held permanently too high, but a too-low scroll is not uncommon (Fig. 21a). This is bad for posture since it encourages pulling down with the instrument; tone may weaken as the bow constantly moves towards the fingerboard; and most bow strokes feel best when the string is not sloping down away from the bridge but is flat or sloping towards the bridge.[1]

Since the neck of the violin slopes down from the body, if you want the strings to be flat the scroll has to be raised so that the instrument itself is at a slight angle.[2]

The angle affects not only tone but also the workings of the bow arm itself: the higher the scroll, the further forward the upper arm goes to keep the bow parallel with the bridge at the point. Raising the scroll has the same effect as shortening the arm:

Experiment

Use exaggerated positions to show how the height of the scroll affects the bow arm:

- Fig. 21a shows the violin held too low, causing the right arm not to extend sufficiently at the point.

- Fig. 21b shows the violin held too high, causing the arm to straighten too much to get to the point.

- Fig. 21c shows the violin at a middle height, the strings flat. The right arm is neither too straight nor too bent when playing at the point.

- To form a new habit of keeping the violin up, sometimes practise with a music stand under the scroll (Fig. 21d). Keep the scroll hovering just above the stand, without ever touching it.

Fig. 21

(a) Violin too low, right arm too bent at point

(b) Violin too high, right arm too straight at point

(c) Violin at correct height, right arm neither too straight nor too bent

(d) Keep the scroll just above the music stand without touching it

Looking at the angles objectively

One of the reasons why students may be slow to correct faults in the tilt of the violin, or in the height of the scroll, is that while they are playing they cannot see the instrument as you see it.

A simple answer is for them to begin playing with the violin in the position that they are used to, and once they have got into the flow of it you suddenly say 'Stop!', at which they instantly freeze and hold whatever position they were in, without moving anything (Fig. 22a).

Then take a firm grip on the instrument (Fig. 22b) so that the student can walk away and inspect the angle or tilt from an objective distance (Fig. 22c).

Fig. 22

(a) Having stopped in mid-action and 'frozen'

(b) Grip the instrument firmly

(c) Looking at the angle objectively

2. Finding the angle to the body

The correct angle of the violin to the body depends firstly on the length of your arms.

- Short arms: point the scroll more to the right
- Long arms: point the scroll more to the left

It also depends on which part of the bow you are using: in a long passage or section at the heel, it is often more comfortable for the right arm if the scroll is slightly more to the left; playing at the point for a long time, it may be more comfortable with the scroll pointing slightly less to the left.

Ideally, when the bow is on the string at the point, the right arm ends up neither too straight at the elbow (Fig. 23a), nor too bent (Fig. 23b), but somewhere in between (Fig. 23c).

Fig. 23

(a) Scroll too far to the left. The right arm has to straighten to reach the point

(b) Scroll too far in front. The arm is near the 'square' position when playing at the point

(c) Scroll in a middle position. The arm is neither too straight nor too bent at the point

(d) Scroll too far in front. The forearm and hand feel cramped playing in the lower half.

Experiment

- Point the scroll exaggeratedly too far out to the left (Fig. 23a). Notice how you have to straighten the arm at the elbow to reach the point, if you want to keep the bow parallel with the bridge.

- Point the scroll too much in front of you (Fig. 23b). Notice how you can now get to the point with the arm still only at the 'square' position, without having to extend the arm to reach the point.

- This leads to restricted bowing in the upper half, since everything is then played with only the forearm; and cramped bowing in the lower half, since the angle at the elbow, of the forearm and the upper arm, has to close too much (Fig. 23c).

- Find the middle position between the two extremes (Fig. 23d).

3. How high or low on the shoulder?

Adjust the position of the violin on the shoulder. A small change at this end of the violin affects the path of the bow more than a small change at the scroll end:

- Short arms: violin higher on shoulder, so that the chin is nearer to, or directly above, the tail piece.

- Long arms: violin lower on shoulder, so that the chin is further to the left of the tail-piece.

Right arm

This adjustment of the position of the violin on the shoulder is often overlooked. It is common to see short-armed players with a chin rest too far to the left, and long-armed players using a centre chin rest.

The lower the violin is positioned on the shoulder, the further you have to reach to bow to the point:

- Short arms: shorten the distance to avoid ending up with an entirely straight arm at the point.

- Long arms: lengthen the distance to avoid ending up at the square position at the point.

Experiment

- Position the violin far too low on the shoulder (Fig. 24a). Notice that you have to straighten the arm at the elbow to reach the point, if you keep the bow parallel with the bridge.

  Even if you point the scroll more in front of you, it is difficult to reach the point without straightening the arm. With the violin so low on the shoulder, there is too far to go to get to the point.

- Position the violin far too high on the shoulder (Fig. 24b). Notice that you can now get to the point without having to extend the arm.

  Even if you hold the scroll out too far to the left, it is still possible to reach the point without straightening the arm – with the violin so high on the shoulder, there isn't so far to go.

- Find the middle position between the two extremes (Fig. 24c).

Fig. 24

(a) Violin too low on the shoulder   (b) Violin too high   (c) Middle position

Left hand and arm

The angle of the violin also has an effect on the left arm. The more the scroll points in front, the more the forearm has to rotate clockwise to keep the knuckles in the correct line with the neck. Too much rotation is a great cause of tension.

Experiment

- Experiment by using extremes: with your left fourth finger kept down on the G string, hold the instrument exaggeratedly pointing to the left, and low on the shoulder (Fig. 25a); and exaggeratedly in front of you, and high on the shoulder (Fig. 25b).

- Notice how, as you bring the scroll in front of you, the forearm rotates clockwise; and how there is a point beyond which strain begins to appear as the forearm rotates further than is comfortable.

- Find a middle point of greatest comfort, where the right arm can bow to the point sufficiently easily, and the left fingers can reach the strings without over-rotating the forearm.

Fig. 25

(a) Low on the shoulder, scroll out to the left, the forearm does not have to rotate so far.

(b) High on the shoulder, scroll in front, the forearm has to rotate clockwise.

4. The tilt of the violin

Right arm

1 The more tilted the violin the easier it is to play on the G string (Fig. 26a), but the worse it is to play on the E string because the bow is too vertical.

   Then it feels as though you are bowing against the side of the string (Fig. 26b). The string lends no support to the bow, and the arm cannot relax into the string.

2 The flatter the violin, the easier it is to play on the E string (Fig. 26c). The bow movement is more horizontal, the string supports the bow and the bow arm can relax into the string.

   However, the flatter the violin, the higher the right arm has to play to reach the G string (Fig. 26d)

- Therefore, it is logical to suppose that a position midway between the two extremes - where it is easy-enough to reach the G string, and at the same time the E string supports the bow sufficiently without the bow being too vertical - must be the ideal.

However, a better approach is often to keep the violin as flat as possible, or to tilt it 'only as much as necessary but as little as possible'. Because it is not just the E string that feels better with a flatter violin: just about all bow strokes on the other strings do too, because there is a different and better feeling in the bow arm. All the lifted bowings, from *spiccato* to *ricochet*, work better with a flatter violin.

Try it for yourself and see: keeping the elbow more-or-less on the same level as the bow, play a few strokes with the violin quite tilted (Fig. 26a), and then again with the violin quite flat (Fig. 26c). With the instrument flat it is like having a completely different bow arm because you are using different muscles, or the same muscles in different ways.

You have to find your own best position, which depends partly on your physique and partly on your choice of chin rest or shoulder rest, if you use one (though the rule is to fit the instrument and the equipment to you, not the other way round). Some may not be comfortable with the violin less tilted than it could be; others are perfectly comfortable with a very flat violin. But if you don't want the violin too flat, the essential thing is that it must not be too tilted.

Fig. 26

(a) The G string is easy to reach

(b) The bow is playing against the side of the string

(c) The string lends support to the bow

(d) The arm has to be raised very high to reach the G string

Left hand

The tilt also has an effect on the left hand. The more tilted the violin, the more comfortable it is for the left hand to play on the G string.

However, if the violin is too tilted it becomes difficult to place the fingers on the other strings, unless the left elbow moves exaggeratedly to the left. So again a compromise can be found where the violin is not quite flat. The best tilt often depends on the exact notes you are playing.

Use fourth-finger D on the G string as a point to measure from.

● Tilt the violin at an angle of about 45°, and position the tip of the fourth finger so that it is almost touching the G string (Fig. 27a).

   Position the hand and elbow so that the little finger is curved, relaxed and comfortable, and requiring the least effort to reach the G string.

● Using your right hand, move the violin to a horizontal position, but without the left arm or hand moving with it: leave them 'frozen' in the air and move only the violin.

   Note how the fourth finger, which had been above the G string, is now above the A string because the strings have moved to the left (Fig. 27b).

   Note how much the elbow would now have to move to the right if you wanted the finger to reach the G string.

Fig. 27

(a) See how easily the fourth finger reaches the G string

(b) Use the right hand to move the violin. The left hand and fourth finger have barely moved, but the violin is now flatter.

Setting yourself up for playing first or second violin

Violinists who always play second violin (perhaps full-time in an orchestra or a quartet) often hold their violin with an exaggerated tilt, while those who play first violin tend to hold it flatter.

This makes sense because if you play second violin you usually spend more time playing on the lower strings than on the upper strings. You can always flatten the violin more during phrases or passages on the higher strings.

If you play first violin you often spend more time playing on the upper strings, and you can always tilt the violin more during passages on the lower strings.

Holding the bow

The bow hold changes constantly

What is the best way to hold the bow? There is no single answer since the exact bow hold changes according to what you are playing. What is the best way to hold the bow to play *what*, exactly?

- To play heavily or strongly, you might grip the bow quite solidly, and spread the fingers more widely to get more leverage.

- To make a particular *dolce* quality you might hold the bow with barely any feeling of contact at all; and allow the fingers to remain a normal, natural distance apart rather then 'spreading them out'.

- It is difficult to play a *sotto voce*, *dolce* tone, like the one at the opening of the Brahms D minor Sonata, if you hold the bow with a 'strong' bow hold:

Brahms: Sonata in D minor, op. 108, *mov. 1, b. 1*

- Similarly, it is difficult to play strong chords or *martelé* if you hold the bow as if to play *piano dolce*. At the beginning of each *martelé* you have to hold the bow firmly to bite the string:

Kreutzer: 42 Etudes ou caprices, *no. 6, b. 1*

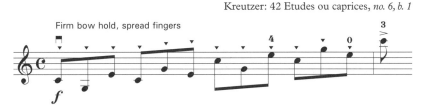

- To play *spiccato* the fingers may be more upright on the bow to allow a little space between the first finger and the top of the bow (Fig. 28j).

- To play *sautillé* the fingers may be more leaning on the bow, and the fourth finger (and at times, even the third finger) may come off the bow entirely.

- At the heel the hand is more upright or 'supinated' (Fig. 28j), balancing the bow with the little finger; at the point the hand leans towards the first finger or is more 'pronated' (Fig. 28k).

  Since the change from more upright to more leaning happens gradually, centimetre by centimetre up the bow, the exact bow hold is slightly different at every place in the bow.

- The tilt of the bow changes all the time, from the hair being flat on the string to tilting so much that only the outer edge of the hair contacts the string.[1]

  The more tilted the bow, the less contact between the pad of the first or third finger and the bow.

[1] See *The tilt of the bow*, page 265

However, although there is not one bow hold but several, and nothing must be 'fixed' in one place, there is still a basic finger-placement, a basic bow hold, from which you start and to which you return.

Naturalness

A correct bow hold is one that feels entirely natural and comfortable, so that you simply forget about it. You are in complete control of the bow as it dances over the strings, but without being particularly aware of holding it.

If you find yourself too often conscious of 'holding' the bow – especially if it feels uncomfortable in any way – it may mean you have an idea of how to hold it that is at odds with what your hand (or the bow) is telling you it wants. In something like this, naturalness must always win over reason or theory.

How to set up the basic bow hold

Begin with a pencil; then repeat using the bow.

- Hold your forearm level with the floor and allow your hand to flop limply from the wrist (Fig. 28a).

  Note how the fingers find their own natural distance from each other.

  It may encourage the hand to be completely loose if you shake the hand vigorously first, before allowing it to drop limply from the wrist.

- Place the pencil slantwise across the fingers, from the tip of the little finger to a contact-point with the first finger at the crease of the first joint (Fig. 28b).

  Note how the natural spacing of the fingers has not changed.

- Place the tip of the thumb almost opposite the second finger, but slightly to the right of centre.

- At the same time lower the knuckles. You may find it more comfortable if at this stage you also push your first finger half a centimetre higher up the bow (Fig. 28c).

Repeat with the bow:

- Place the bow slantwise across the fingers, from the tip of the little finger to a contact-point with the first finger at the crease of the first joint (Fig. 28d).

  Note how the natural spacing of the fingers has not changed.

  Note the continuous line made by the edge of the little finger, and the edge of the frog (Fig. 28e).

  Contact the bow on the upper, inside edge of the octagonal.

  Note the contact-point of the first finger with the bow, at the crease of the first joint (Fig. 28f).

- Place the tip of the thumb in its normal position, half on the bow and half on the thumb-piece (Fig. 28g). At the same time lower the knuckles (Fig. 28h).[1]

[1] See also *Freeing the thumb*, page 53

Fig. 28

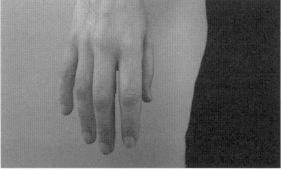

(a) Note the natural spacing of the fingers

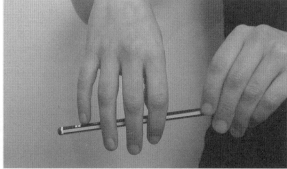

(b) Place the pencil slantwise across the hand without altering the natural spacing

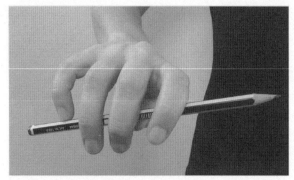

(c) Place the thumb opposite the second finger and flatten the knuckles

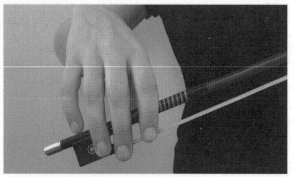

(d) Place the bow slantwise across the hand

(Fig. 28)

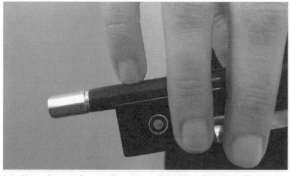

(e) Note the continuous line down the edge of the little finger and the edge of the frog

(f) Note the contact-point of the first finger with the bow

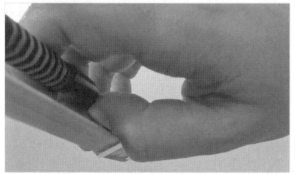

(g) Contact-point of thumb with bow

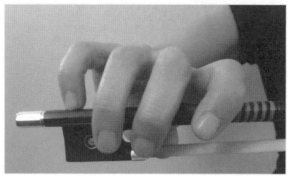

(h) The basic bow hold

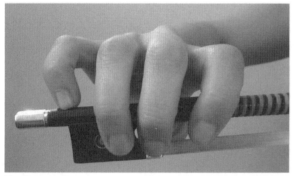

(j) Supinated

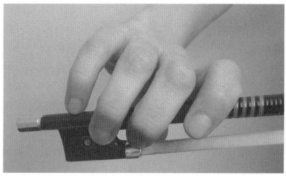

(k) Pronated

 Q **What is the difference in the bow hold for larger and smaller hands, or for longer and shorter fingers?**

If you start with your thumb resting diagonally against the thumb-piece (Fig. 28g), the bow hold ends up much the same whatever the size of hand. Large hands or small, the third finger sits in basically the same place between the curve of the frog and the pearl 'eye'(Fig. 28h).

If your hands are small the line of the outside edge of the fourth finger may not be in line with the edge of the frog as it is in Fig. 28e. Also, the first finger will not be as far up the bow.

The Russian teacher Raphael Bronstein recommended that players with very short arms – but using a full size bow – should position the thumb a little higher up the bow a centimetre or so away from the curve of the thumb-piece. The other fingers then take their usual positions relative to the thumb or to each other, the second finger slightly left-of-centre to the thumb, and so on.

First finger: leverage

Do not hold the bow so that the first finger is too near to the thumb (Fig. 29a). The chances of playing with effort, or a small or pressed tone, are much greater than if the first finger is positioned a little further up the stick away from the thumb.[1]

[1] See also *1. Using the second finger*, page 47; *Adjusting the bow hold for power*, page 293

There are two major disadvantages if the first finger is too near to the thumb:

1 There is an unbalanced distribution of the fingers on the bow, with three fingers one side of the thumb and one finger the other side (Fig. 29a).

2 The first finger is too near the thumb. Any downward pressure from the first finger has a greater effect the further away from the thumb it is. A simple experiment illustrates this clearly:

Fig. 29

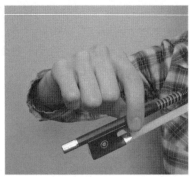

(a) The first finger is too close to the thumb

(b) Holding the bow with as little contact as possible

(c) Pressing the wood to judge the resistance at different distances from the pivot

Experiment in leverage

The teacher or assistant

● Hold the violin in playing position with the middle of the bow resting on the D and A strings (so that the bow is near horizontal). Support the bow at the other end with only the thumb and first finger. Place the tip of the first finger on top of the bow, opposite the thumb, to help steady the bow and prevent it from falling (Fig. 29b).

The student

● Pressing at the place where the bow is resting on the string, press the assistant's bow slowly down towards the hair until the wood touches the hair; then slowly release it again (Fig. 29c).

Repeat several times, pushing and releasing very slowly, noting exactly how much weight is necessary to make the wood touch the hair (which is not much).

● Do the same thing a few centimetres lower, i.e. push the bow down until the wood in the middle of the bow touches the hair. Note how a little more weight is now required.

● Repeat lower and lower in the bow until the pressing finger is right next to the thumb.

More and more weight is needed as you press lower and lower on the bow until, when your finger is right next to the assistant's thumb, an enormous amount of weight is required to make the wood (in the middle of the bow) touch the hair.

Naturally, downward pressure directly above the supporting thumb has no effect at all, and any pressure to the right of the thumb lifts the bow away from the string.

This experiment makes it clear that the *further away from the thumb downward pressure is applied, the less pressure is needed to produce the same effect.*

Think of a see-saw: a small child sitting at the extreme end on their side can easily balance a large adult, on the opposite side, who is sitting closer in to the centre. A door handle is fixed on the opposite side to the hinges: great effort would be required to open the door if the handle were positioned close to the hinges. Try playing notes on a piano with your finger at the back of the key.

Therefore, a bow hold that places the first finger close to the thumb requires much more downward pressure, i.e. effort, to produce a good, carrying tone, than one where the first finger is positioned higher up the stick.[1]

Avoiding tension in the base of the thumb

Although you should not place the first finger too close to the thumb, when you move it further away the second finger moves up the bow slightly as well. If this is done too much (so that the third finger is closer to the thumb than the second finger is), there may be tension in the base of the thumb:

● Position your right hand in the air, with the thumb opposite the first finger.

● With your left fingers, feel the softness of the muscle between the base of the right thumb and the base of the first finger (Fig. 30a).

[1] Carl Flesch recommended positioning the first and second fingers on either side of the thumb, but this places the first finger impossibly close to the thumb. Flesch influenced generations of teachers, as did his student Max Rostal; yet it is interesting to note that none of Flesch's famous students – Ginette Neveu, Henryk Szeryng, Joseph Hassid, Ida Haendel and so on – held the bow in the way he described. They all placed their second finger opposite or slightly to the left of the thumb.

Fig. 30

(a) With your index finger, feel the softness of the muscle at the base of the thumb

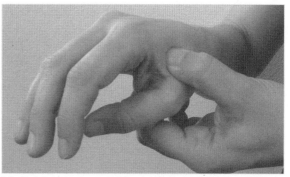

(b) Feel the muscle contracting as the thumb moves towards the little finger

- Slowly move the tip of the right thumb towards the little finger.

  Feel how the muscle at the base of the right thumb immediately begins to contract as the thumb starts to move to the right. By the time the tip of the thumb actually touches the tip of the little finger (Fig. 30b) the muscle is at its maximum contraction and hardness.

Key point: There is a place where the second finger can sit, almost opposite the thumb but very slightly to the left-of-centre, where there is a balance of two fingers one side of the thumb, and two fingers the other side, but with the least contraction of the muscle at the base of the thumb.

Feeling the creases

What are the contact-points of the fingers with the bow?[1] The thumb and fourth finger contact the bow with the tips of the fingers. The first, second and third fingers contact the bow at the crease between the nail joint and the middle joint.

[1] See also *How to stop the fingers climbing up the bow*, page 43

The only contact of the second finger with the bow is at the crease, opposite the thumb and countering it. This is the centre of the bow hold and often needs to be strong. The nail joint has no job to do whatsoever in holding the bow. The tip must not curl in and try to touch the thumb, but the feeling of contact between the crease and the bow is an alive one.

Playing in the lower half, the pad of the third finger contacts the frog of the bow. At the same time feel the crease firmly contacting the top, outer edge of the bow.

Playing in the upper half it is natural for the pad of the third finger to come away from the frog slightly; but the contact with the bow at the crease remains strong throughout.

The contact-point of the first finger changes depending on where in the bow you play; but at the heel – and further down the bow as well – much of the contact is at the crease of the first joint.

Experiment with the sensations of firm contact at the creases:

- Without the other fingers on the bow, squeeze the bow between the tip of the thumb and the crease of the second finger (Fig. 31a).

- Without the second or fourth fingers on the bow, pull in with the first and third (Fig. 31b). Do not push with the thumb, but feel the contact at the creases as you counter the fingers with the thumb.

- Without the thumb or fourth on the bow, feel the creases of the three middle fingers (Fig. 31c).

Fig. 31

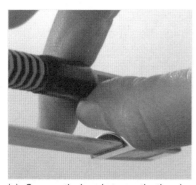

(a) Squeeze the bow between the thumb and the second

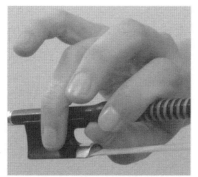

(b) Pull in with the first and third, countering with the thumb

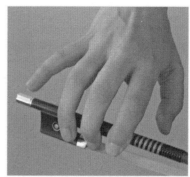

(c) Pull against the bow with the arm, feeling the creases on the bow

- Then find the same sensations of contact at the creases while playing with a normal bow hold.

The changing contact-point of the first finger on the bow

[1] See also *The changing contact of the first finger with the bow*, page 123

At the heel the hand is more upright or 'supinated' (Fig. 28j, page 39); at the point the hand leans towards the first finger or is more 'pronated' (Fig. 28k).[1]

As the hand leans, the contact-point of the first finger with the bow changes from closer to the nail joint to closer to the middle joint:

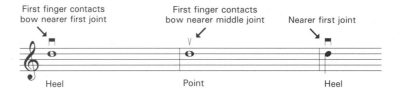

The exact contact-point of the first finger, when playing at the heel, affects the rest of the hand:

- The nearer to the nail joint the finger contacts the bow, the more the knuckles are parallel with the bow and the lower the wrist (Fig. 32a).

- The nearer to the middle joint the finger contacts the bow, the higher the wrist and the more angled the knuckles as the forearm rotates slightly anticlockwise (Fig. 32b).

Fig. 32

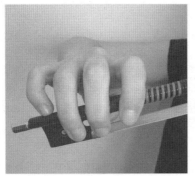 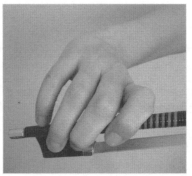 

(a) The knuckles are more parallel with the bow

(b) The knuckles are at an angle to the bow

(c) Playing in the point position too low in the bow without adjusting

A common fault is to play everywhere in the bow with the hand always in the point position (Fig. 32c). On the down-bow it is natural to change from the heel position to the point position; however, it can also seem natural to keep that position of the hand all the way back to the heel.

Then, having arrived back in the lower half with the first finger still contacting the bow near to (or beyond) the middle joint, it is natural to leave it there and carry on playing everything with the hand permanently in that position.

Instead, begin at the heel with the fourth actively balancing the bow and a first-finger contact-point near the nail joint – play to the point and allow the contact-point of the first finger to move closer to (or on top of) the middle joint – then, on the up-bow, let the entire hand move back on to the fourth finger while at the same time the first-finger contact-point gradually moves nearer to the nail joint.

Q **If the contact-point of the first finger with the bow changes all the time, doesn't that make the bow hand feel unstable?**

This changing point of contact of the first finger does not produce any feeling of instability in the right hand because the contact-point of the finger on the *side* of the bow remains constant.

To demonstrate the stable contact on the side of the bow, make a bowing movement in the air while holding your first finger against the bow with your left hand (Fig. 33a).

See how the nail joint of the first finger, on the side of the bow, remains in one place under your left finger during the journey from heel to point; yet the contact-point of the first finger on top of the bow changes from nearer the nail joint at the heel to nearer the middle joint at the point (Fig. 33b).

Fig. 33

(a) Hold the first finger against the bow with the left hand

(b) Note the different point of contact of the first finger on top of the stick

How to stop the fingers climbing up the bow

A common problem in teaching children is that although they may start off playing a piece with a good bow hold, the hand gradually creeps a few centimetres up the bow.

One way to cure this is for them to establish clear mental pictures of the exact role and position of each finger, and to link these with a firm physical sensation on the bow. Go through each finger one by one, describing its precise position. These are the key points to make:

- The tip of the **thumb** contacts the bow, one side leaning against the black thumb-piece and the other side on the bow (or the thumb leather). These contact-points are 'home' to the thumb.

- The **first finger** has two jobs to do, on top of the stick and on the side of the stick (Fig. 28h, page 39). The first finger should never contact the stick between the knuckle joint and the middle joint (the old Leopold Auer method), but between the middle joint and the nail joint.

- The only contact-point of the **second finger** is at the crease near the nail joint.

- There is an alive contact between the pad of the **third finger** and the side of the frog, the finger sitting between the round part of the thumb piece and the pearl eye in the centre of the frog. At the point, the contact between the third and the bow is not the pad, but the crease near the nail joint.

- The **fourth finger** sits on top of the bow, or on the upper inside edge, depending on the tilt of the bow. To keep it curved place the finger on the tip not on the pad. Think of the line of the right edge of the frog continuing up the right side of the finger.

Once these details of the bow hold are clear in the student's mind, the fingers instinctively rebalance and reorganise themselves to find these contact-points during playing, and there is little chance of the hand wandering up the bow unconsciously.

Fig. 34

'Bow-hold' or 'bow-balance'?

It is often said that the terms 'bow-hold' or 'bow-grip' are misleading, since they may encourage the player to 'grip' the bow rather than to 'balance' it in the hand.

While at times the bow does need to be held firmly, at other times you should not be 'holding' the bow by squeezing it between the fingers, but balancing it in the fingers with little sensation of holding.

The bow balanced in the hand rather than held

Q **How can you get the feeling of balancing the bow rather than of holding it?**

To find the feeling of balancing rather than 'holding', simply support the bow in the air without the second or third fingers on the bow (Fig. 34).

Feel the weight of the bow pushing up into your little finger (the finger curved, the tip on the top of the bow). Feel the weight also pushing into the thumb, and into the first finger on the side of the bow. If you took any of these off the bow, the bow would fall; but there is no feeling whatsoever of 'holding the bow'. The bow pushes into your fingers rather than your fingers pressing against the bow.

The string itself supports the bow when the bow is sitting on the string, making it even easier to balance and guide the bow within the hand instead of actively gripping it.

Q **When should you 'hold' the bow, and when should you 'balance it in the hand'?**

The moment just before the bow touches the string, before beginning to play, is an example of when you might balance the bow in the hand more than hold it. Balancing the bow often happens during the many moments *between* strokes, and during rests; as well as during many strokes themselves, from *spiccato* and *sautillé* to ordinary *détaché* strokes along the string.

Whether you 'grip' or 'balance' the bow often depends on the strength or 'bite' of what you are playing. The more powerful the stroke, the more strongly you hold the bow. So long as it is not a fixed state, there is nothing wrong with 'gripping' firmly when necessary.[1]

Key point: 'Gripping the bow firmly' happens only for moments at a time, against a general background of 'balancing the bow in the hand'. To avoid tension, it must never be the other way round, i.e. odd moments of balancing against a general background of gripping.

Proportions

Thinking in terms of proportions makes it clear that there must be a spectrum of possibilities from only balancing the bow with the fingers, to squeezing it between the fingers; and that each degree of balancing or holding is probably going to be good at some time or other.

Think of the degrees of balancing or of gripping the bow on a scale from zero to 10:

- In the moment just before placing the bow on the string the balance is 10:0, i.e. the bow may be entirely balanced in the hand rather than 'held'.

- Playing *martelé* you have to hold the bow firmly to bite each stroke. For a moment the balance is 0:10. After the bite the fingers release and the ratio of balancing to gripping may be closer to 5:5.

- Playing heavy chords the balance may be 0:10 throughout each chord, with a release in between.

- The complete range must be 10:0 (all balancing, no gripping); 9:1, 8:2, 7:3, 6:4, 5:5, 4:6, 3:7, 2:8, 1:9, 0:10 (all gripping, no balancing).

Holding the bow firmly or strongly does not mean that the hand and fingers have to become stiff or tense: you can still be flexible and springy in the fingers and hand.[2]

The perfect sense of contact we are born with

Think of the way babies grip your finger when you place it in their hand. They close their fingers around your finger in the firmest but gentlest grip. They neither squeeze too hard, nor are too flimsy, but instinctively form the closest, best-possible contact. This is a perfect image to illustrate the best contact of the fingers with the bow.

Shaking hands with somebody is another good example: you don't want either a too-weak or a painfully-strong handshake. Between the two extremes is the adult equivalent of the baby's grip.

The alive bow-hold

The fingers on the bow should not be static or immobile, but always alive to the bow, injecting subtle influences into the bow and into the string.

Imagine that there are little electronic, touch-sensitive key-pads or sensors at each of the contact-points of the fingers with the bow. The slightest extra impulse from any part of the finger tips or pads is picked up by the sensor and turned into some effect on the bow.

If you only hold the bow, using the fingers like pincers, and then use the arm to move the bow up and down along the string, none of the sensors would register anything. Instead, use every opportunity to feel the bow in your fingers and press the 'electronic buttons' in endless different combinations according to what you are playing.[3]

Does the fourth finger stay on the bow in the upper half?

Leopold Mozart would tell you to keep the fourth finger on the stick in the upper half:

> ...The little finger must lie at all times on the bow, and never be held freely away from the stick, for it contributes greatly to the control of the bow and therefore to the necessary strength and weakness, by means of pressing or relaxing.[4]

Carl Flesch's advice was the opposite of Mozart's. Flesch was in favour of turning the hand on to the first finger in the upper half ('pronation'), and at the same time allowing the fourth finger to leave the bow entirely. According to this view, the fourth finger is active when playing in the lower half, where it balances the weight of the bow, and is completely redundant in the upper half:

[1] 'To hold the bow as lightly as possible, means as lightly as is possible for the application of the power required at the moment. Everyone knows that less grip is needed on the knob of a door which opens at the slightest touch, than on one which requires the use of considerable force. The player should therefore hold the bow especially lightly for pianissimo, and always avoid a coarse, insensitive grip.'
Percival Hodgson: *Motion Study and Violin Bowing* (Illinois, 1958), 15.

[2] See *The push–and–pull test*, page 51

[3] There are eight contact points – the tip of the fourth finger, pad and crease of the third, crease of the second, two creases of the first and two contact-points of the thumb – so imagine that each key-pad plays a note of the scale. Imagine the different 'tunes' the button would play as you use the bow.

[4] Leopold Mozart: *A Treatise On The Fundamental Principles Of Violin Playing* (Augsburg, 1756; Eng. Trans. Editha Knocker, Oxford, 1948), 58.

Indispensable as is the activity of the little finger at the nut, it is just as unnecessary and injurious when playing at the point...because here it weakens the very necessary pressure of the first finger.[1]

[1] Carl Flesch: *The Art of Violin Playing* (New York, 1924), Vol. 1, 54.

Yet it is precisely in order to counter the first finger, and to stop any hint of pressing, that you *should* keep the fourth finger on the bow in the upper half.

Although the bow in Mozart's day was different from the modern bow and the strings were made of gut, the arguments against Flesch's are that if you lean the hand on to the first finger in the upper half there is a danger of squashing the tone; and that the fourth finger, as well as having the important job of balancing the bow in the lower half, has the sometimes equally important job of balancing the first in the upper half. Therefore the fourth should usually stay on the bow in both the lower and upper half.

Accordingly, the only reason for taking the fourth finger off the bow in the upper half is if your arm is too short to leave it on, and you cannot play to the point without leaning the hand to the left and letting the fourth come off the bow.[2]

[2] According to Dorothy DeLay, the only reason Leopold Auer developed his bow hold, which then was used by Jascha Heifetz, Nathan Milstein and many other Russian players, was that he was a very short man, with short arms, and he could not reach the point unless his first finger contacted the bow between the middle joint and the base joint, and he turned his hand anticlockwise and allowed the fourth finger to leave the stick.

Pulling in with the third finger

Ivan Galamian might have told you to practise a piece without your second or fourth fingers on the bow, i.e. holding the bow with only the thumb, first and third fingers.

The point of the exercise was to sensitise the third finger to its contact with the bow. Lucien Capet, one of Galamian's teachers, described the central role of the third finger:

> This finger is in a sense the Spiritual guide in the domain of general sensitivity of the fingers on the stick.
>
> While the thumb and middle finger stay always at their post, being the very centre of all the principal movements, one must view the 3rd finger as a watchman who, by his artful presence, complements the role established by each finger; it increases the sweetness or strength, the sensitivity or assuredness. It is this finger which must bring ultimate sensitivity in this mysterious communication among the fingers which unite in the realization of an infinitely varied ideal.[3]

[3] Lucien Capet: *La Technique Superieure de L'Archet*, 13

Sándor Végh called the third finger 'the tone finger of the bow'.

This sensitive and important contact of the third finger with the bow is a subtle detail of technique that surprisingly seems to be generally ignored by many players and teachers. Flesch dismissed it entirely in his bow hold, saying that 'the third finger plays a subordinate part, and is passive rather than active'[4]; as did Leopold Auer; yet the difference an active third finger makes is always immediate and obvious.

[4] Carl Flesch: The Art of Violin Playing (New York, 1924), Vol. 1, 54.

In many strokes – particularly in firm, deep-in-the-string playing, or for example during the 'bite' of *martelé* – if you pull in firmly with the pad of the third finger, a great strength, focus and control comes into the bow hand. Feel the third finger sitting on the bow between the pearl eye and the rounded part of the thumb-piece (Fig. 35a).

- Help students find this feeling by gently pulling the bow away from them while they try to resist by using only the third finger. Or they can hold the bow themself in the left hand and pull against it with the right (Fig. 35b).

- They can then find a similar feeling of pulling in with the third finger while holding the bow normally.

Fig. 35

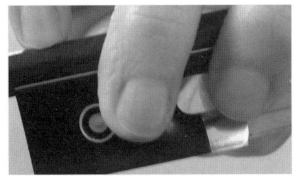

(a) Many strokes need the contact of the third finger with the bow to be firm

(b) Pull the bow using only the third finger

Should the knuckles be flat, or should they stick up?

Every hand is slightly different, and must be allowed to be itself in whatever ways naturally suit it. Some hands will want the knuckles to stick up more, some less.

However, a useful guide is to try to avoid, where possible, 'white' in the knuckles. If the knuckles stick up at all too much, the skin at the knuckles turns white. To see the most white at the knuckles, clench your fingers into a fist. Notice how the white disappears as you relax the fingers again.

The natural shape of the hand playing a keyboard is a useful image for holding the bow (and for the left hand). The knuckles are far more likely to be flat (Fig. 36a) than sticking up (Fig. 36b).

- Gently push down into the base joints (Fig. 36c), and release again. When there is some degree of this give or springiness in every bow stroke, a wonderful softness comes into the tone (however forceful it is); but the give naturally disappears if the knuckles push up even the slightest amount.

Fig. 36

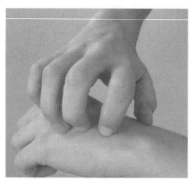
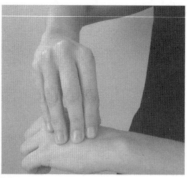
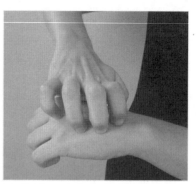

(a) Natural position to play the piano   (b) Knuckles sticking up   (c) Gently push down, feeling the give and springiness

Avoiding pressing in the upper half

To play with a sweet, singing tone, it is essential to avoid any hint of pressing with the first finger – either direct pressing with the finger itself, or pressing by leaning the hand into the finger too much. This is rarely a problem in the lower half, where the hand is less turned on to the bow and you have to lift weight out of the string to avoid scratching. But in the upper half it is easy to squash the tone if you lean too much onto the first finger or use too much active first-finger pressure.

[1] See Fig. 56a, page 120

One exception is when you begin a note with a 'click', as in *martelé* when you use direct, downward, first-finger pressure to 'pinch' the string for a moment[1]; but in general you should avoid pressing with the first finger, or at least always use it as little as possible.

However, there is an argument in favour of leaning the hand into the first finger, in the upper half, which is important to understand – if only so that you do not do it too much.

This argument says that the natural tendency is to play too heavily in the lower half and to scratch; and to play too lightly in the upper half without enough contact:

- The point-of-balance is below the centre of the bow, so the bow is heavier in the lower half and lighter in the upper half.

- The hand is more directly above the strings in the lower half (Fig. 37a). Below the point-of-balance, it feels as though you can rest the weight of the whole arm into the string. Higher in the bow this does not seem possible (Fig. 37b), though you can have a *perception* of 'relaxing the arm into the bow' in the upper half.

Fig. 37

(a) The hand is directly above the strings   (b) The hand is far from the strings

According to this, weight should therefore be taken *out* of the string in the lower half, and put *into* the string in the upper half.

- Weight is taken out by supinating the hand (Fig. 38a). This takes the weight of the hand away from the first finger and into the fourth finger. The fourth finger balances the bow.

- Weight is injected into the string in the upper half by pronating the hand, putting the weight of the hand into the first finger (Fig. 38b).

Carl Flesch advocated this approach and described it precisely:

> [The bow] is too *heavy* at the *nut*, i.e. prevents the string vibrations, and too *light* at the *point*, i.e. unable to set the strings vibrating; and only in the middle will it produce tone through its own weight. Hence, the bow must be pressed down upon the strings at the *point*, and at the *nut* it must be slightly raised. The pressure at the point is produced by the *index finger*, the raising of the entire bow at the nut by the *little finger*. The first is paired with pronation (turning outward), the second with supination (inward turning)…It is the index finger, therefore, which in the main acts in a *tone-producing* way, and the little finger in a *tone-preventing* manner.[1]

The argument against Flesch's is as follows:

It is clear that you have to take weight out of the string in the lower half, as Flesch describes; and this is done by balancing the weight of the bow with the fourth finger, and by lifting the bow out of the string with the arm so that it 'floats'.

But while Flesch did not mean literally to press the first finger downwards (he was careful to say that the pressing is coupled with leaning the hand anticlockwise into the bow), it is still an approach based on weight and the application of pressure by the first finger.[2]

[1] Carl Flesch: *The Art of Violin Playing* (New York, 1924), Vol. 1, 53.

[2] It was Flesch's bow hold that led him to think so much about pressing with the first finger and pronating. He positioned the first and second fingers on the bow either side of the thumb, so that the thumb was between them. But this goes against the laws of leverage, since it puts the first finger too close to the pivot (the thumb). See *Experiment in leverage*, page 40.

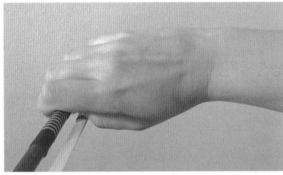

Fig. 38

(a) Supinating the hand in the lower half   (b) Pronating the hand in the upper half

Q **What is the answer to the problem of the bow being too light in the upper half, if you avoid using first-finger pressure and pronation?**

There are three principal ways of producing an even tone without having to 'press' with the first finger:

1 Using the second finger to share the work of the first finger

2 Creating weight from the hand

3 Using faster bow speed in the upper half.

1. Using the second finger

If the nail joint of the second finger is positioned just slightly to the left of the thumb (Fig. 39a), the middle joint of the second finger contacts the bow a considerable distance to the left of the thumb when the hand pronates (Fig. 39b).

Then the second finger can exert leverage on the bow, reducing the amount the first finger has to do.

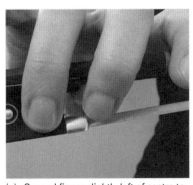
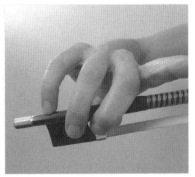

Fig. 39

(a) Second finger slightly left of centre to the thumb   (b) The second finger can exert leverage   (c) Positioned this side of the thumb, the second finger cannot push the bow down into the string

If the second finger is positioned directly opposite the thumb, or any degree to the right of the thumb, it cannot contribute to tone production. A quick experiment illustrates this clearly:

• Play *f*, sustained strokes without the first finger on the bow, with the second finger positioned well to the left of the thumb (Fig. 39b). Play into the string with the second finger.

- Try to do the same with the second finger slightly to the right of the thumb (Fig. 39c), and see how all the leverage is now lost:

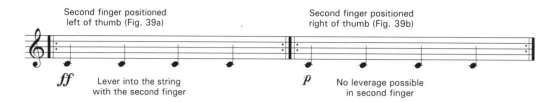

Second finger positioned left of thumb (Fig. 39a)

Second finger positioned right of thumb (Fig. 39b)

ff   Lever into the string with the second finger

p   No leverage possible in second finger

2. Creating weight from the hand

Playing into the string from the hand is a major aspect of right-hand technique (looked at in detail in *Playing from the hand in the upper half*, page 130). The feeling of application of weight that it gives is subtle, and quite different from arm weight or forearm rotation. Curiously, no mention of this is made in many of the most comprehensive treatises on violin playing, while at the same time others possibly take it too far:

> Particular attention should be directed to the development of lightness of bowing and one should be constantly alert in detecting undue bow pressure in any style of bowing. Of the greatest importance is the warning that "ALL NECESSARY PRESSURE IN TONE PRODUCTION MUST COME FROM THE WRIST AND NOT FROM THE WHOLE ARM."[1]

(The block capitals are the same as in the original.) When Yost said that the movement comes from the wrist, he must have meant that it comes from the hand, moving *at* the wrist.[2] He must also have meant only in the upper half of the bow, not in the lower half.

Leopold Auer said exactly the same. 'Tone, in whatever degrees of volume it may be needed, *must only be produced through pressure from the wrist.*' The italics are the same as in the original.[3]

But does all necessary pressure in the upper half come from the hand? I once had a lesson from a leading soloist/teacher who said that all pressure into the string *comes from the upper arm*.

To say either that the weight comes always from the hand, or always from the upper arm, goes against two principles: first, Proportions; second, 'The more delicate the action, the closer to the fingers'.

Proportions

The principle of proportions suggests that sometimes the weight would come from the hand, sometimes from the arm, and usually from some sort of mixture of both.

Number the amount of upper arm weight, and the amount of weight into the string from the hand, on a scale from zero to 10:

- In the most powerful playing, all the weight may come from the upper arm. The balance is 10:0.

- In gentle or expressive playing, or in the delicacy of playing, say, a *dolce spiccato*, the upper arm is 'too far away'. All the weight and perception of control may be in the hand. The balance is 0:10.

- The complete range must be 10:0 (all upper arm, no hand); 9:1, 8:2, 7:3, 6:4, 5:5, 4:6, 3:7, 2:8, 1:9, 0:10 (all hand, no upper arm).

The more delicate, the closer to the fingers

The size of an action determines the part of the arm or hand you use. Sometimes there is a feeling of playing into the string from the fingers; sometimes from the hand; sometimes from the upper arm.

The smaller or the more delicate the action in the bow arm, the closer to the hand or fingers the action originates; the bigger or the more powerful the action, the closer to the upper arm the action originates.

Imagine holding a pen in your fingers, but writing with it by moving only the upper arm; imagine trying to polish a large mirror by moving the cloth only with the hand.[4]

(1)   (2)   (3)   (4)

pp   <   >   *mp*   *f*   *ff*

espressivo

[1] Gaylord Yost: *The key to the mastery of bowing* (Pittsburgh, 1938), 2.

[2] The wrist is the place where the hand joins on to the forearm; it is not something in its own right and cannot do anything on its own. For the same reason, the old term 'wrist vibrato' has been replaced with the modern term 'hand vibrato'.

[3] Leopold Auer: *A Graded Course in Violin Playing, Book 1* (New York, 1926), 20.

[4] The principle of 'the more delicate, the closer to the fingers' applies equally to the left arm. Shifting is led from the fingertip, rather than from the forearm or upper arm (see *Leading from the fingertip*, page 144). Vibrato is led from the fingertip also, regardless of whether it is a hand or an arm vibrato. Naturally, this is only a perception rather than a physical fact: no physical action occurs at the fingertip to make the shift or the vibrato.

The softest, most subtle changes of tone may require only a slight change of contact of the fingers on the bow; playing heavy, three-string chords may require a powerful movement of the upper arm. Between the two extremes many strokes use some degree of 'playing into the string from the hand'.

(1) Creating a delicate, expressive nuance in the middle of a long bow, you might use only the slightest, most subtle movement in the fingers to create the effect.

(2) Playing *spiccato*, the feeling of playing may be more in the fingers and the hand.

(3) Playing accents or *martelé*, the feeling of playing is higher up the arm in the hand and forearm.

(4) Playing heavy chords, much of the feeling of weight comes directly from the upper arm.

Feeling the difference between 'arm weight' and 'hand weight'

Fig. 40

Rest your right hand lightly on your left forearm (Fig. 40).

1 Keeping the remainder of your right arm 'passive' and 'floating', push your hand down heavily into your left forearm.

Move the hand only from the wrist.

2 Then use the weight of the whole arm to bring the hand down heavily into the left forearm. Feel the weight of the upper arm channelled through the right hand into the left forearm.

Feeling the difference between 'hand weight' and 'arm weight'

Notice the different qualities or sensations of weight feeding into the left forearm, depending on whether you use the hand or the arm.

Supporting the wrist, and playing into the string with the hand, is quite a feature of the typical Eastern European bow arm, as opposed to the Flesch or Galamian. It may be no co-incidence that one of Yost's teachers when he studied in Berlin in the early 1900s was the Russian pedagogue Issay Barmas.[1]

[1] Another key feature of the typical modern Eastern European bow arm (but not the old Leopold Auer bow hold) is that there is much more general leaning towards the fourth finger (supination) throughout the whole bow stroke, in contrast to the pronation of the typical Flesch or Galamian bow arms.

3. Using faster bow speed

Use extra bow speed, rather than pressure alone, to compensate for the lightness of the bow in the upper half. This produces a silky, sweet, ringing tone quite different from the sound you get if the speed remains more constant and you 'press' with the first finger or lean the right hand on to it.

An illustration of pressing to sustain tone in the upper half, while keeping the bow speed even:

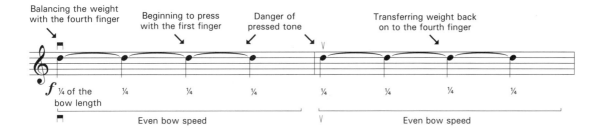

Instead of this, the way to use bow speed instead of pressure is to have a slow–fast pattern on the down-bow, and a fast–slow pattern on the up-bow.

The difference in bow speed is so slight that someone who does not know what to look for should not easily be able to notice what you are doing:

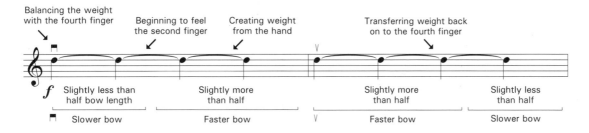

Flexibility

Springiness

The bow hand is often likened to a system of springs:

> To understand the functioning of the bow, one has to realize from the very outset that the whole right arm technique is based on a system of springs. These react in much the same way as do mechanical springs...nothing really constructive can be accomplished unless...the joints of the fingers, thumb, hand, and arm are flexible and spring-like. There has to be this resiliency and springiness in the functioning of the whole arm from shoulder to finger tips or else the tone will be hard and ugly, the bowing clumsy and uncontrolled.[1]

[1] Ivan Galamian: *Principles of Violin Playing and Teaching* (New Jersey, 1962), 44.

The springs in the hand act as shock absorbers. The classic analogy is of bending the knees when you land after jumping. Without 'giving' at the knees a tremendous shock would be transmitted throughout your entire skeleton.

However, being flexible and springy does not mean you have to make a lot of visible finger movements. There is a degree of flexibility in the fingers of the bow hand that is so slight you cannot see it; yet it gives you all the flexibility and springiness that you need.

Even though you cannot see the movements, or barely see them, there is a big difference between a bow hand that is stiff and one that has this imperceptible give.

Allow just so much movement in the fingers that you can see it; and then do just the slightest amount less than that.

Experiment

Do the following experiment on the back of your hand:

- With the hand resting in 'piano position' (Fig. 36a, page 46), gently push the knuckles down with a feeling of springiness, buoyancy and elasticity in the muscles and joints (Fig. 36c).

- Repeat, pushing the knuckles down far less, but with the same feeling of springiness.

- Continue doing less and less until the movement of 'sinking' at the knuckles is only just visible, but you still have the same feeling of springiness and elasticity.

- See how little movement you can make, yet at the same time combine this with finding the clearest possible feeling of flexibility.

Noticing the difference

Even when you think that your hands are free of any tightness, and you think they are completely 'springy', there is often still another degree of springiness, softness and buoyancy that you can find.

The first step is fully to appreciate the difference imperceptible flexibility makes to the sound.

- Play sixteenth-notes (semiquavers) in the upper half, first holding the bow with stiff fingers, and then with lighter fingers which have an imperceptible degree of sympathetic movement or 'give':

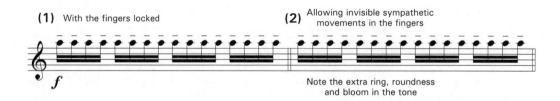

(1) With the fingers locked   **(2)** Allowing invisible sympathetic movements in the fingers

Note the extra ring, roundness and bloom in the tone

(1) Note how there is a 'click' at each bow change when the fingers are locked, and the tone may be harsh or have a hard edge.

(2) Note the smoothness and sweetness of tone when the fingers give.

Do not try to fake the result of harshness or edginess with tight fingers, and of sweetness with flexible fingers. Try to play as well as you can in both cases, and note the often subtle difference in the sound.

You can feel and hear the same difference when playing simple whole bows:

(1) With the fingers 'locked'   **(2)** Allowing invisible sympathetic movements in the fingers

Experiment in passages with loosening and tightening the 'springs' in the fingers:

Pugnani-Kreisler: Praeludium and Allegro, *Praeludium, b. 35*

Begin with floppy fingers: exaggerate by deliberately flexing slightly just before each down-bow, and straightening slightly just before each up-bow.

- Repeat with less and less finger movement.

- Finish with an unnoticeable 'give' in the fingers that is an identical (but imperceptible) version of the flexing and straightening that you used in the beginning.

- Make an exercise out of it by going round and round between the two extremes:

Much finger movement - - - - - - - - - less - - - less - - - - - unnoticeable 'give' - - - more movement - - - - - more - - - more - - -

Repeat several times

The push–and–pull test

Sometimes you need to balance the bow in the hand, with no sense of gripping it between the fingers; at other times you need to hold it more firmly.[1] But however firmly you hold the bow, flexibility must never be lost.

[1] See *'Bow-hold' or 'bow-balance'?*, page 43

Without the violin, hold the bow in playing position.

- With your left hand, pull the bow to the left in the direction of a down-bow, and push it to the right in the direction of an up-bow.

- As you pull the bow, allow the right-hand fingers to flex slightly (Fig. 41a); as you push, allow the fingers to straighten slightly (Fig. 41b).

- Make the bow, pulled or pushed by the left hand, move the right-hand fingers, rather than moving the fingers yourself.

- Experimenting with firmer and looser grips, discover how to combine maximum flexibility with maximum 'holding the bow'.

Fig. 41

(a) Pulling the bow to the left

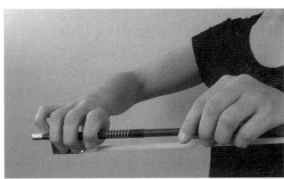

(b) Pushing the bow to the right

The shake test

A good test of flexibility is that while you hold the bow with a normal bow hold, someone can grip your forearm just before the wrist and shake your hand up and down vigorously, without you dropping the bow.

The student:

Fig. 42

- Stand without the violin, holding the bow parallel to the floor.

- Point the bow somewhat towards your left shoulder, as it does when playing (Fig. 42).

- Find a feeling of balancing the bow in your hand, rather than one of gripping it between your fingers.

The teacher or assistant:

While the student holds the bow, take hold of their arm just below the wrist.

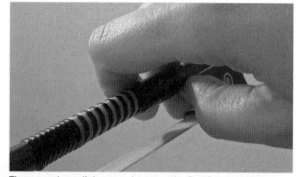

The hand moves freely at the wrist while continuing to hold the bow

- Gently shake the arm in an up-and-down direction – not so much that you can see the forearm actually move up and down more than a centimetre, but enough that the impulse causes the hand to move up and down a little.

The student should be able to hold the bow sufficiently firmly that it does not fall from the hand, yet without the wrist becoming tight so that you cannot shake the hand easily.

The bow 'moving within the hand'

Imagine a see-saw. The pivot is at the centre. One end of the see-saw goes up a certain distance; the other end goes down by the same amount.

Imagine moving the pivot away from the centre. Most of the see-saw is now one side of the pivot; a small amount is the other side. Now a tiny movement at the short end produces a much bigger movement at the long end.

Fig. 43 The way the bow works is similar. The pivot is the thumb; a tiny movement of the bow at the frog produces a much bigger movement at the point.

The fingers contacting the bow must be sensitive to these impulses in the bow, both allowing them and sometimes encouraging them. The first finger must often remain light on the stick so that it does not prevent these natural movements from 'feeding down' into the frog.

At times the first finger should even come away from the top of the stick (so slightly as to be unnoticeable), particularly during lifted strokes

There may be a slight space between the first finger and the top of the bow.

like *spiccato* (Fig. 43). This happens naturally as the hand turns slightly more towards the fourth finger (supination), rather than as the result of the first finger actively lifting away from the bow.

Spiccato and string crossings

It is easy to feel the bow 'moving within the hand' during *spiccato*. Look at the little dipping movements at the point of the bow, and feel the effect of these movements in the movements of the bow within your fingers:

Large-movement spiccato
at the point-of-balace

Experiment by tightening the fingers on the bow so that the hand and the bow are locked into one, immovable unit. See how awkward and unnatural the *spiccato* immediately feels.

Wide string crossings may involve large movements at the point of the bow. You can feel the effect of this in your fingers clearly:

- Look at the distance the point moves, from its place in the air after the first down-bow A on the G string, to its place in the air at the beginning of the down-bow A on the E string. Experiment with a range of bowings to find different feelings of the bow moving within your fingers:

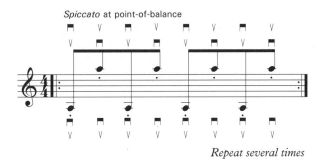

Spiccato at point-of-balance

Repeat several times

- Experiment by playing these patterns without the first finger contacting the stick. Keep it in the air above the bow (Fig. 39b, page 72).

- Feel the extra movement of the bow within the hand. Then find similar feelings of movement within the hand when holding the bow normally.

Freeing the thumb

Three joints, not two

- There are three joints in the thumb, not two.

  Many players have a mental picture of the thumb beginning at its middle joint rather than at the base joint.[1] This causes the entire operation of the right hand to feel restricted, compared to the feeling of ease when the thumb is working from the base joint.

[1] See *Freeing the thumb*, page 181

Tip, not pad

- If you place the tip of the thumb on the bow, the thumb will naturally want to curve outwards; if you place more of the pad on the bow, the thumb will naturally want to straighten. If the thumb straightens, flexibility is lost.

Give

- Every muscle and joint acts like a shock absorber to smooth out the activities of the bow. Flexibility depends on the thumb. The thumb makes giving, bending and straightening movements throughout the course of every bow stroke, without which it is difficult to be flexible elsewhere.

  Most of these movements of the thumb are so small as to be imperceptible, yet if they are prevented the entire right hand may lose flexibility.

The thumb and fourth finger

- The thumb and the fourth finger generally work together as a 'team': when one straightens, the other straightens; when one bends, the other bends. Feel the two fingers moving together.

  To make sure that it remains an unconscious part of your bowing technique, from time to time exaggerate this movement of the thumb for a few moments: consciously straighten and bend it during a few whole bow strokes, enlarging the movement:

Bend - - - straighten - - - bend - - - straighten - - - bend, etc.

The changing contact-point

Fig. 44

- The contact-point of the thumb changes depending on which part of the bow you are playing in (Fig. 44).

  Place the bow on the A string at the heel. Note the contact-point of the tip of the thumb with the bow: is it more to the left of the tip, in the centre, or more to the right? (See also Fig. 28g, page 38.) Play to the point. Note how the contact-point of the thumb has moved to a slightly different place. This movement is something that you would rarely do deliberately, rather than letting it happening naturally on its own. Equally, you must not prevent it from happening.

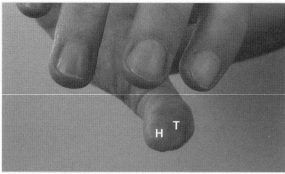

Playing at the heel (H) and tip (T)

Leverage

- During f playing, if you get too deep a 'dent' in your thumb, and it begins to hurt, it may mean that you need more leverage: move the first finger further up the bow away from your thumb.[1]

[1] See *Experiment in leverage*, page 40

The intonation lesson

Clear mental pictures

To play in tune, first you have to 'pre-hear' the note in your mind, and then listen. Beyond that, it is your mental picture of each note that develops as your intonation becomes more and more reliable.

The mental picture includes the exact place of the note on the string, the feeling of the hand and finger, the shape of the finger, the tone-semitone relationships of the fingers to each other, and the aural relationships of each note to the surrounding notes.

The complete picture may include the feeling of the width of the fingerboard and neck for that particular note, the feeling of the height of the string above the fingerboard, and all the other physical sensations of playing.

Many players have a clearer mental picture of some notes than others; or a clearer picture of particular fingers on a note than other fingers on that same note. The picture of some notes may be entirely blank; or consist more of memories of tension or insecurity than of knowledge, familiarity and understanding of the note.

Then either you play those notes out of tune; or you *hesitate* instead of going straight to them.[1]

The hesitation is caused by needing time to think, to put together a mental picture 'on the spot'. The hesitation may often lead to bigger technical hitches than simply playing a note out of tune.

- Practise different finger patterns and intonation exercises (and scales and arpeggios) in the area of the fingerboard where you need to sharpen any blurred pictures of any fingers on any notes.

Self-test

It is easy to discover how clear your picture of a note is:

- Without the violin, first picture a note that feels entirely comfortable, secure and familiar – say, 3rd finger D in 1st position on the A string.

- Then picture, say, 2nd finger F♯ in 5th position on the G string. Can you 'see' and 'feel' it just as clearly?

The answer lies in the amount of detail the picture contains, as well as in how long it takes you to see the complete picture.

The amount of detail in the picture of each note, and of each finger playing that note, leads to four basic levels of intonation.

Four levels of intonation

1 Structured intonation

- Every note is tuned relative to another note or notes. This gives the intonation a sense of musical structure and consistency.

- In the first three notes of a major scale, the whole tone distance (aurally) between the tonic and the second, and between the second and the third, is the same. The semitone distance between the third and fourth degrees of the scale, and the seventh and eighth, is the same. In a three-octave arpeggio each major third is the same distance from the tonic as it is in any other octave.

[1] See *Hesitating before playing*, page 106

- The intonation 'holds': the same notes in a passage played several times will be in tune the same way each time.

- While some or many notes may not be exactly what the player intended, they are 'out of tune' to such a small degree that no other listener would detect any error whatsoever.

2 Structured intonation with mistakes

- As No. 1, but with slips where a note or small group of notes is out of tune. There may be many on each page, or only a few, but they are noticeable only to an experienced listener.

3 Unstructured intonation

- Each note is considered in isolation: it is not compared or related to any other note; it is not tuned in relation to its place in the scale or harmony.

- Some notes are in tune, some are not. The intervals between notes are not consistent, i.e. in a major scale there may be a wider or narrower whole tone between the tonic and second, than between the second and third; there may be a wider or narrower semitone between the third and the fourth degrees of the scale, than between the seventh and the octave. In a three-octave arpeggio, each major third may be slightly wider or narrower than another in a different octave.

- The intonation does 'hold', however. The same notes in a passage played several times will be in tune, or out of tune, the same way each time.

4 Unstructured intonation with mistakes

- As No. 3, but with slips which make the out-of-tune playing noticeable to anyone.

Of course nothing is as clear-cut as this, and many players will move between levels as they play different notes, phrases or types of passage. But the big difference is between 'structured' and 'unstructured' intonation.

It is unlikely that a player who has Level 1–2 intonation will suddenly not know what they are doing, lose their good ear, and start to play on Level 3–4; equally, it is unlikely that a player who has no concept of the structure of intonation can suddenly play on Level 1–2, without re-thinking their tuning and gaining a deeper understanding of how to approach it.

 But surely you don't need to 'know' anything at all, to be able to play beautifully in tune. If you are talented, and have a good ear, playing in tune is a matter of musical instinct, not of intellectual knowledge.

This is clearly true, as proved by the countless examples of players who have had excellent intonation without knowing enough to be able to explain what they are doing. They play well simply because they have a good ear, a good feel for the instrument, and a natural feel for music.

Equally, if you do not at first play on Level 1 or Level 2 naturally, this does not mean that you cannot learn how to play as in tune as someone who does it without knowing how.

How long realistically does it take to improve intonation?

Many players under-estimate the complexity of violin playing; at the same time they over-estimate how hard it is to develop really good intonation, tone production, and all the rest.

Intonation is not difficult to improve. The mental picture is not difficult to gain. A reasonable timescale in which to expect to go from Level 4 to playing with the real measuring and crafting of Level 2, can be one week, or even one day, depending on how much focus you give it.[1]

[1] See also *How long realistically does it take to improve?*, page xxii

After that, you might want to continue to work on your intonation for the rest of your life; but the initial move to Level 2 is not a process that has to take place gradually over months or years. It is one of those things that takes 'a minute to learn and a lifetime to master'.

If you do not play well in tune, getting better is not a question of more practice but of gaining a clearer understanding. Assuming that the left hand is sufficiently free and relaxed, with the clearer understanding comes instantaneous improvement rather than gradual improvement.

Improving listening

Listening is the most important thing of all. Nearly everybody can benefit either from listening better, or from beginning to listen properly in the first place.

Many players do not really hear the sounds and pitches that come out of their instrument. This is one reason why they are surprised if they hear themselves on a recording, and notice for the first time poor intonation, or bulges instead of *legato*, or a wobbly vibrato, or lack of variety or tonal contrast.

Most players, at some point in learning the violin, have to go from not listening, to listening; from not really hearing the sounds that are coming out of the instrument, to so 'hanging their ears on the sound' that they hear every single tone, intonation or vibrato.

Some move from not listening, to listening, earlier; others later. Even at conservatoire level, helping students improve their listening is routine, as well as being one of the great tricks of teaching.

The effects of better listening are so powerful that it often seems as if you do not need to tell a student anything in each lesson except to listen, and their improvement will already be phenomenal – before you have said anything at all about technical or musical matters.

The various ways to sharpen listening all use something in the sound to focus on in particular.

1 Tone-production exercises (page 11) are a good way to 'hook' the ears onto the quality of tone.

2 Intonation exercises (page 73) provide points of reference with which to compare other notes and provide new ways of hearing them.

3 Listening to sympathetic vibrations (page 60).

4 Listening to third tones (page 90).

5 Listening to the background resonance (page 4).

6 Listening to acoustic beats (page 57).

7 Hearing the surface noise of the friction of the bow-hair with the string:

- Play notes high on each string with the bow near to the bridge, where the surface noise is at its loudest.

- Listen closely to the surface noise. Move the bow with even speed, pressure and soundpoint so that the surface noise is regular and even.

- Repeat lower down on the same string where the surface noise may not be so clear. In the back of the sound, identify the same quality that you heard in the higher position.

Tuning and acoustic beats

In the first lesson with a new student the first topic is often the question of listening; and the very first thing to point out is the curious phenomenon of acoustic beats.

The reason why listening, and acoustic beats, immediately become the first issues to tackle is that, more often than not, the student has just tuned the violin with difficulty and apparently without noticing the 'throb' of the acoustic beat.

 What is an acoustic beat?

An acoustic beat is a throbbing sound that you can hear in the background when you play two notes together as a double stop.

When the two notes are exactly the same, i.e. a perfectly in-tune unison, there is no acoustic beat. An in-tune unison is pure and sweet, and at the same time sounds broad and thick because the two notes seem to 'sit alongside' each other.

If the two notes of the perfect unison move just slightly out of tune with each other, the throbbing of the acoustic beat immediately begins.

How to demonstrate an acoustic beat

Acoustic beats are a prime example of an aural blind spot (or 'deaf spot'). Many string players do not know about them at all, while others may hear them without consciously registering them. Players of all ages are astonished and entranced when acoustic beats are first brought to their attention, having never noticed them before.[1]

Acoustic beats open the way to true listening by giving the ears something to hook onto in the sound. Once a student has identified acoustic beats for the first time, and spent some time playing around with them – making them faster and slower – their general level of listening will increase quickly as they listen to all of their playing in the new way.

Acoustic beats are simple to demonstrate:

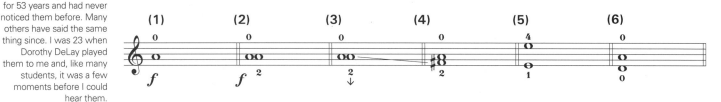

(1) Play the open A string on its own. The note is vibrating at 440 cycles per second.

Imagine a wavy horizontal line going up and down 440 times.

(2) Now play a double stop unison – A on the D string in unison with the open A. Play the stopped A exactly in tune with the open A string, at exactly 440 cycles per second.

Imagine a second wavy line placed on top of the first one; both go up at the same time, and go down at the same time, moving in perfect synchronisation 440 times each second.

(3) Now move the stopped A very slightly flat to the open A string – less than a quarter-tone – say, to 437 cycles per second.

Imagine the two wavy lines. Now the ups and downs get out of synch with each other. Sometimes one is going up while the other is on the way down. The point at which they meet (and cross over each other) produces the effect that is called a 'beat'.

The further out of tune you move the stopped A, the faster the beat. Gradually move the finger down as low as an F♯. You can hear the notes as a very fast beat even with them this far apart.

(4) The next step is to notice beats in octaves. Sustain an octave slightly out of tune: listen to the beat getting faster and slower as you adjust the fingers up or down.

Notice how you cannot hear a beat when the octave is perfectly in tune.

(5) Then listen to the open strings as you move the pegs to tune the perfect fifths, as you ordinarily do when you tune the violin.

Notice the beats getting faster and slower.

Experiment in acoustics

Make an acoustic beat happen across a room or a small hall. Stand on one side of the room and play the A (on the D string) while someone else plays an open A on the other side.

You may both have to play your A's loudly, depending on how far apart you are, but as you adjust your stopped A slightly up or down you will hear the beat getting faster or slower. Somebody else in the room may hear three distinct sounds: one violin one side of the room, the other violin the other side, and a throbbing acoustic beat coming from an invisible instrument in the middle of the room.[2]

Acoustic beats are the reason why one of the first things a string quartet must do is to play in tune. If not, the listener is bombarded with beats and a sense of conflict in the sound, instead of the smoothness and sweetness when intervals are beautifully in tune with each other and the beats disappear.

Super-effective ear tests

The following ear tests are so effective that often the result is almost like simply flicking a switch from off to on. A student's intonation is poor; you give them the ear tests; when they next begin to play they immediately listen in an entirely new way and play far more in tune.

There are three stages. The tests could not be simpler, and the whole sequence takes only 5 minutes.

[1] One of my earliest students was a sixty-three year old violinist in the London Symphony Orchestra who came for occasional lessons. When I demonstrated acoustic beats for him he was astonished, and said that he had played the violin for 53 years and had never noticed them before. Many others have said the same thing since. I was 23 when Dorothy DeLay played them to me and, like many students, it was a few moments before I could hear them.

[2] You can do the same thing with 'third tones'. See *The difference between single-stop and double-stop tuning*, page 90.

The teacher or assistant

- At each stage all you have to do is play two notes, making them almost the same pitch as each other, but playing the second one very slightly higher or lower than the first.

  In the first two stages these two notes are all you play; in the third stage you play random notes as well, between the two similar notes.

The student

- Turn away so that you cannot see the assistant's fingers on the string.

- Say whether the last note the teacher or assistant played was higher or lower than the first note.

Stage 1

- (Teacher or assistant) Play two notes, first one and then the other, so close together in pitch that they are almost the same note but not quite.

- Having played the first note, stop. Do not move your finger. Roll the fingertip the tiniest distance on the string to the second note: do not lift the finger and place it again, and do not slide the finger along the string.

- The goal is to be able to tell the difference between notes that are so close together they could not be any closer without actually being identical, i.e. much closer than the narrowest pitch-difference of vibrato; but in the beginning it is often best to start wider apart than that.

- When somebody is doing the test for the first time, play each note for about three seconds with a silence of about three seconds between them. Later, you might play each note just by touching the string lightly for a fraction of a second:

Stage 2

The same as Stage 1 except now add a time delay between the two notes.

- Play the first note; wait 5 seconds; play the second note.

  Play the first note; wait 10 seconds; play the second note.

  Then wait 15 seconds between the two notes, 20 seconds, and longer.

- Listening to the first note, the student must make a mental recording of the pitch and keep playing it back in their mind while they wait for the second note.

  Then compare the pitch of the second note with the memory of the first note and decide whether it is higher or lower:

Stage 3

Play a completely different note, between the two actual notes, as a distracter.

- First play one distracter note, then two, three, and so on:

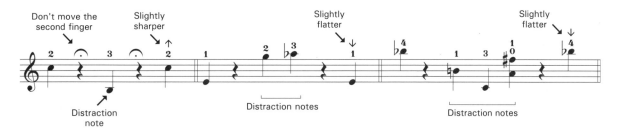

Ensuring success

These ear tests can easily be tailored to suit every level. Make sure at every stage that students are successful and score 10/10. If they do not, gradually make it easier until they do score 10/10:[1]

[1] In any field, a principle of teaching or coaching is that you always set goals the student can achieve. You never 'set them up to fail'. You always arrange things to be like stepping stones across a river, so that they can step easily from one 'success' to the next. Of course, sometimes you deliberately set a goal just outside the current range or ability, or even set an as-yet unreachable goal as part of an overall programme, but that is clearly a different matter.

- In Stage 1 begin with the intervals as wide apart as necessary for the student to get each one right. Then gradually make them closer until they are almost identical.

  If the student again starts to score less than 10/10 as you play the two notes gradually closer and closer together, widen the interval slightly until they get them all right again. Then begin to narrow the distance again.

- In Stage 2 adjust the length of time between the notes, as well as adjusting how close together the notes are, until the student scores 10/10.

  Gradually lengthen the delay, and pitch the notes closer together.

- In Stage 3 adjust how many distracter notes there are; how discordant they are; and how far apart the principal notes are, so that the student can score 10/10.

  Gradually play more distracter notes, more discordantly, while pitching the principal notes closer and closer together.

Increase your confidence

If you are a teacher beginning to work on intonation with a student, these ear tests are often the best thing to do first. But players of all levels should try the tests for themselves. Either you get all the tests right all the time, or you do not. Either way, you benefit.

If you consistently score 10/10 it boosts your confidence, since you then know without doubt that you have an excellent ear. The tests prove to you that you can perceive the slightest differences in pitch. Then you trust yourself more, and this allows you to concentrate all the more on the music.

If you do not consistently call out the right answers, the beauty of these simple tests is that they quickly sensitize your listening, and concentrate your attention so much that it does not take long before you *do* get them right. Few players of any age or standard need more than a couple of brief sessions before they score 10/10 consistently on pairs of notes that are so close together they could not be any closer.

How to think of each note

How do you know if the open A string is in tune? You compare the pitch to something else: either the same note on the piano, or a tuning fork, or an electronic tone, or your memory of an A, and so on.

Without relating the A to something else it is neither in tune nor out of tune; it simply is what it is. When there is a point to relate it to, you can measure and hear whether it is higher, lower, or the same.

The same principle applies to tuning every other note on the violin: each note must be measured against, or related to, at least one other note.

Tuning to the open strings

One of the first steps for an elementary violinist is to check all the open-string notes with the open strings. It is the same for an advanced violinist: when working on intonation in any way, keep checking open-string notes with the open strings as a matter of course, just as much as if you were a beginner.

One way to test these notes is to play unisons or octaves:

Another way is to play only the stopped note, and watch the open string vibrate in sympathy. Leopold Mozart mentions sympathetic vibrations in his Violin School:

[2] Leopold Mozart: *A Treatise On The Fundamental Principles Of Violin Playing* (Augsburg, 1756; Eng. Trans. Editha Knocker, Oxford, 1948), 163.

It is irrefutable that a string, when struck or bowed, sets in motion another string tuned in unison with it…this was already known to the Ancients…Hang a stringed-instrument, the strings of which are not stretched too tightly, near an organ, and if the notes to which the open strings of the string-instrument are tuned be touched on the organ, those strings will immediately, although not touched, sound also, or will at least show a strong movement. Or on a violin, not too thickly strung and tuned rather low, play the G with the third finger on the D string, and the open G string will at once vibrate of its own accord.[2]

With a modern piano you can also do it the other way round: hold down the sustaining pedal to free the strings from the dampers. Play a note on the violin: the corresponding piano string will ring in sympathy.

On the violin, when the vibrating open string is *above* the stopped note (i.e. you play first-finger A on the G string and the open A string vibrates), the open string vibrates in one piece from the nut to the bridge.

A fascinating point that Leopold Mozart does not mention is that when the sympathetically-vibrating open string is *below* the stopped note (i.e. you play third-finger G on the D string and the open G string vibrates), the open string divides into distinct sections.

Playing third-finger G on the D string, the open G vibrates in two halves: it vibrates separately from the bridge to the centre point (the place where you would play a G harmonic), and again from the centre point to the nut.[1]

It is often easy to see the blur of the vibrating string in the lower octave; and another blur in the upper octave; and no blur whatsoever at the exact midpoint of the string between the nut and the bridge.

If you cannot see the two halves of the string vibrating separately, it does not matter or make any difference. After all, you are not going to be looking at the width of the vibrating string when you are playing music. Instead, listen to the timbre of the stopped third-finger G on the D string.

What is the 'timbre' of a note?

The timbre is the quality of tone that makes a note sound different from other notes of the same pitch and volume.

When the finger is exactly in the centre of the note G in 1st position on the D string, and the open G string is vibrating the widest, there is a soft and open quality in the stopped note. When the finger is sharp or flat to the smallest degree, a tight, hard-edged quality comes into the stopped note.

Adjust the finger by rolling slightly up and down on the string: a fraction higher, a fraction lower (like tuning a radio to exactly the right frequency by moving fractionally either side of it), until you are certain you are right in the middle of the note and the open G string vibrates widely.

The bold notes represent the stopped notes; the light notes represent the vibrating open strings:

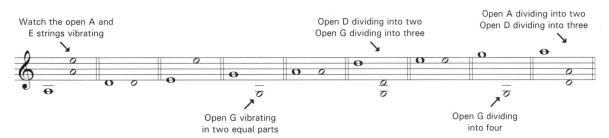

Because of the sympathetic vibrations of the open strings, intonation is a part of tone production. You can make almost any violin sound like a Stradivarius when you make the open strings resonate.[2]

Can a G, D, A or E ever be correct when tuned out of tune to the open string?

A safe approach is to decide that except in rare instances, every G, D, A or E should be exactly in tune with the open strings. There are times when you can depart from this:

[1] How clearly you can see the string sub-dividing is not a question of the quality of the instrument. Sometimes cheaper violins may have extremely wide subdivisions of the string, while they may be barely visible on a more expensive instrument. It also depends on the strings.

[2] The purity of the open strings, and the ringing quality of notes played in tune with them, has clearly not been lost on the composers who have written for the instrument. It is no coincidence that nearly all the concertos, sonatas and other pieces by the great composers are in G, D, A or E, or their relative minors.

Here, playing in the key of E♭ major, and with the chord of E♭ played on the piano, the E♭ in the violin part should not be played too flat otherwise it will clash with the higher, tempered E♭ in the piano. The same could apply if it were played by a string quartet.

To make the D sound like a close 'leading note' to the E♭ in this instance, you may play it considerably sharp to the open D; but because it is quite fast it sounds perfectly in tune.

Playing the same passage Adagio, you would need to play the D exactly in tune with the open D, perhaps compromising by squeezing the E♭ down 'as low as you dare'.

One situation where you should ignore the resonance

Suppose your violin is in tune with itself, but then you decide that the A is flat. You decide to retune the violin a little higher.

You move the peg of the A string up and down, looking for the right A. Finally you decide on what you think is a new, correct A that is a little higher than it was before.

So you begin to tune the violin to that new A, but as soon as you play a perfect fifth with the D string you realise that this A is exactly the same as the one you had before, and the fifth is still perfectly in tune.

This happens because while tuning the A string you listened for the sound of the greatest resonance. When the A string is in tune with the open D and E strings, the tone is more soft-centred and resonant; when the open A is slightly sharp or flat to the open D and E strings, the A gains a hard-edged tone.

So when you tuned the A higher, into its correct pitch, it sounded hard-edged and strained; and when you moved it back to where it had been before, it sounded the most resonant again. In that situation the A sounds wrong when it is right, and right when it is wrong.

Keep checking

Working on intonation in a scale, study or piece, check every G, D, A and E with the open string. If you check, say, an A with the open A in one bar, and then in the next bar there is another A, check that A with the open string as well. Then, suppose two bars later there is another A: check it with the open string as though it were for the first time, and so on through the whole piece.

Warm-up exercise

Simple warm-up exercises which include every finger on every open-string note are a time-effective way to maintain the 'skeleton' or basic structure of the left hand finger-placement.

This exercise consists of all the open-string notes played with every possible finger.

- Play separate bows as well as slurred, aiming for a ringing intonation throughout:

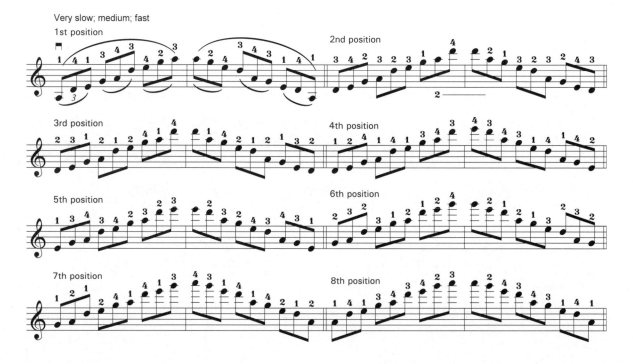

Sharps and flats: gravitational attraction

On a keyboard C♯ and D♭ are the same note. This is called 'tempered intonation'. Sometimes these notes are also the same when played on a string instrument; but sometimes the sharps are sharpened and the flats are flattened, so that G♯ is then somewhat higher than A♭. Pablo Casals called this 'expressive intonation'.

Casals used the term 'gravitational attraction' to describe how A♭, say, seems to want to move down towards G, and G♯ seems to want to move up towards A. This is how the great Russian violinist Mischa Elman described good intonation:

> Its control depends first of all on the ear. And a sensitive ear finds differences and shading; it bids the violinist play a trifle sharper, a trifle flatter, according to the general harmonic color of the accompaniment; it leads him to observe a difference, when the harmonic atmosphere demands it, between a C sharp in the key of E major and a D flat in the same key.[1]

Think of sharps as 'leading notes' to the natural a semitone above, like the seventh degree of the scale wanting to resolve into the tonic. Think of flats as 'leading notes' in the opposite direction, as though they wish to resolve down a semitone to the natural below.

[1] Frederick H. Martens: *Violin Mastery: Talks with Master Violinists and Teachers* (New York 1919), 14.

Warm-up exercise: quarter-tone scale

● As a good test of listening, and to discover how far you can go in squeezing semitones together expressively, practise quarter tone scales. Afterwards a semitone seems a huge distance:

Quarter tone scales sensitise your ears and fingers to the difference between the middle, tempered tuning of a sharp or flat, and the expressive pitches very slightly either side of it.

How to tune each note

It does not take long to consider all the notes of the octave one by one, and to find how to tune them. With many students it can be done within one short segment of a single violin lesson.

One thing that helps keep it simple is that once you have decided how to tune the first half of the octave on the G string – G, A♭, G♯, A, B♭, C♭, B, C, D♭, C♯ – you have already done what you need for the second half – D, E♭, D♯, E, F, G♭, F♯ – since these notes are symmetrical with those on the G string.

Start on G and work up through each note of the octave, semitone by semitone. After G the next note is A♭, not G♯. A♭ is just above G; G♯ is just below A, so the ascending order is usually:[2]

G – A♭ – G♯ – A – B♭ – A♯ – B – C – D♭ – C♯ – D – E♭ – D♯ – E – F – G♭ – F♯

If you include C♭, it would come after B♭ and before B; but it is normally tuned the same as a B. F♭ barely exists on the violin; but when the correct spelling requires it, it is played as an E.

[2] This was not always so. In certain parts of Europe during the Baroque period, sharps were considered close to the natural below, and flats close to the natural above. The order then was G – G♯ – A♭ – A.

In 1752 Johann Quantz said that to play semitones in tune 'the notes marked with a flat must be a comma higher than those that have a sharp before them'.

G

● Tune each G to the open string:

When you play second-finger G on the E string, the open G vibrates in four distinct sections. On some instruments you can see this easily. On others you cannot, but either way you can easily hear the hardness or softness in the tone, according to whether the second finger is in tune or not:

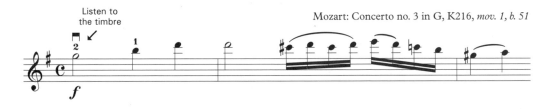

While pausing on one, long, held G, roll the second finger a fraction higher on the string, then a fraction lower, and find the exact centre of the note.

Notice how, when the finger is a fraction sharp or flat, a hard edge comes into the sound. When the finger is exactly in the middle of the note, the hard edge disappears and the note has a soft centre instead.

- Tune A♭ close to G.

Sometimes you have to play an A♭ higher, the same as a tempered, keyboard-type A♭; but for the present purposes of feeling the A♭ in relation to the G, exaggerate slightly by playing an A♭ that is clearly flatter than the same note played on the piano.

- Find each A♭ in 1st position:

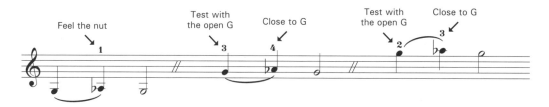

Leopold Auer said that when you play first-finger A♭ on the G string, first-finger E♭ on the D string, first-finger B♭ on the A string and first-finger F on the E string, you should 'place the tip of the first finger as close to the nut as possible for the first half-step'.

Fig. 45a shows too large a distance between the tip of the finger playing first-finger B♭ on the A string, and the nut. Fig. 45b shows a more 'expressive' B♭.

When Auer said 'as close as possible to the nut' the emphasis should be on the word 'possible'. Pressing the tip of the finger up against the nut, as shown in Fig. 45c, makes the note too flat.

Fig. 45

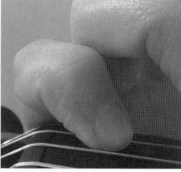

(a) Too much space between the first finger and the nut

(b) Feel the nut with the first finger

(c) Auer did not mean this close

- Tune G♯ in relation to A.

Find each G♯ in 1st position:

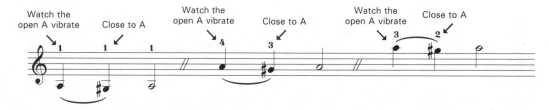

- For practice purposes, exaggerate slightly by playing a G♯ that is clearly sharper than the same note played on the piano.

- Check each A by watching the open A string vibrate: adjust the finger a fraction higher, a fraction lower, until you are definitely right in the middle of the note and the open A string vibrates widely.

How high you should tune a ♯ depends on the key. It is not always a leading note. When G♯ is the tonic rather than, say, the leading note in A major, you have to play it more tempered, i.e. lower.

In *Havanaise*, it is not possible to play a high G♯ here:

Saint-Saëns: Havanaise, op. 83, b. 48

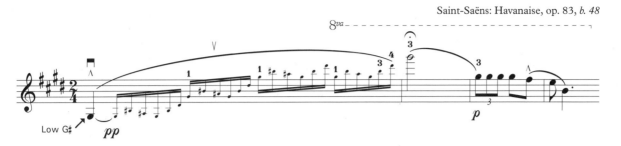

Low G♯

In many cases you can play a 'high' G♯, e.g. as the major 3rd in E, which makes the key 'brighter'. Then, because you play the G♯'s higher, you have to play the F♯'s higher as well:[1]

[1] See *How to play scales in tune: 1–4–5–8*, page 85

J.S. Bach: Concerto no. 2 in E, BWV1042, *mov. 1, b. 1*

A

● Tune each A to the open string:

Listen to the increased resonance of the violin when the stopped note is exactly in tune. Playing in tune with the open strings makes almost any violin sound mellow and resonant:

Listen to the resonance
of the open A and E strings

Sarasate, Playera, op. 23, *b. 4*

B♭

● Tune B♭ in relation to A.

● Find each B♭ in 1st position. Exaggerate slightly by playing it quite low, squeezing it next to the A.

● Check each A by listening to the timbre:

Listen to
the timbre   Close to A   Feel the nut

Listen to
the timbre   Close to A

Here, for the purpose of establishing the intonation, play quite a flat B♭. However, the B♭ that you would choose in a piece depends entirely on the key. In the opening of the Tchaikovsky Concerto, the B♭ is low, dark and expressive, so quite close to A:

Tchaikovsky: Concerto in D, op. 35, *mov. 1, b. 23*

Similarly in the Bruch G minor Concerto, the character would be lost without a low, expressive B♭:

Bruch: Concerto no. 1 in G minor, op. 26, *mov. 1, b. 6*

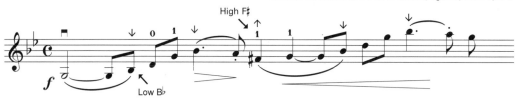

But a low B♭ does not work here:

Mozart: Sonata in B♭, K454, *mov. 1, b. 1*

However, if you tune the second-finger B♭ (on the G string) to the open D string, the B♭ will be too high. Find a place in the middle, between a low, expressive B♭ and a B♭ that is in tune with the D string:

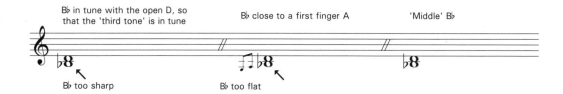

A♯–B–C The next note up is A♯, which is tuned from B. But how do you find a B? B is the leading note to C. But how do you find a C?

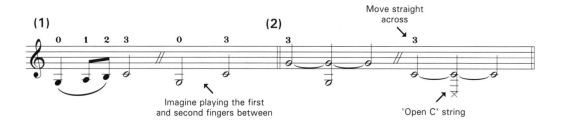

(1) One way to think of a C is that it is a perfect fourth above open G.

(2) Another way to find a C is to play a perfect fifth down from third-finger G on the D string.

If your third finger is playing G exactly in tune on the D string, and then you move the finger exactly across to the G string,[1] the finger should now play a C exactly in tune with an open C string – if you had one.

[1] See *Perfect fifths: back, across, or forwards?,* page 76

(3) Although the notes of a perfect interval are usually better as reference points than those of major, minor, augmented or diminished intervals, you may like to tune C as a minor third above open A.

The danger of taking C from a minor third is that it might be too low; but if you hear G at the back of your mind, using a minor third often ends up with the same pitch as tuning from the open G:

- Having found the C, then take the B from the C:

Feel the B as a
leading note to C

- Then take the A♯ from the B:

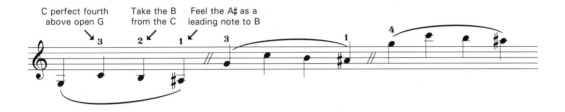

C perfect fourth
above open G

Take the B
from the C

Feel the A♯ as a
leading note to B

Another way to find a B is to pitch it as a perfect fifth above E. However, if you play the fifth exactly in tune the B may be too sharp. Test this by playing B, one octave up on the A string, with the open E, and then find that same B on the E string. It may seem high, even though it is 'in tune':

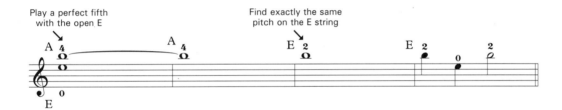

Play a perfect fifth
with the open E

Find exactly the same
pitch on the E string

Similarly, the B in 1st position on the A string is too sharp if it is exactly in tune with the E string; at the same time, it is too flat when it is in tune with the open D string. The best tuning is often between the two extremes.[1]

[1] See *Tuning to a higher or lower string*, page 91

In the opening of the Mendelssohn Concerto the B may seem sharp if it is a true perfect fifth above open E. Play it very slightly flat:

Mendelssohn: Concerto in E minor, op. 64, *mov. 1, b. 2*

Aim for a
'low' B

B on the D string, played in tune with the open G string, comes out impossibly flat if you play it so that the 'third tone' is in tune.

Brahms: Sonata no. 1 in G, op. 78, *mov. 1, b. 3*

In this example, the B is a bright major third above the G. If you played that same B with the open G, it would sound considerably too sharp:

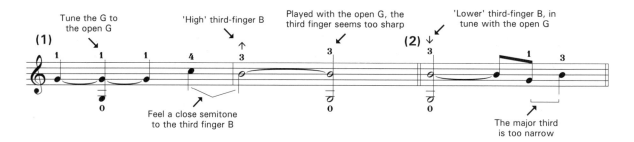

(1) Find the B by first finding the perfect fourth from G to C; then put the B next to the C.

If you then play this B with the open G, it will seem too sharp.

(2) You have to tune the B very flat if you play it with the open G with the 'third tone' in tune.

 • Tune C♭ in relation to B♭:

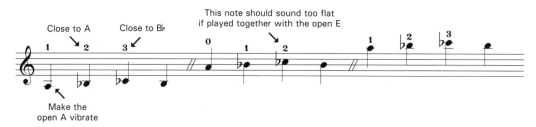

You cannot always squeeze C♭ close to a B♭. More often the C♭ has to be the same as a B♮:

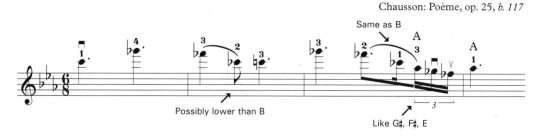

G♯ • Tune B♯ in relation to C♯:

In many cases B♯ is too sharp if it is played as a 'leading note' to C♯, and then works better when you think of it as a straightforward C.

Sometimes a sharp B♯, with a 'gravitational attraction' to the C♯, is possible and produces an entirely different character. Here, the harmony in the piano easily allows it:

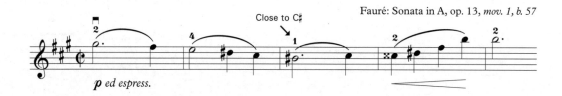

D♭

• Tune D♭ in relation to C:

Sometimes you have to play a D♭ higher, the same as a tempered D♭.

C♯

• Tune C♯ in relation to D:

This C♯ is a classic example of one that must not be tuned to the open A:

Mozart: Concerto no. 5 in A, K219, *mov. 1, b. 40*

This note is exactly like the B in the Brahms G major example (page 67). It should be tuned closer to the D than the lower C♯ which would be in tune with the open A string.

The chromatic scale in the following example is in unison with the piano, so none of the notes can be tuned expressively. The C♯ must be played low:

Beethoven: Sonata in C minor, op. 30 no. 2, *mov. 1, b. 19*

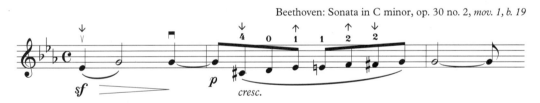

The first E♭ of the example can be played expressively low, but the E♭ in the second bar must be higher because of the unison. The F in the second bar cannot be played low, and the F♯ cannot be played high.

D

• Tune each D to the open string.

E♭

• Tune E♭ in relation to D. Approach this note the same as A♭.

D♯

• Tune D♯ in relation to E. Approach the same as G♯.

E

• Tune each E to the open string.

First-finger E on the D string is in a similar position to first-finger B on the A string. If you tune the E to the open G it will be too flat; if you tune it to the open A, it will be too sharp.

Like the B, a mid-point between the two extremes is often the right place to put it. If the first-finger E on the D string is exactly in tune with the open E, it may be a fraction flat to the open A anyway.[1]

[1] But see *Tuning in narrow fifths*, page 92

F

- Tune F in relation to E. Approach the same as B♭.

In typical passage work in, say, a Beethoven violin sonata, the piano part often leaves the violin free to play expressive intonation. However, with the piano sustaining an F, you cannot play a low F here:

Beethoven: Sonata in E♭, op. 12 no.3, *mov. 1, b. 23*

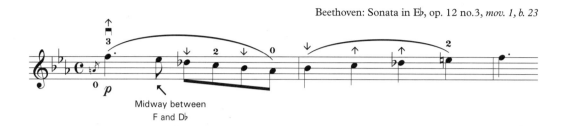

Play the F higher, in tune with the piano. After that, the E♭, D♭ and B♭ can all be played expressively.

In the second bar you can play the same expressive B♭ as in the first bar; but the C and D♭ need to be played higher to match the same notes in the piano.

A piece such as the Cesar Franck Sonata is full of individual notes and melody lines that are in unison with the piano, and at least half the time it is impossible to use expressive intonation without the unisons jarring. But in a passage like the following it is essential to play a low F and a high G♯, and there is nothing in the piano part to go against this:

Franck: Sonata in A, *mov. 2, b. 95*

E♯

- Tune E♯ in relation to F♯. Approach the same as A♯.

E♯ must often be played the same as an F. At other times E♯ can be considerably higher than an F, when it is played as a close leading note to F♯:

Brahms: Sonata no. 1 in G, op. 78, *mov. 1, b. 212*

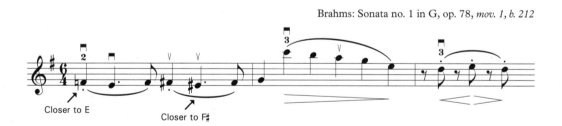

G♭

- Tune G♭ in relation to F. Approach the same as C♭.

F♯

- Tune F♯ in relation to G. Approach the same as B.

In the opening of the Schubert Sonatina no. 1 in D major the violin is in unison with the piano. It may sound out of tune unless you play tempered F♯s, C♯s and D♯s:

Schubert: Sonatine in D, op. 137 no. 1, *mov. 1, b. 1*

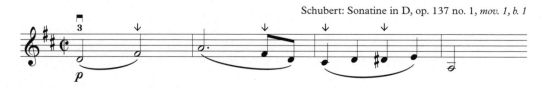

Then at bar 13, when the violin has the melody to itself and the piano begins to accompany, you can let the tuning become more expressive. Even then, any 'colouring' of a note must be slight to avoid clashing with F♯'s in other octaves, as well as to avoid being out of tune with other notes in the piano:

Understanding the differences between the positions

The higher up the string you play (i.e. the shorter the string) the closer together the notes are. This is not a subject only for beginners. Playing in 3rd position, say, but with the same spaces between the fingers as if in 1st position, is one of the most common causes of less-than-perfect intonation and can be heard at all levels of playing, including in the performances of the great violinists.

Perhaps this apparently obvious, elementary factor is so easily overlooked because it is associated only with high positions where, at the top of the string, the fingers are all on top of each other. Yet the difference in spacing between playing in 1st position and playing in 4th position is already striking:

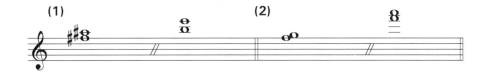

(1) Play a major third in 1st position (both fingers on the E string). Keep both fingers on the string. Move to 4th position, keeping the fingers exactly the same distance apart. Now the same spacing plays a perfect fourth.

(2) Play a major second in 1st position. In 8th position the same spacing plays a major third.

Even when you are playing within one position, the space between the fingers gets smaller as you ascend, and larger when you descend. Play a whole tone scale on the A string:

(1) Ascending, avoid over-reaching with the third finger, as if trying to match the distance you played from first to second. Also avoid over-reaching with the fourth finger, which happens partly because the distance is now very much closer than between first and second, partly because the fourth often feels weaker than the first and second fingers, which makes you want to 'do more' with it.

(2) Descending, you have to reach back further with each finger.

One exception to the principle of notes getting further apart the lower the position, is in the difference in the feeling of the semitone between the first and second fingers in 1st position and in half position:

You would expect the semitone in (2) to feel wider than in (1) because the notes are lower down the string, but they feel closer together:

...one might reason that because it is a lower position there is more distance between the fingers. In this case the reasoning does not hold true because when moving back to play these notes the thumb stays in first position and so creates an abnormally cramped feeling in the hand. The second finger must be placed lower than expected to counteract the pull on the hand by the thumb.[1]

[1] Raphael Bronstein: *The Science of Violin Playing* (New Jersey, 1977), 5.

The following examples show typical spacing miscalculations:

Example 1

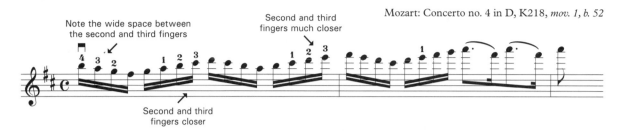

A frequent example is the difference in spacing between playing a simple whole tone (major second) in 1st position, and playing it in 3rd position.

The E at the end of the first bar, in 5th position, feels surprisingly close to the second-finger D when both notes are in tune. You have to be careful not to place this finger too sharp to the open E.

Example 2

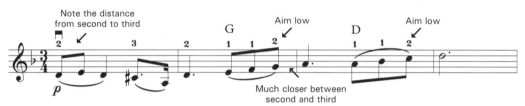

A simple way to check the tuning is to play the phrase in 1st position and see if there is a difference:

Example 3

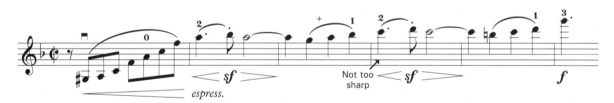

The distance between G and A, played first-finger to second-finger on the E string in 2nd position (marked '+'), feels far wider than the same interval played in 4th position.

Example 4

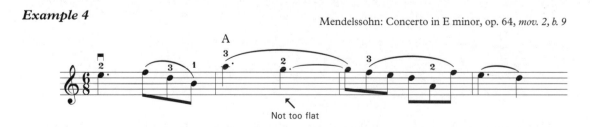

The same naturally applies equally in descending notes. In this example, having shifted up to the A, and with only the third finger on the string at that moment, it is all-too-easy to allow the second finger to play the G too flat.

Example 5

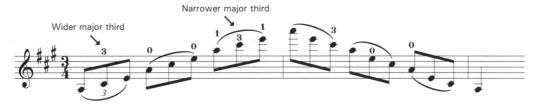

The major third between the first and third fingers feels wide in 1st position, and much closer together in 3rd position. You have to be careful not to play the third-finger C♯ on the E string too high.

Two essential intonation exercises

These exercises are as good for the left hand as essential tone exercises are for the right hand (page 11). Like them, these are equally suitable for professionals and for less advanced players.

Both these intonation exercises have the effect of *tuning the whole hand*, so that your fingers naturally fall in tune wherever you play on the fingerboard, and in whatever finger patterns – instead of you having to work on individual passages to get them in tune while other passages remain out of tune.

Saving time by spending time

Intonation exercises are a good example of how you can save time by spending time:[1]

- Play a three-octave scale a few times, just getting the feel of it and seeing how in tune it is. Then practise either of the following intonation exercises for 5 or 10 minutes.

Practise the finger spacing exercise (Exercise 1) on one string only; or practise the finger patterns (Exercise 2) in the key of the scale only.

- Then play the scale again. You may be amazed at how much better it already feels or sounds.

Suppose you had practised the scale itself for 5 or 10 minutes instead. The question is could you have improved it as much, in that time, as you had improved it by practising the intonation exercise. The results of the exercises are so good it is doubtful that you could have achieved as much.[2]

That does not mean that the actual scale should not be practised also, for fluency and evenness etc. – only that intonation exercises are an exceptionally quick way to get the scale in tune in the first place.[3]

[1] See *Investing your time*, page 327

[2] It is simple to demonstrate this. A new student plays a three-octave scale. They score 5/10 for intonation. Then they spend ten minutes on either of these exercises, and then play the same scale again. Now they score 9/10. Try it for yourself and see.

[3] See *Why practise scales?*, page 301

Exercise 1: Finger spacing

- Play entirely on the A string, continuing each sequence further up the string.

- Feel the clear difference in spacing with each progressive step higher.

- Play also back down the string again, feeling the intervals progressively widening.

- Repeat the same patterns on the other strings.

● In the following numbers 4–9 the x-notes indicate to remember the feeling of playing the missed-out notes, and to measure the played notes from them:

Exercise 2: Note patterns repeated with different fingering

This uniform intonation exercise consists simply of a random group of notes that you make up as you like. Play the group everywhere on the fingerboard, with every possible fingering, using the following easy-to-remember finger sequence.

● Take a short group of notes, or make up a little phrase.

● Begin on the A string in 1st position. Throughout the exercise, often come back to this first bar to check the tuning.

Although you are playing a different fingering in each bar, each bar should sound identical, as though you are actually repeating the same notes with the same fingering.

● Repeat each bar as many times as necessary until you are certain that each note is absolutely in tune, before moving on to the next bar.

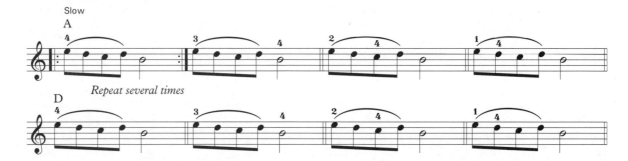

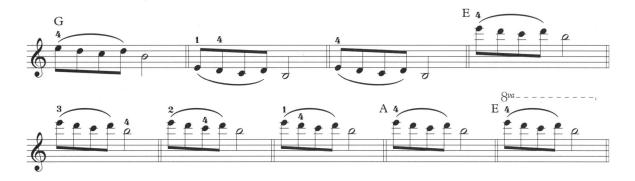

- Use any notes in any order. Examples:

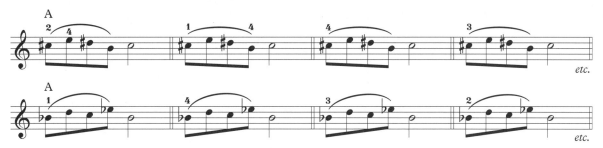

Playing two-octave scales across the strings without shifting, with different fingerings starting on the third finger, then the second finger, then the first finger, is another excellent uniform intonation exercise.

If it is out of tune there is always a reason why

Beyond the most elementary levels of playing, notes that you play out of tune are usually out of tune in the same direction each time. They will not sometimes be sharp, sometimes flat, completely randomly. This makes intonation much easier to correct since it is entirely predictable.

There is a three-step process to follow:

1 First you have to listen so carefully that you catch every note that is not in tune.

   Then the question is whether a false note is a random occurrence, or is it consistently sharp or flat. Repeat a phrase several times and notice which notes are out of tune two out of three times, or three out of five times, and what the direction is – always too high or always too low.

2 Then decide what is the reason for the note being out of tune.

3 Then replay the phrase several times with the new tuning until it becomes a habit, and you no longer have to think about it.

The following are some of the usual reasons for notes being consistently out of tune.[1]

Tension: five areas to release

The first essential condition for playing in tune, after pre-hearing the note and listening, is that the left hand be entirely free of tension. Then the hand and fingers make thousands of instantaneous, natural corrections to the intonation which results in overall in-tune playing.[2]

It is difficult to keep the left hand free if there is tension elsewhere in the left arm, because of all the knock-on effects.[3] There are five areas to keep checking to make sure that they are entirely free, i.e. that there are no muscles or tendons in a state of permanent contraction:

1 **Across the base joints and the palm of the hand.** As part of this, make sure that when using one finger the other, unused fingers remain free. (See Fig. 82, page 139.)

2 **Thumb.** Keep neutral, without squeezing back against the first finger, or counter pressing hard against the neck of the violin.

3 **Wrist.** Keep soft and yielding. In 1st position, normally keep a straight line without pushing the wrist out or pulling in.

4 **Upper arm.** Keep free and mobile, without pulling in against the side of the chest.

5 **Head.** Keep free in the neck and shoulders by resting the head on the chin-rest without clamping the violin between the chin and the shoulders.

[1] See also *Keeping the thumb in one place*, page 305

[2] See *Playing with a soft hand*, page 20

[3] See *Chain reactions*, page 164

The in-built tendencies of each finger to play sharp or flat

One of the essential things is that the position of the hand does not change for each finger, leaning more one way or the other depending on whether an upper or a lower finger is being played. The habits of holding fingers down, and of keeping unused fingers above the string, are a general cure for this.

But then, even if there is stability in the hand, there is the question of moving between one string and another.

Perfect fifths: back, across, or forwards?

Playing from lower strings to higher

Playing in low positions the first finger must often aim not 'directly across' to the next string, but 'slightly back'. This is because the finger is slightly straighter on the G string and more curved on the E, so the finger pulls in as it plays on each higher string.

For example, if you play first-finger A on the G string, then first-finger E on the D string, B on the A string, and F♯ on the E string, you have to pull the finger back very slightly flatter each time, to avoid getting progressively sharper on each string:

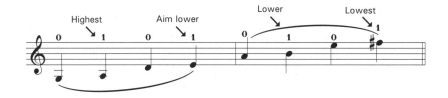

In high positions you have to do the opposite and push the first finger slightly forwards:

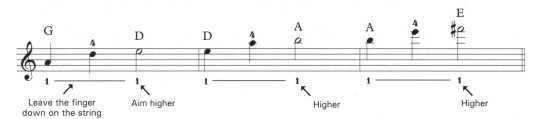

In middle positions the feeling may be of moving straight across, without needing to compensate forwards or backwards. It depends partly on the individual hand. Here, the first finger may move straight across:

Just one semitone lower, there may be more a feeling of aiming upwards:

Dvořák: Romance, op. 11, *b. 43*

Even in third position, especially playing from the A string to the E string where the finger is the most curved, there may be a feeling of aiming upwards:

Schnittke: Suite in the Old Style, *Fugue, b. 41*

Playing from higher strings to lower

Since in 1st position there is a feeling of the fingers moving slightly back, as they cross from the G string to the E string, you could expect them to move slightly forwards when crossing down from the E to the G string; but in fact you have to aim slightly back on the way down too.

This is because the fingers naturally want to move forwards – rather than across – on to the next string anyway. You can see this clearly in the difference between the following patterns.

Tap the fingers silently on the strings, without the bow. Remember to keep the hand in one position and move only the finger:

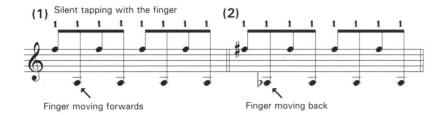

1 The finger opens and closes naturally, extending forwards to the G string and pulling in to the E string. This is the natural direction of the finger and is a very easy movement to make.

2 The finger has to move backwards against its natural direction.

Moving to a lower string the first finger must resist the natural thing of opening forwards, so there is a similar feeling of aiming backwards on the way down as there is on the way up.

Stopping two strings at once

One way to make intonation feel very secure is, where possible, to stop two strings at once:[1]

[1] See *Placing the fifth for single notes*, page 312

Pugnani-Kreisler: Praeludium and Allegro, *Allegro, b. 41*

Warm-up exercise no.1

- Use the following simple sequence as an instant warm-up exercise. It quickly sensitises each finger to the necessary degree of 'pulling back' in 1st position: the first finger the most, the second less, the third almost exactly straight across, and the fourth straight across.

  Naturally, everything depends on the build of the individual hand. Mark your own arrows to suit your own tendencies. For example, if your hand is not wide across the knuckles you may need to aim the fourth finger slightly sharper on each lower string when descending (in the final bar).

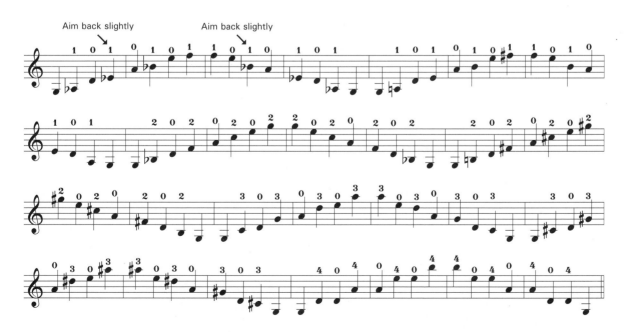

Warm-up exercise no.2

- Playing in high positions you have to do the opposite and aim the first finger very slightly sharper (playing from lower strings to higher) because of the pull the thumb exerts on the finger.

  Playing from higher strings to lower, the second, third and fourth fingers move 'across' from the E string to the A string; but you have to aim higher when reaching to the D ansd G strings because of the extra distance.

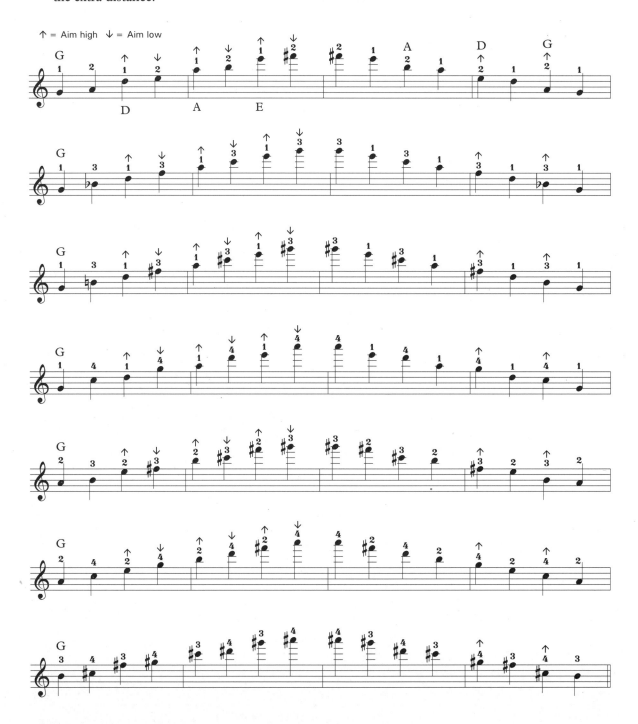

Reaching down to a lower string

When playing, say, first-finger F on the E string, followed by third-finger A, the feeling of the distance of the major third seems less than if you play third-finger D on the A string:

This is because of the extra distance the finger has to reach to get to the A string, or the other strings. There is more widening at the base joint, which makes it seem a larger distance.

Warm-up exercise no.3

Use this sequence to explore the different sensations of reaching for the notes. Each hand is slightly different, so change or add to the arrows to match your finger's needs to aim low, high or across:

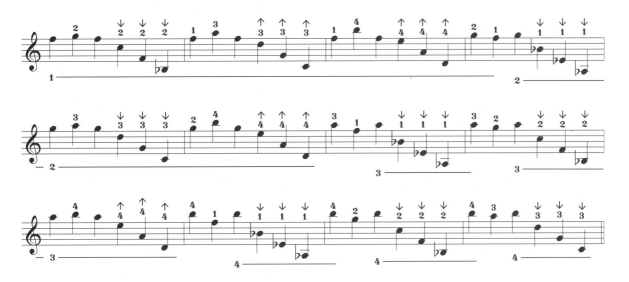

- Play the same notes one octave higher. Notice that many arrows now need to point the other way.

Square and extended finger shapes in moving passages

In moving passages in low positions, fingers are more 'square' or more 'extended' (Galamian's terms) depending on the note. However, in slow, expressive playing you may need more of the pad on the string for a warm vibrato, so then many officially 'square' fingers are played flatter, or more 'extended'.[1]

Playing first-finger B♭ on the A string, the finger is square (□). Playing B♮, the finger is extended (◇). Second-finger C♮ is square (Fig. 46a), C♯ is extended (Fig. 46b), third-finger D is square, D♯ is extended.

The fourth finger is never really square, but less extended when playing E♭ in 1st position on the A string, more extended when playing E or E♯.

It is common to see players putting their hand out of position by using the wrong finger shape, e.g. playing first-finger B on the A string with the finger square, or third-finger D with the finger extended.

[1] Playing with the fingers too square may lead to too thin a vibrato, so strictness about the 'correct finger shape' must not be taken too far.

Then are many occasions when third-finger D (A string), say, or second-finger B♭ (G string) should be put down 'not too square' so that there is enough pad for a warm-enough vibrato.

You do not want to have a thin vibrato every time you put a finger down 'square'.

Fig. 46

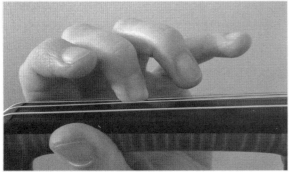

(a) 'Square' position, or 'low' 2

(b) 'Extended' shape, or 'high' 2

Example 1

Playing a natural on one string, and then using the same finger on the next string to play a sharp or a flat, is a common reason for a note being out of tune. The finger must change sufficiently from square to extended, or *vice versa*:

Key point: The hand stays in one position and the fingers change their shape to reach the notes – not, the fingers stay in the same shape and the hand moves to accommodate the fingers.

Example 2

When you are working on the tuning of a phrase, and thinking about how the notes and fingers relate to each other, keep in mind the shape a finger was in when you last used it – even if the note the finger last played, and the note it is currently playing, appear to have no relation to each other.

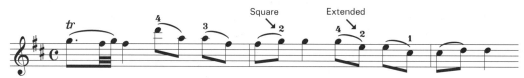

Mozart: Violin Concerto no. 4 in D, K218, *mov. 1, b. 49*

Here, the E in 3rd position on the A string should be played with a slightly straighter finger than if it played an E♭. It may easily be too flat after the square finger playing the G in 1st position on the E string two notes earlier.

- Try playing the passage with an E♭ and then repeat with the written E. Feel the difference in the shape of the finger.

- Practise going from one to the other:

Shifting between one finger shape and another

In moving passages the shape of the finger must often change during a shift.

If you shift with one finger (i.e. 1–1, 2–2, 3–3, 4–4) from square to extended, or from extended to square – but the shape of the finger does not adjust during the shift – the result is that the hand arrives very slightly not quite in the right position; or else the finger has to sit in an uncomfortable shape when it arrives on the end-note of the shift.

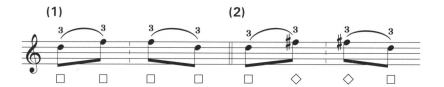

(1) Shifting from a square finger to another square, the shape of the finger does not change during the shift (at least, not in the large sense of changing from square to extended).

(2) Shifting from a square to an extended finger, change the shape of the finger during the shift.

   Shifting up: if you keep the square shape that you had on the D as you shift up into 3rd position, and play the F♯ with a square finger, the entire hand will be positioned a little higher up the neck than true 3rd position. Any notes that follow could easily be out of tune.

   Shifting down: if you keep the extended shape that you had on the F♯ as you shift down into 1st position, and play the D with an extended finger, the entire hand will be positioned a little lower down the neck than true 1st position. The notes that follow could be out of tune.

Instead, change the shape of the finger during the shift so that you arrive in the most comfortable shape for the finger as well as the correct position of the hand.

You can't just put fingers down next to each other

As children, we learn that in playing a whole tone the fingers have a space between them, and playing a semitone the fingers are placed next to each other. Years later, we may still have this idea at the back of the mind. But even in 1st position, if you put the fingers 'next to each other' they will often still be too far apart.

Look at the too-wide space between the contact-point of the second finger with the string, and the contact-point of the third finger (Fig. 47a). It is too wide for a semitone. Instead, the third finger must often move in more closely (Fig. 47b).

Fig. 47

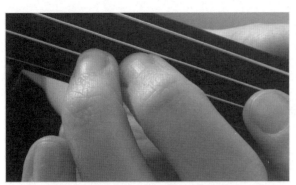

(a) Placed together so that the fingers are touching, the semitone may still easily be too wide

(b) The fingertips are squeezing more closely together

The thing to avoid is the spacing of a semitone being influenced by the thickness of a particular finger:

In **(1)** the semitone may be too narrow if your little finger is particularly narrow at the tip; in **(2)** it may be too wide if the tip of the finger is particularly broad.

The three notes should sound the same whatever the fingering, and be tuned according to the music, not according to the shape of the finger.

 My fingers are too thick and wide at the fingertips to be able to play in tune high up on the fingerboard, where the notes are all so close together. What can I do to help this?

There is little difference, playing in high positions, whether you have large hands or small. With the thinnest fingertips, you still cannot leave a finger down in a high position and place the next finger very close to it on the string, a semitone higher or lower, in tune. You still have to 'skip' the fingers out of the way to make room for the next finger, in exactly the same way that players with larger hands, or wider fingertips, have to do.

The Israeli violinist Itzhak Perlman is an example of a player with very large hands and fat, wide fingertips. His full-size violin looks small in his hands, yet he can play immaculately in tune in high positions. Everybody else can then say that since it is possible to play in tune with much wider fingertips than their own, the shape of their fingers can be discounted as a factor.

Some of the best players have had small hands, and some have had large hands – so the level of your intonation must depend not on your physique but on other qualities of technique or musicianship.

Filling the gap

When you play from the first to the fourth finger – e.g. playing B–E in 1st position on the A string – you can much more easily gauge exactly where to put the fourth finger down if you feel also where the second and third fingers would go if they were on the string.

If you try to measure where to put the fourth finger by thinking only of how far away it is from the first finger, it is far more difficult to sense the correct distance.

Exaggerate the feeling by positioning the second and third fingers *under* the neck of the violin (Fig. 48a). Play B–E–B–E a few times, feeling how difficult it is to know where the E is with the middle fingers unable to help.

Then, with the second and third fingers hovering just above the string over a C (or C♯) and D, feel how much easier it is to measure the E from the first finger.

Fig. 48

 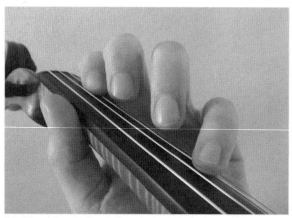

(a) The feeling of measuring the fourth finger only from the first

(b) Measuring the fourth finger using the second and third fingers

The same applies to the other finger combinations:

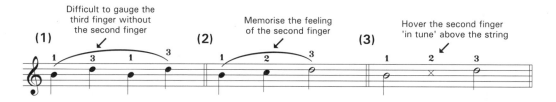

(1) Playing from B to D without the awareness of the second finger.

(2) Play the second finger and memorise the feel of the spacing of the three fingers.

(3) Rather than playing the second finger, hover the finger above the string and measure the third finger from the memory of how the second finger felt in **(2)**.[1]

[1] See also *Exercise 1: Finger spacing*, page 73

Fingers pulling other fingers with them

Example 1

A minor third is 'narrow' or a 'small distance'; a major third is 'wide' or a 'large distance'; but if you play a major third directly before an extension you have to think of it as a small distance because of the way the extending finger tries to pull the lower finger up with it:

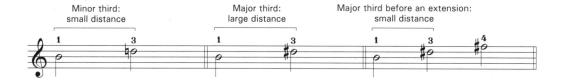

Example 2

Any extension or stretch may have an effect on the notes before or after. Particular care must be taken with the second and third fingers when playing a tone-and-a-half. In most hands these fingers are less happy to separate than the first and second or third and fourth:

(1) Aim low with the second finger, placing it close to the E, since the F may be pulled up too high by the third finger; aim high with the third finger, feeling the G♯ as a leading note to A, since it may be pulled down by the F.

(2) The second finger may again be pulled up too high after the third finger.

Example 3

Other fingerings and note patterns may easily pull a finger away from its right place also:

(1) The fourth-finger D may be flat in anticipation of the next note, second-finger F. If the next note was an F♯ instead, the fourth-finger D would not be likely to be flat.

(2) The F may be too sharp, having been pulled up by the fourth-finger D.

(3) The F may again be too sharp, this time in anticipation of the fourth-finger A.

(4) The fourth-finger may be flat, coming after an F. If instead it came after an F♯, it would not be likely to be flat.

Example 4

Example 5

Example 6

When playing from one double stop to another, where one finger moves a whole tone and the other finger moves a semitone, you have to be particularly careful to prevent the fingers from pulling each other one way or the other.

In this example, in the ascending shifts the first and third fingers both move one whole tone. (They do not actually move the same distance, since from B♭ to C is wider, being nearer the end of the string, than the distance the third finger moves from G to A – but at least both fingers move the same interval.)

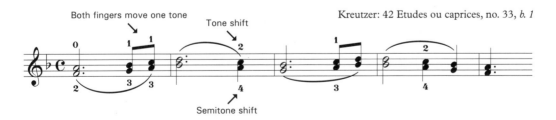

In the descending shifts played with the second and fourth fingers, the second finger moves a whole tone from D to C, but the fourth finger moves a semitone from B♭ to A.

You have to be careful to keep the fingers independent, and not allow the second finger to pull the fourth down too low, or play the second finger too sharp because of the fourth moving only a semitone.

As a general rule, it often helps to think only of the finger that moves the bigger distance, and 'let the other finger look after itself'.

Bow-pressure and pitch

The left hand fingers are often blamed for out-of-tune notes that are actually the fault of the bow. Too much bow pressure, too far from the bridge, 'bends' the pitch of the note flat.

- The further from the bridge the softer the string, and the less pressure the string can take from the bow before the pitch wavers.

- The shorter the string the less pressure it can take.[1]

[1] Few students avoid the following playful trap you can set. You ask them, 'So, the nearer to the bridge the more bow-pressure, yes?' They reply yes. 'And the higher up the fingerboard the left fingers, the nearer the bow must be to the bridge, yes?' Yes, they say. 'So, the higher the note, the nearer the bridge with more pressure?' Yes, is the usual answer. No! The shorter the string, the nearer the bridge, but with *less* pressure.

Pugnani-Kreisler: Praeludium and Allegro, *Praeludium, b. 21*

The top B marked '+' can sound as an A♯ if played too heavily with the bow, even if the left finger is exactly in tune.

Party trick: Für Elise

Play the opening of Für Elise on the open E string without using fingers until the last three notes.

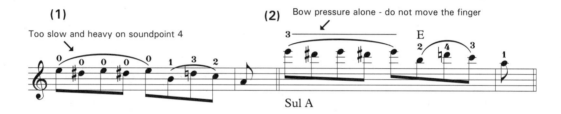

(1) Alternate between open E and D♯ by using too much bow pressure. Bowing on soundpoint 3–4, keep the bow speed the same while increasing the pressure until the note changes pitch.

(2) The pitch of the note is easiest to 'bend' when playing in higher positions because of the shorter string length.

Pulling or pushing the string

The finger stopping the string must not alter the straight line of the string. The pitch sharpens if, at the same time as stopping the note, the finger pulls the string to the right or pushes it to the left.

Normally fingers should be placed as lightly as possible, or dropped on to the string with a feeling of 'drop–release' rather than 'drop–press'. Pulling or pushing the string is an indication of tension since in order to move the string the finger must be pressing it quite hard.

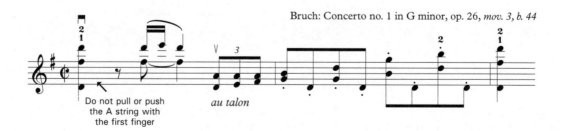

Bruch: Concerto no. 1 in G minor, op. 26, *mov. 3, b. 44*

This chord in the Bruch G minor concerto is often out of tune, but not only because of any difficulty in finding 5th position. Even if the second-finger D is in tune on the E string, the first finger is often sharp on the A string – not because of where it is put down on the string, but because it 'bends' the note upwards by pulling or pushing.

Semitones with one finger

When shifting a semitone with one finger you have to be careful not to make the semitone too narrow, with it ending up almost like a quarter tone:

● Note how far apart the fingers are, then shift the same distance:

How to play scales in tune: 1–4–5–8

The following method of tuning scales was the one taught by Dorothy DeLay. I knew that she had devised the system herself, but some years after I had finished studying I discovered that Pablo Casals had also taught scales in this way.

I teased Miss DeLay about it, saying that I had not realised she had stolen the idea. She laughed and said that she had not known that Casals had done the same thing. 'All I was trying to do', she said, 'was to find some way of getting my students to play their scales in tune!'

> The principal challenge confronting the string player whose sensibilities have been dulled by the mechanical pitch produced by the piano is to establish the proper placement of semitones. Here we must distinguish between diatonic and chromatic semitones, the former being invariably characterized by a sense of connectedness which Casals likened to 'gravitational attraction'.[1]
>
> Casals considered the tonic, subdominant and dominant of a given tonality (the first, fourth and fifth degrees of a scale) to be points of repose to which the other notes are drawn. Thus, the principle of gravitational attraction is at work within each of the two tetra chords of which a scale is composed. The diatonic semitone within each tetra chord has a natural tendency to be drawn upwards: the third degree towards the fourth and, most particularly, the seventh degree – the leading note – towards the octave. The pitch of the leading note needs to be raised high enough for us to feel the inevitability of its resolution to the tonic.
>
> If the semitones are placed higher, the intermediate tones are affected; they must adjust accordingly.[2]

When I first heard this idea of tuning the scale in two symmetrical halves, I realised why I had had a faint sense of something being not quite right when, as a 12-year-old student in the Junior Department of the Guildhall School of Music, I had learnt in the theory class that a major scale consisted of the following sequence: tone, tone, semitone, tone, tone, tone, semitone.

Although I didn't know why at the time, the feeling of dissatisfaction came from the fact that this sequence does not sound balanced or symmetrical, whereas the major scale does, i.e. 'tone–tone–semitone; tone–tone–semitone'. The two halves are joined by a tone, but including that tone in the sequence unbalances the true structure of the scale.

(1)

● There is a perfect fourth in each half of the scale.

(2)

● The tone-semitone pattern in each half is the same: tone–tone–semitone, tone–tone–semitone.

[1] When the notes of a semitone are on the same line or space (i.e. C–C♯) the semitone is chromatic; when one note is on a line and the other on a space (i.e. C–D♭) the semitone is diatonic. In expressive intonation chromatic semitones are played 'wide'; diatonic semitones are played 'narrow'. In tempered intonation they are equally spaced.

[2] David Blum: *Casals and the Art of Interpretation* (London, 1977), 103

(3)

- The seventh degree of the scale is called the 'leading note'. The third degree of the scale has the same relationship with the fourth as the seventh with the octave, and equally can be thought of as a 'leading note' to the fourth. These are the notes that Casals described as having a 'gravitational attraction' to resolve into the note above.[1]

How high to tune the two leading notes is a matter of taste; some prefer higher, brighter leading notes; others prefer them lower (more like the tempered tuning of a keyboard).

[1] It is easy to disagree that the third, in the major scale, is the same to the fourth as the leading note is to the octave.

Although few would question that the leading note seems to want to resolve into the octave, you can easily argue that the third does not always have the same inclination to resolve into the fourth.

Nevertheless, for the purposes of setting up the intonation of the scale (at least in the beginning) it is useful to treat the third and seventh as having a similar inclination.

(4)

- The second and sixth notes of the scale must be tuned relative to the third and seventh. If your personal taste is for a higher leading note in each half of the scale, the second and sixth must be tuned higher; if you prefer the leading notes lower, then the second and sixth must be lower.

If instead you play a low 2 and 6 but a high 3 and 7 – or you play a high 2 and 6 but a low 3 and 7 – you get the following unbalanced tuning:

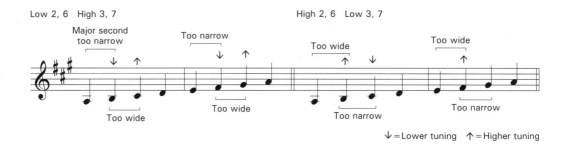

In each case, the A is fixed and must be in tune with the open A string; the D is fixed, in tune with the open D string; and the E is fixed, in tune with the open E string. These are not a question of choice.

The C♯ and G♯ are a matter of personal taste; and then these notes dictate the tuning of the B and F♯, which again are not a matter of choice.

Q **Does this work for every key? Since all G's, D's, A's and E's must be played exactly in tune with the open strings, doesn't the position of the open string notes in the scale affect which notes can be played higher or lower?**

To a certain extent, the position of the open strings in the scale helps create the distinct character of each key. For example, in the scale of C major you cannot decide 'as a matter of taste' that you want a particularly high E (creating a 'bright third'), since then it would be out of tune with the open E.

Even if you could play a high E, you would also have to play a high D (the second of the scale), and this would then be too high for the open D string.

One solution is to play the C as low as possible. But still, this note must be as near as possible to a perfect fourth above the open G, so it cannot go down too low.

The second half of the C major scale has a similar problem: if you tune the B high, as a bright leading note to the tonic, you have to tune the A, the sixth of the scale, high as well; but then it is too sharp for the open A. If you play the B high, but the A in tune with the open string, the whole tone from G to A is disproportionately smaller than the whole tone between A and B.

The result is a lower 3 and 7, and 2 and 6, than is possible in A major or E major, giving C major a 'plainer' character than A major. We see, therefore, that each key has its own tuning requirements.

Before playing complete scales tune each note in the following order:

1 Begin with only the 'skeleton' of the scale, the notes of the perfect intervals: I – IV – V – VIII

2 Then add the two 'leading' notes: III – VII

3 Add the II and the VI to give the whole scale, tuning those notes in relation to the III and VII respectively.

Example: A major

Stage 1

- Play the 1st, 4th, 5th and 8th degrees of the scale. In this key they are all tuned to the open strings:

Stage 2

- Add the 3rd and the 7th. It is a matter of taste exactly how high the C♯ and G♯ are; but whether higher or lower, tune or feel them in relation to the 4th and the octave.

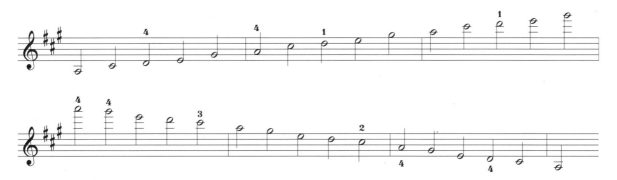

Stage 3

- Add the 2nd and the 6th. If you play high leading notes (C♯, G♯), the 2nd and 6th (B, F♯) must be slightly higher. If the leading notes are not so high the 2nd and 6th must be slightly lower.

Hovering fingers in tune above the strings

- As you play up or down the scale, pause on the first note of a group of fingers that all fall within one position (after a string crossing, or before or after a shift).

- While pausing on this note, prepare the notes that follow by hovering the fingers over the strings (shown as x-notes). Measure the exact distances between the fingers; then place the fingers on the string at the exact locations that you have calculated:

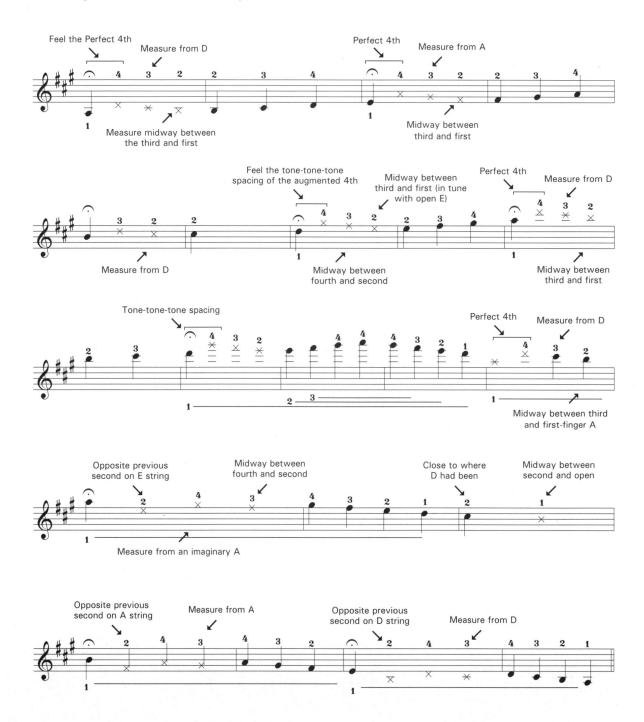

Alternatively, play the measuring-notes instead of hovering the fingers above the string:

Applying scale tuning to the repertoire

The next step is to think and hear in the same way in the repertoire:

Mozart: Concerto no. 4 in D, K218, *mov. 1, b. 45*

Here, the D at the beginning must be in tune with the open D, and the A with the open A. The C♯ is measured in relation to the D, and then the B is placed higher or lower depending on the C♯.

The impossibility of playing in tune

Part of the art of playing in tune is to adjust notes that are fractionally out of tune so quickly that nobody else notices. This makes it possible to give an *impression* of playing in tune.

Sometimes this instinctive, instant adjustment – which occurs at the very start of the note – is hidden in the vibrato, which should be wider than the infinitesimal pitch correction anyway.

Sometimes the adjustment is made by fractionally altering the exact angle that the finger leans into the string – again at the very start of the note as the fingertip first begins to contact the string.

Carl Flesch tried to prove that it is 'impossible' to play in tune by measuring the distance between A and B♭ played halfway up the A string.

The notes are 60 vibrations apart in pitch and 9 millimetres apart in actual distance, i.e. there is one vibration to each 1/6 of a millimetre.

> Therefore, granting that I have played the A in tune, in order to play the B♭ mathematically correct, I would have to place my third finger at so true a point as not to vary 1/6 of a millimetre, which would seem only possible with some implement which had a surface breadth of 1/6 of a millimetre, and not the finger, which is with some players 10 millimetres broad at its tip.
>
> Even were I to assume, however, that some fortunate chance would make it possible for me to touch the exact spot at 1/6 of a millimetre it would be impossible to do so in a sequence of tones such as represented by the scale. Hence…*in the physical sense "playing in tune" is an impossibility.*
>
> Hence what we call "playing in tune" is no more than an extremely rapid, skilfully carried out improvement of the originally inexactly located pitch. When playing "out of tune," on the other hand, the tone [pitch], as long as it sounds, remains as false as it was at the moment of its production.[1]

[1] Carl Flesch: *The Art of Violin Playing* (New York, 1924), Vol. 1, 20.

In a famous anecdote about Jascha Heifetz, someone asked him: "How do you play so in tune? You play so incredibly in tune. How do you do it?"

Heifetz replied: "I don't. But I adjust anything that isn't before you notice it was out of tune in the first place."

Adjusting for out-of-tune strings

Instantaneous adjustment, and the ability to give an 'impression' of playing in tune, is so much part of playing that Ivan Galamian advised not to tune the violin too often while practising. You cannot stop in the middle of a performance to tune, if your strings have slipped, so within reason you have to be able to play in tune whatever happens to the open strings.

It is a great party trick to be able to un-tune your strings but still play perfectly in tune.[2] A less advanced violinist plays out of tune on an in-tune violin; a more advanced violinist plays in tune on an out-of-tune violin.

[2] The Russian violinist Nathan Milstein liked to let his strings down slightly, overnight, to allow his violin a chance to breathe. A favourite trick of his was to arrive in front of the orchestra the next morning for the rehearsal, take the violin out of its case without tuning it, and stand there playing a few tricky passages from various concertos or show-pieces. The members of the orchestra would look on and admire his effortless and perfect playing. Then, smiling, he would play the open strings, and everyone would realise for the first time that the violin was completely out of tune. Yet nobody had noticed while he was playing.

Playing with a soft hand

Since instantaneous adjustment is part of good intonation, the first condition for playing in tune is that the left hand is free, since these lightening-fast, microscopic adjustments are blocked if the hand is tense. The muscles have to be in a state of balance and freedom, so that any part of the hand or finger is free to move in any direction without initial resistance.

The lightning-fast adjustments cannot happen if each resistance to movement lasts even one hundredth of a second, let alone if the hand is so tight that it takes an entire second to make one adjustment.

In sport and athletics it is at the 'big moments' that you are most at risk of tightening. It is common to see tennis players, just about to win or lose a game, unable to get the ball over the net because they keep tightening. Tightening in preparation for an action is something to guard against consciously all the time. Even an imperceptible amount of preparatory tightening has a disabling effect.

Playing a string instrument, every note may be a 'big moment'. The left hand is always at risk of tightening and players need to take constant care to see that it remains soft and responsive.

The difference between single-stop and double-stop tuning

The most frequent problem in tuning double stops is whether the 'third tone' should be in tune, or whether you should ignore it.

The third tone is a low note, often lower than the open G, that drones softly in the distance. It is called the 'differential tone' since its pitch is the difference between the frequencies of the two notes:[1]

[1] There is also a fourth tone called the 'summation tone'. It is the pitch of the two frequencies added together but is too high for us to hear. Presumably dogs hear them as clearly as we do the third tones.

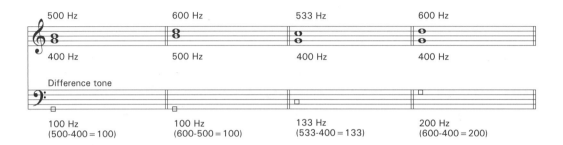

Campagnoli wrote out examples of third tones in his Violin School (c. 1800):

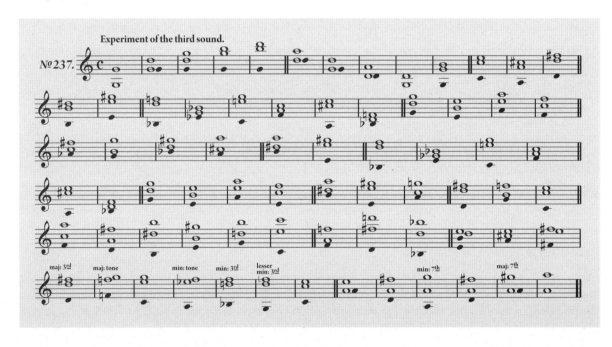

[2] Stand in opposite corners of the room to each other, playing one note each of major thirds or sixths. A listener standing somewhere in between will hear the third tone distinctly, and the players may be able to hear it themselves. This happens even in a hall with the players standing a hundred metres apart.

You can do the same thing with acoustic beats. See *Experiment in acoustics*, page 58.

The third tone magically appears 'out of nowhere' when the two notes are played together as a double stop; but it is also created when the double stop is shared by two players, each playing only one note.[2]

● Use the following examples as a guide to find the third tones of other double stops. You can hear the third tone more clearly the higher the double stop. Experiment with playing the examples one octave higher than written:

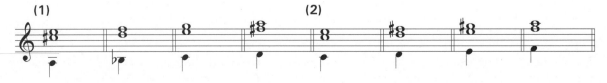

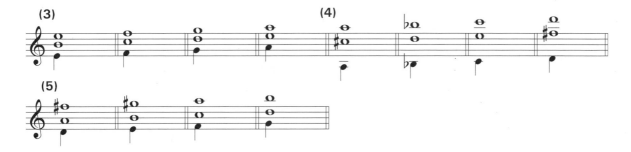

(1) Minor thirds: the third tone creates a major triad

(2) Major thirds: the third tone doubles the tonic

(3) Perfect fourths: the third tone doubles the upper note, creating an 'empty' perfect chord of I–V–VIII without a major or minor third

(4) Minor sixth: the third tone creates a major chord with the tonic doubled and no fifth degree of the scale

(5) Major sixth: the third tone creates a major chord with the tonic in the bass.

Tuning to a higher or lower string

One factor that complicates tuning is that you get an entirely different pitch depending on whether you tune a note to a higher or a lower string.

The classic example is of tuning first-finger B on the A string to the open D. If you want the third tone to be in tune you have to play the B quite flat. If you then play that same B with the open E, it sounds out of tune.

If instead you tune the B to the open E so that the third tone is in tune, the B will have to be quite sharp, and then sounds out of tune played with the open D:

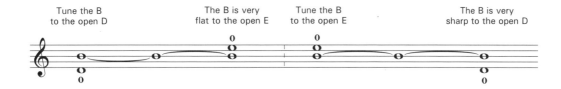

Key point: To get the third tone in tune, if the fixed note is the lower of the two notes, the upper note has to be flattened. If the fixed note is the higher of the two notes, the lower note has to be sharpened.

To play that B on its own, as a single note rather than as part of a double stop with either open string, a place midway between the two extremes is often the note you have to play.

This can lead to interesting problems of tuning caused by the difference between playing double stops with the third tone in tune, and ignoring the third tone and playing the same pitches as if the notes were single notes. The problems are in major thirds and major sixths, not so much the other intervals.

Sometimes you can tune major thirds and sixths with the third tone in tune; but often it is important to consider the key you are playing in, and tune them as if they were divided between two players. Then two notes played separately, or played as a double stop, would be tuned exactly the same.

Q **But if you play first-finger B on the A string so that it is flat to the open E, it means the perfect fourth from B to E will be out of tune. Is it not true that although you can slightly adjust the tuning of major, minor, augmented or diminished intervals, any perfect interval must be exactly in tune? Surely the B must be tuned to the E?**

It is true that perfect intervals *played* as a *double stop* are either in tune, or not in tune, and can never be 'a matter of taste'. While you can play a doubled-stopped major third slightly wider or narrower, depending on the context, and it is still 'in tune' either way, you cannot play an out-of-tune perfect fourth or octave and say 'you like it like that'. It is simply out of tune.

But the notes of perfect intervals *played on their own* do not have to be exact in the same way. In the course of a flowing melody the ear hears them differently, even when they would not be correct if played together as a double stop. Therefore the note B may sometimes be exactly in tune with the open E, sometimes not.

Ignoring the third tone

It was Dorothy DeLay who first introduced me to the idea of *not* getting the 'third tone' in tune in major thirds and major sixths. The question was how to tune the opening of the last movement of the Brahms Concerto:

Brahms: Concerto in D, op. 77, *mov. 3, b. 1*

The problem is that if the F♯ is in tune with the D, with the third tone in tune, the F♯ seems too flat; but if it is a normal, bright F♯ as a major third in D major, the third tone is then a long way out of tune.

"But why do you want the third tone to be in tune?" she immediately asked. "The audience's ear catches the upper line as the melody, so the theme would sound dull if you played a low F♯."

"You're telling me that the third tone does not have to be in tune?" I said. "After all these years of trying to get the third tone in tune…!"

It is interesting how so many people react with exactly the same words when they first hear this principle: "After all these years of trying to get the third tone in tune…!"

Tuning in narrow fifths

If you tune the D string exactly one perfect fifth below the A – and then tune the G string exactly one perfect fifth below the D – the G may be too flat.

Solve this problem by tuning in 'narrow' fifths. This is particularly important when playing with the piano, but also helpful when playing unaccompanied Bach because the chords and harmonies are all built up from the bass. String quartets typically tune in narrow fifths to avoid the C string on the viola and cello being much too flat in relation to the E string on the violin.

 How do you tune in narrow fifths?

Tune the D very slightly sharp to the A; then tune the G very slightly sharp to the D. Tune the E string an in-tune perfect fifth above the A, or tune it only infinitesimally flat to the A.

Although A is the centre point around which you are tuning, and making the D slightly sharp is perfectly acceptable to the ear, making the E slightly flat does not always work – or, if you do tune it flat, it has to be so slight that it is truly unnoticeable when you play the two open strings together.

However, suppose you had a 5th string – a 'B string'. If you tuned the E as a perfect fifth above the A, and then tuned the 'B string' a perfect 5th above the E, the B would be too sharp (see also page 66).

The answer would be to choose a 'B string' that is very slightly flat to a very slightly flat open E.

Quantz described how to tune the violin in narrow fifths in 1752:

> To tune the violin quite accurately, I think you will not do badly to follow the rule that must be observed in tuning the keyboard, namely that the fifths must be tuned a little on the flat side rather than quite truly or a little sharp, as is usually the case, so that the open strings will agree with the keyboard. For if all the fifths are tuned sharp and truly, it naturally follows that only one of the four strings will be in tune with the keyboard. If the A is tuned truly with the keyboard, the E a little flat in relation to the A, the D a little sharp to the A, and the G likewise, the two instruments will agree with each other.[1].

[1] Johann Joachim Quantz: *Essay of a Method for Playing the Transverse Flute* (Berlin 1752; trans. Edward R. Reilly, London, 1966), 267.

Background essentials 1

Pitch–sound–rhythm–ease

What is the ideal performance? I used to think that it consisted of five headings: pitch, sound, rhythm, style and expression.

I reasoned that if every note was in tune and had the desired sound, and was musically in time, and if the style suited the period or the composer, and if it were played with feeling, then it would be 'perfect'.

Later it became clear that those five headings should have been only three – pitch, sound and rhythm – and that after them comes a fourth heading of how you play physically and mechanically.

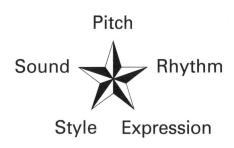

Pitch
Sound — Rhythm
Style   Expression

Finding the music: pitch, sound, rhythm

The three main aspects of playing music are pitch, sound and rhythm:

- To play anything, the first question is what note you want to play; the next question is what sound you want that note to have; the last question is when do you want that note to sound.

- In other words, every note must be in tune; played with the desired sound quality for the note, phrase or passage, and free of scratch or other distortion; and sounded at the right moment rhythmically.

Many instruments work along the same lines. Playing a xylophone, the first question (pitch) is to decide which steel bar to strike with the mallet. The next question (sound) is how hard does the mallet hit it, and partly the angle of the impact. The final question (rhythm) is when does the mallet hit it.

The breath is part of all three factors of pitch, sound and rhythm in playing a wind or brass instrument.

First, to make the pitch you create the right length of pipe or tube with your fingers or hands, and/or regulate the pressure of the breath or the shape of the embouchure. (For a string player, this would be like making the pitch partly with the left finger, partly with bow pressure.)

You create the tone partly by the force of the breath and sometimes (e.g. playing an instrument like the flute) partly by the angle of the breath across the mouthpiece; finally there is the question of when you blow, or when you change the length of pipe by stopping or unstopping a hole, and so on.

Why is a harp the shape it is?

A good question to ask children is why is a harp the shape it is? Or a grand piano, or organ pipes?

On fixed-pitch instruments such as these, all the notes you might need are ready for you before you begin to play. Each string on the harp or piano is already the right length and tension; each pipe on the organ has already been cut to the right length and shape; each block on the glockenspiel is ready to be hit; but on string instruments you have to create the different string lengths as you play.

So to play any note on the violin the first thing is to decide on the exact string length; next you have to bow the string in order to hear it; the final question is when to bow it.

Pitch–sound–rhythm IS the style and the expression

Style or expression, and the exact pitch–sound–rhythm, are the same thing. You cannot separate one from the other. After 'pre-hearing' the sound and the expression in your musical imagination, the precise pitch, sound and rhythm *creates* the expression, style or character. Playing musically, or in the right style for the composer, is not a matter of 'putting feeling into it' after 'learning the notes'.

- Intonation and expression are inseparable. Expressive intonation, in contrast to neutral 'piano' (tempered) intonation, is as much a part of expression as volume or attack. To change the expression you change the tuning, which means you play flatter flats or sharper sharps to get a particular expressive colour into a note (e.g. B♭, second note of the Bruch G minor Concerto).

- Sound and expression are inseparable. If the sound is dull, or without the right character or expression, and then you add expression, in doing so you must you change the sound.

  In the same way vibrato is expression. If you change the character or expression of the vibrato, you change the width and speed, or the area of the pad or tip that is contacting the string; and if you change those things, you change the expression.

- Rhythm and expression are inseparable. For a particular effect you might play more (or less) metronomically in time, or make a dotted rhythm ever-so-slightly more dotted, or sustain a held note right to the very end rather than ever-so-slightly shorter, and so on. In changing the rhythm you change the expression.

- Style is also not a separate issue. The only way to create style, or to change it, is through changing the exact intonation, sound (type of stroke and vibrato), and rhythm.

Ease: the master formula

Master musicians, athletes, dancers or acrobats always make what they do look easy, largely because by the time you are that good at something it *is* 'easy'.

Every athlete strives to develop greater and greater 'maximum power and minimum effort'. Imagine putting all your might and effort into hitting a golf ball, but the ball travels only a few metres. Then an expert takes the same golf club that you used and, seemingly without any effort at all, makes the ball travel hundreds of metres.

But suppose you too can hit the ball so that it travels hundreds of metres. Apparently F.M. Alexander was particularly fond of saying this to everyone he worked with:[1]

> When you are pleased with yourself – when you have got there, when you have made it, when you have achieved what you set out to achieve, when you have got the result that you wanted – then try it again and see if you can get the same result, but using less effort. Then, do it yet again and see if you can get the same result with even less effort than that!

This is the Master Formula in any field or activity.

[1] F. M. Alexander (1869–1955), originator of the Alexander Technique, a method of improving posture and movement taught in many schools of music, dance and drama world-wide.

What is a good performance?

The goal is always the same

Thinking in terms of 'pitch–sound–rhythm–ease' is endlessly helpful in both playing and teaching because when you listen to someone play, or if you analyse your own playing, there is nothing else to think about *except* pitch, sound, rhythm and ease.

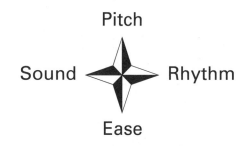

These headings are the starting-point for every question of phrasing, colour, expression, and of the mechanics or techniques involved.

Suppose you want to improve a passage of sixteenth-notes (semiquavers). You decide to work on it using rhythm practice.[2]

[2] See *Rhythm practice*, page 114

If the passage could be improved, the specific things that could be better must be something to do with pitch, sound, rhythm or ease, or a combination of them.

So you begin to practise in rhythms. So now what is the goal?

The goal remains the same, to be able to play the passage in that rhythm and in any other, with every note in tune, every note completely pure and resonant, and every note musically in time without hesitation of any sort, and all this with the minimum of physical or mental effort.

Until you can play the passage in any rhythm, with all four conditions satisfied, and at any tempo, it means there is still work left that you can do to improve it even further.

Whenever you hear someone play, or consider your own playing, thinking in terms of pitch–sound–rhythm–ease provides a perfect framework within which everything else finds its place.

If all four elements of pitch–sound–rhythm–ease are good, the result is a performance of a few notes, a phrase, a passage or a whole work, where:

1 Every note is musically and expressively in tune

2 Every note has exactly the desired sound, free of tonal blemish, one which creates the phrasing, style and character that you want, and contains within it the chosen mood, drama, emotion and expression of the phrase

3 The timing of every note is precise, and at the same time full of musical character and expression

4 Every note is played with real ease, and with complete absence of unnecessary action or effort.

Uniting technique and music

Following your musical conception, the expression of music is the result of what the hands and fingers are doing to the instrument:

● What the bow does to the string, and sound; where the fingers touch the string, and pitch; when the fingers touch or leave the string (or when the bow moves on one note, or to another string), and rhythm – all these are obviously the same thing, or like two sides of the same coin.

● If 'musical expression' and 'pitch–sound–rhythm' are inseparably one thing – and if 'pitch–sound–rhythm' and 'what the hands and fingers are doing to the instrument' are one thing – then it follows that 'the music', and 'what the hands and fingers are doing to the instrument', are one thing.

A 'musical instrument' is an 'instrument of music', and *the direct making of the music is by way of what the hands and fingers are doing to the instrument.*

● Then there is a marvellous feeling of the instrument, and the player, and the music, all being one. The physical sensations of playing, and the musical expression, are fused together. A sobbing quality in the vibrato, for example, and the physical sensation of vibrating the finger on the string, and the musical feeling, all become one in your perception as a player.

This was stressed in earlier centuries just as much as today:

> In Geminiani's eyes the technique of playing the violin was inseparable from the expressive intention of any particular piece of music. Different manners of playing the same passage are linked to different types of emotional expression (i.e. the 'Affect'). His instructions with respect to the mordent ('Beat') begin 'This is proper to express several Passions'; and these passions, ranging from mirth to horror, depend for their expression on the manner of performing the mordent.
>
> A similar range of emotions may be noted in his description of the manner of performing the vibrato, in itself one of the most expressive devices of violin playing.[1]

[1] Francesco Geminiani: *The Art of Playing on the Violin* (London, 1751; Facsimile edition, David D. Boyden, London 1952), viii.

Of course the important thing is always to be a musician first and an instrumentalist second; but once you know that the musical expression, and what you physically do to the violin, are one thing, you can let go and play the violin without fear of losing the music or of playing only mechanically.

This explains how it is perfectly possible to focus completely on the music and at the same time maintain complete control of the playing: the musical idea and the physical playing are one thing.

However, many players fear that the more they control their playing, the less musically they will play. The result is often that they do not develop a real fineness of technical control that they could otherwise have trained into their playing quite easily.

The final result: only two questions to ask

When you think in terms of pitch, sound, rhythm and ease, you end up asking only two questions with every note you play, not four questions:

● Does it sound right, i.e. is this the pitch and the tone I want, and with exactly the right rhythm?

● How can I work less hard but get the same result?

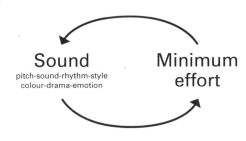

Sound
pitch-sound-rhythm-style
colour-drama-emotion

Minimum effort

The magic word

Whatever your occupation – whether you are a musician or sculptor, poet or painter, cook or carpenter, or scientist, farmer, racing driver, hairdresser, athlete – and whatever you do in your everyday actions, e.g. measuring how many tea leaves to put in a tea pot, or judging how fast to walk across the road in relation to the speed of the approaching traffic, and so on – in some way you will be dealing with proportions of one thing to another all day every day.

The master key

Proportions is the magic word in playing the violin. When you stay at a hotel you have a key that opens only your door, but the staff have a master key that opens every door. If you liken the whole of violin playing to a vast building, with each of the thousands of aspects of playing represented by thousands of rooms, then Proportions is the master key which opens every door.

'Divine proportionality', as Leonardo di Vinci called it, is also the basis of every musical factor, e.g. dynamics, intonation, tempo, and so on. To make a *crescendo* or *diminuendo*, you play each note proportionately louder or softer than the note before. To make an *accelerando* or *ritardando*, you play each note proportionately sooner or later than the note before.

Everything must be a matter of proportion, since you cannot think of louder–softer, faster–slower, higher–lower, darker–lighter, harder–softer, and so on, without these things being in proportion to some other degree of the same thing.

Generating ideas by thinking in terms of proportions

The beauty of thinking in terms of proportions is that, as soon as you do, you never get 'stuck' any more. As a player, you never reach the point where, although you know that your technique or music-making could be still better, you do not know what is 'wrong' or what you should do next.

As a teacher, you never reach the point where you know that your student could be playing better or improving faster, but you just do not know what to suggest next.

Instead, as soon as you think in terms of proportions you begin to be flooded not only with answers, but with new questions that you had not asked before.

Then it is usually that you run out of *time* long before you run out of ideas as to what to do next, with either your own or your student's playing. The date of the concert arrives; a student comes to the end of their course; but if you had had more time there would always have been something more that you had wanted to do.

Technique is describable from A to Z

Artistry, musicality, expression, communication, charisma etc. are abstract terms with different shades of meaning, and cannot be described or defined exactly. But the entire physical side of playing – the concrete reality of the hands and fingers, the bow and the string, and how they work – is completely describable (and therefore teachable), from A to Z; and the language used to describe everything is the language of proportions.

- Every sound the bow makes is the result of certain proportions of speed, pressure and soundpoint.

- Everything about intonation is a question of proportions. The major scale begins with two tones. If you play a narrower tone from the tonic to the second, and then a wider tone from the second to the third – or *vice versa* – it sounds wrong because the tones are not even.

- An out-of-tune octave sounds wrong because it is unbalanced. The proportions should be exactly 2–1, e.g. one A played at 440 and another at 880.

- All the lifted strokes like *spiccato*: different proportions of height of bounce to length of bow.

- All the many qualities of vibrato: different proportions of speed and width.

If something is not working or could be better, you need to change the proportions of the factors that are involved in it, i.e. change the size or amount of one thing in relation to another.

Q **What is an example of making something work better by changing the size of one action in relation to another?**

When you experiment with different bow strokes and sounds, you are dealing with proportions in the same way as a cook experiments with different proportions of ingredients.

To change the sound of a *martelé* stroke, you have to change the amount of bow speed in relation to the pressure, or in relation to the degree of 'bite' at the start of the stroke.

In a simple *détaché* stroke, the speed–pressure–soundpoint balance must remain entirely even.

If the position of the left hand could be improved, it means that the proportions of one aspect of the left hand could be changed in relation to another aspect: the hand could be positioned higher or lower, the elbow more to the left or more to the right, the fingers falling more on to the fingertips or more on to the pads; there could be more widening between the base joints, and so on.

True stories: Deborah

Deborah was a postgraduate violin student who had focused on music until she left school, but had then decided to go to university to read mathematics. Having got her degree, she had now returned to the violin at music college and, knowing she needed to make up for lost time, was practising hard.

One lesson early in the first semester she asked how she should position her left hand to play a high note at the top of the E string. I quickly arranged her left arm and hand so that it looked comfortable, and made a few explanatory comments.

She immediately understood what to do and what not to do, and was happy with the new arrangement of her hand; but then she complained that she often felt frustrated when she was practising. She said that I knew all the answers to technical questions such as these, but she did not have that information.

She could not phone me every five minutes to ask questions, she said; but meanwhile she was wasting time working so hard when either she was making mistakes that she did not know about, or else having problems that she was aware of but which she did not know how to solve on her own.

What was she supposed to do all week long, she asked, practising for hours every day, having to wait many days until her next lesson?

I explained that actually I did not know as much as she thought I did, and until she asked that particular question I did not know the 'answer'. How could I have a ready-made answer to how her particular hands and fingers should best be positioned to play a particular note? But to find the answer to her question, I had only to look at her hand on the violin, and the finger on the string, in terms of proportionality.

In arranging her finger on the note, I had to find what would look right: what was the most gracefully curved, the most balanced, symmetrical, natural-looking, all-of-a-piece, comfortable, normal and ordinary-looking hand position.

So instead of having to learn 100 'facts' about violin technique before she would be able to practise without 'wasting her time' – and without having to wait for a lesson – she needed to learn only one thing: to think in terms of proportions.

Practice is not a matter of playing things over and over again until they are 'correct', but more a question of constantly experimenting with different proportions of actions or factors.

Asking simple questions: 'more' and 'less'

The process of finding the right proportions – e.g. to find the best position of the left or right hand – is a matter of asking simple questions: should the hand be higher, should it be lower; should it be more to the left, more to the right, more curved, less curved, more on the tip of the finger, more on the pad, and so on. Whatever looks balanced and feels comfortable is likely to be the correct position.

You do not have to consult a book or a teacher to find this 'correct' position, because finding the right proportions is almost entirely just a matter of instinct and common sense. The process consists simply of trying more, and trying less, going either side and narrowing the distance between the extremes until you find a perfect balance point.

Of the hand positions shown in Fig. 49, it is clear that (f) looks the most balanced, the most all-of-a-piece, natural and comfortable.

In (a) the hand is too high, so that the finger is too tilted over on the fingertip towards the bridge; in (b) the hand is too low, the finger is too straight, there is too much pad on the string, and the palm of the hand is resting on the shoulder of the violin.

In (c) the elbow is too far to the right, and in (d) too far to the left, each resulting in an off-balance feeling in the hand. In (e) the fingers have squeezed together, locking the hand instead of allowing the hand to remain in a state of balance.

Fig. 49

(a) Hand too high

(b) Hand too low

(c) Elbow too far to right

(d) Elbow too far to left

(e) Squeezing fingers together causes tension

(f) Good, balanced hand position

Q What about the actual rules of violin technique? Taking this high note as an example, how do you know whether the hand should touch the shoulder of the violin or not, just by thinking about proportions? Is it correct to lean the hand on the shoulder of the violin, or should there be a space? Don't you need a teacher to tell you a technical fact like that?

If you could go away and practise the violin for long enough, you could probably work it all out for yourself; but a teacher's job is to save you time. A teacher can bring you to the same point now by simply telling you, and save you years. There's nothing wrong with that.

However, the answers to technical questions are often obvious once you approach the question from the point of view of proportions. In this case, the degree of freedom of the left hand, or the degree of it feeling immovable, is in direct proportion to the degree of its pressing on the upper rim of the left shoulder of the violin.

When the hand is entirely clear of the rim, pivoting or resting only on the thumb, it is naturally much freer or more mobile than when it presses hard on the rim and becomes immovable.

But the hand often needs to know where it is by keeping a slight, fleeting, brushing, sensitive contact with the instrument. In 1st position, the first finger brushes against the neck to use it as a reference point.[1] In high positions the hand uses the rim of the shoulder of the violin for the same purpose.

 See *The principle of the double contact*, page 183

There must be a certain degree of sensitive, fleeting contact with the rim, to orientate the hand, which is the 'correct' amount between too little contact and too much; and you can discover this principle yourself, and the right amount, by first looking for the middle point. No contact, you lose security; too much, you become fixed. Between the two extremes you end up with the fleeting contact.

The same experimenting applies to every aspect of technique. The typical questions are to do with 'how much': higher or lower, more to the left or right, more forwards or backwards, heavier or lighter, faster or slower, harder or softer, and so on.

Some of the chief areas to look at in terms of 'more' or 'less' are these:

General

- Violin higher or lower on the shoulder (chin more to the left of the tailpiece, or more directly above it)

- Scroll pointing more to the left or more in front

- Scroll higher, lower

- Chin heavier or lighter on the chin rest

- Head rotated more to the left or to the right

- Feet further apart, closer together

Left hand

- Contact-point of the first finger with the neck of the violin: higher or lower

- Contact-point of the fingertip with the string: more on the tip or more on the pad

- Knuckles more parallel or less parallel with the fingerboard

- Thumb higher or lower

- Thumb further forward or further back

- Forearm rotated more, or rotated less, to bring the knuckles closer to the neck

- Wrist further in or further out

- Elbow (i.e. upper arm) more to the left or more to the right

Right hand

- Thumb more curved or less curved

- Thumb contact-point more on the tip or more on the pad

- First finger contacting the stick nearer to, or further from, the middle joint

- First finger nearer to, or further from, the thumb

- Second and third fingers higher or lower on the frog

- More space, less space, between the fingers

- More, less, pressure of the fingers on the bow

- Fourth finger contact-point more on the tip or more on the pad

- Fourth finger contact-point more on the top of the bow, or more on the upper, inside edge

- Knuckles higher or lower

- More, less, visible flexibility in the fingers

- Hand more pronated or supinated

- Higher, lower wrist

- Elbow higher or lower than the hand

- Upper arm moving forwards more, less, in the upper half of the bow

- Bow more or less tilted for more or less hair

Working on fundamentals

Keep on starting again

The fastest way to advance your technique, or to solve specific problems, is to keep on starting again from the very beginning.

- Practise basic elements of technique by playing exercises that deal with only one thing at a time, e.g. tone exercises on one note, vibrato, intonation and shifting exercises, finger movement, etc.

Adding twenty floors to the skyscraper

A classic analogy is that when you look at a construction site that is in its early stages, you can tell how tall the building will be when it is finished. The taller the building, the deeper (and often the wider) the foundations.

The same principle applies to improving skill in violin playing or music-making. The higher you want to go, the deeper you must build your foundations.

There is an important difference. Suppose you have already got a seventy-story skyscraper, and then you decide you want to add thirty floors to it. You cannot simply lift the building up and place it on one side, dig deeper foundations, and then put the skyscraper back and add the new floors.

But whenever you want to 'raise the level' of anything like playing the violin, you can always work on your foundations to strengthen and deepen them.

Another important difference is that even if you could add to the foundations of the skyscraper, you would still have to build the extra floors. But when you add to the foundations of your technique, the 'extra floors' appear magically on their own, without you having to do anything else.

Advanced tennis training

Imagine the high level of a typical 16-year-old today who has been selected out of thousands to be part of a junior national tennis team.

An important part of their training will typically be to spend many hours each week practising with a partner or their coach by simply knocking the ball backwards and forwards across the net.

They will do this without trying to win points or competing in any way, but just calmly and evenly knocking it to-and-fro, continuing for as many as 1000 shots each session.

The fact that these 16-year-olds are already such good tennis players, and would be fearsome opponents for any ordinary player, is not the point. What they do is focus on the fundamentals, and return to them again and again.

Advanced violin training

Yuri Yankelevich was one of the foremost violin teachers in Russia at the height of the Soviet Violin School, and worked with many violinists who went on to have full international careers. He held regular performance classes for his students which were open to the public and were always a big event, with people travelling hundreds of miles to attend.

Imagine the high level of a typical 18-year-old studying with Yankelevich in Moscow in the 1950s or 1960s. They would already be playing the big concertos and virtuoso repertoire without there being anything remarkable about it: all the students could play pieces like that.

Yet what would Yankelevich typically teach these 18-year-old students? They would work together on Kreutzer no. 2 with bowing variations:

Kreutzer: 42 Etudes ou caprices, *no. 2, b. 1*

There are hundreds of useful possibilities, but here are typical examples of basic patterns to practise. Most editions of Kreutzer suggest a dozen or more:

Of course these students could already play advanced pieces, but the point is always to develop finer and finer musical control of the instrument. The simplest and fastest way to do this is by working on the foundations and basic elements of playing, however good you already are. Proof of how such work improves your playing is easy to find:

- Play through a piece once; then spend twenty minutes practising Kreutzer no. 2 with a few bowing patterns in all parts of the bow. Pay close attention to keeping an appropriate soundpoint, good contact with the string, and complete purity of tone.[1]

  Then play through the original piece again. You will notice an immediate improvement.

How to build technique

Violin 'technique' is made up of 'techniques' in the plural, like a mosaic or an engine where the whole is made up of many smaller parts.

When technique as a whole is excellent, each individual component must therefore be excellent also. If the technique as a whole needs further development, the way to improve it is to deal with each individual technique on its own.

Many wind, brass, percussion or keyboard instruments are quite straightforward to play compared with the violin. What you have to do to play these instruments in terms of blowing or hitting, or moving your fingers, is often really quite simple. You may be able to play a lot of notes with these instruments; but the number of different things you have to do to play those notes is actually quite limited.

[1] The way to practise these patterns is to play them using little bow at the heel, in the middle of the bow, and at the point; to play using more bow in the lower half, the 'middle half', and the upper half; and also to use whole bows. Also use different bow strokes such as *martelé* or *spiccato*. Apply the usual goals of pitch, sound, rhythm, and ease: work the patterns until they are in tune, with every note pure, rhythmically precise, and feeling easy.

Also practise in rhythms and accents

(see *I haven't got time to practise in rhythms and accents*, page 114).

Naturally it takes extraordinary talent, skill and dedication to be able to play these instruments to the highest artistic level; but in terms of the sheer physical actions required to make them work, they are relatively simple.

6 different techniques to play 6 notes

Even the piano falls into the category of 'relatively simple instruments to play'. A cat, walking along a piano keyboard, plays in-tune, recognisable notes; yet a complete beginner with a violin and bow may be quite unable to make any sort of recognisable violin tone.[1]

Pianists usually disagree if you say that playing the piano is simple compared with the violin. They will point out that the number of different shades of technique required to colour a phrase on a piano is infinite. Even so, six notes on the piano may require basically the same 'technique' to play each one: you press the key down; yet on the violin even a simple phrase may require a large number of different techniques to be performed one after another, sometimes at great speed.

For example, this phrase from Brahms *Sonatensatz* must be smooth and even, yet six notes in a row each require a slightly different technique to play them:

Brahms: Scherzo (Sonatensatz), WoO2, *b. 3*

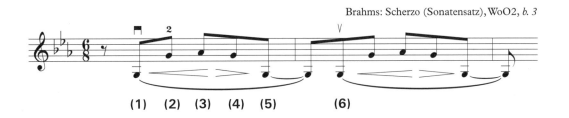

(1) (2) (3) (4) (5)   (6)

(1) The bow is placed on the string, and then the first note is started by pulling the bow.

(2) The physical actions of beginning this note are entirely different from those of beginning the first note. While playing **(1)**, the bow pivots clockwise until it reaches and plays the D string. The 2nd finger must already be on the string.

(3) Without having any effect on the bow, the third finger drops on to the string. Dropping a finger to create a new string length, while sustaining the bow on one string, clearly feels entirely different from the sensations and actions of playing the first two notes.

(4) Without affecting the bow, the third finger lifts. The feeling of lifting a finger, to play a note during a slur, is quite different from the feeling of dropping it, and the timing is different. You have to lift *when* you want the note to sound, whereas you have to drop *before* you want it to sound.

(5) The bow pivots anticlockwise over to the G string. This is an entirely different physical operation from pivoting clockwise, as in playing from **(1)** to **(2)**.

(6) This note must sound the same as the first note, but begins on the string, up-bow, without first having to be placed on the string.

Combining techniques

When technique is taken apart, or stripped down to its individual components and principles, everything is simple. If anything seems complex, it means that there is further to go in stripping it down to its most basic parts.

The individual actions of playing are all straightforward, e.g. placing a finger on the string; crossing on a slur from one open string to another; changing direction from down-bow to up-bow at the point; making a vibrato on one note. It is when we have to do lots of these things at the same time that 'technique' feels complex.

This is why practising simple exercises that focus on only one aspect of technique at a time is the fastest and most efficient way to develop technique. Otherwise, you are trying to improve several things all at the same time, which must be less focused than when concentrating on only one at a time.

To combine the techniques in the form of more complicated exercises or studies is the next essential step that comes later; but the way to build, maintain, and endlessly expand your playing as a whole is to continually revise and refine the individual techniques.

[1] This difference in how 'easy' it is to play the piano, compared with the violin, continues until quite advanced levels on each instrument. Meanwhile, the piano makes up for the ease with which each note is created, by the sheer number of notes that must be played. For every single note the violinist plays, the pianist might have twenty to play. Then, at the highest levels of playing, who can say which instrument is more 'difficult' – to play a Mozart Sonata on the violin, or at the keyboard; to play the Brahms violin concerto, or a Brahms piano concerto? The Russian pianist Vladimir Horowitz said that in the beginning the piano is the easiest instrument in the world, and in the end it is the most difficult. But perhaps he never tried to play a violin, which is arguably the most difficult instrument in the beginning when you cannot yet play proficiently, and the most difficult in the end because of the technical complexity of the important music written for it.

Practising like a beginner

One of the beauties of playing the violin is that most of the technical challenges that apply to advanced, virtuosic players apply equally to a beginner. Obviously there are things that you have to do when you play advanced technical features in Paganini or Wieniawski that are never required in elementary playing; but the basic issues are all exactly the same, e.g.:

- Not squeezing at the base joint of the left thumb
- Raising and dropping the left fingers from the base joints
- Widening the left hand at the base joints
- Not pressing fingers too hard into the strings
- Keeping the fingers hovering over the strings
- Knowing how to think of tuning each note, and to tune them in relation to each other
- Keeping the bow parallel to the bridge

- Changing the direction of the bow smoothly
- Playing with a singing tone created by the right proportions of speed, pressure and soundpoint
- Pivoting early with the bow during smooth string crossings
- Not tightening before performing an action; not rushing into an action
- Not 'pulling down' with your back, and 'pulling in' with your shoulders; and so on.

All of these issues apply equally whether you are playing elementary pieces or the Tchaikovsky Concerto. The language used to describe what is happening is therefore the same in both, too.[1]

[1] 'Sometimes I wonder why anybody is ever interested in anything I have to say about playing the violin, since everything I say is so simple.' – Dorothy DeLay

The language used in talking about playing Paganini is not more complex than the language used to describe an easier piece. Even strictly 'virtuoso' techniques, e.g. a springing bowing such as *ricochet* (which you do not find in elementary pieces) require the same language as other, non-virtuosic strokes.

For example, the important questions in *ricochet* are 1) where in the bow you play it, 2) how much hair you use, 3) the proportions of length of bow (and therefore speed) to height of bounce.

Improving any detail of technique – playing in tune, drawing a straight bow, vibrato, lightness of shifting, etc. – is the same whether you are a beginner or an advanced player. In either case, the exercises and practice routines are exactly the same as well.

Fig. 50

The typical lesson: different level, same issues

Whether a student is an advanced or an elementary player, many parts of the lesson are exactly the same.

Suppose at the start of the lesson the student begins by playing, say, a few pages of a virtuoso piece.

Suppose there seems to be a certain lack of flow or flexibility in the right hand which is constantly getting in the way of the music (by affecting the tone quality, the smoothness and evenness of the tone, and the connections between strokes). As soon as the playing stops and the lesson begins, attention is focused on the right hand.

Balancing with the fourth finger

The question is, what are the student's concepts of holding the bow, of balancing it in the hand, or of flexibility? Do they have sufficient sense of balancing the bow with the fourth finger, rather than of gripping the bow tightly?

A quick check is easy to do; and so within moments of finishing playing a concerto, the student is standing without the violin, holding the bow with only the thumb and fourth finger (Fig. 50).

The point is that if they were complete beginners they would probably find themselves standing there, without the violin, balancing the bow in their hand in exactly the same way.

The problems just get smaller

The less advanced the player is, the more obvious all the issues or problems are – e.g. problems of tension, intonation, poor tone or co-ordination, and so on. The more advanced the player, the smaller each of these issues becomes, until finally they are either so slight that they are unnoticeable, or else now really completely absent. But they are all still the same issues.

Often it is only after seeing a glaring error in an undeveloped student that you then notice the tiniest trace of it in a very advanced one, or in yourself.

Pablo Casals once taught an amateur cello student who was not very good. A friend asked him, 'Pablo, why do you teach this man? You can teach the best talents and musicians in the world – why him?'

Casals answered, 'Because from him I learn how to teach the good ones!'

The language of the violin

The word 'fluent' derives from Latin, with the original meaning 'capable of flowing'. The word can be used to mean 'moving smoothly and easily', e.g. 'the fluent movements of an athlete'. The word 'fluid' comes from the same root.

Learning a foreign language, you have to build up a large-enough collection of words that you understand and know how to say; and you have to learn how to string those words together into phrases and clauses, and larger sentences, in ways that obey the laws of grammar.

Playing the violin, each element of technique is like a syllable or a word, or a nuance of pronunciation or other feature of grammar; and the combinations of technical actions that you need to be able to play a group of notes is like putting all those 'words' and other things together into a sentence.

The first technical 'words' we learn are perhaps how to pluck each open string. Each single pluck, on each string, is a 'word' or 'syllable'.

Later, each finger that is added – until all four are being used, on each string, in each position – is another word or syllable; so is each string crossing, each shift, each extension, each tiny moment of finger preparation, or of lifting the finger off the string to create a 'ping'.

Just as you can make one single new word by joining two other words, so does each new combination of actions on the violin begin to feel like an individual 'word' in its own right. For example, play from first-finger F to fourth-finger E:

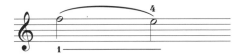

Keep the first finger on the string until after you have begun to play the fourth.

This pair of notes, which can feel like quite a big stretch for many players (you need to open at the base joints between the two fingers), is a feature of violin playing. It is something you are bound to encounter. It is 'one of the things you do' when you play. There's no getting away from it. It is a 'word' you need to be able to 'say' easily.

So is shifting from first-finger B on the A string, to first-finger D, a 'word' you need to be able to say easily. Shifting from B♭ is a similar word, but not pronounced quite the same:

Playing one down-bow *martelé* stroke in the upper half, on, say, third-finger A on the E string, is like saying a particular word or syllable; playing the same stroke on the same finger on the G string feels completely different. This is because of the extra thickness of the G string, so it is almost a different 'word' entirely:

Both are individual 'words' that you need to be able to 'speak' fluently, as are *martelé* strokes on every other note on the violin.

Every extension is an individual word: to play first-finger B on the A string, and then to be able to reach up to fourth-finger F♯ effortlessly and in tune – and to be able to repeat that extension over and over again and get it as easily each time – is like having a word that you know perfectly how to say, and you do not notice when you use it:

By practising a sequence of extensions such as those shown on page 162, or a sequence of shifts (page 240), you are adding to your vocabulary, or polishing your pronunciation of words that you have already encountered in the past.

It is not only less-advanced players who need to find the gaps in their technical vocabulary. During a recent lesson on the Brahms Violin Concerto it was striking how the violinist, a young free-lancer a few years out of college, would shift the whole left hand into half position when she played notes such as first-finger G♯ on the G string, and then shift back into first position in order to continue. Instead she could have kept the hand in first position and simply extended the first finger back on its own to play the D♯.

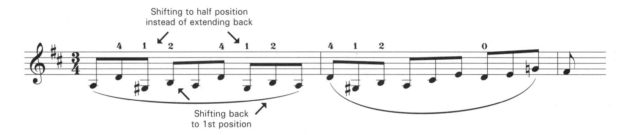

You could say that when it came to playing those G♯s she had no technique. But 'technique' is how you do something, and she did have a way of doing it – by shifting the whole hand – only this was a very inefficient technique compared to reaching back with the finger. And then because her playing had 'technical inefficiencies' her overall playing ability was limited.

So just as things may be said clumsily if there are words the speaker does not know, which would do the job more quickly and effectively, so this violinist had some clumsy ways of playing because she didn't have the 'technical vocabulary'.

It is in learning technical 'vocabulary' on the violin that basic technical exercises are so useful. They offer a way of continually revising and improving the 'language' of your playing, syllable by syllable.

Study with a great teacher: yourself

Imagine how you might be playing today if, having begun to play the violin at the early age of five or six, you had had an organised, systematic, step-by-step, perfect training from the very beginning:

● Suppose new technical challenges were added only gradually, and you never moved on to the next stage before completely mastering the previous one.

● Suppose, at the same time as mastering every technique one at a time, you gradually climbed a ladder of repertoire, always proceeding little by little in a carefully planned order, from simple to ever more complex pieces, again never moving to a new level of difficulty without first completely mastering the previous one.

Assuming that you have a musical imagination and a musical ear, and all the other necessary qualities, you might easily have been able to play virtuoso pieces with complete technical security by the age of 10 or earlier.[1]

Suppose you did not have the advantage of a step-by-step 'perfect' training from an early age. It does not necessarily matter.

Now that you are an adult, and have gained some knowledge and experience of violin playing, why not give yourself the training that you think you missed as a child?

It is easy to do. You simply start at the beginning, i.e. open strings, and add the techniques one by one.

Starting from the point of complete security

Whatever the subject, if there is anything you find difficult it must mean that there is a word, or meaning, or way of doing things, that you do not know about or you have not understood. The logical thing to do is to go back to the point before it became difficult.

Suppose you have an average grasp of mathematics. If you went back further and further to earlier and earlier levels of maths, there must be a level you can arrive at where you could take a test today, at that level, and score 100%.

That level of maths where you could immediately score 100% may be the level that you think is suitable only for a 5-year-old. It does not matter. The point is that if you would not score 100% above that level, it means that there are some things you need to know or think about differently. Then, once you do know those things, you would be able to score 100% at the next level up, and so on.

Working on this basis, anyone can take any subject and by starting at the level at which they know everything they need to know, they can build up detail by detail from there to whatever level they wish.

Applying this to progressing on the violin, the obvious thing to do is to keep returning to the roots, foundations and fundamentals of technique – by practising basic exercises, scales and etudes – so that you are forever adding to your fundamental knowledge and ability, and filling in the gaps.

- Basics exercises which focus on one element of technique at a time are the perfect, easiest and fastest way to build and rebuild technique.[1]

- Intermediate and advanced players can also relearn elementary etudes such as those by Hans Sitt and Kayser. Pretend that you are five years old again but be your own teacher, and learn to play them completely without blemish. By doing that, you can give yourself the sort of rigorous foundations you may not have developed when you actually were that age.

[1] See *Investing your time*, page 327

I am too scared of difficult pieces even to start learning them

Command–response

'Command–response' is the process of the mind issuing a command and the muscles responding. Every technical stumble can be traced back to a delay either in sending the command or in responding to it.

To play a passage completely fluently the mental picture (of the musical intention and the whole act of playing) must be clear; and the hands have to be set up on the instrument so that every muscle is in a state of balance and freedom, and capable of instantaneous response to the mental command.

Improving a piece is a matter of discovering the weak or blank areas in your mental directives, or of speeding up the physical responses if they are too slow for the passage.

Mind not muscles

The single most important thing to understand about practising is that it is all about training your mind, not your muscles. Ivan Galamian called command-response 'correlation' and states that it is the cornerstone of all technique:

> It is the improvement of this correlation which provides the key to technical mastery and technical control and not, as apparently is commonly believed and taught, the training and building of the muscles. What counts is not the strength of the muscles, but their responsiveness to the mental directive. The better the correlation, the greater the facility, accuracy, and reliability of the technique.[2]

[2] Ivan Galamian: *Principles of Violin Playing and Teaching* (New Jersey, 1962), 6.

The first thing is to be clear, musically and technically, how you want to play the beginning, middle and end of each note; then to think a little ahead of whatever you are playing (the faster the passage, the further ahead of the current notes you have to be); and then to concentrate. Dorothy DeLay used to say that the moment you make any sort of error, the question to ask is: what was I thinking about a fraction of a second before I made the mistake? Where was my mind?

Hesitating before playing

It is easy to discover how good the command–response is, in any group of notes or passage. The thing to measure is the amount of hesitation, either in knowing what you want to do, or in being able to do it instantly. When you know the passage fluently there is absolutely no hesitation before going straight to the new notes: no delay before the command, no delay before the response.

Suppose you are playing a passage of double stops, or a series of chords where you have to put each finger in a different place on a different string in rapid succession: can you play them instantly, and without first thinking them through?[1]

[1] See *Silent placing exercise*, page 299

Alternating clockwise-anticlockwise

A challenge for many string players lies in rapid string crossing passages where you have to alternate moving the bow in one direction and then in the other:

Bach: Partita no. 3 in E, BWV 1006, *Preludio, b. 17*

The movement from the A string to the E string is clockwise; from the A string to the D string anticlockwise. This causes a command-response problem:

The arrows show the direction of the movement. It is easy to move the bow fast one way **(1)**, or fast the other **(2)**, but the brain may seem to seize up when it has to do one and then the other **(3)**.

Improving command-response

Ivan Galamian's main answer to the question of how to improve command–response ('correlation'), how to speed up the mind-muscle 'unit', was that you should *increase* the demands of the passage by adding accent and rhythm patterns.[2] The process of learning how to play these patterns forces the mental directive to sharpen, and the muscles to respond more quickly.

[2] See *I haven't got time to practise in rhythms and accents*, page 114

In a sense any practice method improves command–response, since whatever you do improves your knowledge – technically and musically – of what you are doing. Some particularly direct ways include:

- Breaking the passage down into smaller units.

- Playing more slowly

- Playing slowly, but with exaggeratedly fast left finger speed, moving at the last possible moment before the note must be played.[3]

[3] See *Fast fingers: the key to a great left hand*, page 152

'You should have heard it yesterday'

It is common to hear someone lament how badly their examination, audition or concert went, and that it had been so much better the day or the hour before, and that they cannot understand why it all felt so difficult when it came to the actual event.

One reason can be that it went better beforehand because the player was managing to get through passages by 'thinking fast' – actively controlling each phrase or passage with lots of determined thinking, lots of remembering what to do or what to aim for, all based on the decisions made during the lessons and preparation that preceded the performance.

But when we are under pressure it can be very difficult to think clearly, or even to think at all. Then the playing falls down because the 'command' part of the command–response becomes sluggish.

Instead, when you really know a piece well you can play it without all the moment-by-moment directions. The entire command-response moves on to an involuntary, unconscious level instead of a conscious one. Until you reach that stage, you have not really got to the end of learning a piece.

The traditional, age-old test of whether you really know a piece is that you could be woken up in your bed at 3am, handed a violin and bow, and be able instantly – without any warming up or preparation – to play perfectly any phrase or passage from your piece or concerto.

Understanding percentage shots

'Percentage shot' is a term commonly used in sport. Hitting the ball over the net in tennis, you might hit the ball very hard, and at the same time aim so low that the ball almost touches the top of the net. If you misjudge by the smallest amount, the ball may hit the net. This is a low percentage shot.

Or you might hit it somewhat more gently and lob it higher, well above the net. You really cannot miss. This is a high percentage shot.

Whether a shot is high or low percentage depends on your ability. In a game such as golf the way to decide what a high, medium or low percentage shot is for you is by asking this question: "If I hit 10 shots from here, how many times could I do it well?"

- High percentage   7–10 out of 10
- Medium percentage   4–6 out of 10
- Low percentage   0–3 out of 10

It is obvious that a passage of fast double stops, high up the fingerboard, will be lower percentage than a passage of slower single notes in 1st position; but each composer, or each distinct style of playing, can also have a tendency towards low or high percentages.

Why is Beethoven, Mozart or Schubert so exacting to play? Why is the opening of the Beethoven Violin Concerto so much more of a challenge than the opening of the Brahms Violin Concerto? It cannot be only because one begins p and the other f:

Beethoven: Concerto in D, op. 61, *mov. 1, b. 89*

Brahms: Concerto in D, op. 77, *mov. 1, b. 90*

Why is a typical Mozart passage so much more fragile than Sibelius?

Mozart: Concerto no. 3 in G, K216, *mov. 2, b. 9*

Sibelius: Concerto in D minor, op. 47, *mov. 1, b. 4*

Why does Franck often feel so much safer than Schubert?

Franck: Sonata in A, *mov. 1, b. 5*

Schubert: Sonatina in A, op. 137 no. 2, *mov. 1, b. 31*

In each example no note must be too loud, but neither must it be too soft; it must not be too long, but not too short either; the vibrato must not be too wide, but neither may it be too narrow; the shifts must not be too fast, nor too slow; the accents not too sharp, but not too soft either; and so on.

In the Beethoven, Mozart or Schubert examples, every note seems to be a 'low percentage shot' because the range between 'too much' and 'not enough', i.e. the range within which anything is acceptable or 'good', is extremely narrow.

Playing Brahms, Sibelius or Franck, the range within which everything is good is often much wider. There is a far greater distance between 'too much' and 'not enough'. You can play slightly louder, softer, longer, shorter, wider, narrower etc., and whatever you do is still easily within completely acceptable boundaries.

The Bartok First Rhapsody is very high percentage:

Bartók: First Rhapsody, *mov. 1, b. 2*

The forcefulness of the writing is not the reason why this is a high percentage piece. The slow, expressive section that follows is equally high percentage:

Bartók: First Rhapsody, *mov. 1, b. 38*

To say that this is 'high percentage' is not to say that it does not have to be played *as well* as something that is lower percentage. It is simply that this is a different sound-world to that of Mozart or Schubert.

Q **How does thinking about 'percentage shots' help in violin playing?**

The knowledge that whatever you are playing is 'higher percentage' leads to a feeling of ease and confidence, since you know that you can play a little heavier into the string, or lighter – or you can vibrate a little wider or narrower, faster or slower, and so on – and still what you play will be fine.

Appreciating that something is 'lower percentage' (either a particular composer or a certain phrase or passage) does not necessarily make it any easier; but it may affect your approach to it, so that you are particularly careful not to rush, to tighten, or to over-try.[1]

[1] Three things that sportsmen and musicians equally have to guard against constantly: rushing into an action; tensing before an action; and trying too hard, which may result in getting in the way and 'interfering' instead of 'letting it happen'.

Expand your range of comfort

- Practise fast passages so that you can comfortably play them faster than you need to, and slow passages slower than you need to.

- Practise fast passages with the left fingers closer to the string than you need to.

- Practise *forte* passages so that you can comfortably play them louder than you need to, and *piano* passages softer than you need to.

- Practise the vibrato of certain notes or phrases wider, narrower, faster, slower, than you need to.

- Practise chords longer than you need to play them, and with exaggerated vibrato.

- Practise long strokes longer than you need to play them, and so on.

I can't play fast

The Russian who couldn't play fast

Dorothy DeLay once mentioned that she was very pleased with the recent progress of one of her students, a Russian in his early twenties called Vladimir.

Vladimir had had a big problem: he had never been able to play anything if it was fast. He was a good musician, and as long as the tempo was slow enough he could play well. But as soon as he had to play something tricky and fast, he could never get it to a high standard.

Apparently his previous teachers had given up with him and advised him to take up a different profession. Miss DeLay explained how, for many months, she had tried everything she could think of to help him, but there had been little progress. He just couldn't get anything working really well if it was at all fast and brilliant.

Then one day he arrived at his lesson beaming, took out his violin, and said: "Listen to this!" He started to play some difficult passages very fast and accurately, and with evident ease.

Miss DeLay was astonished. "Fantastic!" she said. "What have you been doing to get this result?"

Vladimir explained what had happened. He had been in a practice room on the fourth floor of the Juilliard School, and in the room next to him a brilliant and successful Russian violinist called Yuri was practising. Vladimir could hear Yuri faintly through the wall.

Yuri was practising a piece that was fast and tricky. It was obvious that he was at an early stage of learning it – he could not yet play it fluently – yet he was practising it at performance tempo.

Vladimir was surprised. He had always been told that you should not play anything fast until you can play it perfectly at a slow tempo. You cannot run before you can walk. He had never practised fast passages at performance tempo. Since he couldn't play them fast, he would practise them slowly; but because he practised only slowly, he couldn't play them fast.

The moment he started to practise, *up to speed*, the passages that he could not yet play fluently – as well as practising slowly, and in all the other ways of practising – the new results were extraordinary.

Playing through without stopping

The idea that you should not practise passages at performance tempo until you can play them fluently more slowly, belongs in the same family as the idea that you should always stop if you make a mistake, i.e. that playing through without stopping is bad practice.

Stopping and correcting, and doing all the different types of technical building work, is naturally a part of practising that everybody has to do; but at the same time, it is at least equally important to play through as a non-stop performance, and often more important.

Like a gymnast always regaining balance after the slightest mishap, you have to know how to be able to rescue yourself in performance, either when things go wrong or when they may be about to. You cannot practise doing that if you always stop every time you make a mistake, or if you spend little time playing as you would do in a concert.

Groups

When you play slow passages there is time to think. You can consider each note one by one if you like. In faster passages a speed limit is soon reached where you begin to struggle to keep up with each note. This is perfectly natural, but the problem is not that you cannot keep up, but that you are trying to keep up in the first place.

Instead, you have to begin to think in larger groups. Two or more notes (up to as many as 9 or more) combine into one 'unit' which is set off by one mental command. In other words, one command sets off several notes at the same time, instead of each note requiring a separate command to itself.

Spiccato clearly illustrates how you reach speed limits in mental control, and how you then have to form groups:

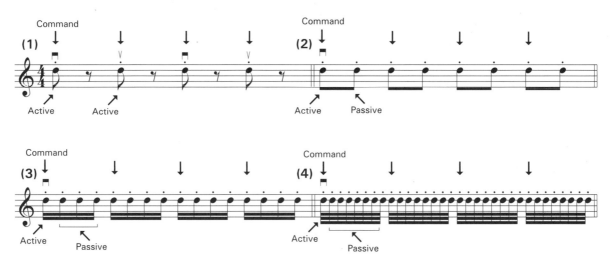

(1) At slow speeds you can control each *spiccato* stroke individually.

(2) As the tempo increases you soon need to think in pairs of notes – the down-bow 'active' and the up-bow 'passive', like a rebound. Each pair of notes is set off by one mental command.

(3) As the tempo increases still further you soon need to think in groups of four notes, the first note active and the next three passive. Each group of four notes is set off by one mental command.

(4) As the tempo increases still further, the stroke develops into *sautillé*. It may feel like 'one active, seven passive', or there may be an underlying sense of two groups of four.

Sándor Végh likened slow and fast playing to driving cars. When you drive slowly, he would explain, you can sit up in your seat and look carefully just ahead of you, and to left and right; if you wanted to, you could press your face up quite close to the windscreen and peer just in front of you, if you were driving slowly enough.

But when you drive fast, you have to sit back in your seat and look much further ahead. Imagine how difficult it would be to drive at high speed if you leaned forward, your face close to the windscreen.

During fast passages you have to 'sit back' and take a larger view at the same time as playing each note. If you mentally 'lean forward' and get 'too close' to the fast passage, you may find yourself forever stumbling at one place or another.

- Join smaller groups together so that you think in larger units. In passages like the following, think in groups of 4, 8 or 16, rather than thinking of each note as you come to it:

Dont: 24 Etudes and Caprices, op. 35 no. 3, *b. 1*

Just 'one of those'

Before you can set off a group of notes with one command, you have to have a feeling that the group is 'one thing', rather than a collection of notes or actions joined together quickly.

You can easily make the group feel like one thing simply by repeating it over and over again.

After a while you forget about the individual notes, and the group as a whole becomes just 'one of those'. Here is another of them: you play it. It is one thing. You want another? Here it is.

Once the group has reached that stage, you can play whole runs with few commands: you simply play 'one of those', and then 'one of those', and so on.

How to play faster than Heifetz

Dorothy DeLay was fond of asking students, "Did I ever show you how to play *Scherzo Tarantella* faster than Heifetz?" Pausing before playing, and putting on an act of great seriousness and earnest concentration, she would play this:

She had played only two, slow notes. But then she would explain that she had actually 'played' four notes but the middle two had been so fast the student hadn't even heard them.

She would show how, after playing the open A, she had dropped the first, second and third fingers together, in a 'block'. Although all three fingers had dropped onto the string at the same time, she had shaped the three fingers of the block like a fan, so that the first finger would contact the string first, then the second finger, and then the third:

So in a passage like the following, you could drop your fingers together and 'play' faster than Heifetz:

Wieniawski: Scherzo-Tarentelle, op. 16, *b. 40*

- Practise by first putting the fingers down at the same time in 'blocks':

Then keep some of that feeling as you play the passage with a normal finger action.

- It can also be helpful to practise the middle notes as very short grace-notes:

Speeding up with the metronome

Gradually speeding up with the metronome is one of the simplest ways to build a passage up to speed.

There are two main things to keep in mind:

- At every speed, from the slowest to the fastest, the goal is good pitch–sound–rhythm–ease. Learn how to play the phrase or passage so that every note is musically in tune, tonally and expressively right, musically in time, and you can play it with the least possible effort.

- At every speed, pretend that this is the actual tempo that you are going to take when you perform the passage in a concert. Replace a tempo indication such as '*allegro*' with '*adagio*', and then practise it at that speed until it is musically convincing, as well as technically without blemish.

Adagio molto

Bruch: Concerto no. 1 in G minor, op. 26, *mov. 3, b. 19*

Flow

One of the hallmarks of excellent technique is smoothness and flow throughout every action and series of actions. No stops interrupt the flow.

A clear example of flow can be seen in playing the piano. In a simple scale, the thumb passes under the second and third fingers, and then the third and second fingers move over the thumb, in a non-stop, continuous flowing motion (see the example on page 205).

To maintain flow on the violin, one of the most important things is that you do not stay too long on the note before a shift. The time for the shift must be stolen from the note before the shift (see *Understanding timing*, page 243).

Examples of other typical areas important for maintaining flow:

- **Pivoting**   Moving to another string while playing the previous one (see page 294).

- **Bow changes**   Feeling some degree of imperceptible circular motion when changing direction (see *Making imperceptible circles at the bow-change*, page 128).

- **Vibrato**   Not stopping the vibrato during or between notes (see *Continuous vibrato*, page 259).

- **Tone**   Sustaining the bow evenly (see *How can I make my bowing feel really smooth?*, page 261).

- **Pulse**   Feeling the underlying rhythmic pulse (see *Feeling the pulse*, page 218).

Thinking ahead

Playing a scale or arpeggio on the violin, or anything for that matter, one of the secrets of control and flow is to be always thinking ahead:

Example 1

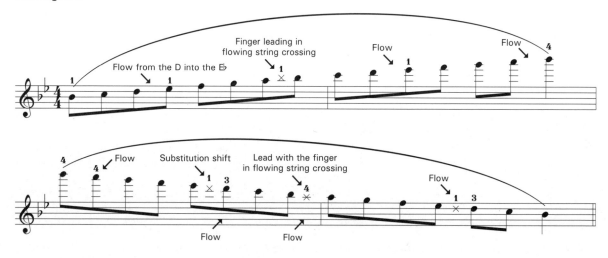

Example 2   Kreutzer: 42 Etudes ou caprices, no. 35, *b. 12*

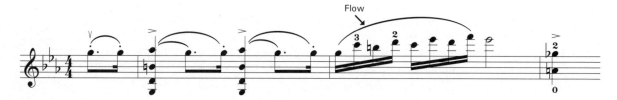

Example 3

Sarasate: Carmen Fantasy, op. 25, *Introduction, b. 49*

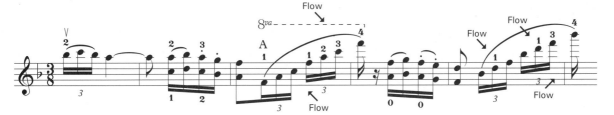

Remembering to play music not notes

When students play the Bach E major Praeludium (or fast passages within pieces), the impression they often give is that they have only two thoughts in their mind: first, 'it's got to be fast, got to be fast,' and second, 'I mustn't stop, mustn't stop.'

Instead, the thing to do is to concentrate as much on the expression, phrasing and dynamic shading of each phrase as you would in a slow passage.

The speed, and the technique to play it, then develops out of the music. It does not work so well (or at all) the other way round – if you go for the speed, and hope that the music will come out of that. The fingers, and other elements such as co-ordination or shifting, simply do not work well unless you are 'first being a musician'.[1]

[1] See *Practising musically*, page 221

Don't speed up when things get tough

In both music and sport, one of the things performers must learn is not to hurry when faced with a difficulty or something they are worried about.

In the Paganini 24th Caprice the first four bars of each variation are repeated:

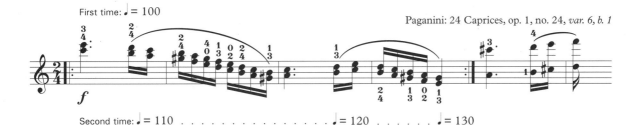

Paganini: 24 Caprices, op. 1, no. 24, *var. 6, b. 1*

It is common to hear someone trip up in some way the first time they play it, and then on the repeat *play it even faster*. Instead, they should pull back slightly.

  But if you slow down, even if you play well it will still not be good because then it will be too slow.

It all depends on how slow. Suppose you are playing a piece at, say, ♩ = 60. Everything feels comfortable, and you continue along at a steady 60. But then you find yourself at a tricky passage.

So you slow down to, say, ♩ = 57. This is not enough for anyone in the audience to notice. They are not all going to look at you in astonishment and wonder why you are suddenly playing so slowly.

But instead, suppose you are playing along at 60, find yourself at a tricky passage, and immediately increase the tempo to, say, ♩ = 63. Again, this is not enough for anyone in the audience to notice. They are not all going to wonder why you are suddenly playing so fast.

But the difference to you is six points on the metronome, which is a big difference.

I haven't got time to practise in rhythms and accents

Rhythm practice

I was first shown how to practise in rhythms when I was 11. I can remember it clearly – not being told how to do it, particularly, but the feeling of playing the passage afterwards. I just couldn't believe how easy it felt.

It was this passage from the Handel Sonata in D major:

Handel: Sonata no. 4 in D, op. 1, no. 13, *mov. 2, b. 24*

I began with the following basic dotted pattern:

Then I played the pattern round the other way:

The whole process took perhaps five minutes, and then I played it normally again. My left hand and fingers felt light and effortless, and I could barely feel the fingers moving up and down. I watched in amazement, as if from a distance, as my fingers seemed to play the passage on their own.

After this I did not need any encouragement to practise in rhythms. It was more that you could not stop me. This was not because I was such a good student or so keen to practise – I was neither – but because it was such a quick and painless way to learn things and to 'get them out of the way'.

Yet what has always puzzled me is the difficulty I have so often had in trying to get my students to practise in rhythms. Rather than seeing rhythm practice as a 'power-tool' that takes all the effort out of a task, as an electric saw does, they more often seem to think it will be too much hard work, and that there must be an easier, quicker way to get there. But this *is* one of the easiest, quickest ways.

Many explain that they do not have enough time to practise in rhythms and accents. In most cases, the truth is that they do not have time *not* to practise in these ways, since these practice methods save much more time that they ever take to do.

 For how long should you continue to practise a particular phrase or passage in rhythms and accents?

A single session of rhythm practice can give quick results, and is sometimes enough; but several sessions of concentrated work in a variety of rhythms (and/or accents) will yield fantastic results.

- Imagine that you are actually going to give a public performance of the passage in rhythms – as though that is how the passage should be played in the piece – and you want to practise each rhythm until it is completely polished.

- There are always four main goals to achieve.[1] Each rhythm should be practised until the three elements of playing – pitch, sound and rhythm – are all good: every note in tune, every note clean and resonant, and the rhythms mathematically precise. The fourth goal is for all this to feel *easy*. Until each rhythm is in tune, clean, in time, and feeling easy, you have not really mastered it yet.[2]

[1] See *The goal is always the same*, page 94

[2] The great cellist Pablo Casals said, 'Good intonation is a question of conscience!' The same can be said of everything: is the pitch/sound/rhythm/ ease really impossible to improve even by a small amount?

- However, it is often a mistake to carry on working on each rhythm (or other practice technique) until it is 'perfect' before moving on to the next. Having made some progress with one rhythm – it is more in tune, cleaner, more in time, and feeling easier than it was five minutes ago – it is better to move on to the next rhythm. Solving some of the problems of playing the new rhythm will improve the former rhythm at the same time.

Basic rhythm patterns

There are endless combinations and variations of rhythms you can use, but for normal practice purposes it is rarely necessary to go beyond the following simple two-note, three-note and four-note dotted patterns.

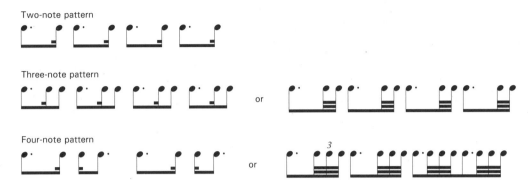

Using just these rhythms you can cover every possibility if you begin on different notes of the phrase:

- Begin two-note patterns on the first and on the second note of the passage

- Begin three-note patterns on the first, second and third note of the passage

- Begin four-note patterns on the first, second, third and fourth notes of the passage

Basic accent patterns

Accent practice is the twin of rhythm practice, and everything that can be said about one applies equally to the other. Examples:

Sometimes it is helpful to go further than these basic patterns, and it is also powerfully effective to combine accent and rhythm practice.

Practising difficult fast passages, or long non-stop pieces such as the Bach E major Praeludium, you might put together groups of 3s and 4s to create dotted and/or accented patterns in groups of 7 notes – anything to try to give yourself new problems.

 Q **Why would you want to give yourself new problems, when the point is to try to make the passage easier to play?**

The idea of rhythm or accent practice *is* to give yourself problems to solve. It is in the solving of the problems that you gain true knowledge and mastery of the passage.

When you first play a particular rhythm, and find that it throws you so completely that you do not seem to be able to play it at all – and you immediately think: 'Oh no, this is so difficult, it is impossible, I wish I did not have to do this!' – in fact this is the time to be pleased, because by solving the problems you are going to improve your playing of the passage immeasurably.

If playing a rhythm was not tricky in some way, there would be no point in doing it. The greater the difficulty, and the bigger the problems that you solve by learning how to play the rhythms cleanly, the easier it feels when you then play the passage normally.

Therefore, not only do you want problems, but if something is or becomes too easy, you need to find a way of making it more difficult again.

● A simple way to 'raise the bar', like an athlete always wanting to jump higher, is to play rhythms with the metronome. Increase the speed of the click each time you satisfy the four conditions of pitch, sound, rhythm and ease.

Example 1

Mozart: Symphony no. 39 in E♭, K543, *var. 6, b. 1*

Rhythm practice

Accent practice

Example 2

● Apply rhythm and accent practice to a variety of note patterns:

Example 3

● Use rhythm or accent practice for double stop passages:

[Andante]

Provost: *Intermezzo, b. 25*

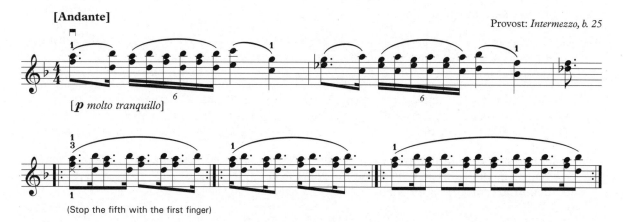

[*p molto tranquillo*]

(Stop the fifth with the first finger)

Setting up the bow arm

lesson 5

Finding the violin position

Fit the violin to the bow arm rather than the other way round. The best violin position is more the one that suits your right arm than the one that suits your left.

The ideal is to be able to arrive at the point, at the end of the down-bow, with the bow parallel to the bridge but with the arm neither too straight nor too bent (Fig. 51f).

Fig. 51

(a) Balanced, 'middle' position

(b) Upper arm too far back

(c) Upper arm too far forwards

(d) The bow and the upper arm are parallel

(e) The strings and the right forearm are parallel

(f) Playing at the point the arm will be neither too straight nor too bent

1 Make a right-angle at the elbow.

   Allow the arm to find its natural, balanced, 'middle' position (Fig. 51a). The upper arm should not be too far back (Fig. 51b) nor too far forward (Fig. 51c).

2 Without moving the right arm, place the bow in your right hand. Notice how the bow and the upper arm are parallel (Fig. 51d).

3 Again without altering the positions of the bow or right arm, put the violin under your chin and adjust the angle so that the strings and the right forearm are parallel (Fig. 51e).

   Notice how there is a right-angle at the elbow, and between the bow and the strings; and the forearm and strings are parallel, as are the upper arm and bow.[1]

4 Now if you bow from the square to the point, you should end up with the arm neither too straight nor too bent (Fig. 51f).

[1] Make sure also that the position of the violin on the shoulder is suitable for your length of arms: shorter arms, higher on the shoulder (chin nearer to or above the tailpiece); longer arms, lower on the shoulder (chin further to the left of the tailpiece).

See *3. How high or low on the shoulder?*, page 34

Drawing a straight bow

The image of the compass

There are three 'levers' in the arm: the upper arm, the forearm, and the hand. Each moves in an arc: the largest is the upper arm, the smallest the hand. In bowing, if any one lever is used alone the bow moves in a circular motion. It is easy to see this in a simple experiment:

Without the bow, hold your right arm horizontally in the air, with a right angle at the elbow, and with your fingers pointing straight forwards (Fig. 52a).

- Imagine that your arm is a huge compass. Your shoulder is the fixed point of the compass, and the pencil that draws the line is attached to your elbow.

- Imagine that there is a large sheet of paper under your arm.

- Move your elbow to left and right. The pencil draws a large arc.

- Then imagine that the fixed point of the compass is the elbow, and the pencil is attached to your wrist (Fig. 52b).

  Keeping the elbow still, move the wrist to left and right. The pen draws a smaller arc.

- Then imagine that the fixed point of the compass is the wrist, and the pen is attached to your fingertips (Fig. 52c).

  Keeping the wrist still, move the hand to left and right. The pen draws the smallest arc.

To move the bow parallel to the bridge, combinations of these arcs must be used at the same time.

Fig. 52

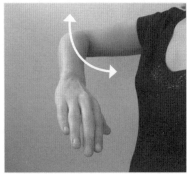 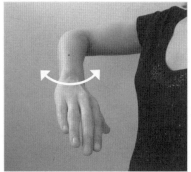 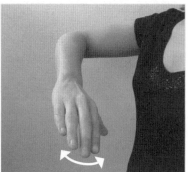

(a) Largest arc   (b) Smaller arc   (c) Smallest arc

Bowing out to the side

Your mental picture of what to do directs your actions and determines the results that you get. Many players have an unhelpful mental picture of the right arm moving to and fro from left to right. This results in an awkward, cramped bowing action (Fig. 53a), since most of the time the right arm does not so much move to the right and left, as much as forwards and backwards.

Fig. 53

(a) The hand and arm do not move   (b) Draw the bow to the point, parallel to   (c) Note the position of the hand in front
     sideways   the bridge   of the shoulder

Experiment

- **Student** – Draw the bow to the point, keeping the bow parallel with the bridge, and stop there with the bow on the string (Fig. 53b).

- **Teacher or assistant** – While the student holds this position, take the bow out of their hands. Fig. 53c shows the same position as (b) but with the bow removed. Note where the right hand is: directly in front of the shoulder, not out to the right.

The best straight-bow exercise in the world

The first thing is to know what drawing a straight bow feels like. This exercise is excellent because you learn by feel instead of by learning rules. It is ideal for children, who can thus improve their bowing without needing an intellectual understanding of the principles; and just as good for adults for the same reason.

Using a mirror can also be helpful when working on your bow arm, but it does not give you the feel of the arm as this exercise does.[1]

With someone holding the bow for you, parallel to the bridge, simply run your hand along the stationary bow. Since the bow is parallel to the bridge, your arm is forced to perform the perfect combination of movements to draw a straight bow.

Instead of the bow being straight because the arm movement is perfect, the arm movement is perfect because the bow is straight.

It is easiest to do this exercise if someone holds the bow for you (Fig. 54a), but you can do it by yourself if you rest the end of the bow on a music stand (Fig. 54b).

- Lightly run the hand many times up and down the entire length of the bow.

(a) Running the hand up and down the bow

(b) Rest the bow on a music stand

(c) Do not allow the hand to lose its bow hold shape

- **Teacher or assistant** – The most important thing is to keep checking that the bow is parallel to the bridge. Hold the bow sometimes on one string, sometimes on another.

- **Student** – Make sure you hold the violin in a position that allows the arm to be neither too straight nor too bent at the elbow when your hand is at the point (Fig. 51f, page 117). Make sure you keep your hand in a proper bow hold shape. The proportions of the movements of the bow arm change if the hand is held at an abnormal angle to the bow (Fig. 54c).

Aiming the bow

After the pupil has run their hand along the bow, the next stage may be for them to play whole bows while you hold the point of your bow – or your hand – in the place in the air where the frog of their bow should be heading. Then they can aim the moving frog towards or away from it.

Four important places in the bow arm

Notice four important positions of the arm while running your hand up and down the stationary bow:

1 At the heel 2 At the point-of-balance 3 At the square 4 At the point

1: Heel

Ivan Galamian called this position of the arm the 'triangle'. It is formed by the forearm, the upper arm, and an imaginary line from the shoulder to the hand.

- Starting at the extreme heel (Fig. 55), get ready to run the hand along the bow. Make sure the elbow is on the same level as the hand.[2]

  Make sure your hand is in the heel bow hold shape, i.e. the hand more upright and balanced on the fourth finger, rather than leaning towards the first finger (as it does more when playing at the point).

Triangle position

- While not moving away from the heel, move the hand in down- and up-bow movements along the stationary bow, moving only one or two centimetres.

[1] When you use a mirror to see if the bow is parallel to the bridge, stand with the violin parallel to the wall. You should be able to see only the side edge of the bridge. If you can see any of the front or back of the bridge, adjust the angle of the violin until the bridge is a two-dimensional vertical line.

To work on string crossing, stand with the violin pointing directly at the mirror, i.e. at a right-angle to the wall.

Fig. 54

Fig. 55

[2] See *Elbow and wrist: how high?*, page 127

Notice how the elbow moves exactly the same distance, at exactly the same speed, as the hand. If the hand moves one centimetre to the right, the elbow moves one centimetre to the right as well.

Notice how far you can continue along the bow without any opening at the elbow whatsoever. Depending on your length of arm and the angle of the violin to your body, you may be able to move twenty centimetres along the bow before you can feel or see the elbow starting to open.

For that first twenty centimetres of the down-bow, beginning at the frog, the elbow moves at the same speed as the hand.

2: Point-of-balance

The point-of-balance (Fig. 56a) is not at the middle of the bow because the frog is heavier than the tip.

Beginners may find it helpful if you mark the point-of-balance with a white sticker. Another place to mark with a sticker is the square, which is slightly above the middle of the bow if the arm is long.[1]

[1] It is traditional to mark the middle of the bow with a sticker, yet this place has little significance unless it happens to coincide with the square position (which it does in the case of shorter-armed players).

There is a comfortable, balanced feeling when playing at the point-of-balance, created not only by the balanced weight of the bow, but also by the neutral position of the forearm and upper arm (see Fig. 51a, page 117). This makes the point-of-balance a good area for many common *spiccato* strokes, and often an easy place to begin a down-bow.

Fig. 56

(a) The point-of-balance

(b) Holding the bow at the point-of-balance while experimenting with strokes in the upper half

Experiment in balance

- Holding the bow at the point-of-balance (Fig. 56b), play a few strokes in different places between the middle and the point.

- Move the hand a couple of centimetres lower and repeat. Note the difference in the feel of the bow.

- Repeat until the hand is in its normal position at the frog.

Fig. 57

3: Square

The square (Fig. 57) is the place in the bow where there is a right angle between the forearm and the upper arm, and between the forearm and the bow; the upper arm and bow are broadly parallel; and there is an imaginary line, parallel with the forearm, drawn from the shoulder to the bow.

Short arms have the square nearer the middle of the bow; longer arms slightly higher.

The square position

- Run your hand up and down the stationary bow for about 10 centimetres at the square (i.e. from 5 centimetres below the square to 5 centimetres above).

   Make sure the elbow is on the same level as the hand, with no upwards curve at the wrist.

- Notice how only the forearm moves, and the upper arm is entirely still. This is the only place in the bow, and the maximum amount of bow, where the forearm can move alone, and is usually the best place in the bow to play fast, separate-bow passages. Above this area, and below it, the upper arm must move too, if you want the bow to remain parallel with the bridge.

- Move the hand over a larger area of the bow, above and below the square (i.e. from 10 centimetres below the square to 10 above). Notice how the upper arm moves backwards and forwards when the hand is above or below the square.

4: Point position

Make sure that the instrument is positioned so that when you run your hand to the point, the arm ends up neither too straight at the elbow nor too bent (Fig. 51f, page 117).

The question is how to get from the square to the point. According to Galamian, the upper arm 'purposely' pushes forwards ('out') at the end of the down-bow.

Notice this 'in' and 'out' movement of the upper arm when you run your hand along the bow:

- Starting at the square and moving in the direction of the point, feel how the upper arm moves forward ('out'), as the hand runs along the bow to the point.

- At the beginning of the up-bow at the point, feel how the very first movement of the right arm is backwards ('in') with the upper arm.

Feeling the symmetry of the bow arm

When you move the upper arm 'out' (forwards) at the end of the down-bow at the point, and 'in' (backwards) at the very beginning of the up-bow at the point, there is a satisfying feeling of symmetry in the bow arm:

- At the beginning of the down-bow at the heel, the upper arm moves back; it stops moving around the middle section of the bow; it moves forwards during the upper half to the point.

- At the beginning of the up-bow at the point, the upper arm moves back; it stops moving around the middle section of the bow; it moves forwards during the lower half to the heel:

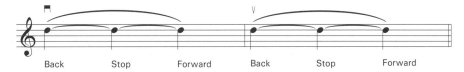

Back   Stop   Forward   Back   Stop   Forward

- Feel the rhythm of the pattern: back–stop–forward, back–stop–forward.

The Flesch and Galamian bow arms

Carl Flesch does not mention this pushing 'out' at the end of the ⊓, or moving 'in' at the beginning of the ∨ at the point. The Flesch bow arm may easily appear to be faulty because Flesch says to use only the forearm when bowing in the upper half, opening and closing the arm at the elbow, without any mention of the upper arm moving as well:

> …horizontal movement of the forearm from the elbow joint. This movement produces the normal *détaché* stroke between the middle and the tip of the bow.[1]

[1] Carl Flesch: *The Art of Violin Playing* (New York, 1924), Vol. 1, 39.

This produces a curved movement which takes the bow away from being parallel to the bridge (Fig. 58). In contrast, Galamian was clear that the upper arm moves 'out' (down-bow) and 'in' (up-bow) near the point:

> The reason underlying the necessary forward motion rests in the circular character of the natural movements of the arm. As the point of the bow is approached, unless the upper arm purposely pushes forward, the lower arm will naturally describe a backward-moving arc as it opens up on the down-bow. This opening out of the arm at the elbow is not sufficient in itself to preserve the straightness of the stroke. The bow hand has to reach gradually frontward as the arm straightens. For the sake of brevity we have called this forward motion on the down-bow the "out" motion. Thus, from the square to the point, the bow moves out on the down-bow.

> …In returning up-bow from the point to the square, the motions are reversed. The elbow gradually bends, bringing the forearm from its straight-line position back to its right angle relationship, as the middle of the bow is approached. The upper arm begins to pull backward as the up-bow stroke starts. This backward motion we shall term the "in" motion.[2]

[2] Ivan Galamian: *Principles of Violin Playing and Teaching* (New Jersey, 1962), 53.

According to the Russian violinist Zakhar Bron, Flesch's apparent misunderstanding was perhaps only a problem of language. Consider the same levers in the left arm, Bron says. Everybody would say that to shift from 1st position to 5th position you bring the left forearm closer in towards your body; but nobody ever says that the left upper arm must fold back at the same time. Yet otherwise the violin would move vertically upwards.

This movement of the left upper arm is so obvious that nobody mentions it; similarly, says Bron, it probably never occurred to Flesch that anyone would try to move the right forearm alone without the right upper arm moving too.

Fig. 58

This is what happens if you move only the upper arm without pushing forwards

Building the bow arm

The ideal is to have a feeling of one down-bow movement, and one up-bow movement, rather than having a collection of many individual movements which you try to join together as you play.

David Oistrakh's bow arm is a classic example. There is no feeling of the different 'bits' of the bow arm in his bowing: he simply moves down-bow from the heel to the point, and up-bow from the point to the heel, as one action, with all the individual actions merged into one unit.

Sometimes, the more a student learns about the bow arm or the left hand, the worse it gets. If you start to think about the movement of the arm here, and the action of the fingers there, and during a down-bow from heel to point you try to stick everything together, there may be a danger that 'conscious interference' will get in the way of your natural feel for bowing.

Kicking a ball, you do not use your conscious mind to pull the upper leg back, and then consciously push it forward again. You know where you want to kick the ball, and how hard; you keep focused on the result you want; you let yourself kick it at the same time as making it happen.

The idea that somebody might consciously pull the upper leg back, and then add some lower leg movement, may seem absurd; yet many string players try to move the arm exactly like that.

This does not mean that you cannot analyse your bow arm and make changes to certain elements of it. Once the new habit has become unconscious, you can return to the perception of only one natural movement for the down-bow, and one movement for the up-bow.

Forearm rotation

Forearm rotation (the forearm movement of turning a key) is something that many players do naturally, without knowing or ever thinking about it. Others do not automatically have it as part of their bow arm, or sometimes get into a habit of blocking it; but it is an easy and simple process to add forearm rotation back in to the playing.

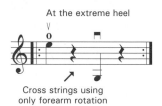

At the extreme heel

Cross strings using only forearm rotation

If it is not part of your bow arm, and then you begin to allow it – or if you play repetitive exercises to encourage it – an immense new feeling of freedom immediately comes into your bow arm.

My first encounter with the idea of forearm rotation was Yfrah Neaman teaching Carl Flesch's Six Fundamental Types (see page 264). The exercise above is No. 4, and is shown in Fig. 59:

Fig. 59

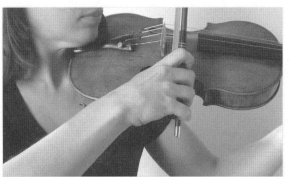

(a) Just after playing the up-bow open E

(b) Just before playing the down-bow open G

For years afterwards, I thought that forearm rotation was entirely something to do with string crossing. Passages like the following are obviously easier if you do not use the upper arm on its own, but use a degree of forearm rotation as well:

Sarasate: Habanera, op. 21 no. 2, b. 26

It was only much later that I realised that this turning movement is used not only in string crossing. It is something that happens all the time, in a multitude of different types of strokes.

You can see it even in the simple operation of drawing the bow from the heel – where the hand is more upright (supinated) – to the point, where the hand is more tilted (pronated):

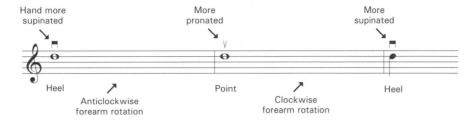

Obviously the amount of the movement may be so slight as to be imperceptible:

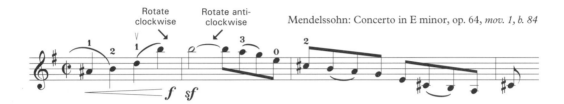

The changing contact of the first finger with the bow

The first finger's changing point of contact on the bow is a key element of forearm rotation.[1]

- Playing at the heel, the forearm has rotated clockwise and the first finger contacts the bow closer to the first joint (Fig. 60a).

- At the point, the forearm has rotated anticlockwise and the first finger contacts the bow closer to the middle joint (Fig. 60b).

The changing contact-point of the first finger, and forearm rotation, have a clear effect on one another: if you keep the contact-point of the first finger fixed in one place, forearm rotation is prevented and the wrist has to bend excessively instead (Fig. 60c).[2]

[1] See *The changing contact-point of the first finger on the bow*, page 42

[2] See *Excessive right wrist movement*, page 193

Fig. 60

(a) Forearm rotated right

(b) Forearm rotated left

Lifted strokes

Forearm rotation is also a key part of lifted or springing strokes. The actual amount may be so little you cannot see it. Exaggerate the movement once or twice, so that afterwards an imperceptible amount happens naturally, on its own, without your being aware of it.

The arrows indicate anticlockwise and clockwise forearm rotation:

(c) Note the excessive wrist movement if forearm rotation is prevented

- The *spiccato* movement into and out of the string is curved: follow that curve invisibly with forearm rotation.

Understanding curves

No bow stroke on the violin moves in a straight line: every stroke curves or moves in a slight arc. The bow plays around the string even if this is so slight as to be imperceptible.

Watch the path that the right hand and frog take through the air:

It is obvious that a note pattern like the one shown in **(1)** is a series of curves and circles; and that the pattern shown in **(2)** produces a wavy line; but the crucial point is that two long notes played on one string **(3)** are not in a straight line either, but actually form a figure eight.

As a pair of notes, the two short *martelé* strokes shown in **(4)** form a figure eight, and each stroke has its own curves within the overall figure eight as well.

True stories: Joe

One of my first pupils was a boy of 9 whom I taught for three years. In that time he went from a rather poor elementary standard to a rather poor intermediate standard. He always had a 'wooden' bow arm, and was never able to find that sensuous quality of bowing that distinguishes a natural string player.

We worked together constantly on his bowing, with no real progress except that as time went by he was able to play more complicated pieces – but still with the same wooden tone and tension. He practised various tone-production and flexibility exercises, but nothing seemed to help much, or for long.

Finally, during a conversation about technique, a new fragment of thought came up which explained why progress had been so limited. *He had always thought that the bow moved in a straight line.*

Perhaps the very first time he saw someone playing a violin, he unconsciously registered the impression of the bow moving in a straight line as a fact. Or perhaps his first teachers, in trying to get him to draw the bow parallel with the bridge, had unintentionally communicated the idea of a straight line.

Wherever it had come from, this single erroneous idea of a straight line, hidden at the back of his mind but active there, short-circuited his every effort to play.

If you want to demonstrate a tense and awkward bow arm, you do not need to try to be tense and awkward. Instead, all you need to do is to try to draw the bow in a straight line, and the symptoms appear at once with startling naturalness.

With sufficient will-power and determination many players can reach quite a high standard even with such a crucial deficiency as trying to play in a straight line – but there will always be an element of strain or 'something not quite right' about their playing.

The moment you encourage more curves into your bowing, every stroke immediately feels more natural and flowing, and free of tension.

 How can you encourage more curves into your playing?

The simple realisation that even one note, played on one string, consists of a curved line, is often already enough to bring about a change: a new physical freedom, and more sense of naturally singing through the bow, often immediately enters the playing.

- Feel the hand playing deeply into the curve of the bow, e.g. following the stick down to the middle of the bow, and then rising again during the last part of the down-bow in the upper half.

[1] See *The give of the wood and the hair*, page 15

- At the heel the hair gives and the wood of the bow is rigid; at the point the wood gives (in the middle of the bow) and the hair is rigid.[1] This adds to the feeling of the hand 'curving down' into the bow during the down-bow from heel to middle, and the feeling of 'ascent' in the curve as you continue from middle to point.

Exercises such as the following can be helpful:

- Feel the curve as the bow travels towards the D or E string while sustaining the A string.

- Continue to make the double stop shorter until you end up sustaining one long A, down-bow and up-bow, while still feeling the arcs in the path of the frog rather than straight lines.

  These are not necessarily the actual arcs that the bow travels during one long down- or up-bow, since they depend on what you are playing; but they help in getting away from any feeling of a straight line.

Playing into the wood of the bow

One of the first things elementary students need to discover about bowing is to play down into the springiness of the stick rather than only move the hair horizontally along the string.

But this feature of bowing is usually either neglected or left out entirely, firstly because of all the other problems already in the way – of holding the bow and of drawing it parallel to the bridge – and secondly because the last thing you would ever encourage somebody to do is actively to press with the bow. The teacher is more likely to be spending all their time trying to *stop* the pupil pressing.

However, years later, the same student may now be doing all kinds of good things in holding the bow, bowing parallel to the bridge, and moving the bow horizontally with a pure tone – and yet still never really be playing deeply into the tensions in the stick. But playing into the wood of the bow is a simple thing to add to the bow arm, and the results are always exciting as new dimensions open up.

First number the distances between the hair and the wood (in the middle of the bow): 5, the bow resting with its own weight on the string; 1, the wood pushed down to the hair.[2]

- With the bow sitting stationary on the string not too far from the bridge, look at the middle of the bow and see how far away the wood is from the hair (Fig. 61a).

- Push the wood down until it is near to the hair (Level 2). Note the distance carefully (Fig. 61b).

- Without allowing the distance between the wood and the hair to change, move the bow up and down along the string. Adjust the speed, and the distance from the bridge, until the sound is pure.

Note that the only place to watch, when you are doing this, is the middle of the bow. It is only there that the hair will be near the wood of the bow.

The nature of a spring is that it always wants to return to its state of least effort, and all that the wood of the bow wants to do is to spring back up out of the string.[1] You have to hold it down and resist the upward push that it exerts, while adjusting the speed and soundpoint so that the tone remains pure.

[1] See *Point-of-contact: not following the line of least resistance*, page 6; *The bow wants to bounce*, page 280

Fig. 61

(a) Note the distance between the wood and the hair

(b) Push the wood down towards the hair and hold it at that distance

The place in the bow that is the most difficult to sustain is at the change of direction from down to up or vice versa. The key thing is to be able to keep the distance between the wood and the hair (in the middle of the bow) constant at the moment of changing direction; or, if that is impossible, to disguise the slight releasing at the bow change by keeping it to the absolute minimum:

Experiment in 'hanging'

To get a practical feel for the springiness of the stick, try the following experiment:

- Resting the point of the bow on the D string, so that the bow is approximately horizontal, make your left fingers into a 'hook', and 'hang' the left arm from the bow (Fig. 62a).

  Gently push down into the bow (in the middle) and release again, like gently testing the springiness of a trampoline. Feel the springiness of the wood of the bow.

- Then repeat, but now using the bow hand to do it instead of the left hand (Fig. 62b). Push the wood down towards the string (in the middle of the bow) in exactly the same way as before, feeling the same springiness in the stick.

Fig. 62

(a) 'Hang' the left arm from the bow

(b) Feel the same feeling of springiness in the stick using the right hand

Playing into the wood of the bow during string crossing

The next step is to be able to sustain during string crossing – either in slurred or separate bows.

Playing into the wood of the bow during string crossing is another hidden but essential aspect of bowing technique:

During the string crossing from the A♭ to the B♭ the bow pivots on the D string as it moves towards the A string. To create a seamless, sustained tone, the bow must not lose its grip on the string during the pivot:

(1) Looked at in slow motion, this is the unwanted effect if you do not 'keep the wood of the bow down towards the string' during the string crossing.

There is a lack of connection between the A♭ and the B♭, and a danger of an accent on the B♭.

[1] See also *Smooth string crossing*, page 294 (2) One way to practise string crossings is to play a double stop.[1]

Elbow and wrist: how high?

If you asked the Greek philosopher Aristotle for his opinion, he would probably remind you that the best course usually exists somewhere in the middle between two extremes. Therefore the wrist and elbow must not be too high, nor too low. You have to discover for yourself, through simple experiment, where the exact 'middle' point occurs between the two extremes, and that depends on what you are playing and where in the bow you are.

Fig. 63

Adjust the position of the elbow with your bow

For the simplest and most streamlined approach to the bow arm, keep the elbow and wrist more or less on the same level as the bow – sometimes a little above, sometimes a little below, but nearly always close to it.

- For the most comfortable, all-of-a-piece bow arm, avoid bowing the E string with the elbow on the level of the A or D strings.

- For strength of tone, and for a balanced feeling in the bow arm, avoid bowing the lower strings with the elbow too low, bowing as if you are playing on the upper strings.

Use your bow to make frequent adjustments to the height of a student's bow, so that they can correct it while playing (Fig. 63).

Lower half of the bow

Suppose you are going to play a down-bow beginning at the heel. Stop with the bow just above the string. Without moving the hand, you can put the elbow on the same level as the bow (Fig. 64a), or above it (Fig. 64b), or below (Fig. 64c).

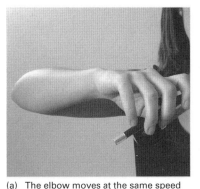 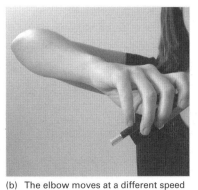 

Fig. 64

(a) The elbow moves at the same speed as the hand

(b) The elbow moves at a different speed to the hand

(c) The elbow moves at a different speed to the hand

Key point: If the elbow starts off much higher than the bow hand, and starts to move lower while the right hand moves the bow to the right – or if it starts off much lower than the bow hand, and begins to rise as the hand moves to the right – the elbow and the frog of the bow do not move in the same direction or at the same speed.

Then it is much harder to control the speed of the bow and get absolute evenness. Prove this by experimenting without the bow.

Experiment without the bow

- Hold an imaginary bow in front of you, with the arm in the triangle position, with the elbow more or less on the same level as the hand (as in Fig. 64a).

  Move the imaginary bow in short, horizontal, up- and down-bows at the extreme heel. Move the upper arm only, without opening and closing the arm at the elbow. Notice how the elbow and the hand move in the same direction and at the same speed.

- Then make the same short bowing movements with a high elbow. Exaggerate the height of the elbow so that the difference in the direction is clear (Fig. 64b).

  As the down-bow begins, you can keep the elbow at the same height above the bow without allowing the elbow to move vertically down; or as the down-bow begins, you can allow the elbow to move down at the same time as the hand moves to the right. Whichever you choose, the elbow and the frog of the bow no longer move in the same direction or at the same speed.

> Q Should the elbow always be level with the hand, so that both move at the same speed? Or are there times when the elbow is higher or lower than the hand, and it does not matter if they move at different speeds?

Fig. 65

Sometimes a higher elbow feels right, either in *pp* or *ff*, and it might feel very comfortable to move the elbow in a way that breaks the speed connection between the elbow and the frog.

If the elbow starts off higher than the bow hand, you can get a feeling of 'gearing' where a faster downward movement of the elbow happens at the same time as the bow moving more slowly, producing a feeling of great control and flow.

Finding the feeling of keeping the elbow more or less on the same level as the bow

[1] See *Raising the elbow*, page 282

Spiccato, and other bounced strokes such as *ricochet*, often work better with a higher elbow.[1]

Generally, however, there is more control if the elbow and the frog move in the same direction; and for that the elbow needs to be more or less on the same level as the hand.

If you have a spare bow handy, use two bows to give students the feeling of keeping the upper arm and bow level (Fig. 65).

Making imperceptible circles at the bow-change

The idea of raising and lowering the elbow at the heel may partly have come from the principle of using a circular movement at the change of bow to add smoothness to the change of direction.

When you are moving towards the heel near the end of an up-bow, and you are going to change direction and begin a down-bow – and you want the connection between up-bow and down-bow to be as smooth and seamless as possible – it is much easier if there is an element of a circle in the change of direction, rather than the bow coming to a dead halt and then going back the other way.

However, the circular movement does not have to be obvious. An almost undetectable amount is enough to add the same degree of smoothness in the bow-change as a much larger movement.

- To find this undetectable circular movement, first exaggerate the elbow movement. Staying in the lower half of the bow, play repeated up- and down-bows:

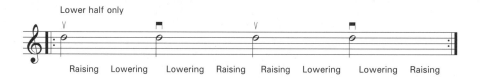

- Begin in the middle of the bow. Begin with your elbow and wrist on the same level as the bow.

- During the first part of the up-bow, move the elbow higher than the level of the bow.

- During the second part of the up-bow, move the elbow back down to almost the same level as the bow, but slightly higher.

- Continue the downward movement of the elbow so that it is still moving down as the bow changes from up-bow to down-bow.

- During the first part of the down-bow, continue the elbow's downward movement so that it reaches the same level as the bow. It does not matter if the elbow goes very slightly lower than the bow.

- During the second part of the down-bow, move the elbow back up so that you arrive at the beginning of the up-bow with the elbow very slightly above the level of the bow.

- Continue the upward movement of the elbow so that it is still moving up as the bow changes from down-bow to up-bow (in the middle of the bow).

- Feel the smoothness the circle adds to the bow-change, in contrast to the 'stop' that must happen if the bow moves in a straight line, comes to a halt, and then starts off in the other direction again.

- Repeat several times, each time making the movement of the elbow smaller and smaller. In the beginning the path the elbow travels in the air may be almost a full circle.

  As you make it smaller, the arc becomes flatter and flatter until finally the elbow appears to stay more or less on a level with the bow throughout. Notice how the smoothness at the bow-change remains, despite the fact that the curved lines are now imperceptible.

Upper half of the bow

As in the lower half, the elbow in the upper half stays basically on a level with the bow.

Playing on the G string, there may be many occasions when it is natural to allow the elbow to be slightly lower than the the bow, to avoid raising it needlessly; at other times, the elbow will be on a level with the bow or even higher.

Playing on any string in the upper half, you can raise the elbow slightly above the level of the bow to produce leverage into the string, and is another way to create extra power without extra effort (Fig. 66). Feel the elbow-raising movement led from an anticlockwise turning in the upper arm.

Fig. 66

Lever the bow into the string for extra power

Raising the elbow above the level of the bow in the upper half, to get extra weight from leverage, seems to be one of the great secrets of the bow arm. Perhaps the reason why it remains generally unknown is that the correct amount of raising is so slight as to be imperceptible. If the right amount made it point up almost vertically when playing powerfully in the upper half, then everyone would know about it.

Wrist

An old-fashioned approach to the right wrist, which is still sometimes taught today, is called 'hills and valleys'. When approaching the heel at the end of the up-bow, the wrist is raised into a hill or arch (Fig. 67a), and allowed to sink down almost as far at the point (Fig. 67b).

There may be a little of this pattern in a natural bow arm, but it can be kept to a minimum so that the bow arm is basically 'flat' – or there is a graceful, slight arc between hand and elbow in the lower half.

Fig. 67

(a) 'Hill': the wrist is too high   (b) 'Valley': the wrist is too low   (c) The forearm and hand in splints

- If the wrist is too high at the heel, at the beginning of the down-bow, it must move downwards as the down-bow begins. This makes the wrist travel at a different speed from the bow – leading to the same situation as when the elbow does (page 128).[1]

  This may not create many problems in a slow stroke, but in a fast down-bow it is simply less complicated if the wrist is more on a level with the bow.

- If the wrist is too low at the point, power may be lost because the energy of the right arm does not get as far as the string. It 'leaks out' at the wrist. Think of a hose that has a puncture: the strength of the jet of water is diminished.

Imagine the wrist drawing a line through the air. In 'hills and valleys' the waviness of the line, above and below the level of the bow, is extreme; in a 'flat' bow arm the line still curves, but much less.

[1] See also *Lower half*, page 265

Experimenting with splints

At the other extreme, some players try to keep the hand and forearm in an almost entirely straight line. It depends on your length of arm, and the angle of the violin, as to whether you can do this comfortably. For most people, a little raising the wrist at the heel, and a little dipping at the point, is a natural middle point between the two extremes of either too arched or too straight.

However, a powerful way to approach the issue is to play for a few minutes with the arm in splints (Fig. 67c). Use a couple of rulers inserted inside the sleeve; and a scarf, or tape, to secure the rulers tightly. Position them so that they go across the hand, ending just before the knuckles, on both sides.

Playing will naturally feel very awkward. The hand can move only sideways, with no vertical movement, and the thumb and fingers have to make exaggerated movements to compensate.

Afterwards, recapture some of this bow arm without the splints. If you are not used to a more flat bow arm, you may be amazed at how uncomplicated and streamlined it feels.

Playing from the hand in the upper half

Playing more deeply into the string by using the hand is a subtle area of technique. Many players simply hold the bow and control it from the arm, perhaps with some hand movements in certain string crossings, but rarely feeling this specific control from the hand.

As soon as they add 'playing from the hand' to their existing bow arm, it always leads to a complete transformation of many different types of bow stroke, and their approach to bowing in general.[1]

[1] See 2. Creating weight from the hand, page 48

Playing from the hand reduces the slight downward curve at the wrist (Fig. 68a), when playing in the upper half. Fig. 68b shows the wrist when it is 'supported'. The amount shown is slightly exaggerated for the sake of clarity: if you can see the wrist raised, it is probably too much.

The downward curve is often more natural than a straight line from the forearm to the back of the hand; but there are two reasons for supporting the wrist to prevent – or at least, to lessen – the curve:

- Playing into the string with the hand, in the upper half, injects tone directly into the string without needing weight from the rest of the arm. This has the effect of raising the wrist slightly, as though trying to create a straight line from the forearm to the back of the hand.

- Supporting the wrist channels power from the arm directly into the string without 'leakage' at the wrist.

[2] See The more delicate, the closer to the fingers, page 48

Supporting the wrist, to produce sensitive and expressive bow contact directly from the hand, rather than from the whole arm, follows the principle of 'the smaller, the closer to the fingers'.[2]

Fig. 68

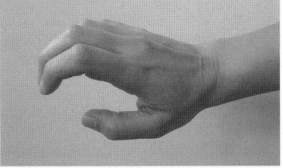 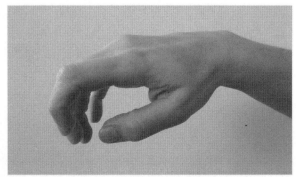

(a) Natural slight downward curve when playing in the upper half   (b) Supporting the wrist to channel power into the string

All the different proportions or combinations of arm weight and hand weight are needed for different strokes and effects: all arm, no hand; all hand, no arm; half arm-weight, half hand; and all the combinations in between.

In the following bowing pattern, which is played near the point with very short, *martelé*-type strokes or *collé*, feel the arm transporting the hand up and down; feel the hand making the strokes:

Kreutzer: 42 Etudes ou caprices, *no. 36, b. 1*

Catch the string with the fingers
and 'playing from the hand'

- To make the accents, bite the string using a combination of forearm rotation (feeling the first and second fingers leaning heavily into the string), and playing from the hand.
- Feel the weight seemingly spread through and across all the fingers evenly.

Imagine a crane on a construction site. The arm of the crane moves horizontally to the place where the hook can descend to pick up the load. Similarly, the right arm transports the hand to the place where the hand can act on the bow as it needs to. This is the basis of the bow arm and 'playing from the hand'.

Warm-up exercise

The movement of the hand in this exercise is so slight as to be almost imperceptible. Before doing it, make a large version of the movement in the air:

Put your arm out in front of you as if playing on the D string, with a straight line from the forearm to the back of the hand (Fig. 69a). Then lower your hand to an angle of 45° while keeping your forearm level with the floor. This is a 'high wrist' (Fig. 69b). Return your hand to the straight-line position.

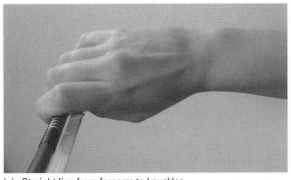 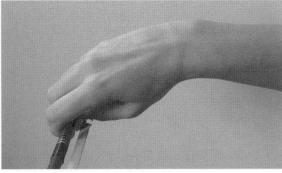

Fig. 69

(a) Straight line from forearm to knuckles   (b) Moving the hand down creates a 'high wrist'

Use a tiny amount of that movement in this exercise. Play the following pattern in the upper half.

- Use only the hand movement to play the stresses. Do not play each note with a fast–slow bow speed: use one, even bow speed for the whole bar. Use the arm to transport the hand and the bow along the string; move the hand down from the wrist to make the sound.
- Lever the bow into the string with the hand moving at the wrist. Do not press the first finger to exert pressure, or turn the hand on to the first finger. Feel the extra weight from the hand distributed evenly amongst the fingers.

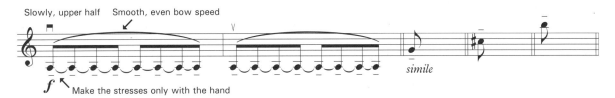

- Play upper-half passages using only hand weight to make the dynamics and bow articulations. Of course the result will be lumpy and impractical in that you cannot actually perform like this, but it is an exaggeration.

Afterwards, add a small amount of this hand movement to whatever else you do with the bow arm in the upper half.

Playing from the back

- The shoulder is a ball-and-socket joint: the rounded ball at the end of the upper arm fits into the shoulder socket and can move in any direction (unlike the elbow joint which works like a hinge and can only open and close).

  Do you have a picture of your bow arm 'beginning' in the shoulder socket?

- Your back and shoulders should remain entirely still while you are moving the bow (apart from any obvious 'follow-through', sympathetic movements). There should be a feeling of only the arm moving, entirely independently of the rest of the body.

  Do you keep everything else still and try to move just your arm?

- The muscles in the upper arm and shoulder are the main ones working to move the arm.

  Do you think of those muscles as being the ones that hold the arm up in the air, as well as being the muscles that move the bow?

Of course you are right to answer 'yes' to these three questions, and yet there is a certain type of awkwardness, or woodenness of movement, that comes from thinking of the bow arm like that. You can bring about an instant transformation if instead you gain a feeling of 'playing from the back'. You can easily get a new picture by doing the following simple experiment:

Fig. 70   **'Window-cleaning' experiment**

Feel bow strokes originating from the lower back

- Place the fingers of your left hand on your left hip joint. Push your thumb into the large muscle on the left of your spine (Fig. 70).

- Then make a window-cleaning movement with your right arm. (Make sure you move your right *upper* arm, not your forearm.) Feel the muscle under your left thumb contracting and releasing as your right arm moves in circles.

This is actually where the bowing movement begins, not in the arm. This is why lengthening the back – and not pulling down, not twisting, and always remaining balanced and supported – has such a positive effect on the bow arm.

Naturally you are not going to be thinking about muscles in your lower back while playing a concert. Having just once gained the picture of the arm not 'beginning' at the shoulder, but working from lower down in the back, you barely need ever to think about it again. But from then on the difference in the feel (and sound) of the bowing is clear.

Setting up the left hand

lesson **6**

Developing a 'classic' left hand

It is natural to think that how your hand looks on the violin is mainly to do with the build of the hand. If it does not look right or feel comfortable you have to accept whatever you were born with, and make the best of it. You cannot make your fingers longer or shorter, or your hand wider or narrower.

Yet almost any hand can look and feel like a 'classic' violin hand. It is more a question of what you do with your hand and what you do not do with it, than of its structure.

 What does a 'classic' violin hand look like?

Because every hand is slightly different everyone finds their own subtly different ways of playing; but whatever the size or shape, a left hand that is set up well on the violin looks natural, balanced, and all-of-a-piece with the instrument. The fingers fall easily and naturally on to the strings without effort or strain, the hand and fingers remaining rounded and soft throughout.

The classic poor hand shape to avoid is the one where you always balance or tilt the hand on to the first finger, with the first and second fingers squeezing together. The third and fourth fingers then almost have to straighten to reach their notes (Fig. 82a, page 139).

You immediately have a different hand on the violin if you base the hand position a little more on the upper fingers and reach back with the lower fingers (Fig. 82b, page 139).

Widening at the base joints: the secret of a good left hand

One of the most important things is that the left hand does not contract, the fingers squeezing together, but that the hand constantly widens at the base joints. It is easy to feel how to do this:

- Hold the left hand in front of you in playing position, the fingers naturally curved (Fig. 71a).

- Keeping the fingers curved, and the second, third and fourth fingers almost touching, move the first finger sideways so that a V-shaped space opens between the base joints of the first and second fingers (Fig. 71b). The same, though less, widening is possible between the other pairs of fingers.

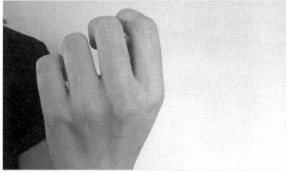 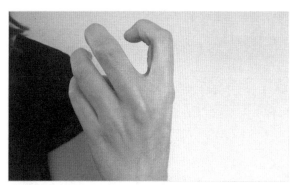

Fig. 71

(a) Begin with the fingers naturally rounded

(b) Move the curved first finger sideways to create a V with the second finger

This possibility of opening between the first and second fingers is one of the most important features of the hand. Tension or squeezing at this place are frequent technical faults found in players of all levels.

Lesson 6: Setting up the left hand **133**

Another approach begins with the fingers straight:

- Begin with the fingers straight and lightly touching each other.

- Move the first finger sideways to form a wide 'V' with the second finger (Fig. 72a).

- Then, while keeping the angle of the 'V' wide but keeping the entire hand as soft as possible, curl the tips of the fingers down (Fig. 72b).

- Make the same angle of the fingers on the back of your hand (Fig. 72c), making sure that you do not squeeze or press between the thumb and the first finger; and then do the same on the violin.

Fig. 72

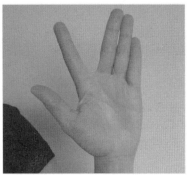 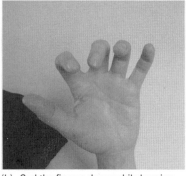 

(a) Make a 'V' with the first and second fingers
(b) Curl the fingers down while keeping the 'V'
(c) Make the same 'V' on the back of your hand

- The greatest possible widening is between the first and second fingers; but you can turn this into a powerful exercise for widening at the base joints by doing the same with the second and third fingers, and with the third and fourth.

Be careful, once you have spread the fingers to form the 'V', when you then curl the fingers down. Doing this for the first few times uses muscles and tendons in a way that they may not be used to.

It would be easy to cause a sprain by **(1)** widening too far all at once, instead of getting there by degrees; **(2)** by curling the fingers down hurriedly; **(3)** by forcing in any way, i.e. forcing the fingers apart while at the same time forcing them down too far.

Q **Should you always be able to see a 'V' shape made by the first and second fingers?**

The habit of squeezing the first and second fingers together is something that gets in the way and holds up the progress of many players, perhaps even the majority. It is one of the first things the average player needs to change if they want to move their playing on to the next level.

However, although the fingers should never squeeze together, whether or how much they should open depends on the passage. Sometimes the hand should open at the base joints, with a space between the first and second finger; sometimes it feels natural if the first and second fingers are more parallel.

For example, in playing sixths the fingers will probably be more parallel (Fig. 73a). Playing them with angled fingers (Fig. 73b) may feel unnatural (unless the fourth finger was just about to be played).

But if you play a trill with the fingers parallel (Fig. 73a), the action may feel far less comfortable or less agile than if you open at the base joints (Fig. 73b).

Fig. 73

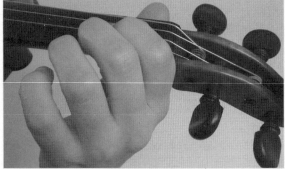 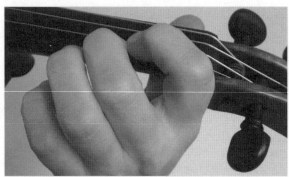

(a) Sixths with less-angled fingers may feel natural
(b) Angling the fingers in sixths may feel awkward

- Find the same angles in the finger-placement in everyday playing.

Separating the fingers

Help students find a new sensation of moving the fingers up and down without squeezing them together, by putting your fingers between theirs while they play simple patterns using all four fingers (Fig. 74).

This sequence covers all the possibilities of moving from one finger to another. Include semitones, since they are the most awkward to play like this:

12, 13, 14, 23, 24, 34; 43, 42, 41, 32, 31, 21

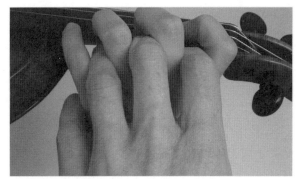

Fig. 74

Keeping the student's fingers apart

Fingertip placement: left, middle, right

Widening at the base joints, and choosing the exact part of the tip of the finger that you place on the string, are like two sides of the same coin. You cannot have one without the other.

Divide the area of the fingertip that contacts the string into three parts: left, middle and right (Fig. 75a).

- If two fingers both sit on the string on the left side of the fingertip, the fingers are more parallel and may touch each other or squeeze together (Fig. 75b).

- If the lower finger sits slightly more on the left side of the finger tip, and the upper finger slightly more on the right side, the fingers open (Fig. 75c).

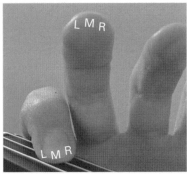

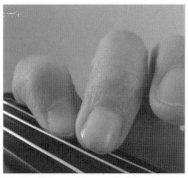

Fig. 75

(a) Left, middle, right, placement of finger on tip

(b) First and second fingers both more on left side of tip

(c) First finger more on left side, second finger more on right

True stories: Andrew

In my first few years of teaching the violin I often had pupils whose left hand did not seem suited to playing the violin. Andrew was one, his left hand looking like the one shown in Fig. 76.

I told him all the right things: do not stick your wrist out, do not stick your elbow out, do not squeeze your fingers together, get your knuckles more parallel with the violin neck, and so on. None of it helped. He could not make any of these changes despite his best efforts to carry out my suggestions.

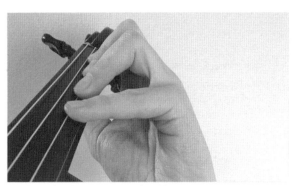

Fig. 76

The fingertip placement is causing this awkward hand position

I decided that he simply did not have the right kind of hands for the violin. That seemed to be the only answer. Then one day I was re-reading *Principles of Violin Playing and Teaching* by Ivan Galamian. I had read this particular section several times before, but this time I suddenly took in what he was saying:

"If the fingertip placement is correct then the arm, hand and fingers all take their natural position automatically."[1]

[1] Ivan Galamian: Principles of Violin Playing and Teaching (New Jersey, 1962), 14.

This was the answer to Andrew's hand position problems, and other students'. He was putting all his fingers down too much on the left side of the fingertip. The effect of this fingertip placement was that his elbow and wrist stuck out, each finger was too parallel to its neighbour, and the angle of the knuckles to the fingerboard was too steep, making the finger action awkward. He needed to place the fingers a little more upright (Fig. 77).

Fig. 77 Although I had been telling him to change the effect, I had not shown him the cause. As long as he kept trying to put his fingers down on that area of the pad, all the other symptoms would remain; but if he made that one, slight alteration, everything else would fall naturally into place.

You can see examples of this uncomfortable hand position in many players. In every case it is caused simply by the fingertip placement.

If the fingertip placement makes the wrist stick out in low positions (there should generally be a straight line from the elbow to the back of the hand), equally if you push your wrist out, you force the fingers on to an incorrect part of the fingertip.

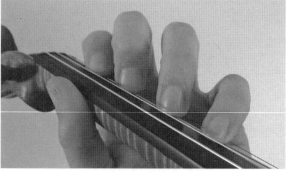

The fingers are more upright on the middle, or bridge side, of the pad

Daily warm-up exercises for widening the hand

Exercise 1

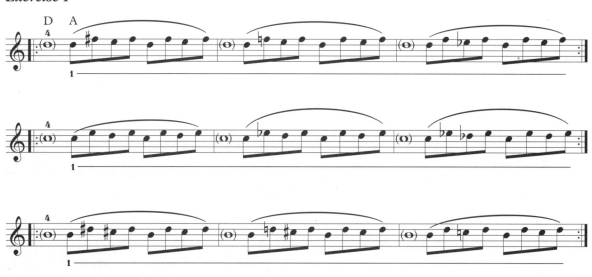

- Hold the fourth finger down on the D string without playing it.

  Keep the hand soft, without counter pressing with the thumb.

- Position the hand to favour the fourth finger so that it is curved, relaxed and comfortable.

- As far as possible, keep the fourth finger curved as you reach back with the other fingers.

- Widen at the base joints by placing the fourth finger very slightly more on the side of the finger furthest from the thumb; place the first finger very slightly more on the side of the finger closest to the thumb.

Exercise 2

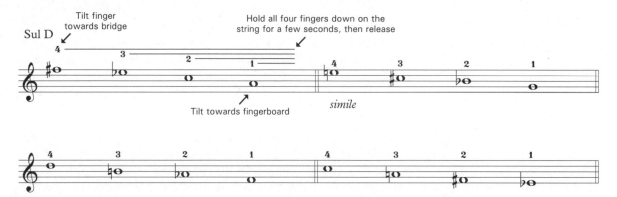

- Hold down the fourth finger, with the entire hand feeling soft and free. Then reach the third finger back as far as you can, and then the second and the first, ending up with all four fingers on the string widely spaced (Fig. 78a).

- Position the hand to favour the fourth finger so that it is curved, relaxed and comfortable. Reaching back with the other fingers, do not disturb the shape or balance of the fourth finger – or at least change as little as possible.

- Exaggerate widening at the base joints by tilting the fourth finger slightly more on to the right side of the finger; tilt the first finger slightly more on to the left side.

- Avoid allowing the hand to collapse back on to the first finger (Fig. 78b). Note the difference in the angle of the base knuckle joints to the neck of the violin in the two pictures.

Fig. 78

(a) Note how the upper three fingers have remained more upright (b) Hand position has collapsed backwards with each new finger

Keeping fingers above the string

The ideal is for the fingers of the left hand to be rounded, and for the shape of a finger not to change as it moves up and down.

Naturally the shape of the finger changes as it reaches over to another string, or when it extends out of position and so on; but the principal up-and-down movement is with a curved finger, moving from the base knuckle joint, without any movement at the middle joint (Fig. 79a).

If the hand is turned away from the neck too far (i.e. the forearm is rotated too far anticlockwise) the fingers have to lengthen forwards as they go down, and curve again as they lift off. See the third or fourth finger in Fig. 79b, or the fourth finger in Fig. 92a, page 157.[1]

[1] The position of the left elbow affects the angle of the knuckles to the fingerboard, which in turn affects whether the fingers have to straighten to reach the strings.

See *The angle of the knuckle joints*, page 144.

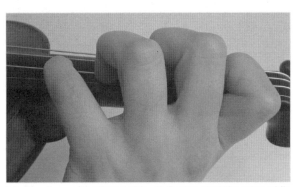

Fig. 79

(a) The shape of the third and fourth fingers stays the same while dropping or lifting (b) The third and fourth fingers straighten and curve to touch or leave the string

The problem is how to keep the fingers hovering above the strings without having to over-rotate the left forearm. The further clockwise the forearm rotates the less freedom there is in the whole arm and hand.

Again, widen the space between the fingers at the base joints and bring the base joint of the fourth closer to the neck. Because of the natural curve of the knuckles, widening helps bring the base knuckle joint of the fourth finger closer in to the neck of the violin without having to use extra forearm rotation.

At first, bringing the base joint closer in and widening the space may feel awkward and unnatural; yet it is actually quite easy to form a new habit which you quickly get used to and forget about.

The following simple exercise rapidly transforms the entire shape and balance of the left hand.

Warm-up exercise: pulling in the base joint

(1) Place the fourth finger, on its tip, high up on the G string somewhere in the region of a B.

Push the base knuckle joint of the fourth finger down as though trying to touch it against the string (Fig. 80a). Allow the base joint to remain soft, giving and 'springy'.

Fig. 80

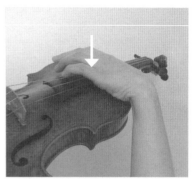 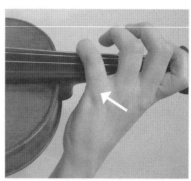 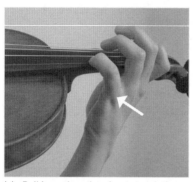

(a) Push down the base joint of the fourth as though trying to touch the fingerboard

(b) Pull the base joint in as though trying to touch the neck of the violin

(c) Pull in as though trying to touch the neck of the violin

(2) Then place the tip of the fourth finger on the note D on the G string (Fig. 80b).

Place it on its tip to ensure that the finger is rounded, not straight or with its base joint sticking out as in Fig. 91a, page 155.

Pull the base joint in as though trying to touch the neck of the violin.

Feel every joint in the finger, hand, and wrist, soft and springy. Do not contract a single muscle anywhere in the hand except those directly required to pull the base joint in towards the neck.

(3) Repeat with the tip of the fourth finger on the D string, on the note A.

(4) Repeat on the A string, on the note E.

(5) Repeat on the E string, on the note B (Fig. 80c).

Fig. 81

If there is any feeling of resistance or difficulty, gradually and continually push against the boundaries (while always remaining gentle and never ever forcing). By progressing little by little, you may be amazed at how quickly you discover an entirely new ability to give and to be free in that part of the hand.

Try practising this on the back of your hand first (Fig. 81). Softening the hand is the first step towards doing anything. Make the whole hand light and soft as you push down into the knuckles and allow them to give.

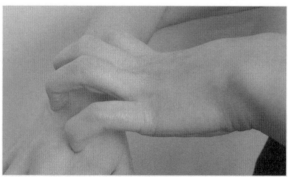

Allow the hand to give at the base joints

Using the exercise during practice

The fourth finger, more than the others, is often more in danger of straightening on certain notes than on other notes, e.g. playing the arrival-note after a descending shift to a fourth:

If the fourth finger tends to end up too straight playing the B♭ after the shift (marked '+'), briefly pull the base joint in as shown in Fig. 80c. Then recapture that feeling when you shift down to the B♭.

Keeping fingers close to the strings

Keep the unused fingers close to the string, i.e. while shifting with the first finger, hover above the string with the fourth finger. If the unused fourth finger were to touch the string, the note should be in tune, or at least nearly in tune.

- Playing the first finger, keep the second, third and fourth fingers close to the strings (Fig. 82a). Do not bunch them all together with the first finger, while at the same time leaning the balance of the hand over on to the first finger (Fig. 82b).

Fig. 82

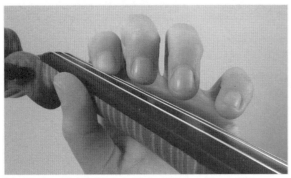

(a) The hand is balanced on the first finger, with good finger distribution

(b) The first and second fingers are squeezing together, as are the thumb and first finger

- Playing the second finger, keep the first, third and fourth fingers close to the strings (Fig. 82c). Do not squeeze the third and fourth together with the first finger (Fig. 82d).

(c) The hand is balanced on the second finger

(d) The second, third and fourth fingers should not squeeze together

- Playing the third finger, keep the first, second and fourth fingers close to the strings (Fig. 82e). Do not squeeze the fourth finger together with the third finger (Fig. 82f); do not tilt it towards the bridge (Fig. 82g).

(e) The hand is balanced on the third, which is independent of the fourth

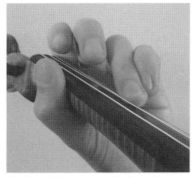

(f) Hand tilted towards the first; third and fourth are squeezing together

(g) The finger should not tilt towards the bridge

- Playing the fourth finger, keep the first finger close to the string, and keep the third finger apart from the fourth (Fig. 83a). Play more on the tip of the fourth than on the pad, so that the finger remains curved.[1] Playing too much on the pad causes not only the fourth finger to straighten, but makes the others want to straighten as well (Fig. 83b). Do not tilt it towards the bridge (Fig. 83c).

- Elementary players often need to be reminded not to let the fourth finger stray off underneath the neck (Fig. 83d), or leave it resting it on top of the third finger (Fig. 83e). Find a sense of widening the space between the bass knuckle joints of the third and fourth fingers (Fig. 83f).

[1] See *Aiming onto the tip or pad*, page 158

Fig. 83

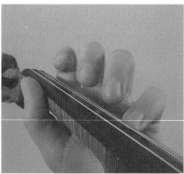
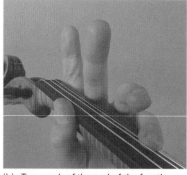
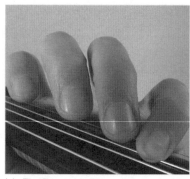

(a) The hand is balanced on the fourth finger

(b) Too much of the pad of the fourth is on the string; the first and second have tensed backwards

(c) The finger should not tilt towards the bridge

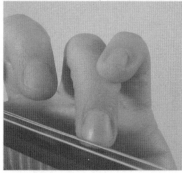

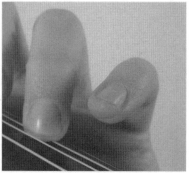

(d) The fourth finger should not rest on top of the third

(e) The fourth finger must not go underneath the neck

(f) Widen at the base joints between the third and fourth fingers

Fig. 84 **Preventing the fingers from lifting**

Help students find a new feeling of playing with their fingers very close to the strings by cupping your hand over theirs for a few moments while they play (Fig. 84). Forcibly prevent the fingers from lifting more than the slightest amount.

They might play a scale in one position, or a scale in broken thirds, or a passage in one position from a piece. They can even play a passage that includes shifts if you move with them as they change position.

It will probably all sound terrible as the fingers do

Prevent the fingers from lifting

not clear the strings properly and the fingers are cramped and unable to move properly. But afterwards, with the constraining hand removed, it is easy to recapture the feeling of keeping the fingers close to the strings.

Setting the left hand position using double stops

The 18th-century approach

In the eighteenth century the Geminiani chord was a standard way to find the position of the left hand:

> ...a Method of acquiring the true Position of the Hand, which is this: To place the first Finger on the first String upon F; the second Finger on the second String upon C; the third Finger on the third String upon G; and the fourth Finger on the fourth String upon D. This must be done without raising any of the Fingers, till all four have been set down; but after that, they are to be raised but a little Distance from the String they touched; and by so doing the Position is perfect.[1]

[1] Francesco Geminiani: *The Art of Playing on the Violin* (London, 1751; Facsimile edition, David D. Boyden, London 1952), 3.

In Germany in 1756 Leopold Mozart gave similar advice, and made a little exercise out of it. After giving the same instructions to place the first finger on F, the second on C and so on, he continues:

> ...in such a fashion that none are lifted, but all four fingers lie simultaneously on the right spot. Then try to lift first the index-finger, then the third; soon the second, and then the fourth, and to let them fall again at once, but without moving the other three from their places. The finger must be lifted at least so high as not to touch the string and you will see that this exercise is the shortest way to acquire the true position of the hand and that thereby one achieves an extraordinary facility in playing double stopping in tune when the moment arrives.[2]

[2] Leopold Mozart: *A Treatise On The Fundamental Principles Of Violin Playing* (Augsburg, 1756; Eng. Trans. Editha Knocker, Oxford, 1948), 57.

Given the benefits of reaching back from the upper finger, both Geminiani's and Mozart's instruction to begin with the first, and then place the second, third and fourth in that order, is not good advice. If you begin with the hand balanced to favour the first finger, and then reach forward from there to find the other notes, there is a danger that you will end up in the position shown in Fig. 85a.

Instead, it is completely different if you begin with the fourth finger, and only then reach back with the third, second and first fingers in that order (Fig. 85b).

- Before placing the other fingers, make sure the fourth is curved. Then, as you reach back with the lower fingers, change the curve of the fourth finger as little as possible.

Fig. 85

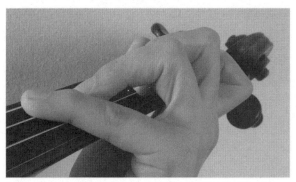

(a) The hand is based on the first finger with the other fingers reaching forward

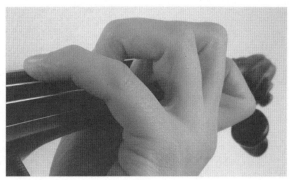

(b) The hand is based on the fourth finger with the other fingers reaching back

Clearly you cannot play with the hand fixed in this position;[1] but after setting it in this exaggerated shape for a few moments a normal, 'middle' position feels more comfortable than usual. A less drastic approach is to place all four fingers on one string:

- Place the fourth finger on, say, A on the D string. Then place underneath it the third finger on G, the second on F, and the first on E (Fig. 86a).

- Leave the first down and lift the second, third and fourth fingers just above the string (Fig. 86b).

Fig. 86

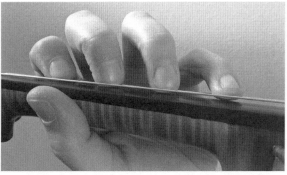

(a) Having placed the fourth, third, second, and first finger, in that order, on the D string

(b) Leaving the first finger down, raise the second, third, and fourth fingers just clear of the string

Practising thirds, fourths, sixths

Another way to build a good left hand position is to practise double stops. Thirds are an obvious choice, but broken sixths and fourths are good for this too.

(1)   (2)   (3)

4-2 almost touching the strings while playing 3-1   3-4 almost touching the strings while playing 1-2   3-4 almost touching the strings while playing 1-2

(1) While playing one double stop, hover the fingers of the next interval over their notes almost touching the string. For example in thirds, while you play 1–3 keep the fourth and second fingers curved (Fig. 87a) not straight (Fig. 87b).

Note the open space between the first and second fingers in Fig. 87a.

(2) Practising broken sixths hover 3–4 over their notes, almost touching the strings, while you play 1–2.

(3) Broken fourths may be even more helpful at encouraging the fingers to stay above the strings because you have to bring the hand round much further

[1] The German violinist Andreas Moser commented on this position of the hand in 1905: 'Since Corelli's pupil, Geminiani, in his Violin School of 1740, identified [this chord] with the normal position of the fingers of the left hand, this notorious "grip" has wrought confusion in all the later treatises, most of which are based on Geminiani. In the time of our forefather, however, this position of the left hand was by no means so absurd…the neck of the violin was, until well into the second half of the eighteenth century, two or three centimetres shorter than it is at present…to play this chord in the first position involved only that stretch, which would nowadays be required were it played in the third or fourth position. Every experienced teacher must have observed that not one half of his pupils can execute without effort the Geminiani "grip" on the violin of today, with its increased dimensions, and that indeed the position causes difficulty to many a distinguished violinist all through his life.'

Joachim–Moser: *Violinschule* (Berlin 1905), 10.

Fig. 87

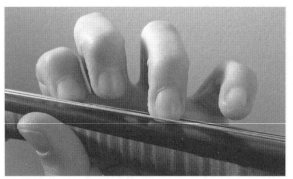

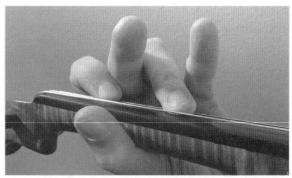

(a) Keep the 'hovering' fingers curved

(b) Straightening the fingers is both a cause and effect of tension

What is the correct position of the left elbow?

Keeping the upper arm free

The left elbow should be mobile underneath the violin, which is called 'elbow steering'. A locked, immovable left upper arm is a common (and highly visible) technical feature which is easy to improve.

The correct position of the left elbow (i.e. upper arm), changes according to finger, string and position. There are three basic principles:

(1) The elbow is more to the left when the fingers are playing on the E string; more to the right when playing on the G string.

(2) The elbow is more to the left when playing in lower positions; more to the right in higher positions.

(3) To a certain extent, or at certain times, the elbow is slightly more to the left when playing on the first finger, and more to the right when playing on the fourth finger. (More often, though, it is desirable to have one hand position for all four fingers, the fourth finger hovering close to the string while you play the first finger.)

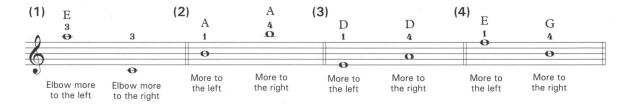

(4) Therefore the elbow would be most to the left when playing first-finger F on the E string, and most to the right when playing a note high on the G string with the fourth finger.

Playing from a lower to a higher string

There is no problem in the elbow getting stuck in one place playing down the strings in the direction E–A–D–G, but only playing up from the G string to the E string.

• Suppose you are playing on the E string, with the elbow and hand in the E string position (Fig. 88a), and then you move to the G string (Fig. 88b). There is no danger that you would try to move only the hand or fingers to the G string, while leaving the elbow in the E string position, because you cannot reach the G string like that.

• But suppose you are playing with the elbow and hand in the G string position, and then move to the E string. You have to be careful that you do not move only the hand to get to the E string, ending up with the hand and wrist as shown in Fig. 88c.

In a passage like the following, it is common to see somebody start off in a good position (Fig. 88a), and play down to the G string with the elbow naturally following; but then leave the elbow behind as they play back up to the E string (Fig. 88c):

Fig. 88

(a) The hand and elbow in the E string position

(b) The hand and elbow in the G string position

(c) Moving only the hand to the E string, leaving the elbow in the G string position

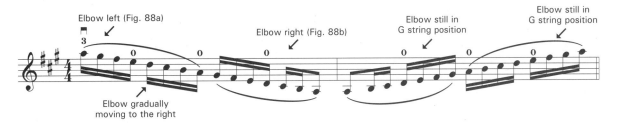

Getting stuck when shifting down

Many players start off in a low position with the elbow correctly to the left; shift up into high positions with the elbow moving naturally to the right; but then keep the elbow fixed to the right as they shift back down again, without allowing the elbow to return to where it started:

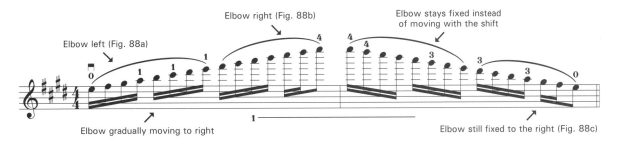

- To focus on the sensation of the upper arm adjusting under the violin, use a two-octave *glissando*, keeping the finger as light on the string as if playing a harmonic:

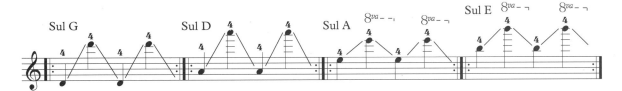

- 'Swing' the arm underneath the violin from more to the left (lower position) to more to the right (higher position).

Finding the position by 'hanging' the arm

Fig. 89

Support the scroll

Rest the scroll on a shelf or other support, or hold the scroll with your right hand (Fig. 89).

- Using, say, the third finger of your left hand, make the finger into a kind of hook, and 'hang' the arm from the fingerboard on it. Make the finger quite stiff and strong, while the rest of the hand and arm hangs loosely with a feeling of 'flop'.

- Notice how, if you hang the arm from the finger on the E string, the elbow naturally finds its correct, balanced position more to the left. If you hang from the same finger on the G string, the elbow will automatically find a new position more to the right.

- Hang from each finger shown in numbers **(1)**–**(4)**, *Keeping the upper arm free* (page 142), and notice how the elbow hangs in a different position each time. Whatever position the elbow naturally finds for itself will usually be the best position for playing that particularly finger, in that position, on that string.

The position of the elbow that is best for one single note may not be exactly the same as the best position for a group of notes; but by 'hanging' in this way from a single finger you will be close enough for it to be a good guide as to where the elbow should be for a phrase as well.

The angle of the knuckle joints

The position of the left elbow also affects the angle of the knuckle joints to the neck of the violin: the more to the left the elbow, the more parallel the knuckles are to the neck (Fig. 90a). If you pull the upper arm in too far to the right the knuckles may be at 45° to the neck (Fig. 90b).

Fig. 90

 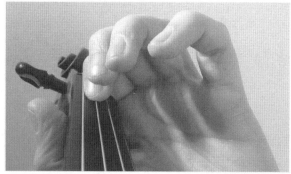

(a) Good angle of the knuckles to the neck of the violin

(b) The position of the elbow, too far to the right, is making the knuckle joints too tilted

The angle of the knuckles has a direct effect on the action of the fingers. If the elbow is positioned too much to the right when playing on the upper strings, the knuckles become too tilted and the fingers then have to straighten slightly as they drop, in order to reach the strings. One of the principles of good left-hand finger-action is that the shape of the finger on the string, and the shape of the finger when it is lifted, remains more or less the same.[1]

[1] See *Keeping fingers above the string*, page 137

Remember that where the elbow should be depends on the tilt of the violin. The flatter the violin, the more to the right the elbow needs to go.

A further knock-on effect of the elbow position, and therefore the tilt of the knuckles, is the amount of space between the fingers: the less tilted the hand in relation to the neck, the more the fingers can widen at the base joints, giving freedom and independence to each finger. The more tilted the knuckles, and therefore the more straightening the fingers as they reach the strings, the less space there can be between the fingers.

Of course there is no one setting that is correct. It depends entirely on what you are playing, and each player has to find the right balance for their hand, between the knuckles being too parallel with the neck, and them being too much at an angle.

How can I get my fingers and bow to work together better?

Co-ordination

One of the first issues facing the beginner is that of having to do one thing with one hand while doing something else with the other. This remains an issue even in the most advanced playing.

'Co-ordination' refers to timing the left finger and the bow to work together perfectly.

The left finger stops the string at a certain distance from the bridge to create a certain pitch; only when this string length has been fully established should the bow set that string into vibration.

Poor co-ordination is nearly always a question of the bow already beginning to play a note before the finger has fully stopped the string. It is rarely the result of the finger being too early.

Leading from the fingertip

Feel your way around the fingerboard by going from one left fingertip sensation to another.

[2] See *Leading from the fingertip*, page 234

Clearly you have to feel the string with the fingertip when shifting,[2] but you can focus on two sensations in the fingertip when playing in one position:

- When playing ascending slurs on one string, the fingers fall on to an already-vibrating string. There is a momentary tingle in the fingertip as the finger stops the string. You can also find a slight tingle as the finger lifts during a descending slur, particularly when playing f.

- Playing all other notes – descending slurred or separate bows, or ascending separate bows – the finger is placed on to a motionless (or near motionless) string.

Part of the sensation is the give of the flesh of the finger; part is in the give of the string.

Everything else follows from that initial clear feeling of the physical contact of the tip of the finger contacting the string. The fingertip contact is the trigger without which nothing in the bow should begin.

Practising by opposites: overlapping

When co-ordination is less than perfect, the finger is always very slightly late for the bow; so practising by doing the opposite would mean putting the finger down very slightly too early.[1] This produces a dotted effect and is called overlapping:

Fiocco: Allegro, b. 18

When you practise by overlapping, the aim is to try to put the fingers down the same degree too early as they might have been too late, i.e. only an instant too early:

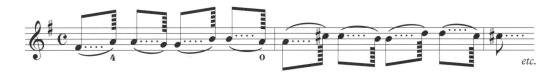

The most important thing to focus on is the sense of the bow following the fingers. Use this practice method on almost any type of passage when the finger and bow need to connect better.

Reinventing the wheel

When I show students the 'overlapping' practice method, I sometimes tell them about a conversation I had with my friend Bogusluv during a rehearsal break. Bogusluv was an excellent Polish violinist who had played the Wieniawski F♯ minor Concerto on the radio when he was 17.

I mentioned how Emanuel Hurwitz often said to me that, in a field as old as violin playing, it is impossible to discover anything new, and that the most you can hope for is to bring to the present and future generations the findings of the previous ones; but, I said to Bogusluv, I was proud to be able to say that I felt that I had indeed discovered original ways of thinking about the violin or of practising, and that many of the exercises in *Basics*, and practice methods in *Practice*, are in fact original.

'Tell me, please, an example of an original idea you have had,' said Bogusluv in a disbelieving voice.

I showed him overlapping practice.

He listened to my description and explanation without saying a word. 'Huh!' he said at the end. 'I was taught that in Warsaw 30 years ago!'

I told Hurwitz this story.

'And Yankelevich was teaching it in Moscow 30 years before that!' he said.[2]

Finger preparation: the secret of legato

Before I went to study with Yfrah Neaman as an undergraduate at the Guildhall School of Music, I happened to hear him playing on the radio one day. I noticed a striking and beautiful quality of seamless legato in his playing.

Soon after I had begun to work with him, I asked him how to develop that quality of smoothness.

'Finger preparation is the answer,' he said. 'You should always have the fingers ready on the string in advance of playing them.'

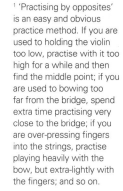

[1] 'Practising by opposites' is an easy and obvious practice method. If you are used to holding the violin too low, practise with it too high for a while and then find the middle point; if you are used to bowing too far from the bridge, spend extra time practising very close to the bridge; if you are over-pressing fingers into the strings, practise playing heavily with the bow, but extra-lightly with the fingers; and so on.

[2] Nevertheless, I still maintain that many of the exercises in *Basics* or here, or practice methods in *Practice*, are entirely original in the sense that it seems impossible to find them elsewhere – certainly not in print, but neither is there ever any evidence of them having being taught verbally. Of course, great players have played in the ways that these methods encourage you to play, but they did it instinctively and without knowing or being able to say exactly what they were doing.

Q **What is finger preparation?**

Finger preparation means that you get the finger ready on the string before the bow sets the string into vibration. The left fingers lead the bow and the bow follows.

If you play the piano or the harp, all the different string lengths you might need – all the notes – are already there, waiting for you should you wish to play them.

Playing the violin, you have to create the different string lengths as you need them. First you stop the string, and then you bow or pluck it in order to hear the note.

The finger must be there first. You cannot play, with a clean tone, a string length that has not yet been completely stopped.

Stepping down a ladder: one finger; two fingers; one finger

- When you step down a ladder, you lift one foot off the rung you are standing on, and put all of your weight into the foot remaining on the rung. For a moment you have only one foot on the ladder.

- While you stand on that one foot, you place the other foot on the rung below. For a moment you have two feet on the ladder, your weight partly going into the upper rung, partly into the lower.

- Having positioned the foot on the lower rung, you then remove the foot from the upper rung and put all of your weight into the lower foot. Now you have only one foot on the ladder again.

Finger preparation works in a similar way: first you have one finger on the string; then you place a lower finger, so now you have two fingers on the string; then you lift the upper finger (to uncover the lower finger), so you have only one finger on the string again.

Brahms: Sonata no. 3 in D minor, op. 108, *mov. 2, b. 1*

The notes to prepare

- Playing any descending notes – e.g. in a descending scale or arpeggio – the next finger that is about to be played needs to be placed on the string before you lift the current finger.

[1] See also *Finger preparation*, page 202

- Any first note on a new string must always be stopped before the bow plays it:[1]

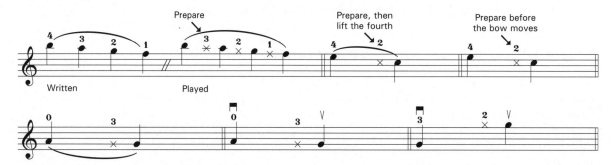

The important thing is to know the type of places where there may be a danger of the finger being late. For example, in an ascending scale the first finger must not be late on each new string (shown as '+'):

● Practise preparing and placing fingers exaggeratedly early, like a syncopation:

● Descending, all the fingers need to be prepared, but pay particular attention to the fourth finger:

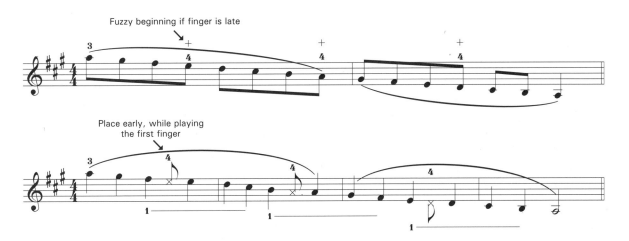

Oddly, teachers who continually stress the need and value of finger preparation are rare. It seems that most players or teachers never mention it.[1] This might be because finger preparation is one of those technical issues where you can get the same result whether you work from a musical or a technical angle. If you concentrate on wanting a seamless, legato quality, the fingers may automatically and naturally prepare; or, doing it the other way round, because you prepare your fingers you get a seamless, legato quality.

Clearly, there is magic and artistry in preparing fingers the 'musical' way. Getting there by means of a conscious, controlling, 'placing the finger early' technique, or by practising exercises, seems to some musicians as too detached or intellectual, rather than artistic or expressive.

They argue that if you listen carefully to your sound you will instinctively prepare: while practising, the student hears the slightly raspy sound at the beginning of the note which comes from bowing the incompletely-stopped string and, not liking the impurity, they find how to make the note sound pure without actually knowing what they did to put it right.

So if you listen properly you don't need to know about 'finger preparation'. And what is the correct timing anyway? 'Just in time' is good enough for a pure-sounding note; so if you look at it like that, finger preparation becomes just part of good co-ordination.

Yet even otherwise advanced students often do not prepare fingers well, and the effect of playing a half-stopped string for an instant is plainly audible. Despite the fact that they can run up and down the fingerboard with ease, if you listen closely you can hear many notes that are not actually pure, and one of the reasons for these constant impurities is simply the lack of good finger preparation.

There is no harm in concentrating on preparing fingers until it becomes a habit, so that afterwards you can forget about it again, and, you can easily instil finger preparation into your playing with simple warm-up exercises. They quickly engrain the habit so that preparation happens automatically in the normal course of playing, without you having to think about it.

[1] The classic objection to thinking about technique on this minute level of detail is that if a centipede began to think about which leg to put forward next, he would soon get confused and be unable to walk. In the same way, as the objection goes, if you think about how to play every note and make too many conscious directions, it is impossible to play the violin. Therefore, finger preparation should be left to instinct.

Typical warm-up exercises

● Place and lift the silent x-note fingers in time underneath the playing fingers:

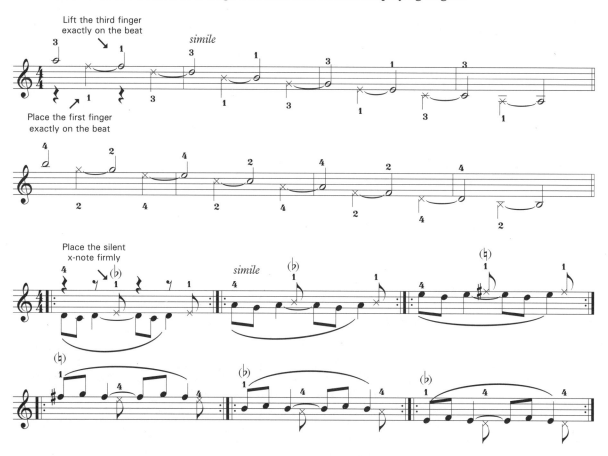

Pizzicato practice

Curiously, while poor co-ordination in bowed passages is something that for most players crops up again and again, when we play *pizzicato* there is a sort of natural instinct that makes us unable to pluck the string before getting the left finger firmly in place. Unless the tempo becomes too fast there is an automatic feeling of stop-the-string – pluck; stop – pluck; with never any danger of pluck – stop.

Try plucking a moderately-fast scale, or a passage from a piece: notice how you always place the left fingers just before the pluck, and how clever the timing is, even at speed – left fingers and plucking finger moving absolutely regularly and at the same speed, but just slightly apart in timing.

Using *pizzicato* as a practice method

Practising bowed passages with *pizzicato* seems to be a little-known practice method, but it brings instant and obvious improvement. It works so well because the timing of the co-ordination that you automatically fall into when you play a passage *pizzicato*, remains with you afterwards when you play it again with the bow.

Also, since plucked notes ring better the more the string is stopped, *pizzicato* is an exception to the rule of minimum finger-pressure. Of course, you may want to produce a veiled, non-ringing *pizzicato* by only half stopping the string, but for maximum ring you need as good a stop as possible.[1]

The extra weight that you automatically use to stop the string, when playing the *pizzicato*, also stays with you when you play the passage again with the bow, but without it making you feel as though you are over-pressing. Rather, it is more a new feeling of strength, and a sort of confidence in knowing exactly where the note is on the string under the finger.

● Take a problematic passage from a study, piece or concerto; practise it for a short while using only *pizzicato*; then play it again with the bow. You will undoubtedly notice an immediate improvement in all respects, not just in co-ordination.

Spiccato

In *spiccato* passages, the bow is usually blamed when certain notes scratch, or the sound is splashy or not ringing. Sometimes it may be the bow or bow-arm's fault, but just as often the cause actually lies with the left finger being slightly late to the bow, so that the string is not properly stopped; yet for the purest, most ringing *spiccato* you need to stop the string firmly, almost as in playing *pizzicato*.

[1] In normal playing the correct amount of finger-pressure is always 'as little as possible', i.e. just enough to make the tone entirely pure. Sometimes we might want to use more than that, to change the tone quality or as part of rhythmic emphasis in the left hand, but continual over-pressing is obviously a waste of energy and may cause tension.

See *How can I stop pressing the strings too hard?*, page 189

So *spiccato* passages benefit very well from short bursts of *pizzicato* practice. Afterwards, you may be surprised at how well co-ordinated the bow is with the finger, and how pure the *spiccato* note sounds.[1]

Once you discover the quick results that *pizzicato*-practice brings, you may find yourself using it regularly throughout every practice session.

[1] See also *Pizzicato*, page 287

Leaving fingers down on the string

One of the great secrets of left hand ease and security is the art of keeping fingers down on the string. As a general rule avoid the feeling of 'playing the piano on the violin', i.e. one finger automatically coming up as the next finger goes down. It is true that sometimes left finger action on the violin is similar to keyboard finger action (particularly in the very fastest passages), but the moment you start to keep fingers down as anchors, or when you prepare fingers on the string ahead of playing them, the action on the fingerboard is markedly different from that of playing the piano.

Holding fingers down on the string gives the hand a point on which to balance, and from which to measure other fingers. Look at the trouble the Belgian violinist Léonarde went to, to mark all the held-down fingers in a simple scale or passage of broken thirds:[2]

[2] H. Léonard: *La Gymnastique du Violiniste* (Mainz, 1911), 21, 23

(The 'diamond head' notes are Léonarde's instruction to place the first finger on two strings, rather than placing it only on one string and then picking it up and replacing it on the next.)[3]

[3] See *Placing the fifth for single notes*, page 312

One argument against holding fingers down is that vibrato is freer if you have fewer fingers on the string. A single stop is easier to vibrate than a double stop, which is easier than a triple stop. Holding fingers down, in a single-note passage, makes it feel as though you are playing chords.

The answer must be that sometimes you hold fingers down and sometimes you do not. But while it is often good or natural to let fingers off the string when they are not used, it is safest to have a default that you hold fingers down – so that lifting is the exception – rather than the other way round.

- One finger to leave down whenever you can is the first finger, which gives a great feeling of stability. In a three-octave scale the first finger can stay on the string the whole time, except for the brief moment before it is needed on a new string.

- Ascending, the fourth finger should stay on the string while you cross to the next higher string.[4]

[4] See *Holding down the first and fourth fingers*, page 302

Hold fingers down at the top of a scale, otherwise you have to find each of the notes again:

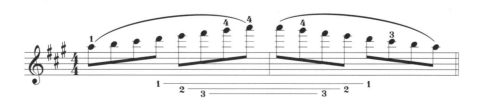

You would not leave your first finger down in the opening of the Tchaikovsky Concerto, even though you are returning to it after the second note:

But in moderate-speed passages save energy, and make tuning consistent, by keeping fingers down on the string just as often as you allow them to come up immediately.

Practise holding fingers down even if in the end it might be more natural to let them come off the string a little. Afterwards, when you are playing musically and listening, and not thinking about your fingers, they will stay down or lift as a matter of instinct; and anyway, the held-down fingers touch the string so lightly that often you will not know whether the finger is actually on the string or not.

String crossing

Keeping fingers down on the string is part of the technique of playing from one string to another. It is easiest to see this principle in slurred notes but it applies equally to separate bows too. For example, in an arpeggio the finger on the lower string must remain in place until the new finger on the new string is actually played:

- Try doing it the 'wrong' way deliberately: lift the third finger at the same time as you place the first finger. Even if you try very hard to play smoothly and evenly, with either slurred or separate bows, notice how there is no real connection between the notes.

- Then see how very much smoother and more even it is when you do leave the third finger down until after beginning to play the first finger.

The importance of keeping the finger on the previous string a little longer becomes obvious when you consider that when the notes in a string-crossing are joined seamlessly within a slur, for a brief moment the two separate notes are played together as a double stop.

One of the pieces that post-graduate students often bring is the Mozart D major violin concerto, since this is a typical audition piece for jobs in orchestras. You would think that by the time the student is at this stage, such a simple thing as finger preparation would be automatic and no longer an issue. Yet time after time one hears the following:

[1] See *Understanding technical and musical timing*, page 205

The problem is that they are placing the second finger F♯ on the D string at the same time as bowing the note, and placing the third finger G at the same time as lifting the fourth finger A. The key point is that there are two types of timing: technical timing and musical timing. Musical timing is when you want the notes to sound, but technical timing is earlier: the finger must be placed before you want to hear it.[1]

Holding fingers down on the string is a close cousin of finger preparation, and in this same Mozart example the first finger A must be held down on the string until after the F♯ has begun to be played, even though the note will not be played again. It is simply impossible to play a true legato between the two notes if the first finger A lifts off the string before the second finger F♯ is in place.

Try it for yourself and see: first, try to play a real legato but lift the first finger as you drop the second finger. Then do it again, this time holding the first finger down. The difference is obvious. But since countless advanced students make the elementary mistake of lifting the first finger as they drop the second finger, the 'listening without knowing what you are doing' approach does seem to be inadequate (unless you are a Yehudi Menuhin or Joseph Hassid).

As usual, the way to practise it lies in exaggeration: play a longer double stop and gradually shorten it:

You can make this principle into a quick all-combination warm-up exercise:

Add different key signatures, and also play the exercise on the other pairs of strings.

How can I improve my trills?

Picture the perfect trill

The first step, before performing any action, is to picture the result you want; and then, while performing the action, to keep on 'seeing it perfect' in your mind.

When you are not happy with a trill, e.g. it is too slow, or the finger feels tight, and you would like to improve it, what typically happens is that all you do is see, hear and feel what is happening in the finger or the sound – you fill your mind with images of what is already happening.

Instead, if first you visualise a perfect trill, and see it as clearly as if it really is happening like that – and then if you continue to hold that image in your mind as you play the actual trill – the immediate improvement in the trill is always obvious.

Here are some of the factors that may be included in your picture of the trill:

- Every note is clear and clean
- The hand is entirely relaxed, free and balanced
- The wrist is free, neither pushing out nor collapsing in
- The thumb does not squeeze against the neck
- The trilling finger stays close to the string
- The held-down finger remains light and springy
- The fingers move freely from the base joints
- Each pair of fingers plays as good a trill as every other
- The fingers can trill very fast
- At any speed the trill is rhythmically even

The student plays a trill. It is uneven and slow (not enough notes), and the intonation is unsteady. You ask them to stop and to 'picture it perfect'. The picture must be full of detail, rather than just a hope or a vague, undefined 'wish'.

When they begin again, the accuracy of the trill and the speed, ease and smoothness, is always much better than the previous time.

To make the trill better still, repeat the process, continuing to refine and perfect the inner picture of what you want to do. With each improvement in the picture, the actual trill will improve as well.

Practise the trill exercise

The trill exercise is easy and straightforward, yet trains all the essential components of the trill.

- First play only one note in the trill – i.e. begin with a mordant – and then two notes (a double mordant), three notes, four, five, six, seven, and eight.

Stage 1

(1) Before dropping the finger raise it slightly – like raising a hammer before striking with it.

(2) Drop the finger very fast, and lift off very fast, as though testing something hot with your finger.

(3) Release the finger back to a natural place just above the string, i.e. go back to the starting place, before you raised your finger in **(1)**.

Stage 2

(1) Raise the finger slightly before dropping it. **(2)** Drop the finger fast. **(3)** Raise the finger just enough to clear the string. **(4)** Drop fast. **(5)** Lift off fast, and release the finger back to the starting place.

Stage 3

(1) Raise the finger slightly.

(2) Drop fast.

(3) Raise just enough to clear the string.

(4) Drop fast.

(5) Raise just enough to clear the string.

(6) Drop fast.

(7) Lift off fast, and release the finger back to the starting place. Continue adding notes until it becomes a continuous trill.

Although Dorothy DeLay called this 'the trill exercise', it is more than that since it improves all kinds of things in the left hand, e.g. the speed of the finger movement, the movement of the finger from the base joint, the clarity of fast notes, and localization of activity in the left fingers.

Try practising the trill exercise using all the finger combinations (01 – 02 – 03 – 04; 12 – 13 – 14; 23 – 24; 34). Afterwards you will notice your left hand feels very light, free and accurate.

Other work on trills

1 See *Tapping exercises*, page 187

- Tapping exercises make the fingers feel light, quick and free, so they naturally help trills.[1]
- Practise Ševčík-type repetitive finger patterns
- Learn and continually re-visit all the Kayser, Kreutzer and Dont trill studies, as well as any other trill studies you can find in the technical literature:

  Kayser: 4, 15, 22; Kreutzer: 9, 15–22, 40; Dont: 6, 9, 15, 22

Fast fingers: the key to a great left hand

One way to measure or assess technique is to look at the speed of the movements of the left hand. You want fingers that move with quickness and alacrity; light, quick shifts, and fast, narrow vibrato. There is also the question of the degree of energy in the bow speed, particularly at the beginning of accented strokes.

It is relatively easy to improve someone's playing considerably simply by concentrating on speeding up these key areas. Then the entire energy and brilliance of the playing increases. Of course, there are as many musical occasions when you want slower fingers, slower shifts and slower vibrato, but what we are talking about here is how to bring more life and brilliance into the playing in general.

'Fast fingers' is to do with the speed of the left hand finger movements. Sometimes it is also about the timing of shifting, but it is mainly a sort of 'waiting' before moving a finger, and then a fast movement of that finger.

Fast fingers is one of those things that is obvious once you see it; but until then it may be so subtle that you miss it entirely. Compare any two players – one who is not yet very advanced with one that is more advanced. The more-advanced player will undoubtedly be moving their fingers faster. Any of the top players move their fingers very, very fast, with no resistance anywhere in the hand or fingers that would cause heaviness or sluggishness. Without that, they could not be a 'top' player in the first place.

Training fingers to move quickly is one of the 'master methods' of improving the left hand.

 Why is 'fast fingers' so important or beneficial?

If you want to arrive somewhere at 09.00, and it is going to take you 60 minutes to walk there, you will have to leave at 08.00; but if you decide to take a taxi, you may be able to leave instead at 08.45. You can leave later because you will get there faster.

In the same way, developing fast fingers transforms your playing because it makes everything feel slower:

- The faster the fingers move, the later they can move and still arrive in time
- The later they move, the longer you can wait between each movement
- The longer you can wait between each movement, the slower the passage feels.
- The slower the passage feels, the more time you have to think, and the more in control you feel.

By speeding up all the movements, an extraordinary lightness, quickness and ease comes into the hand.

 How can I develop fast fingers?

It is easy to build fast fingers into your technique. You can practise fast fingers directly into a piece; or instead of that, or as well as, you can practise fast-finger exercises.

- To practise fast fingers into a phrase or passage, simply play at a very slow overall tempo but move the fingers very late and very fast. The feeling is one of moving at the last possible moment: if you were to move an instant later, you would not get there in time.

- Before placing the finger on the string – or before moving it across to another string, or whatever the movement of the finger – keep the finger still for as long as possible before moving; then go so fast that there is only a blur as the finger moves.

If you practise like this for only a short while, you will notice a striking difference in the movement of the finger and the feel of the hand when you play normally again. Even better, the gain in facility is also clear in everything else you play.

Making a 'ping' with fast fingers

There are also tonal benefits in playing with fast fingers. Notes that are slurred under one bow gain a new clarity and articulation as the finger drops on to the string or lifts from it.

- Sustain long bows, playing first-finger B in 1st position on the A string. Play loudly, using fast bow strokes and experimenting with balances of speed–pressure–soundpoint until the string vibrates as widely as possible.

- Get ready to drop the fourth finger on to the string on the note E. Before dropping the finger, look at the place on the string where it is going to land. See how widely the string is vibrating there. The finger must actually 'stop' the string.

When it does this very, very quickly, there is the sound of a sort of 'pop' or 'ping' as the finger contacts the string and the new note begins. This is similar to the satisfying 'pop' as the tone hole on a flute is opened or closed[1]. Feel the momentary 'tingle' of the vibrating string on the pad of the finger as it first contacts the string.

Make sure the finger drops during a stroke, not at the same time as changing bow.

[1] Flautists as well as string players can suffer from notes not sounding well due to a faulty stop. The metal key cup (the part of the flute which comes down to close the tone hole) has a felt pad which closes off the hole completely, creating a hermetic seal. If the pad is not seated correctly in the key cup, there will be an air leak when closed that will affect the quality of the note it produces. This is similar to the sound of a finger, during a slur, stopping or unstopping the string too slowly.

- Having played the E, play a few more fast strokes to make the string vibrate widely, and then lift off again very, very fast. Notice the 'ping' as the finger leaves the string and the B sounds:

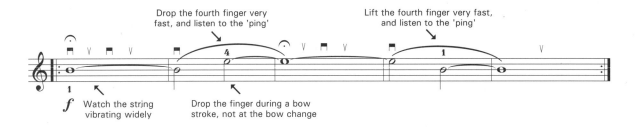

When musically appropriate, this crisp, articulated beginning to a note produces brilliance and energy in the tone.

The sound of lifting the finger quickly should not be confused with the articulated brilliance that you get by lifting the fingers with a partial left-hand *pizzicato*:

This effect has to be saved for special occasions. When used too much, it leads to brittleness and steeliness of tone. In contrast, the brilliance of fast fingers does not rob the tone of warmth or sweetness.

Lift-off exercises

One of my teachers used to say that to drop a finger on to the string required an active finger movement; but that to raise a finger required a passive movement, i.e. more a releasing of the finger.

Later I found out that this is the wrong way round: although you often need an active, fast movement to place a finger on the string, you often need an even faster movement to raise it. This is because dropping a finger is like allowing a spring to release; raising a finger is like pulling a spring out.

One traditional exercise for developing fast lift-off uses simple left-hand *pizzicato*:

The idea is that the plucking will make the finger automatically lift off fast. However, this exercise often fails to help because instead of pulling the finger back to pluck the string (moving the finger from the base joint), the student plucks with a sideways–downward movement from the middle joint.

The answer is first to hold fingers down on the string to stabilize the hand. This forces the finger to pull back in one piece from the base joint:

- Begin by holding three fingers on the E string. Pluck the lower strings with the remaining finger:

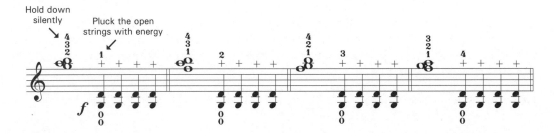

- You can also place the held-down fingers on the A, D or G strings:

Enabling the third finger to move easily

In this exercise, many players find that the third finger seems weaker or less able than the others. It may feel too weak to pull the string back and pluck at all. The answer is simple:

- If, before you pluck with the third finger, you press the second and fourth fingers hard into the string – and continue to press them as you pluck – you will find that the third finger feels weak.

- Instead, if the second and fourth fingers rest lightly on the string, the third finger regains all its power and agility.

- Prove this by exaggerating: rest the first, second and fourth fingers on the string as lightly as if playing harmonics. The third will now be able to pull back with the same agility as the second.

  Then press the second and fourth fingers down as hard as possible; now the third finger may feel heavy and slow again.

Heifetz exercise

Dorothy DeLay told how if you were sitting on a tram in San Francisco in the 1960s you might well find yourself sitting opposite someone carrying a violin case; and if they had a violin case it would be quite likely that they would be sitting there making a curious forwards-and-backwards movement with the fingers of their left hand.

If so, you would know that they were on their way to their violin lesson from Jascha Heifetz, since this is an exercise he would have taught them, and that they were using every available moment to practise and to stay warmed up.

- Begin with the fingers in a neutral, middle position, neither forward or back (Fig. 91a).

- Then pull the fingers back suddenly (Fig. 91b), pause with them in the pulled-back position, and then push them forwards again suddenly (Fig. 91c). Pulling back uses all the lift-off muscles; pushing forward uses all the drop muscles.

- Keep the fingers together, more or less touching each other; keep them curved throughout.

Thirty seconds of the Heifetz exercise makes your fingers feel as good as they do after thirty minutes of repetitive sixteenth-note (semiquaver) finger exercises.[1]

[1] One situation in which the Heifetz exercise becomes a life-saver, is when you have to perform in a venue which is cold, such as an insufficiently-heated church or in the open air. However cold your fingers, a few moments of the Heifetz exercise can be enough to make you feel perfectly ready to play.

Fig. 91

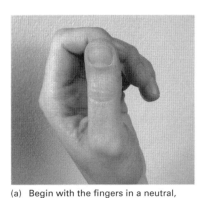

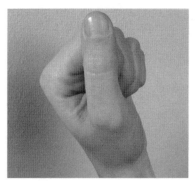

(a) Begin with the fingers in a neutral, middle position

(b) Pulling back uses all the lift-off muscles

(c) Pushing forwards uses all the drop muscles

 When you pause for a moment, with the fingers in the pulled-back position as in Fig. 91b, should the hand feel relaxed?

When the fingers are pulled back, the muscles doing the pulling have to contract. With the muscles in a state of contraction, the hand and fingers will never be able to feel 'relaxed' in the sense of 'floppy'. However, there is an obvious difference between the feeling of the muscles being active, and the feeling of them being tense.

Metronome exercise for fast drop and lift-off

This exercise makes the fingers drop and lift with ever-faster speed and precision of timing.

Drop the finger exactly in time

- Set the metronome to click in eighth-notes (quavers).
- Practise every possible pair of fingers: 01 – 02 – 03 – 04; 12 – 13 – 14; 23 – 24; 34.

Practise on each string.

How can I improve my fourth finger?

Many players find that the fourth finger feels weak, in comparison with the others, in all the different actions of shifting, trilling, vibrating and so on.

The traditional approach is that you should strengthen and improve your fourth finger by using it as often as possible, and not avoid it by using the third finger. Otherwise, it will never get stronger.

Yet many of the great violinists have made no secret of avoiding the fourth finger whenever they get a better effect, or the right effect more easily, by using the third. It is the music that matters, not a display of one fingering over another.[1]

Use the fourth wherever it feels comfortable and secure; use the third if it offers more, so long as doing so does not lead to bad fingerings or intonation problems. At the same time, in the background keep up a continual program of strengthening and development exercises for the fourth finger.

See it as being strong

The first step is to see it in your mind's eye as being strong. If your fourth finger feels tight or weak, or if you cannot get the vibrato you want, many times a day picture the finger how you would like it to be.[2]

I first discovered this during a heavy period of orchestral playing when I was not able to practise much. At that time I often found that I couldn't get the vibrato I wanted in my fourth finger, or my hand felt slightly tight. It was intriguing to discover that if, a bar or two before playing a fourth finger, I visualized it strong, relaxed, secure, in tune – it would always feel much freer when I actually played the finger.

The trick of mental visualization is to picture the ideal image with such clarity that it becomes more real than whatever the current fact may be. Mental visualization is based on knowledge, not on wishful thinking. The more information you have, the more detail and clarity you can work into the mental picture:

- Picture the finger completely free, strong, supple, and capable.

- Picture a cartoon version of your hand with an 'electric' fourth finger.

- Remember the feeling of strength in one of the other fingers, and then 'transpose' that feeling onto a picture of the fourth finger.

- Picture a warm, intense vibrato, the fourth finger effortlessly drawing the note out of the string.

- Picture the entire hand soft, free, relaxed, and not clenching together in any way.

- Picture the wrist free, the upper arm free, and so on.

Run these pictures through your mind as often as you can while you are playing, and whenever you imagine yourself playing. After the shortest period of this, you may be amazed at the results you find.

[1] Apparently Fritz Kreisler would avoid the fourth finger wherever he could. Sometimes David Oistrakh would shift up, say, an octave and arrive on a fourth finger on its own; sometimes he would arrive on the fourth finger but support it with the third finger on the string underneath; sometimes he would instead shift up to a third finger. The Belgian violinist Arthur Grumiaux would constantly use his third finger for important notes rather than his fourth.

Their basic approach was that you can use a third finger anytime you like, when playing lyrical, expressive notes, if it will produce a more 'juicy' or more 'telling' vibrato, or if it feels more secure.

[2] This is one of the secrets of playing with a good fourth finger, but of course it is also the first secret of playing anything at a high level: first you have to see it that way. Whatever the detailed picture is – good or bad – affects or actually creates the results you get.

See *An outline of mental rehearsal*, page 322.

How can I stop my fourth finger from collapsing?

Many players find that when the fourth finger is placed on the string it often collapses in the middle joint and partly straightens. This may make the finger feel clumsy, weak or tense (Fig. 92a). To lift off the string again, the finger then pulls back out sideways again.

Coupled with this there may be a feeling of a resistance point somewhere in the middle of the movement which causes a 'bump': if you move the finger back slowly, you reach a point where it seems to be unable to go any further, and then it suddenly snaps back faster and further than you intended.

Fig. 92

  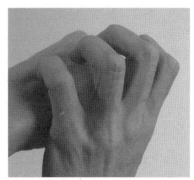

(a) Notice how the fourth finger has straightened and the base joint is sticking out

(b) Placing the fourth finger on its tip makes the finger naturally curve

(c) Practise on the back of your hand

- One reason is the base joint being too far from the neck, causing the finger to move almost horizontally to reach the string. Bring the base joint closer in to the neck (Fig. 92b).[1]

  In Fig. 92a note how the base joint sticks out, and the angle of the hand is turned too far away from the neck of the violin. The finger may have to straighten simply in order to reach the string.

- Place the fourth finger more on the tip of the finger, which makes the finger naturally assume a curved shape (Fig. 92b).

- The angle to the string makes a big difference. Think of keeping the fourth more upright rather than slanting. In Fig. 92b note the 'V' shape between the second and fourth fingers whereas in Fig. 92a they are more parallel.

- When the problem occurs on a specific note in a passage, it is often cured by balancing the hand more on the little finger, with the lower fingers reaching back.

[1] See *Warm-up exercise: pulling in the base joint,* page 138

Exercise

- Alternate between straighter, so that the knuckle collapses (Fig. 92a), and curved – in (Fig. 92b).

- Begin with the finger lightly resting on the surface of the string; as you move the finger in and out, gradually press the string harder.

- You can also do this on the back of your hand (Fig. 92c).

Typical fourth finger exercises

Fig. 93

Moving from the base joint

- With the violin in guitar position, place the hand against the shoulder of the violin (Fig. 93).

- Position the hand so that the base joint of the fourth finger is just above the rim of the violin, and so that the finger can reach the E string.

- With your right hand, press the left hand strongly against the shoulder of the violin to ensure that the hand does not move. Make sure you do not press on the actual base knuckle joints but on the back of the hand below them.

Using the shoulder of the violin to stabilise the hand

- Tap the fourth finger quickly and lightly on the E string, feeling the finger moving from the base joint independently of the hand.

Aiming onto the tip or pad

If you place the finger on its tip, the finger naturally curves (Fig. 92b); if you place it on its pad, it naturally straightens (Fig. 92a).

Placing the fourth finger more on its pad may produce a 'juicier' vibrato than the fingertip gives, so there may be many times, especially in slower or melodic passages, when it does not matter if the finger is a little less rounded when you deliberately choose more of the pad.

Placing the fourth finger more on its tip helps to ensure that the shape of the finger on the string, and the shape when it is lifted off the string, remain much the same.

It also helps ensure that the finger moves from the base joint, essential for fast playing, whereas using the pad of the finger encourages movement of the finger at the middle joint or from the hand.

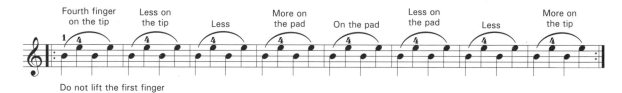

- Begin by playing the fourth finger on the tip of the finger.
- Without stopping, gradually move more on to the pad; gradually move back on to the fingertip.
- Practise the sequence up to a very fast speed.

Aiming into the middle of the finger

Players sometimes need to improve their aim, as they lower the fourth finger, to ensure that the tip of the finger contacts the string in the middle of the finger. It is a horrible feeling when the finger slightly misses the string, and ends up too near to the adjacent string on either side.

Use the following exercise as a quick warm-up. Just a little practice soon improves the aim of the finger:

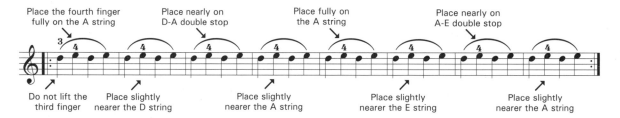

- Do not allow the finger to straighten at any stage. Keep it curved throughout and keep playing on the tip of the finger, adjusting only how near the tip is to the E string or to the D string.
- Practise the sequence up to a very fast speed.

Raising and dropping exercise

- Raise and drop the fingers from the base joint so that the shape of the finger on the string, and in the air, is the same.
- Drop the fourth finger more on its tip so that it is more rounded.
- Hold the lower fingers down as marked.

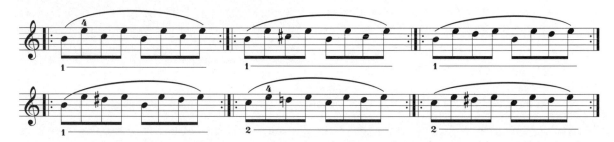

- Begin at a very slow tempo, raising and dropping the fingers very fast, at the last possible moment.[1]

- Also work up to a fast speed so that you can play the whole sequence through like this:

- Practise *p* and *f*. The louder the volume the wider the vibration of the string, and the more energy you need in the fingers to stop the string.

- Play the same notes on the other strings in other positions:

This exercise is more strenuous than it appears. Do not practise it for too long, or too many times within a short period.

Independence exercises

Many players find that their fourth finger is not independent of the third finger but moves with it, e.g. the fourth pulls down (sometimes underneath the neck) as the third finger drops onto the string.

Simple exercises improve this rapidly, so that the fourth finger is not affected by the actions of the third.

Example 1

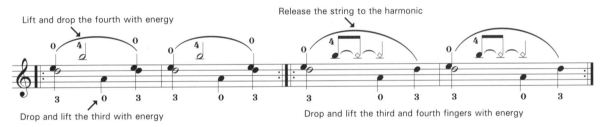

- Keep the fourth finger rounded, without changing its shape as it drops onto the string or lifts.

- Drop the third finger with exaggerated speed and impact to emphasise the contrary movements of the fingers.

- In the second bar, change from a stopped B to a harmonic.

Example 2

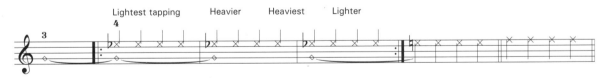

- Playing the harmonic with the third finger, keep the finger curved and as light as possible.

- Without playing the A string, silently tap the fourth finger up and down on the string.

- Keep the fourth finger curved, and contacting the string on the tip.

- Begin with the lightest possible contact with the string. Gradually drop the finger faster and with more impact until you are striking the A string quite heavily; then gradually lighten the impact back to the starting-point.

- Throughout, ensure that there is no reaction whatsoever in the third finger as the fourth moves.

Example 3

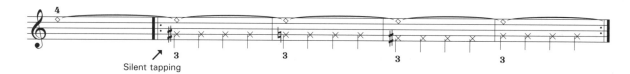

Silent tapping

- Normally a fourth finger harmonic would be played with quite a straight finger, and contact the string on the pad; but in this exercise keep the finger curved and contacting the string on the tip.

- Tap with the third finger on the D string without affecting the fourth finger.

- Tap with energy. Miss out the F♯ if you cannot reach it.

Example 4

Keep both fingers as curved and upright as possible

- For the purposes of the exercise, keep both fingers as upright and rounded as possible.

- Play the same patterns on the other pairs of strings.

Reaching-up exercise

Use this exercise as a quick warm-up before playing scales.

Players with small hands often find that when playing the descending scale, and reaching from a low first finger to a fourth finger on the next string (e.g. first-finger B♭ on the A string, to fourth-finger A on the D string), it seems a long way to have to reach with the fourth finger.[1]

[1] See also *Manipulating the wrist*, page 184

The ideal is for the hand to stay in one position, and for the fingers to find their notes within that setting. A common technical error is to get the fourth finger down on its note by means of a 'shift' from 1st position to 1st-position-and-a-bit, i.e. actually moving the hand a little higher up the neck after playing the first finger and before playing the fourth finger.

If you jump from the first to the fourth finger rather than reach up to the fourth, the notes that follow the fourth are likely to be out of tune because the hand is now slightly out of position.

Jumping means also that the first finger is not on the string at the beginning of playing the fourth finger. It should be held down because of overlapping (i.e. momentarily having two fingers on the string during a string crossing), which is one of the keys to playing really smoothly.[2]

[2] See *Holding down the first and fourth fingers*, page 302

- This exercise exaggerates the distance and makes it feel much easier for the fourth finger to reach the actual note it will play in the scale:

Hold down the first finger throughout

- Increase the reach of the fourth finger by opening the hand at the base joint. Be particularly careful not to squeeze the first and second fingers together.

- Keep the fourth finger curved throughout.

- Make sure that the entire hand remains soft, relaxed and free throughout.

Sliding exercise

- Repeat the same pattern on the other strings.

Dotted exercise

A useful image for fast lift-off in this exercise is of the string being red-hot:

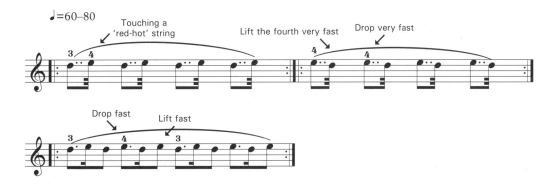

Other ways to improve the fourth finger

- Massage the muscles below the elbow on the fourth-finger side of the arm (see *Squeezing the arm to make the fingers move*, page 170). Move along the muscle in the direction of the elbow.

- Massage the muscles on the side of the palm of the hand below the knuckles of the third and fourth fingers. In particular, massage in the direction of the edge of the hand, as though trying to pull the muscles sideways (Fig. 94).

- Watch the movement of the finger in the air without the violin (see *Moving the finger from the base joint*, page 187).

- Play single-finger scales and arpeggios on the fourth finger (see *Single-finger scales and arpeggios*, page 235).

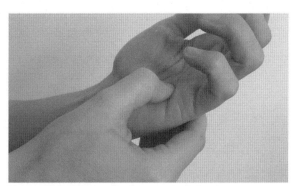

Fig. 94

Massage below the knuckles in an outward direction

- Practise vibrato exercises on the fourth finger (e.g. *Speeding up with the metronome*, page 256).

- Practise the trill exercise with the fourth finger (see *Practise the trill exercise*, page 152).

- Practise all the fourth-finger trill studies in the Kreutzer Etudes and the Dont Caprices, op. 35.

Extending a finger away from its usual note

Extensions are a way of reaching, without moving the hand in a shift, notes that are outside the normal range of notes a finger plays in that position.

The extension of the fourth finger out of its perfect fourth 'frame', which makes it like a 'fifth' finger, is a good example of an extension that you need to have as part of your left hand technique, simply because it crops up again and again. Like one of the 'words' in the 'vocabulary of technique',[1] the 'fifth' finger is essential in playing countless passages in the ordinary repertoire:[2]

[1] See *The language of the violin*, page 103

[2] There are a few editions in which extended fourth fingers like this are actually written as a '5'; but this has never become standard, and extended fourth fingers are usually written simply as '4'.

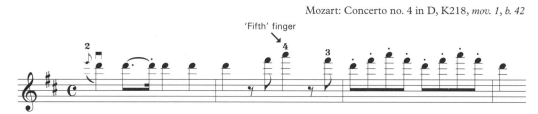

Extensions often take the place of a shift. To move into a new position without shifting, place the finger directly on the new note, without sliding along the string, and then follow with the hand:

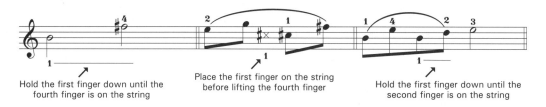

Practising extensions is a good example of spending time to save time. When you feel confident with extensions, a whole new series of possibilities opens up in fingering; at the same time, your sight-reading improves as you develop new ways of reaching notes that before would have required an actual change of position.[3]

[3] "You've got to crawl around the fingerboard, not jump everywhere!" Ruggiero Ricci

Extension exercises

From time to time add extension exercises to your warm-up routines to build greater knowledge of the 'geography of the fingerboard', the knowledge of exactly where every note is. Then everything you play, with extensions or without, feels clearer in the mind and in the fingers.[4] Whenever there is an extension in a piece, you know where to place the finger just as well as if the note were within the four-finger 'frame'.

It is easy to devise simple exercises covering all the possibilities of extending. For example:

[4] If you cannot play extension exercises in tune, it must mean than you do not sufficiently know the geography of the fingerboard; and so once you have practised and learnt them, and raised them to some level of accuracy and fluency, it must mean that your knowledge of the geography of the fingerboard is better.

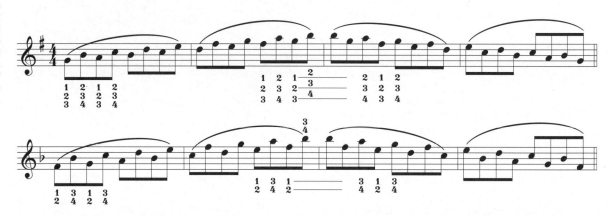

If you play just a few of these exercises up and down each string, and in various keys, it will quickly make a noticeable difference to your general feeling of security as you play in every region of the fingerboard.

Avoiding aches and pains

The basis of all playing must be balance and physical freedom. All too often we spend our practice time working on problems of the left hand or right, when actually what we need to do first is to find a basic balance and freedom throughout our entire system. Then everything works much more easily in the first place.

General tension throughout the body often begins with the neck and shoulders, and tension there has to spread to the arms and then to the hands and fingers. Then it can become less and less productive to practise problematic passages over and over again, trying to get them sounding well and in tune, if the basis of the playing is not one of freedom.

While it may seem very difficult to find such a basis of freedom if you do not already have it – and if it seems that you already have enough to think about just trying to get around the notes – in fact there are certain key issues which make an enormous difference, and more freedom can be gained very quickly indeed.

Understanding the causes

Listening to your body

Imagine that you are busy practising, and the fire alarm goes off. You do not ignore the alarm, saying, 'I have important work to do, I can't stop now.'

Pain is your personal fire alarm going off. Yet many string players, hurting with every note they play, ignore warning signals and carry on playing in the same way. A common approach to practice is this:

> First I have to learn how to play this piece; then I will learn how to play it without getting tense.
>
> I know that all these things my teacher tells me about being balanced in my posture, not squeezing my fingers together, relaxing my shoulders, not pulling my chest down, not squeezing my left thumb back, and so on, are all the right things; and one day I will be able to use all this helpful information, and then I will be glad that I learnt it now.
>
> But meanwhile I can't think about it because if I play in all those relaxed, balanced, non-squeezing ways, I simply cannot play; or if I can, my playing seems boring and uninvolved and unmusical; but if I forget about them, and just play as I have got into the habit of playing, I can play at least quite well.
>
> I can ignore the pain in my left upper arm, and I can still get through the piece even if I am tense. One day, when I can play it and all my worries with it are over, then I will learn how to play it in the way that my teacher is suggesting.

This approach often fails for the simple reason that until you find a way of playing without tension and conflict, you never do reach the stage where you can play it easily anyway.

Forming good associations

From the very beginning of learning a new piece, build good posture, balance and freedom into the musical playing of the notes.

Just as you have a muscle-memory of the feeling of beginning a piece on a down-bow or an up-bow, so that it becomes impossible to begin accidentally on the wrong bow when playing from memory, so do undesirable physical actions (such as tightening) become associated with playing a particular note or phrase. Then that tightening becomes part of how you play that phrase, even if you have got yourself into a generally relaxed state beforehand.

If you form an association of bad posture or tension with the phrase, it becomes more and more difficult to change to a new way of playing without the musical playing suffering. Then you may become reluctant to make the change.

The force of gravity

The effect gravity has on us is one of the first subjects in disciplines from Alexander Technique to Tai Chi. All our lives we are weighed down by this force. From your first attempts to stand up, as an infant, you need to learn how to rise up against it:

> 'Now, the thing that all living things have to cope with…is the force of gravity. The force of gravity is the constant in our environment. It is the one unvarying thing, because air and food and everything else varies, every other thing varies, but gravity doesn't vary…The first requirement of living things is to come to terms with this constant in their lives. As we all know, there are considerable degrees of gradation in how well or how badly we adapt to it.[1]

[1] Walter Carrington (1994), 94

This effect that gravity has, pushing down on you while you are wanting to keep your arms, violin and bow up in the air, and how you react to it, is the first factor to consider in the whole subject of good posture and freedom from aches and pains.

Create a feeling of lightness by visualising that gravity works in the other direction instead, and you are constantly being pulled or stretched up by it: if you were to let go of the violin or bow, they would gently float upwards like a balloon.[2]

[2] See also *Starting from above*, page 29

Chain reactions

When you feel tension or other blockages in your arms, hands and fingers, there are usually a multitude of interrelated factors responsible.

Many of these factors are subtle or imperceptible aspects of technique which, although seemingly insignificant, set off chain-reactions of tension that spreads throughout the entire playing.

> Because the fingers pressed too hard into the strings, the hand was tense
>
> Because the hand was tense, the intonation was unreliable
>
> Because the intonation was unreliable, the player held back and became over-cautious
>
> Because the player held back, the audience was not moved
>
> And all just because of pressing the fingers too hard.[3]

[3] For want of a nail the shoe was lost,
For want of a shoe the horse was lost,
For want of a horse the rider was lost,
For want of a rider the battle was lost,
For want of a battle the kingdom was lost,
And all for the want of a nail.
Traditional

Playing too far from the bridge is the direct cause of many different types of problem in violin playing:

> Because the violinist played too far from the bridge, the string was too soft to take the weight of the bow
>
> Because the string could not take the weight of the bow, there was no attack and the tone was small
>
> Because there was no attack and the tone was small, there was no excitement
>
> Because there was no excitement, the audience was not excited
>
> And all just because of playing too far from the bridge.

There are likely to be many separate chain-reactions all occurring at the same time, starting from different places and reinforcing each other in a complex network of cause and effect.

Pressing and squeezing

Any degree of pressing may cause knock-on effects because the moment there is pressure, there must also be counterpressure – and this leads to a feeling of squeezing.

Squeezing causes contraction in the muscles, leading to loss of elasticity or springiness; and with the loss of springiness, the loss of unconscious instantaneous adjustment and mobility.

The most common examples of squeezing:

- Squeezing together the base of the left thumb and the base of the first finger
- Squeezing the left fingers together
- Squeezing the neck of the violin between the fingers and thumb through over-pressing the strings
- Squeezing the violin between your chin or jaw, and shoulder or collar bone
- Squeezing the bow between the fingers and thumb
- Pressing upwards with the right thumb while pressing down with the first finger.

These are common true-to-life examples, but of course the chain-reactions from such things as squeezing, or playing too far from the bridge, can come from or lead anywhere.

Curing the problems is usually surprisingly easy

Although you can have an endless number of chain-reactions occurring all at once and tangled up together, in fact they all stem from a limited number of areas.

By making sure of only one thing – such as no longer over-pressing the left fingers and thumb – you prevent all the possible chain-reactions that require over-pressing in order to start in the first place. By not over-pressing the chin into the chin rest, your neck and shoulders remain free; they in turn do not reduce the freedom of the upper arms, which then help keep the lower arms and hands free, and so on.

Common first causes of chain-reactions

General

- Feet not providing balance and sense of solid foundation
- 'Pulling down' and 'pulling in'
- Twisting the back
- Rotating the head and dropping the chin onto the chin rest as one action instead of 'first turn, then drop'

Left hand

- Pressing violin between chin and shoulder
- Tensing and raising the shoulder
- Locking the left upper arm
- Locking, or pushing out, the wrist
- Tension in the base joints
- Squeezing the neck
- Finger on the wrong part of the tip
- Hand too high (angle of fingers too steep)
- Fingers over-pressing
- Fingers squeezing together
- Too-slow finger action
- Vibrato speed equal forwards and backwards
- Vibrato finger-pressure equal forwards and backwards

Right hand

- First finger placed too close to the thumb
- First joint of the first finger curling in too forcibly against the bow
- First joint of the second finger not remaining neutral, but pulling in towards the thumb
- Third finger trying to do the job of the fourth finger, i.e. balancing the weight of the bow
- Fourth finger contacting the bow on the pad of the finger instead of on the tip
- Thumb contacting the bow on the pad instead of on the tip
- Thumb bending inwards instead of outwards
- Wrist too high/low
- Blocked forearm rotation
- Not bowing 'out' (forward) in the upper arm at the end of the down-bow (when appropriate)
- Tension in the right shoulder
- Thinking of bowing movements being only in the arm, instead of originating lower in the back
- Bowing too far from the bridge
- Trying to do things with the bow, instead of following the bow's momentum

An introduction to lactic acid

It is common for players to suffer from aching, tired muscles after playing for many hours.

The world of sport and athletics has known, for decades, something that seems to be still generally unknown amongst musicians:

> Endurance is associated with aerobic metabolism. At relatively slow speeds a runner can absorb, transport, and utilize enough oxygen in the muscles to economically split the chemical which is the source of our energy – adenosine triphosphate, abbreviated to ATP.
>
> The ATP stored in the working muscles is limited to only a few seconds' work, but fortunately creatine phosphate (CP) is also there for rebuilding ATP. But CP is also limited and runs out after about 15 to 20 seconds of heavy exercise. So how are milers able to race for four minutes and marathoners for over two hours? Enter aerobics and anaerobics.
>
> If the rate of work is moderate, as in a marathon, a runner can get enough oxygen to economically burn fat and glycogen. This enables ATP to be rebuilt as fast as it is being broken down, and a trained runner can continue for several hours at least. This is aerobic metabolism.
>
> If the rate of work is very rapid, as in the sprints, oxygen cannot be absorbed fast enough for the breakdown of fat and glycogen. The body is able to cheat chemically for a short while and breaks down glycogen without oxygen. This is anaerobic metabolism. Unlike aerobic metabolism, with its innocent waste products of water and carbon dioxide, the nasty waste product of anaerobic work is lactic acid which, as it accumulates, ultimately prevents the muscles from contracting.[1]

[1] Ron Daws: *Running your best* (Massachusetts, 1985), 140.

The problems come from filling your system with lactic acid without getting rid of it afterwards by 'warming down'. A by-product of the presence of lactic acid is greater acidity in the blood, and it is this that causes the soreness and sensitivity.

Warming down

When tennis players go off the court after a strenuous three-hour match, they do not simply flop into a chair and relax. First they make sure they warm down. If they did not do this, when they woke up the next morning their muscles would feel sore and could be almost too stiff to move. They must not immediately stop, as the circulation and respiration drop down too quickly for the removal of the waste products from the body.

What they have to do is keep the blood flowing in order to wash away deposits of lactic acid, but without producing more lactic acid in the process. They alternate hot and cold showers, have deep-tissue massage, lie in an ice bath, gently jog, jump up and down and shake themselves about, and so on.

Q **How do you 'warm down' as a violinist?**

Deep massage is a very good way to eliminate chronic build-ups of lactic acid by increasing circulation and flushing waste products from the muscles. You can briefly massage most areas of your hands, arms and shoulders yourself, and do this at regular intervals throughout long practice sessions. It is not difficult to learn the basic techniques, and any massage is better than none.[1]

Counter-exercising and stretching exercises are excellent for general maintenance and should be done regularly during and between practising. Then the extra step of massage may seldom be needed.

[1] See *Massaging the upper forearm*, page 170; *Massaging the hand*, page 171

Counter-exercising and stretching

Counter-exercising means to move muscles in the opposite direction to those they normally move in. This is extremely powerful in helping to maintain balance in the muscle system and freedom.

Approach any exercise very carefully. Do not force or strain, or hurry into any action. A number of smaller efforts is often much more effective than one larger effort, and there is less – if any – danger of straining something.

- Do the following stretches at regular intervals during practice, as well as using them to warm down.

Example 1

This is a typical sports and yoga stretch:

- Place your left elbow on the crook of your right elbow (Fig. 95a).

- Clasp your hands together, thumbs interlocking (Fig. 95b).

- Slowly and gently raise your hands above your head (Fig. 95c).

Example 2

- Wrap the fingers of your left hand as far around the neck of the violin as you can (Fig. 95d).

- With your left hand, rotate the violin clockwise until the chin-rest end is facing up (Fig. 95e). At that point, hold the violin with your right hand (Fig. 95f).

- Continue to rotate the violin clockwise by turning the violin with your right hand. Move the violin very, very slowly, feeling the muscles in your left arm stretching as you turn with the right.

  Make sure that your left shoulder is complete released. Keep the left hand as low as you can so that you can relax the entire arm while it is rotating.

- Once you have reached the near horizontal position shown in Fig. 95g, grip the violin securely with the right hand. Then simply let go with the left hand and return the arm to its normal position.

Example 3

This yoga exercise was one of Yehudi Menuhin's favourites:

- Begin with your fingertips together behind your back, palms facing down (Fig. 95h).

- Bring your palms together and move your hands up to between your shoulder blades (Fig. 95j).

  Lengthen your back and raise your chest, and allow your elbows to drop naturally.

Example 4

- Drop your left arm by your side. Keep quite straight at the elbow.

- Raise your hand so that there is a 90° angle between the hand and the forearm (Fig. 95k).

- Keeping the elbow straight, slowly rotate the arm clockwise (Fig. 95l) and anticlockwise (Fig. 95m), feeling the muscles stretching all the way up your arm and into your shoulder.

- Rotate very slowly as far as you can go, feeling all the muscles in the forearm stretching.

Fig. 95

(a) Cross your elbows

(b) Clasp your hands

(c) Very slowly raise your hands above your head

(d) Wrap your fingers around the neck

(e) With your left hand rotate the violin clockwise

(f) Take hold of the violin with your right hand

(g) Rotate as far as you can without forcing

(h) Place your fingertips together

(j) Move your hands up your back

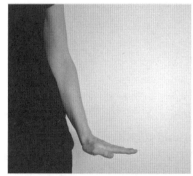

(k) Raise the hand to 90° keeping the elbow straight

(l) Rotate clockwise

(m) Rotate anticlockwise

Muscles: working from the zero point

The following description of how muscles work uses no more than the simplest terms possible. These few images are all that are necessary for the purposes of playing the violin.

Muscles can only contract

An essential thing to know about muscles is that they can only contract. They cannot lengthen by themselves. They can pull but can never push.

> Muscle tissue consists of cells which are capable of contraction...Each skeletal muscle fibre ...acts in an "all or nothing" manner, and the degree of contraction of the whole muscle is proportional to the number of fibres acting. Normally a few fibres are stimulated, maintaining tone even when the muscle is at rest. When many fibres are stimulated together, they produce shortening of the whole muscle or tension between the two ends...If the stimulus is prolonged or too frequently repeated the muscle may become fatigued.[1]

[1] H.G.Q. Rowett: *Basic Anatomy and Physiology* (London, 1973), 32.

The contraction of the muscles is one of the reasons why all of our attention needs to be on constant 'lengthening and widening', and on avoiding 'pulling down' and 'pulling in'.[2]

[2] Continual contraction without release is experienced as 'tension'. When we say of somebody that they are tense, or say 'I feel a bit tense today,' it would be more accurate to say that he or she is 'contracted', or 'I feel a bit contracted today'.

There are always at least two sets of opposing muscles that move a joint or limb one way or the other. For example, to close your arm at the elbow the muscles on the inside of the arm contract, causing the forearm to move towards the upper arm. While these muscles contract, the muscles on the outside of the arm are stretched, but cannot themselves push out.

The muscles that contract are active; the opposing set of muscles are passive. To move the hand away from the shoulder again, the opposite occurs: the muscles on the outside of the arm contract while those on the inside are passive. Sometimes we use activity on both sides in opposition to each other, in order to fine-tune a movement.

The zero point

There is a certain position of each joint or limb where neither set of opposing muscles is active – i.e. the position where, if there were a movement of even a short distance one way or the other, the muscles on one side would have to contract and those on the other side would be stretched.

This is the 'zero point' of activity, and is the best starting position for any action.

When the starting position is not this neutral position, care must be taken that all muscular activity is always as little as possible.

- Hold your left arm out with your hand flopped at the wrist (Fig. 96a). The fingers will fall into a certain shape and position. This is their position when the muscles on top of the fingers, stretching across the knuckles to the back of the hand, and the muscles underneath, stretching across the knuckles to the palm, balance each other so that none are in a state of 'work'.

- Using your other hand to move it, push a finger down (Fig. 96b) and then suddenly release it. The finger will spring back to exactly the same position that it was in before (Fig. 96a). It will not stay pushed down when you take the pressing finger away because the muscle on top of the finger, having been stretched, wants to spring back to its state of least effort.

  Nor will it spring back to a position above the starting place, since here a pull would be exerted on the finger by the muscles underneath the finger.

Fig. 96

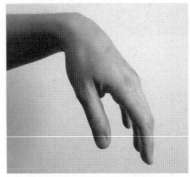 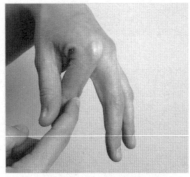 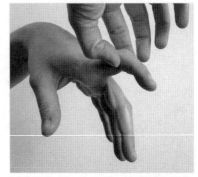

(a) Flop the hand from the wrist, each finger at the middle point

(b) Push the finger down and then let it spring back up to the middle point

(c) Lift the finger and then let it drop back to the middle point

Similarly if you lift a finger (Fig. 96c) using your other hand to do it, and then suddenly let go, the finger will spring back again more to the position shown in Fig. 95a. It will not stay up, since the muscle underneath the finger has been stretched and wants to spring back to its state of least effort. Nor will it spring back down to a place lower than the starting-point.

Find the same 'zero point' in the muscles on either side of each lever in the arms and hands:

- Starting with the right hand flopped from the wrist (Fig. 97a), with your left hand push your right hand down; then let it spring back up to the starting place.

  Pushing down causes the muscles on top of the hand and arm to be stretched, and they naturally want to return to a neutral state. The hand will not spring back past the starting-point.

  With your left hand, lift the right hand and allow it to fall. It will not fall past the starting-point.

- Position your right forearm at a right angle to the upper arm. Make sure the upper arm is neither too far forwards, nor too far back.

  With your left hand, pull the forearm in towards you (Fig. 97b). Then let go and watch how it swings back out, slightly past the starting-point; then swings back in, now only slightly past the starting-point; and finally settles at the starting-point.

  With your left hand, push the forearm away from you (Fig. 97c), and then let it swing back in again. Watch how, after swinging back in past the starting-point, it takes a few seconds to settle back to the starting place.

- Starting again in the position shown in Fig. 97b, do exactly the same with the upper arm: with your left hand, pull the upper arm in towards you and then let go, and push it away from you and let go. The upper arm will perform the same little movements, briefly going either side of the middle point before settling, as the forearm did.

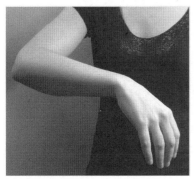 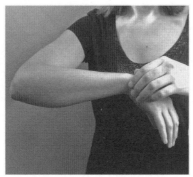 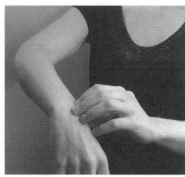

Fig. 97

(a) Suspend the arm with the hand flopped from the wrist

(b) Pull the forearm in, and then let it spring back out to the middle point

(c) Push the forearm out, and then let it spring back in to the middle point

Ideally, each finger is in this neutral state of inaction when not in use, or before beginning any action; similarly the muscles in the bow arm, depending on where you are in the bow, often do not need to be active before beginning a bow stroke.

When muscles remain free or neutral, rather than in any unnecessary state of contraction, everything becomes less effortful.

The key to freedom and ease in violin playing is that you constantly have this point of balance as the starting-point, before any movement one way or the other, and return to it afterwards.

Suspending your arm without using any muscles in it

If you want to move a finger, the main parts of the muscle or tendon involved are in the hand.

To move the hand, the main parts of the muscles used are in the forearm; to move the forearm, they are in the upper arm; to move the upper arm, the main muscles involved are in the shoulders, upper back and upper chest.

So the main part of the muscle used to make the movement is always in the next higher area of the arm, going in the direction of the shoulder.

Therefore, you can suspend your arm in the air using those muscles in the shoulder, upper back and upper chest, without a single muscle in the arm being active. This gives the arm a feeling of 'floating' or being suspended in the air, rather than of being held. It is easy to demonstrate.

Without the bow, float your right arm in playing position (Fig. 98). With your left hand, squeeze the muscles in your right hand, forearm and upper arm. You should find they are all soft and relaxed.

Fig. 98

Squeeze the muscles in your right arm with your left hand

[1] See *Widening at the shoulders: releasing the minor pectoral*, page 174; *Staying free in the upper arm*, page 256

Make sure you are not clenching the minor pectoral muscle.[1]

Once you are holding the bow you need to use certain muscles; but when the basic condition of the arm is one of floating rather than of being held, everything feels lighter and more responsive.

That is the starting-point from which you can go to 'relaxing the weight of the arm into the string', and all the other functions of the bow arm, and to which you can return.

Feeling the contraction–release in the palm of the hand

- Find the muscles on either side of your hand that move the third finger (Fig. 99).

- Move the finger up and down, as though tapping the finger on the string. You can feel the muscle in the palm of your hand, under your thumb, alternating between contraction and release.

- If the muscle there feels permanently contracted as the finger moves, it means that you are resisting a state of release that would produce an entirely new sensation of freedom in your left hand.

Fig. 99

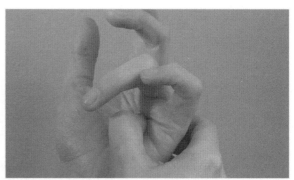

(a) Feel how the muscle is soft   (b) Feel the muscle contract

Squeezing the arm to make the fingers move

The muscles that move the fingers originate in the forearm. If you press there, between elbow and wrist (which has the same effect as shortening the muscle), the fingers move on their own.

Fig. 100

- Without the violin, hold the left arm in playing position. Make sure your hand and fingers are completely relaxed.

- With your right hand, put fingers one side of the forearm and the thumb the other (Fig. 100). Finding the muscle, experiment by pressing in different places until the fingers move downwards at the same moment that you press.

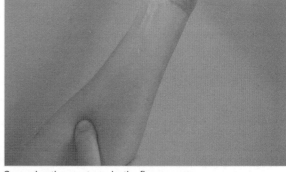

Squeezing the arm to make the fingers move

If your finger action is not free, perhaps because of your hand position, you may feel tired or aching in your forearm; but the problem will not be in the forearm where the discomfort is, but in the finger action. It also works the other way round.

Someone's entire left hand can sometimes be transformed simply by their seeing the fingers move on their own, and feeling the freedom in the fingers, when you squeeze their forearm muscles.

Massaging the upper forearm

Whenever you feel any tension in your hand or fingers – and certainly the moment you feel any pain or discomfort in the muscles or tendons in your wrist, hand or fingers – the place to work on is probably the area of your forearm just below the elbow.

First find the muscles: grip that area of the arm with your right hand and move the fingers of your left hand as though playing (Fig. 101a). Feel the muscles and tendons in the forearm moving under your right hand.

Having found them, massage them with deep strokes along the muscle, always moving in the direction of the upper arm. Always move along the muscle, not directly pressing down in to it.

If the muscles feel sore or tender, this may be a reason to go on rather than to stop. In fact, it is easy to discover places which are extremely sensitive to the touch, but these are the places to concentrate on, not to avoid. A little gentle work – though it has to be as deep as possible – on those muscles instantly creates greater ease and elasticity in the entire left hand.

Fig. 101

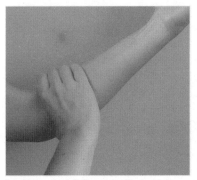

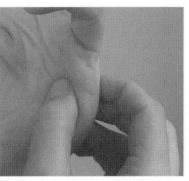

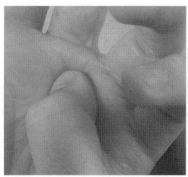

(a) Move the left fingers to find which muscles to massage

(b) The muscle remains soft while closing the finger at the middle joint

(c) Gently massage the muscles on either side of the knuckle joints

A little work on a regular basis completely cures a wide range of different aches or pains that typically appear in a violinist's left arm and hand. Many players have the frightening experience of suddenly feeling sharp pains in their left or right wrist when they play with energy, and often even these can be eliminated almost instantly by massaging the upper forearm muscles.

Simple stretching exercises can be as good as massage or even better. If you regularly do simple, five-second stretches, the balance of the muscles is maintained and massage is less often needed.[1]

[1] See *Counter-exercising and stretching*, page 166

Massaging the hand

Bring freedom to your left fingers by gently massaging the muscles in the palm just below the beginning of each finger as in Fig. 99 (page 170).

There are three movements of each finger: moving only at the nail joint without moving the rest of the finger; moving only at the middle joint; moving the whole finger as a piece from the base joint. Find the muscles with your thumb while moving the fingers.

The first, second and third fingers each use the same muscle or tendon for all three movements.

The fourth finger is different. To move it at the middle joint, the muscle used is between the third and fourth fingers, slightly to the right of the spot shown in Fig. 99; but the muscle that moves the finger forward from the base joint is on the side of the hand.

Feel this by gently squeezing the side muscle between your thumb and fingers while closing the fourth finger at the middle joint (Fig. 101b). The muscle on the side will remain soft and not contracted.[2]

[2] See also *Other ways to improve the fourth finger*, page 161

Another place to work, to free the fingers, is the muscles on each side of the knuckle joint (Fig. 101c).

Minimum muscular effort

A common image concerning the right degree of muscle tone is that the correct amount of strength you need is somewhere in the middle between being 'floppy' and being tense.

According to this image, complete relaxation (in the sense of being floppy and limp) is at one end of the spectrum. This is mainly good for only one thing: going to sleep.

Tension is at the other end of the spectrum; and somewhere in the middle is a balance point where there is enough muscle tone to be able to move around and do things.

However, this image may be misleading in violin playing: a 'middle point' between the two extremes already means far too much tension or over-use (over-contraction) of the muscles. Instead, think of the point-of-use as being only just past the point of floppiness:

'Point-of-use' means the amount of muscle tone required to hold and move the bow, to move the fingers up and down on the violin, stop the strings, vibrate, change position, and so on.

Bringing the point-of-use closer to the point of floppiness, immediately produces a wonderful sensation of lightness and ease. An extraordinary new aliveness and alacrity immediately comes into every action.

Experiment on the back of your hand

It used to be thought that a good left-hand technique meant that you could hear the fingers banging on the fingerboard with a hard impact. Perhaps the display of power and energy of doing this, and the fact that some players are able to make a louder thud than others, became confused with ability.

Instead, a fast finger action should be the norm rather than a heavy one. There may be notes which need firmer finger action for greater articulation or rhythm, but apart from them the only time to drop the finger with energy is when playing ascending slurs – since otherwise there is a moment of 'fuzz' if the finger stops the string too slowly;[1] but even then the fingers should not thud on to the string.

[1] See *Placing fingers gently: the secret of a relaxed left hand*, page 186

Fig. 102

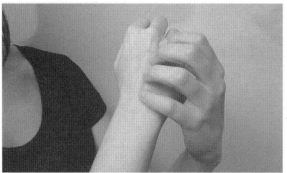
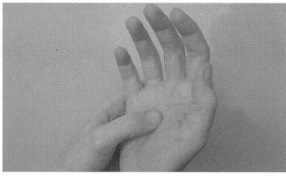

(a) Are your hand and finger completely light, free and effortless?

(b) Make sure the thumb is as light as a feather, never pressing into the hand

The fingers must move quickly to create the different string lengths, but always using minimum power and effort and stopping the strings as lightly as possible.

- Finger with your fourth finger on the back of your hand as though playing the violin (Fig. 102).

Is your hand, and are your fingers, almost 'floppy'; or are they over-active and perhaps even tense and inflexible? Are you certain you cannot release even a tiny fraction more? Make sure that the contact of the thumb on one side of your hand, and the finger on the other, is as light as a feather – 'tickle–light'.

- Finger on the back of your hand as a constant reminder of how your left hand should feel most of the time during the normal course of playing.

Expecting tension produces it

- Without the violin, hold your left hand in the air in playing position. Allow every muscle in the hand and fingers to let go so that the fingers fall into a natural shape (Fig. 103a).
- Move the fingers from there into the position they may be in to play some wide thirds, fingered octaves, or tenths (Fig. 103b).
- Wait! Has your hand now become tight? Are you clenching the muscles at the same time as widening the space between the fingers? Has your wrist suddenly tightened?

    Do you have a mental picture of this feeling in the hand as being an unquestionable part of playing double stops, an automatic by-product of widening the hand in any way?

Key point: Spreading the fingers is one thing; tightening is another. They are two separate factors. After only a short time of playing double stops with a tight hand, when we first attempt them as beginners, we form an association between tension and double stops and forever afterwards expect that feeling.

Instead, picture the hand remaining soft, flexible and free as you widen it. Then find this feeling of letting go, releasing and remaining free as you widen the fingers.

It is perfectly possible to widen the hand a long way and remain soft and free at the same time. You just have to break the association with tension, and begin to expect softness and freedom rather than contraction and hardness.

Fig. 103

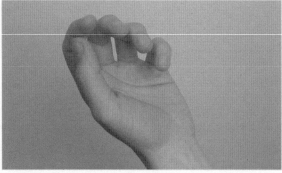
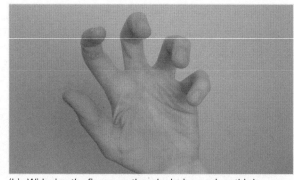

(a) Release every muscle in the hand

(b) Widening the fingers as though playing a minor third

Lengthening and widening

Not pulling down: lengthening the back and raising the chest

'Pulling down' means contracting the muscles in the front of the body so that the upper chest is lowered in the direction of the stomach (Fig. 104a).

Pulling down in the upper chest is one of the occupational hazards of playing the violin or viola. If you work on a building site, an occupational hazard is that something may fall on your head; so wearing a hard hat is essential. Playing the violin, you have to pay constant attention to lengthening the back and raising the chest.

Fig. 104

(a) Lengthening the back and raising the chest

(b) Pulling down

The tell-tale sign is a hump or curve at the top of the back (Fig. 104b). This posture leads to a catalogue of problems in the back and in the working of the arms and hands, and then in the fingers.

It is all-too-easy to link bowings and left hand actions (and musical feelings), with a simultaneous pulling-down, so that the scroll always visibly lowers whenever a particular note or phrase is played.

When you cut the link between these actions, so that (say) playing a strong accent with the bow does not automatically trigger shortening the muscles in the front of the body, an extraordinary new sense of economy, freedom, control, focus and authority immediately enters the overall playing.[1]

[1] See also *Localizing: the key to mastery*, page 198

Go up to go up; go up to go down

As he watched a young violinist pulling down as she crossed from the E string to the G string, the Alexander teacher Walter Carrington observed: 'You have to go up to go up, and go up to go down!'

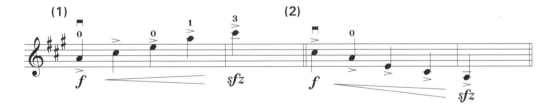

(1) Suppose you play up from the A string to the E string: you've got to go up to go up. If you pull down as you go up, the tone may weaken; the bow may slide away from the bridge; your body contracts and your breathing is constricted, and so on.

Instead, lengthen the back as you crescendo up the arpeggio, with a feeling of raising the chest and becoming taller.

Keep the scroll still, or allow it to rise slightly, with a feeling of buoyancy in the instrument so that it floats on a cushion of air without any hint of dropping with gravity.

(2) Suppose you play down from the A string to the G string: you've got to go up to go down. Lengthen the back, raise the chest, keep the scroll still or allow it to rise slightly as the strings meet the bow-hair, the same as when playing ascending.

One way to avoid pulling down is to have a feeling of the string or violin coming up to meet the bow.[2]

[2] See also *Image of the cat*, page 4

Another way to avoid pulling down is to link lengthening the back, or raising the chest, with flattening the violin. Instead of two unrelated subjects, see them as two parts of the same thing:

- Use a certain amount of lengthening your back in order to flatten the violin
- Flatten the violin in order to lengthen the back.[3]

[3] See also *4. The tilt of the violin*, page 35

Examples

Pugnani-Kreisler: Praeludium and Allegro, *Praeludium, b. 21*

Rode: Concerto no. 7 in A minor, op. 9, *mov. 1, b. 4*

J. S. Bach: Sonata no. 1 in G minor, BWV1001, *mov. 1, b. 4*

Widening at the base joints of the left hand

Sometimes the fingers touch each other during the course of playing, sometimes they do not, depending on the shape of the hand and the note pattern. It makes no difference, but what does matter is that there is never any sideways squeezing-together.

I often remember a student who had an awkward-looking left hand action. I made various suggestions which she seemed unable to pick up. Finally it came out that she had always thought that no finger should ever touch another finger, so she was trying to keep them unnaturally spread apart all the time.

Another common misconception is that all the fingers should point in the same direction. Maxim Vengerov and Joshua Bell are two examples of leading players with hands where the fingers do remain more or less parallel most of the time; but for many hands the fingers should as often form a fan-like shape.

Widening at the base joints encourages this fan-like shape, and gives the left hand increased range, flexibility and mobility.

Widening at the shoulders: releasing the minor pectoral

One of the chief causes of tension in either arm is the minor pectoral, the thick wodge of muscle near the armpit, between the near-top of the chest and the place where the upper-arm fits into the shoulder-socket. (Fig. 105). Clenching here is the explanation for many of the tension-problems violinists experience in the shoulders and arms.[1]

[1] See *Keeping the upper arm free*, page 142

Fig. 105 ### Right shoulder and upper arm

- Put the fingers of your left hand almost into your right armpit so that you can get underneath the muscle, and place the thumb on the other side (Fig. 105).

- Find how you can make this muscle contract. Push your shoulder very slightly down and forwards, and feel how the muscle becomes rigid with contraction. Let the shoulder return to its normal position and feel the muscle release and become soft and pliable again. Learn how to do this rhythmically: tense–release, tense–release.

Squeeze the muscle gently

The crucial point is that this pectoral muscle is not required for keeping the arm suspended in the air. Its job is to pull the shoulder down and forwards, and it must not be allowed to join in the general bowing movements. If it does, the only result is the opposite of what you want, i.e. heaviness and lack of quick, light response in the entire arm and shoulder.

What about moving the upper arm backwards and forwards? Again, this particular muscle between your fingers can remain soft and neutral much or most of the time, while it is the job of other muscles to move the upper arm.

- Make backwards-and-forwards bowing-movements with your right upper arm. Do not allow the muscle between your fingers to contract as you do so.

The feeling of release in the bow arm, when you learn to move the bow without this muscle constantly reacting, is extraordinary. But in many students the muscle sticks out visibly as soon as they bring the bow into playing position, though they could release it; and you can see the muscle contracting and releasing in time with the strokes, though they could minimise this or even stop it entirely.

At first you might find the muscle difficult to control, and it will want to return quickly to its clenched state, but little by little you can release it for longer and longer until it becomes a habit.

Permanent, extreme over-shortening of this muscle (i.e. tension), coupled with pulling down in the upper chest,[1] can ultimately lead to tingling or numbness in the fingertips. Happily, it is not too difficult to remedy by improving the posture, through awareness and the application of will, and by way of simple stretching exercises.

[1] See *Not pulling down: lengthening the back and raising the chest*, page 173

Left upper arm

The same minor pectoral muscle on the left side is equally likely to take part in things when it should be staying quiet, and it is by keeping free here that freedom comes into the whole arm.

It is common for an association to set in between any movement of the left upper arm to the right, and pulling-in with this muscle. Then, if the elbow remains pulled in to the body, the muscle remains permanently contracted. The same tightening is likely also to be associated with any upward shifts, and players with an arm-vibrato are particularly prone to tighten here the more intensely they vibrate. Again, it is easy to prove that this muscular activity or clenching is entirely unnecessary:

Without the violin, hold the left arm in playing position. Hold the pectoral muscle between your fingers and thumb as you did before on the right-hand side. Make sure that it is soft under your fingers.

- Slowly move the elbow to left and right, as though moving from the G string to the E string

- Move the hand towards and away from you, as though shifting

- Make the arm- or hand-movements of vibrato.

- Notice how you can make all these movements without the muscle between your fingers reacting.

Learn how to clench the muscle and then release it again. The more easily you are able to do this, the more you can instantly release it whenever you wish during the course of playing, and the released state soon becomes a habit.

Disassociate the action of vibrato from the action of contracting this muscle:

- Vibrate with great energy while pointing the violin as far backwards as possible (Fig. 106).

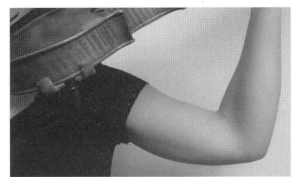

Fig. 106

Vibrate intensely with the violin in this position

Not tightening as the date approaches

It is a common experience that a piece seems to become ever more difficult in the days leading up to a concert. One week before, you are happy with your solo or whatever the piece is that you are preparing. It is at the stage of preparation where it feels easy, free and relaxed, the bow lies smoothly in the string, your left hand seems to play by itself, and you are looking forward to the concert.

Three days before the concert it still feels and sounds good, but you notice a certain feeling of effort, and an edge in the tone, which had not been there before. Also your left hand feels a little tight, so notes which you have never had to think about before keep going out of tune. On the day before the concert, for some reason the piece now seems slightly awkward to play. It isn't that you cannot play it; just that it does not feel quite as easy compared with how very free and easy it had felt the previous week. By the time you get to the concert you are having to try in a way that you were not having to do one week before. Then, a few days later, after the concert, everything feels easy again.

The moment this sequence starts to happen – and any other time your playing does not seem comfortable – one simple thing to check is that your shoulders are free, and the specific place to check is this minor pectoral muscle. If you release this muscle your bow arm will immediately return to normal. The smoothness and evenness of the bow strokes will return, as will the sweetness and roundedness of the tone, and the intonation.

This is one answer to the question of why the playing becomes more difficult as the date of the performance approaches: if, as it gets closer, you become unconsciously more and more ever-so-slightly in awe of the event, you ever-so-slightly tense up in preparation. This is exactly the same as a sportsman tightening in preparation for an action.

Having let go, keep checking to make sure that you are still releasing. At times you may need to remind yourself every few seconds. Find places in the music to mark 'shoulder' or 'release':

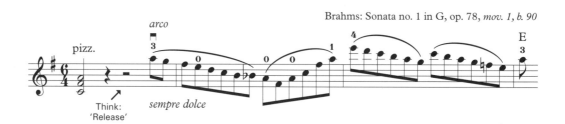

Brahms: Sonata no. 1 in G, op. 78, *mov. 1, b. 90*

This is a place, before the eighth-notes (quavers), to lengthen and widen and release. Then, if you hold the violin quite flat so that the bow can rest on the string – and if you do not so much 'hold' the bow as 'follow it', allowing it its own sense of momentum and flow – the entry on the E string is guaranteed to be effortless and sweetly singing.

Maintaining balance and flow: avoiding fixing

One of the easiest mistakes to make is that once we have found a correct posture or position, we then try to 'fix' ourselves in that position.

Do not 'lengthen the back', or widen at the shoulders, and then try to stay like that. There is no one, fixed place for the left thumb in any position. There is a neutral, middle place from which it starts and to which it may return, but in between it performs countless instinctive readjustments. There is no one, fixed, correct bow hold, or position of the upper arm, and so on. Everything must be mobile and free, and working from a state of balance. Other likely areas to check for fixing:

- Knees (should not lock backwards)

- Hips/upper leg (unconsciously trying to prevent natural swaying and expressive movements)

- Stomach area/solar plexus (clenching)

- Pulling down in the upper chest

- Pulling the shoulders in

- Pressing the head into the chin rest

- Fixing the left wrist in one tight position

- Pressing with the fingers on the string prevents them from maintaining an alive mobility.

- Fixing the position of the unused fingers over the string

Freeing the middle of the back and the costal arch

The costal arch

As you walk, the upper back moves in contrary motion to the lower back. As your shoulders swing clockwise, your hips swing anticlockwise, and vice versa.[1]

- Imagine a cross, the lines going from shoulder to hip (Fig. 107a). The point where the lines intersect is the place where the two halves of your back meet. It is essential not to tighten or 'fix' at this point, but remain free and mobile.

- Similarly, constantly widen and remain free in the same place in the front, the costal arch. This is the place near the solar plexus at the bottom of the rib cage, where the ribs divide.[2]

[1] Next time you are sitting in a restaurant notice how waiters manage to keep trays of drinks level while bringing them to the tables. They keep their arms and shoulders, and therefore the upper body, absolutely immobile. But something has to give somewhere. So the lower half of the body, from the costal arch downwards, swings from side to side much more than normal. If this swinging motion did not occur they would simply fall over within one or two steps.

[2] See also *Unlocking the costal arch*, page 195

Tension in this area (contraction or shortening of the muscles, rather than constant lengthening) leads to loss of balance and loss of freedom through the whole back, which in turn affects how the arms feel.

Playing the violin, whether standing or sitting, keep this area free so that there is an imperceptible degree of movement there during every bow stroke. You can encourage it with a simple exercise:

- Start with your hips and shoulders facing the same direction.

- Play simple long, slow strokes on one string (or just do it in the air without the instrument and bow). During the down-bows rotate your shoulders (i.e. your upper body) clockwise as far as you can go; during the up-bows rotate anticlockwise.

- Feel how all the give occurs at the costal arch because the hips remain still. You can simply think of moving the scroll to right and left, but make sure you do it with the whole upper part of your back rather than just moving your left arm on its own.

- Then, having started off with a large movement from side to side gradually make it smaller and smaller until the movement is barely visible, i.e. you are still rotating to the right on the down bow and to the left on the up bow, but moving only a millimeter either side of the middle point.

- Finally make no deliberate rotational movement at all. Think of a pendulum decreasing to a standstill and ending up at its perfect balance-point. As you continue to bow up and down notice a new sensation of lightness, balance and freedom at the costal arch. Your arms and shoulders will have a new buoyancy about them as well.

Not twisting the back

Keep the shoulders and hips facing in the same direction (Fig. 107b, Fig. 107c). Twisting the back, so that the shoulders face one way and the hips another, prevents easy spring-like mobility in the middle of the back and the costal arch (Fig. 107d, Fig. 107e).

Fig. 107

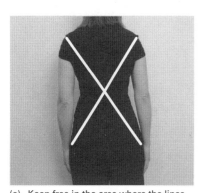

(a) Keep free in the area where the lines meet

(b) Keep the shoulders and hips facing the same way

(c) Do not twist to avoid hitting your right leg: sit upright and bow between your legs

(d) Typical twisted posture

(e) Twisting and bowing to the side of the leg

Freeing the shoulders

Raising or not raising

The most common advice is that you should not raise your left shoulder in holding the violin. However, it may feel unnatural and inhibiting if you do the opposite and purposely 'keep the shoulder down'. Dounis recommended a buoyant, mobile feeling in the shoulder:

> Lift the [left] shoulder slightly. The shoulder will then support the weight of the arm. Otherwise the weight will be in the elbow where it is a burden.[1]

[1] Valborg Leland: *The Dounis Principles of Violin Playing* (New York, 1982), 39.

Imagine that someone about your height is standing in front of you. You reach forwards with both arms to embrace them. Notice what you do with your shoulders as you reach forwards.

- It does not feel natural to force your shoulders to stay down, without any movement whatsoever, so that only your upper arms move (Fig. 108a).

- Nor do you 'raise' the shoulders, i.e. the same movement as shrugging (Fig. 108b). What happens naturally is that your shoulders 'come up' without being raised (Fig. 108c).

- This is a perfect model for what to do with the shoulders when playing the violin. (Fig. 108d, Fig. 108e, Fig. 108f). Of course, the correct height and position of any shoulder rest is crucial.[2]

[2] See *Using a shoulder rest*, page 27

The Alexander teacher Walter Carrington, after listening to a discussion about the left shoulder at a violin teachers' forum, said: "Instead of thinking about raising the shoulders, or not raising the shoulders, why don't you just keep the shoulders free?"

Fig. 108

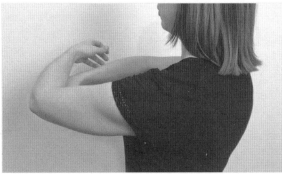

(a) The shoulders forced down unnaturally

(b) Raising the shoulders

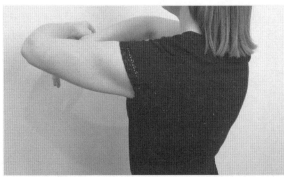

(c) The shoulders are active

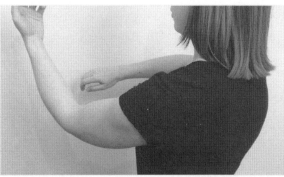

(d) The shoulders are too low

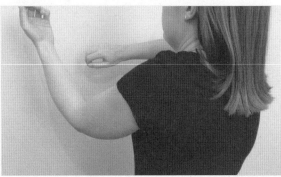

(e) The shoulders are too high

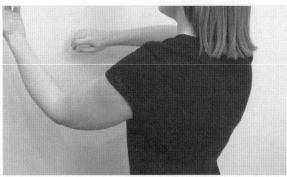

(f) The shoulders are 'up but not raised'

The shoulder and the elbow

It is often helpful to a student to understand the difference between the movements of the arm at the elbow and at the shoulder.

The elbow is called a hinge joint. The forearm can move only backwards and forwards on a horizontal plane, when held level with the floor. If it appears that the forearm can also move up and down, this is due to the upper arm rotating.[1]

The shoulder is called a ball-and-socket joint. The upper arm has the possibility of both horizontal and vertical movements, with a combination of these producing a circular movement.

Teacher or assistant

- With your right hand, take the complete weight of the arm at the elbow joint (Fig. 109a).

- Place your left hand on the shoulder to encourage it to keep still. With your right hand move the upper arm in circles to demonstrate the freedom of movement in any direction (Fig. 109b).

Student

- 'Flop' the weight of your arm into the supporting hand. Do not make any movements yourself.

- Allow the arm to be moved in any direction, feeling it move within the shoulder socket without any movement whatsoever in the shoulder itself.

[1] Curiously, although forearm rotation is a standard term in violin playing, upper arm rotation is rarely ever mentioned throughout the whole of the violin literature. One exception was the American teacher Paul Rolland, who used pegs attached to the students' clothes to graphically illustrate the rotation of the forearm or upper arm

Fig. 109

 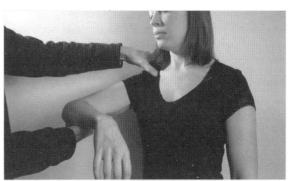

(a) Take the complete, flopped weight of the arm in your right hand

(b) Move the upper arm in circles with your right hand

Keeping the shoulder down and the elbow up

One of the things children often have difficulty with is keeping the right elbow supported without raising the shoulder. Often, if their elbow is too low (Fig. 110a) and you ask them to raise it so that it is level with the bow, they raise the shoulder too (Fig. 110b). If you then ask them to drop the shoulder, the elbow drops too (Fig. 110a). They need to learn how to do one without the other (Fig. 110c):

Fig. 110

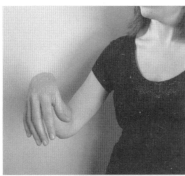 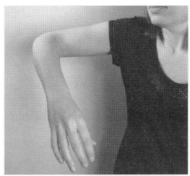 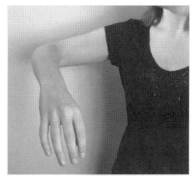

(a) The elbow is too low

(b) Unintentionally raising the shoulder as well as the elbow

(c) Elbow level with the bow

Freeing the left hand

Understanding flexibility

You do not need to try to develop 'flexibility' in your hands and fingers. You already have it most of the time. Whenever you are not playing, and engaged in ordinary, everyday activities, your hands are soft, relaxed and pliable.

What you must do is keep that softness and flexibility when you play the violin. Instead, many players go through the following process:

1 Before you pick up the violin and bow, your hands and fingers are soft and flexible, i.e. no muscles in the hands or fingers are in a constant state of contraction.

2 Every time you are just about to play, first you tighten (i.e. contract) the muscles in your hands, fingers, wrists and arms, so that they feel hard and inflexible.

3 You spend many years doing relaxation exercises on the violin, forever trying to build freedom and ease, relaxation and release into your technique and general playing.

Instead of this, why not miss out stages 2 and 3? Your hands are soft and pliable before you pick up the instrument; keep them like that as you go to pick up the violin and bow; then keep them soft and pliable as you move your fingers around the fingerboard and manipulate the bow.

But aren't children's muscles naturally softer, unspoilt by years of tension, so that if they are taught good technique at an early age they will never develop tension in the first place? Therefore isn't it a much more difficult matter for an older person somehow to undo the tensions they have built up over the years?

The 'build-up of tension over the years' is often an illusion. Tension may feel the same as it did last week and be in the same place, but it is not the same tension. It is more that over the years you build up a long history of being in the habit of contracting certain muscles, i.e. tensing them.

We tend to think: "There is that tight feeling again that is always there," as though it is the same tension that we had last time and now have to deal with again. In fact contracting the muscles, or allowing them to release and lengthen, is something that happens in the present, in the here-and-now.

Most children do not naturally and automatically hold the bow without tension, or move their fingers on the strings without tension. You can prove this with a simple experiment.

- Ask a young child to stand, without the bow, with their right hand relaxed and 'floppy'. Very slowly bring a bow towards their hand: in almost every case they will stiffen their hand and fingers (contract the muscles) in preparation as the bow approaches their hand.

- You can do the same thing with their left hand. Ask them to stand with the violin under the chin, but the left hand down and away from the neck of the violin. Make sure their hand is completely soft. As they move their hand towards playing position, notice how in most cases the hand tightens on the way to the neck and arrives in a state of hardness; and that is before they have pressed the string down too hard and counter-pressed with the thumb, which causes even more tension.

As an adult, the difference is that you have self-motivation and will-power at your command, and can guide yourself to the desired result quickly.

Continual moments of release

Take every opportunity to release and soften the hand. One of the key relaxing moments to take advantage of, is when you play an open string.

- Make sure that your hand does not remain 'active' when playing an open string (Fig. 111a) – after all, there is nothing for it to do. The hand can release completely (Fig. 111b):

Fig. 111

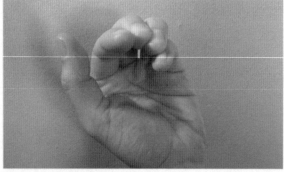

(a) Tight, contracted hand

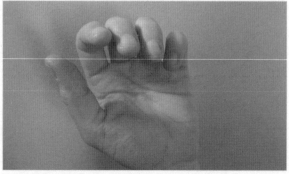

(b) 'Open', released hand while playing an open string

Freeing the thumb

Ask the student to hold their hand out, fingers outstretched. Point to the little finger and ask: "How many joints are there in that finger?"

Some will reply "three" without any hesitation; some will begin a close examination of their finger, looking at it as if for the first time, before answering.

Then point to the third finger and ask: "How many joints are there in that finger?" Again some will answer 'three' immediately; others will once more inspect their finger closely before replying.

Point to the middle finger and ask the question again, and then the same for the index finger.

Then point to the thumb and ask: "How many joints are there in that finger?" Nearly everybody will immediately answer: "Two!" That's not true. The thumb also has three, with the base joint near the wrist.

Many players have a mental picture of the middle finger being the longest on the hand, and the thumb the shortest. Take a ruler and measure from the tip of the middle finger to the base joint (Fig. 112a); and from the tip of the thumb to its base joint near the wrist (Fig. 112b). The thumb is easily the longest finger on the hand.

Fig. 112

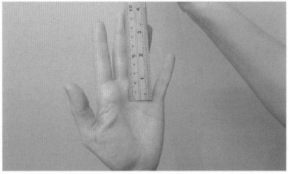

(a)   It is easy to suppose that the middle finger is the longest

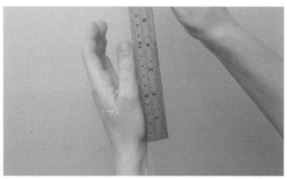

(b)   The thumb is longer

(c)   Many players have a mental picture of the thumb beginning here

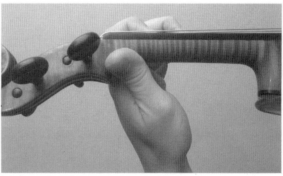

(d)   Clenching with the thumb causes the whole hand to tighten

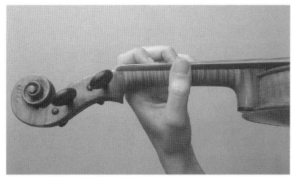

(e)   Practise tapping exercises with the thumb exaggeratedly forwards

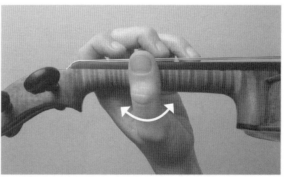

(f)   The thumb can rotate as well as move forwards and backwards

If you have a mental picture of the thumb beginning at the place where it seems to join on to the hand (Fig. 112c), there is nothing you can do when you try to 'relax the thumb' because all the releasing, relaxing and softening happens in the big muscle in the ball of the thumb.

Instead, the moment you feel the thumb working from its base joint a new feeling of release, balance and springy agility comes into the entire hand. Exactly the same applies to the right hand.

Practising exercises with the thumb exaggeratedly forward

It is difficult to free the hand if the thumb clenches backwards against the base joint of the first finger (Fig. 112d). Releasing the thumb is usually the first thing to do to release the left hand.

The thumb should not stay fixed in one position on the neck of the violin, but is naturally mobile and 'clever' in the way it moves in relation to the actions of the fingers. Sometimes the best balance in the hand is when the thumb is quite near the nut; sometimes the thumb may be quite far forward and 'open', almost opposite the second finger.

- Practise not squeezing with the thumb by playing with it exaggeratedly forward, opposite or nearer the third finger (Fig. 112e). Set the thumb in this position whenever you practise finger exercises like tapping (page 187), or the trill exercise (page 152), and so on.

- In extreme cases of locking and clenching, put an eraser or a small, soft ball between the base of the thumb and the first finger. Playing like that for just a few minutes each day, for only a few days, may be all that you need to form a new habit of not squeezing. Afterward, the urge to squeeze backwards will seem absurd.

Thumb rotation

Many players do not realise that the thumb – as well as being able to move forwards and backwards – can also rotate slightly, clockwise and anticlockwise, on the neck of the violin. Move it from all the way down at the base joint near the wrist (Fig. 112f).

- Frequently rotate the thumb one way and then the other, for a few seconds, to make sure it is free.

Experiment: play without the chin on the violin

Fig. 113

[1] 'Preparing' means moving the thumb ahead of the hand, e.g. in a shift from 3rd to 1st position you can keep the hand in 3rd position while moving the thumb into 1st position, and then follow with the hand.

Do not think about the thumb. You never need to use it consciously unless you sometimes like to 'prepare' with the thumb when shifting (and even then the preparation is normally unconscious).[1]

So long as the thumb is not locked backwards, you can leave it alone to look after itself. You can prove this by means of a simple experiment.

Rest the violin on the collar bone without your chin touching the chin rest (Fig. 113). Play something that involves shifting – say, a simple scale or arpeggio.

Playing without the chin touching the violin

Notice how, when shifting up, the action of shifting pushes the violin in against your neck, so there is no danger of dropping the violin.

However when you try to come back down again, the action of shifting has the effect of trying to pull the violin off your shoulder:

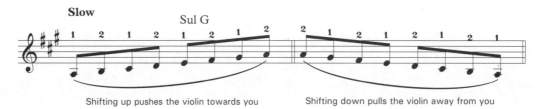

Shifting up pushes the violin towards you   Shifting down pulls the violin away from you

Therefore your thumb, as you descend, has to move down just before the shift; then, using the thumb as a support or a pivot, you can move the rest of the hand into the new position and play the new note.

Playing this descending scale without a shoulder rest, your thumb instinctively moves at exactly the right moment in order to lend support to the shift.

The ability to do something, and the ability to explain or teach it to somebody else, are two entirely different things. You do not need to know anything at all for the thumb to react instinctively, and do exactly the right thing at the right time.

The principle of the double contact

When I was a child my violin teacher told me that in 1st position there must always be enough space for a pencil to fit between the neck of the violin and the side of the first finger (Fig. 114a).

I did not like the feeling of the space and quickly forgot all about it, and carried on in the way that felt comfortable (i.e. not squeezing the neck but often touching it). Fortunately my teacher forgot about it too, or at any rate never mentioned it again.

Ten years later I discovered that my instinct had luckily been correct, and Ivan Galamian even had a name for the need to reference the neck with the first finger: the 'principle of the double contact'.

Countless violinists who had stricter teachers on this point than I did, do try to keep their first finger away from the neck at all times. This causes many problems, including tension and poor finger action, poor intonation and difficulty in shifting, and tense and restricted vibrato.

Experiment

- If there is no contact at all with the neck, it is impossible to find a note accurately.

  Hover the hand very close to the neck in 1st position, but without any actual contact with the violin whatsoever. Keep the thumb half a centimetre away from the neck; do not touch the neck with the side of the first finger.

  Try putting a finger down on a note in tune. Finding it is a matter of chance.

- If there is one point of contact, the thumb, it is naturally easier to aim the finger on to the string (Fig. 114b); but it is still difficult to measure where the note is precisely, and the hand feels tight and the finger action feels awkward.

Fig. 114

(a) The times are rare when there should be this space here

(b) Trying to find a note with only one point of contact

(c) The side of the first finger is the second point of contact

(d) Once the finger is down there are three points of contact

- You need to have at least two points of contact. The thumb is always one of them, and in the lower positions the side of the first finger, lightly brushing against the neck (never pressing, sometimes coming away for a moment, at other times directly touching the neck) is the other (Fig. 114c).

- However, once the finger is down on the string, there are then three points of contact – the thumb, the side of the first finger, and the finger on the string (Fig. 114d). At this point, the first finger can come away slightly from the neck (especially to free the vibrato), but in doing so still leaves any other finger two points of contact with which to orientate itself.

In a fast passage, the side of the first finger continues to reference the neck throughout. Play the following fast scale twice, once with the first finger contacting the neck and then while keeping a space between the neck and the side of the first finger.

Notice the feeling of freedom and ease when you contact the neck, compared with when you keep a space:

Freeing the wrist

Q **What is the correct position of the left wrist?**

In low positions the back of the hand should be in a straight line with the elbow, wherever possible. Sometimes there may be certain chords that feel comfortable only when the wrist moves out slightly, but for normal playing a straight line at the wrist is the most suitable.

Sometimes you can produce a good feeling of release by allowing the wrist very slightly to give in; but a hand position that is based on the wrist sticking out may be prone to tension.

Obviously in higher positions there has to be an outward bend at the wrist.

Relaxation exercise

If you find that your wrist tends to lock, which then makes the hand and finger-action feel less free, practise a few simple notes while moving the wrist in and out:

- Push the wrist out slightly, so that there is an outward bend.

- Pull in slightly, so that the wrist curves inwards. Feel the ease that a 'giving' wrist creates, rather than the feeling of effort – or at worst, strain – when the wrist pushes outwards.

- Experiment with different degrees of finger pressure to stop the notes, and see what effect there is on the freedom in the wrist. Over-press the string, and see if you can find how to keep the wrist free anyway.

Afterwards, with the wrist in a straight line and without over-pressing the string, you will find that your entire hand feels unusually relaxed and free.

Manipulating the wrist

You can get an astonishing result by gently manipulating the eight bones in your left wrist. It is very easy to do and instantly produces great freedom in the left hand. You can also find a new rubbery springiness in the right wrist by doing the same there. A new silkiness and smoothness immediately enters every bow stroke.

You have to use your instinct and common sense as to how hard to do it, but the key thing is that even a slight push, even so *slight as to be barely noticeable*, has a good effect. However, if you feel little resistance and can find a slight springiness in the bones as you move them, you can probably be less cautious. It is this feeling of springiness, rather than rigidity, that is the ideal and the objective.

Key point: Force is not the issue and must never be used. It is more a matter of giving the bones the gentlest, most subtle encouragement to be free. (Of course, it is not the bones themselves that are not free, but everything attached to them.)

- With the left palm facing up, place the fingers of your right hand on the back of your wrist, and use your thumb to push against the large, protruding bones on the right side of the wrist (Fig. 115a).

  Push with the fingers (on the back of the hand) in the direction of the elbow; push with the thumb (against the bone) in the direction of your fingers. As you do so keep the hand free, allowing it to move or rotate or do whatever it likes.

  Push against the large, protruding bone on the left side (Fig. 115b).

- With the palm of the left hand facing towards you, place the index finger of the right hand flat against the top of your left wrist so that it sits on the two protruding bones. Then use your thumb on the other side of the wrist – positioned not quite opposite the first finger but slightly to the right of it (Fig. 115c). Gently push forwards with the thumb while opposing with the first finger. As you do so allow the wrist to give slightly.

- With the palm facing down, reverse the fingers: place the thumb flat against the two protruding bones on the top of the wrist (Fig. 115d). Gently push upwards with the index finger on the two protruding bones on the other side of the wrist (i.e. the first finger is a little closer towards the fingers than the thumb).

- With the left palm facing down, keep your left forearm quite still while you gently turn your left hand with your right (Fig. 115e). There is only a tiny rotational movement possible. Whatever that small distance is that you can move the left hand with your right, move it gently to and fro without any hint of movement in the forearm, giving only in the wrist.

    Or hold the left hand still with your right, and gently rotate the forearm.

- With the left hand in violin playing position, hold the left wrist with the right thumb one side of the left wrist and index finger the other side, exactly on top of those eight little bones (Fig. 115f). Shake the wrist very, very quickly, as though trying to make the narrowest, fastest arm vibrato. Allow the left hand to be completely passive throughout.

- Pressing in the region of those eight bones quite hard with the right thumb one side and the index finger the other, make slow and gentle fingering motions with the left fingers. Move the left fingers from the base joints.

Clearly, there are many other things you can do along the same lines, and once again instinct is your guide as you gently explore and discover new possibilities.

Fig. 115

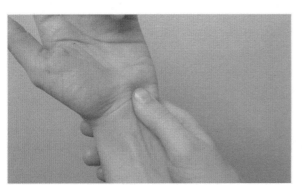

(a) Gently leaning in to the bone on the right side

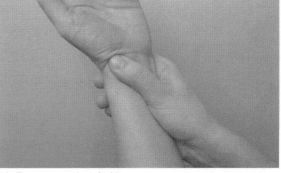

(b) The same on the left side

(c) The thumb positioned just in front of the first finger

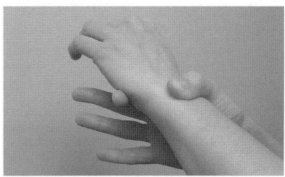

(d) The other way round

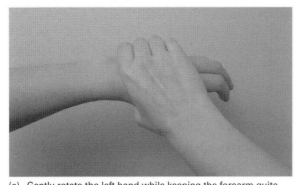

(e) Gently rotate the left hand while keeping the forearm quite still. Or *vice versa*

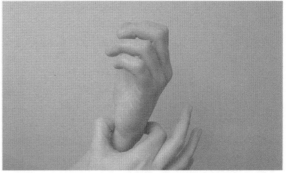

(f) Shake the forearm with a slight, gentle but quick movement

I often witness the powerful, instant effects of doing this. For example, a student with quite small hands (though wide at the knuckles) who was having difficulty playing the extended fourth fingers near the opening of the third movement of the Mendelssohn Violin Concerto (marked +):

I showed her how to free the bones in her wrist, which she did for about a minute, and then she played the perfect fifth again, first finger B to fourth finger F♯ (while holding down the first finger). She was astonished as, with no effort at all, she overshot the F♯ and nearly placed her fourth finger on a G. But this can be repeated over and over again with the majority of violinists.

The effects of the tiniest amount of gentlest wrist manipulation are profound. Even the finest players remark on how, after 30 seconds of doing it, their left hand (or right hand) feels superior to how it did before.

The situation of players who suffer from major feelings of impediment in the left hand, can be likened to someone behind bars in prison for years, yet all the time the keys were just sitting there within reach. The prisoner was 30 seconds from freedom the whole time.

Use a very small, mild amount of wrist manipulation often as a key warming up or pre-warming up exercise. After a while you may find that you no longer have the urge to do it, and you can then return to it briefly whenever you need a 'boost' of freedom.[1]

[1] Gentle manipulation of the wrist is excellent in five ways: you can do it yourself; it is entirely painless and non-aggressive; it takes moments to do; the results are fantastic; and you need to do it less-and-less often

Placing fingers gently: the secret of a relaxed left hand

I could barely contain my excitement when I first understood this principle. The principles behind it are obvious and well-known; yet they add up to a new general rule that I had not come across before:

- The only time that you need to drop a finger on to the string with speed and impact is in ascending slurs. Playing all other notes the finger should be placed.

Notes are either ascending or descending; and either slurred under one bow or played with a separate bow. There are four possibilities: **(1)** descending, separate, **(2)** descending, slurred, **(3)** ascending, separate, **(4)** ascending, slurred.

(1) and **(2)** Playing any descending notes (slurred or separate) the lower finger should be placed on the string before the upper finger is lifted (i.e. finger preparation). Or, playing the first note on a new string, the finger should be placed on the string before the bow gets there.

All that matters is that the finger is ready before the bow plays the string. There is no tonal difference between placing the finger suddenly and purposefully, as though stopping a vibrating string, and placing it gently, except that one takes more energy than the other.

(3) During ascending separate bows there is also no need to drop the finger with energy. If you look at the string vibrating, you can see that it stops vibrating for an instant as the bow changes direction. It is during that moment that the finger stops the string ready for the next bow stroke.

Again, there is nothing gained by dropping the finger as though the string were moving from side to side. Placing the finger in separate bows is a matter of co-ordination, and is entirely different from the feeling of playing ascending slurs.

(4) Only ascending slurs require articulation in the fingers since this is the one time that the finger falls on to an actively vibrating string. Even then, the more quietly the note is played, the less the string swings from side to side, and the more slowly the finger can stop the string.

Key point: The feeling of placing most fingers gently is one of extraordinary effortlessness, as each finger simply gets itself ready for the bow to play it, instead of playing everything with needless extra energy.

Of course this must not be taken too far or the hand may feel too passive. Some notes require more finger energy for musical reasons, e.g. to stress a certain note or as part of the rhythmic feel in the left hand. 'Finger accents' are a normal part of the feel of violin playing.

But if the fingers are already working hard, they have to work even harder to drop with extra musical feeling or articulation. When the normal finger action, except for ascending slurs, is generally 'quiet', you need only the slightest extra articulation when you do want a finger to be more active.

Moving the finger from the base joint

Moving fingers from the base joints, rather than partially moving them from the hand, is another of the most important issues in the whole left hand technique.

- Hold your left hand in playing position without the violin. Look at the angle that is formed by the back of the hand, and the lowest section of the finger (Fig. 116a).

- Move the fourth finger from the base joint, keeping the rest of the hand entirely still (Fig. 116b).

- Keep the shape of the finger the same as you move it backwards and forwards.

- Notice the changing angle between the back of the hand and the lowest section of the finger.

Key point: The essential thing is to avoid moving the finger partially with the hand itself (Fig. 116c).

Fig. 116

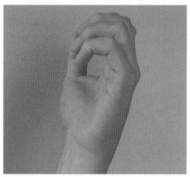  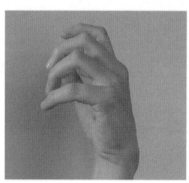

(a) Note the angle between the back of the hand and the lowest section of the finger

(b) Moving the finger from the base joint, notice how the angle changes

(c) The hand has moved forward with the finger

Tapping exercises

Tapping the fingers on the strings, without the bow, is a simple, neat and effortless way to keep your left fingers in good working order.

To get the maximum benefit, it is essential that you raise and drop your fingers from the base joints, rather than from the hand.

- While you should not play the violin like this normally, drop the fingers with enough weight and speed that each finger sounds the note, i.e. in the first bar of Example 1 you should hear 'A A A A, E E E E, B B B B, F♯ F♯ F♯ F♯'. This is produced by the finger going 'down, down, down, down'.

  The second finger produces B♭, F, C, G. What you do not want to hear is the sound of the open strings, i.e. hearing 'G G G G, D D D D, A A A A, E E E E' whatever the finger you are tapping the string with. This is caused by the finger action being 'up, up, up, up'.

- For the sake of rhythm and symmetry tap in regular groups, e.g. do not tap three times (say) on one string, then four times on the next, then five times, and then four again. It helps the rhythmic pulse if you give the slightest extra finger accent on the first of each group.

Example 1

The obvious thing to do first is simply to tap each finger on each string:

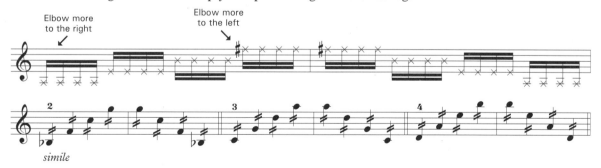

simile

- Tap quickly and lightly, and as evenly as possible.

- Repeat in groups of three on each string, with a slight accent on the first of each.

- Repeat in pairs on each string.

- Repeat with one tap on each string.

- You can take all tapping exercises on to a different level by holding down some or all of the unused fingers on the string.

If you do only this exercise – playing it a few times each day for a few days, for a couple of minutes at a time, moving the fingers well from the base joints – you will notice a new freedom quickly coming into your general playing, as your left hand starts to feel easy and effortless.

However, the better your fingers feel when playing some notes, the more you may notice that there are other notes that do not feel as good.

This is because the finger movements that feel easier will be simple up and down movements like those in the tapping exercise in Example 1. The finger movements that feel less easy, in contrast, may involve the finger lifting or dropping while at the same time moving horizontally to another string.

The following type of exercise, horizontal tapping, is the answer:

Example 2

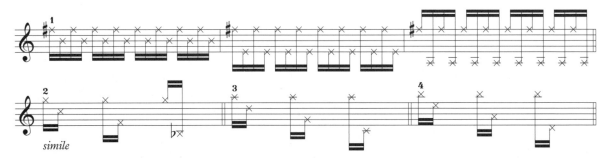

simile

After the horizontal tapping, one more type to add is the movement along the string:

Example 3

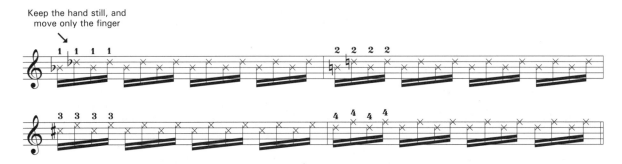

These are examples of the most basic and effective tapping exercises, and are great for warming up. Each time you do them – making sure you drop each finger lightly and freely from the base joints – they quickly get the hand and fingers working.

Pull the note out of the string with the finger

One thing to be aware of in practising tapping exercises, is that most of the time you cannot actually play like that. Tapping the finger on the string is mechanical and unmusical.

Q **If this is not the way you should play, surely tapping would be bad for you? How should the fingers work instead?**

Tapping exercises make the fingers move lightly, freely and quickly; but afterwards, instead of mechanically 'hitting' the string with the finger, you have to return to a feeling of lifting, drawing or pulling the note out of the string with the fingertip. There is often an upward feeling when you stop the string which makes the left hand feel sensual and musical, rather than a downward percussive action.

The idea of the left finger 'pulling' the note out of the string makes no sense if you look at it from a practical point of view. The left finger works in a downward direction, sometimes vertically and more often diagonally, in order to stop the string firmly enough for the tone to be pure.

Yet there is a feeling, or a perception, that is quite easy to find, of the finger drawing the note out of the string rather than of pressing the string.

- Imagine that the sound is not created by the bow but by the finger, and that the place where the finger touches the string is where all the musical expression comes out of the violin.

- Rather than 'putting a finger down on the string', the finger comes down towards the string to meet it and then, as it contacts the string, draws the note and the musical expression out of the string.

Still, the benefits of tapping exercises are clear. You have only to invest a small amount of time in them before you start to notice extra lightness and quickness in your finger action.

How can I stop pressing the strings too hard?

Stopping the string more than necessary wastes energy and makes the fingers feel heavy and slow.

> The degree of pressure is determined by the sound desired. When the tone is clear, the pressure is sufficient. The amount of pressure does change according to circumstance, but should never exceed a necessary minimum.[1]

[1] Yuri Yankelevich

One of the knock-on effects of excess pressing is that the thumb has to counterpress more to equal it, leading to a feeling of clamping the neck of the violin between finger and thumb. Lightening the finger-pressure immediately leads to a lightening of the thumb on the neck of the violin, and vice versa.

Over-pressing the left fingers is also one of the first reasons for a dead or metallic tone.[2]

[2] It is easy to make the mistake of working only on the right arm to improve or sweeten the tone, and to forget about the left fingers.

Then all efforts seem in vain because the one thing that should be changed – the left fingers over-pressing – is ignored.

This is the reverse of practising the left hand for purer intonation when the problem is in the bow, i.e. 'bending' the pitch by over-pressing the bow (see *Bow-pressure and pitch*, page 84).

Changing the mental picture

When working with a student on freeing the left hand, or when working on intonation (which depends on complete freedom of the hand), one of the first questions to ask is whether the student thinks that the left fingers should press the string down until the string makes a firm contact with the fingerboard.

Are they mistakenly thinking of it as a guitarist does, i.e. when playing *pizzicato* the harder you stop the strings the better, since then the instrument rings more?[3]

[3] See *The one time you need to press the left fingers hard*, page 320

Many students answer yes – their mental picture is indeed one of pressing the string down until it touches the fingerboard – when actually the best approach is always to stop the string as little as possible. This is an area where the principle of 'as much as necessary but as little as possible' clearly applies.

Five levels of pressure

The first step is to find exactly how little finger-weight is actually needed to stop the string cleanly:

Level 5   'Harmonic' level, where the string is not pushed down at all.

Level 1   The string pushed down to touch the fingerboard.

Level 3   Midway between 5 and 1.

Level 4   Midway between 5 and 3.

Level 2   Midway between 3 and 1.

Sensitisation exercise

- Place the third finger on D on the A string, as lightly as if to play a harmonic (Level 5).

- Moving the finger down slowly and gently, push the string down until you can feel it contact the fingerboard (Level 1). Feel the elasticity or springiness of the string.

- Release the string back to Level 5. Repeat several times.

    Feel the resistance of the string as you slowly push it down or let it back up again.

- Now find the middle point between Level 5 and Level 1: change between 5–1–3 several times, gauging the degree of weight for Level 3 that is exactly in the middle between the two extremes.

- Then find the middle point between Level 5 and Level 3: change between 5–3–4 several times, each time gauging the degree of weight for Level 4 that is in the middle between 5 and 3.

- Experiment in the same way to find Level 2, changing between 3–1–2 several times:

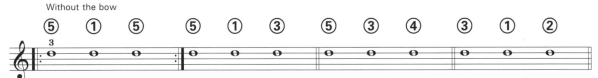

Without the bow

Repeat several times

As a general rule, the level to aim for is between Level 2 and Level 3. Many players use only Level 1 for everything they play, leading to problems of tension and slow fingers.

Playing with a softer finger changes the timbre of the note so that it becomes less focused and often sweeter or less strident. You can always stop the string further when you want a more concentrated or harder tone, or when playing *pizzicato*.

- Silently finger a few notes on each string, in each area of the fingerboard (low, middle and high), with each finger in turn, experimenting with all five degrees of finger pressure.

Starting from nothing and gradually increasing

Rather than starting from the point of too much pressing and then trying to release, work up from the point of too little pressure.

Play a short group of notes, or longer phrase, or even a whole passage, with full weight in the bow but with varying amounts of finger pressure, from too little up to just enough:

- Begin with so little finger-pressure (Level 5), but with a lot of weight in the string from the bow, that the sound is entirely impure.

- Repeat several times, each time gradually stopping the string a little more (Level 4, 3, 2).

- As you gradually increase the weight of the finger, while always keeping the bow heavy, the sound will gradually improve until it is entirely pure and sweet; but the left fingers will still feel light and nowhere near the maximum amount they could be stopping the string.

Replacing finger-pressure with arm-weight

Left-arm weight is something that you can use only in the smallest amounts, and it depends on how you hold the violin as to whether you can use it at all; but if you can find a way to use it a little, the extra feeling of effortlessness in the left fingers is noticeable.

[1] See *Finding the position by 'hanging' the arm*, page 143

Use arm-weight by 'hanging' the arm from the neck of the violin.[1]

- Hang the arm from the left fingers, meanwhile keeping a feeling of supporting the violin with the thumb. (To make it easier you can rest the scroll on a shelf or other support.)

- Feel how you can stop the string enough without 'pressing' the finger down at all, since the weight of the arm pulls the finger down into the string on its own.

- Notice how the thumb feels entirely light and effortless because there is no need for any counterpressure.

  If you do not lean the scroll on a shelf you may find yourself holding the violin more firmly with the chin than usual; but since this degree of hanging is an exaggeration, 'hanging' the arm in the normal course of playing does not lead to tension problems in holding the violin.

Rolling the finger into the string

Rolling the finger into the string is an extremely subtle detail of technique. It is to do with what happens as the fingertip contacts and then stops the string. Rolling produces a magical feeling of stopping the string without pressing the finger into the string.

When you press the finger downwards to stop the string, the thumb counter presses against the neck, leading to a feeling of clamping.

When you roll the finger into the string, the rolling alone is enough to stop the note, without the thumb seeming to have to do anything.

- You can get the feeling of rolling simply by resting your hand flat on a table top (Fig. 117a). Relax the weight of your arm into the hand, feeling the weight spread equally across the hand.

- Then lean the hand slightly on to the thumb side of the hand (Fig. 117b), and then lay it flat again. Notice how, as you lean on to the side of the hand, the feeling of weight into the table increases.

The feeling of rolling the finger into the string is similar, and as the finger rolls forwards the extra weight stops the string automatically.

Fig. 117

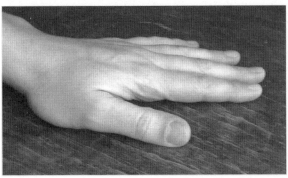

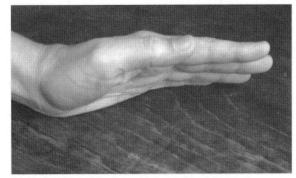

(a) Feel all the weight spread evenly across the palm of the hand   (b) Feel all the weight directed into the side of the hand

Q **If you roll fingers down on to the string, doesn't that affect the intonation, or make each note begin with a slide?**

The one time you can never roll the finger is during ascending slurred notes:

The difference between rolling the finger, and dropping it directly vertically, is often so slight that you can barely see the difference. Imagine looking at the moment of impact through a strong magnifying lens, and seeing it in slow motion: even if you think you are not rolling the finger, as the finger drops onto the string there may be an infinitesimal degree of rolling into the note at the last moment.

Drop fast on to the string without 'rolling'

Even so, the feeling of rolling is quite distinct from the feeling of pressing the finger down into the string.

Any notes preceded by silence can easily be stopped mainly by rolling, with no danger of a false beginning to the note. It is all a question of timing with the bow, so that the string is not played until the exact moment that the finger is in place.

It is also possible to roll into shifted-to notes:

(1) Drop the finger fast   (2) More rolling into the note   (3) More rolling

(1) Shifting up on the first finger, and then dropping the fourth finger down on to its note ('Classical' shift), is much like playing any other slur, and the action of the fourth finger is more 'straight down' than 'rolling' – though there is still a tiny amount of rolling the finger into the G.

(2) Shifting up on the fourth finger, so that the finger glides into the G from beneath ('Romantic' shift), makes it possible to stop the note entirely just by rolling. There is an enormous difference in freedom and ease in the hand, between rolling into the G and pressing it.

(3) Playing either shift with separate bows, it is possible to time the connection with the bow so that you roll into the note, just as in any separate bow notes.

Understanding balance

Key areas

Everything in nature is a constant striving to maintain balance, or to return to a state of balance when it is lost. Examples of key areas in which to maintain a sense of balance in violin playing:

- Balanced position of the feet
- Balanced posture – not pulling down, twisting, leaning to left or right
- The head balanced on top of the spine, not fixed in place
- The right arm working from a constant point of balance
- Balanced bow hold
- Balancing the bow in the hand, rather than gripping it, before placing it on the string

- Balanced feeling of the bow sitting in the string – the tilt, angle to bridge, string level
- Balance in the left upper arm – not pulling the arm one way or the other
- Balanced position of the left hand, giving each finger maximum advantage
- Correct part of the fingertip contacting the string to give balance to the finger and the hand
- Balanced left thumb position relative to the hand position and finger.

Hyper and hypo

One of the meanings of 'hyper' is 'excessive' in the sense of hypersensitive, hyperactive. It derives from the Greek 'hyper' meaning 'over'. 'Hypo' means 'less than normal', deriving from the Greek 'hypo' meaning 'under'.

The body strives to maintain balance at all times. If you are inflexible in one part of your body, you often need to compensate by becoming more flexible in another part of the body. If you are too loose in one area, you often need to compensate by becoming less loose in another.

Problems caused by compensation are common amongst athletes, who may all-too-easily over-train certain groups of muscles to the neglect of other groups.

Suppose you have aches and pains in your upper back, between the shoulder blades. You hurt there, so you think something must be wrong there. Your lower back feels fine, so you think you do not need to think about that area. You receive massage or physiotherapy on your upper back and shoulders. This brings relief, but the relief wears off quickly and you find yourself often in pain.

In fact, the cause of the pain might easily be that you are *hypo mobile* in the lower back, i.e. there is not enough mobility or movement there. In other words, the lower back is tight and locked solid.

To maintain balance, you have to give somewhere else if you are not giving in the lower back; otherwise you will fall over.

So because the lower back is *hypo mobile*, i.e. not moving, the upper back moves much more than it should do, and becomes *hyper mobile*. Then, because the upper back has too much movement it starts to hurt. But although the pain is in the upper back, the cause is in the lower back, and no amount of treatment in the upper back will make any permanent difference.

Knowing to look somewhere else

When you are analysing any physical actions in violin playing, keep the idea of the balances of hyper and hypo at the front of your mind all the time.

- Whenever you see something excessive in one area of playing it is often necessary to look to another area of the body entirely.
- If there is too much or too little of something, it is likely that a balancing will be going on somewhere else.

String instrument technique is full of examples of hyper and hypo compensations.

Unlocking the right elbow

Create a vivid example of hyper and hypo by playing rapid sixteenth-notes (semiquavers) with a slightly locked elbow:

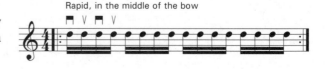

- Playing standing up, with your feet a natural distance apart, put the bow on the string in the middle of the bow (Fig. 118).

- Play quite rapid, short strokes, using only an upper arm movement, without allowing the right-angle at the elbow to change. Move the arm all in one piece, without any movement at the elbow.

Notice how your hips rotate in a counter-motion to the arm movement. The hypo mobility of the bowing arm causes hyper mobility of the whole torso.

The moment you see any movement like that in the hips, you always know immediately to look at the right elbow to see how free is the movement there. The slightest amount of extra opening and closing at the elbow always cures the hip movement immediately.

Excessive right wrist movement

Because of the slight change in the angle of the fingers as the bow moves from the heel to the point (hand more upright at the heel, more leaning at the point), the contact-point of the first finger with the bow changes. In Fig. 119 the 'H' shows the approximate contact-point with the bow when playing at the heel, 'P' the position at the point.

If this movement is restricted and is therefore hypo mobile, the give has to occur somewhere else. Typically the wrist becomes hyper mobile, raising too high above the level of the hand at the heel, and sinking too low at the point. This excessive wrist motion is called 'hills and valleys', and may easily disturb the smooth passage of the bow.[1]

Lack of forearm rotation (hypo mobile) may be another reason for excess movement in the right wrist.

Keeping the left upper arm free

If the left elbow remains locked in the G string position (i.e. positioned more to the right), the hand has to make excessive movements (bending at the wrist) to get the fingers on each string, particularly when playing on the E string.

Unlocking the left nail joint

The amount of give in the nail joint of the finger ranges from loose and almost floppy, to almost completely tight.

A hypo-active (locked) nail joint may be the cause of too-wide vibrato movements, both in hand or arm vibrato, because if a give does not occur in the nail joint it must happen somewhere else.

In the same way that a small amount of hand movement, during string crossings, takes away a far larger amount of right upper-arm movement, a small amount of movement in the nail-joint takes the place of a far larger movement in the rest of the left finger and hand.[2]

- If your vibrato is too wide or difficult to speed up, experiment with letting the nail joint go so that it is completely loose. Then 'tighten' it by degrees, until finding exactly the right freedom and energy that you want in the vibrato:

Fig. 118

The locked forearm causes the hips to rotate

[1] The old bow hold taught by Leopold Auer was nothing like this. He said, 'Always hold the bow firmly with the fingers but keep the wrist loose. Never loosen the fingers nor stiffen the wrist.'

In his bow hold, the contact-point of the first finger with the bow did not change between the heel and the point; but the hand was arranged so that the wrist was not low at the point of the bow.

Leopold Auer: *A Graded Course in Violin Playing*, Book 2 (New York, 1926), 20.

See also the margin note on page 45.

Fig. 119

Different points of contact of the first finger with the bow at the heel and the point

[2] Fingers, arms and legs all consist of three levers. The upper leg, upper arm and upper finger; the lower leg, forearm and middle joint of the finger; the foot, hand and nail-joint, are all roughly equivalent.

You can learn a lot about how the levers of one limb function by seeing how those of another one do. For example, the strongest levers of the arms and legs are the upper arm and upper leg, and all the large movements come from these. In the same way, the main movement of the finger should be the 'upper finger' moving at the base joint. Just as you cannot walk only by moving your lower legs at the knees, or throw a ball only by moving the forearm at the elbow, so the main movement of the finger must not be from the middle joint.

In the case of unlocking the left nail joint, see how big all the other movements become if you try to walk without any movement at the ankles, or use your hands without any movement at the wrists.

Repeat several times

Unlocking the left hand

Sometimes hyper movements in the arm are caused by hypo movements in the hand:

Flexibility in the base joints helps
the fourth finger to reach its note

Keep the first finger down
until playing the fourth finger

The way to get from the first finger to the fourth is to widen at the base joints, particularly between the first and second fingers, to help the fourth finger reach the lower string. Widening at the base joints brings the fourth finger base joint closer in to the neck without having to make other changes.

When the hand is not soft and flexible in the palm of the hand or at the base joints, the only way to get the fourth finger across to the next lower string is to move the elbow to the right (after playing the first finger), and move the entire hand into a slightly new position.

Conscious softening and widening of the hand, and simple flexibility exercises, are quick solutions.

Unlocking the fingers on the bow

The fingers holding the bow need to be ever-changing and adjusting to the different conditions of playing. This is a separate issue from that of adjusting between playing at the heel and at the frog.

If the fingers holding the bow lock, allowing no movement (hypo mobile), too much activity transfers to the arm and shows as excessive movement (hyper mobile) of the hand at the wrist, and in the forearm.

If the change from the hand being more upright at the heel, to more slanted at the point, is blocked during the first part of the down-bow – and then happens all at once somewhere around the middle of the bow – the bow may judder. The hand needs to 'follow the curve of the bow', and even if the amount of adjustment is hardly visible, the hair will remain smoothly in the string.

Excessive head movement

Many players fall into a habit of moving their head in contrary motion to the bow, i.e. moving to the right during the up-bow, and to the left during the down-bow:

Mozart: Concerto no. 4 in D, K218, *mov. 1, b. 42*

L   R   L   R   L   R L   R   L R L R etc.

L = Left   R = Right

The moment you stop extra movements like these, an entirely new level of freedom, precision and control enters the bow arm, and the playing gains in authority.

Fig. 120

(a) During the up-bow, moving the head to the right   (b) During the down-bow, moving the head to the left

Bowing smoothly

Suppose the bow is not smooth as it first contacts the string, but shakes or judders on impact. If the bow is shaking, you could say that it is being hyper mobile. So something somewhere must be hypo mobile. A typical reason is lack of give in the fingers and in the thumb at the moment of impact.

The fingers and thumb act as shock absorbers. Something has to give somewhere, even if the amount is so slight as to be imperceptible. If it is not in the fingers then it must occur somewhere else, so the bow itself shakes. A flexible, shock absorbing right thumb is one of the most essential aspects of the bow hand, enabling silky-smooth legato and clean *spiccato*.

Vibrato (particularly arm vibrato) may be another reason for the judder. If the vibrating left finger is tense (hypo mobile), the violin itself moves too (and therefore the string under the bow-hair). The most common reason for the scroll of the violin shaking during vibrato is tension in the base of the thumb.

Unlocking the costal arch

If you do not allow freedom at the costal arch or in the middle point of the back, any rotation of the upper body has to happen all-in-a-piece from hip to shoulder.[1] Whether you play standing up or sitting down, the result is a particular and visible constriction in all the playing.

[1] See *Freeing the middle of the back and the costal arch*, page 176

Constriction occurs because the lack of smaller movement in the middle of the back causes larger movements of the whole back to occur. This leads to a feeling of general holding back because every movement feels too large and unwieldy and you are forced to contain them.

Keeping the knees free

When playing standing up, keep checking that your knees remain free and never locked backwards. Locking the knees has two disadvantages.

- The first is that all the 'shock absorbing' springiness is lost from the knees, and this again translates into larger, less subtle or less fine movement in the upper body.

- The second is that if you lock your knees backwards it is natural for the pelvis to want to swing forwards (in order to keep your balance). This in turn creates a downward pressure onto the small of your back, which over time can lead to lower back pain.

If a violinist frequently needs to relieve pain in the lower back by bending forwards, one of the first places to check is the knees. The second place to check is the upper back, that you are not pulling down there.

Unlocking the shoulders

One of the most frequently-given instructions to violinists is 'do not raise your shoulders'. This advice is in itself incomplete,[2] but even if the advice is basically good it must not lead to 'holding the shoulders down' and fixing them there rigidly.

[2] See *Freeing the shoulders*, page 178

Preventing freedom in the shoulders makes every action in the arms feel like much harder work than when the actions are invisibly shared beyond the arms into the shoulders and back.

Any sign of a player having to 'work hard' in bowing, or in moving around the violin, may be an indication that they are tight in the shoulders and need to understand the importance of not 'fixing'.

Positioning the feet for balance

The feet must have sufficient space between them to form a solid base.

- The feet cover the smallest possible area when they are side by side and touching. Spreading the feet further apart creates a larger base.

- Turning the feet slightly outwards increases the area further.

- Positioning one foot slightly more forward increases the area still further.

Apart from the weight moving from foot to foot as the player sways, if weight is to rest on only one foot it should be on the left foot. This is the stable side, while the bow arm is the unstable side.

Although there is greater stability when the left foot is positioned slightly behind the right (because of the increased surface area), the best position of the feet is probably when they are side by side and the weight is distributed equally between both of them. Then there is no twist in the spine.

However, so long as nothing is 'fixed', a small imbalance caused by the right foot sometimes being slightly more forward does not cause problems.[3]

There are three points of the foot to stand on (Fig. 121). Stand with your balance slightly more on the forward two points than on the single, rear point.

Fig. 121

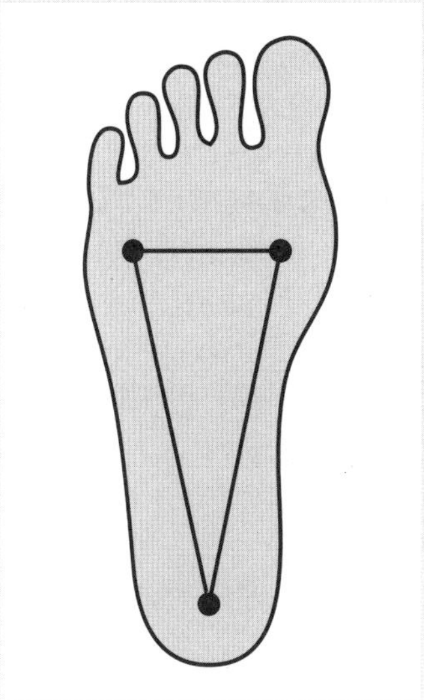

Stand slightly more on the forward two points

[3] 'The player must stand erect with the weight of his body resting on the left foot, and with the right foot slightly in advance. It should be mentioned that certain modern authorities favour a straddled position of the legs, in which the full weight of the body rests upon both feet, a solid but rather ungainly attitude as a whole.'

Leopold Auer: *A Graded Course in Violin Playing*, Book 1 (New York, 1926), 9

Q **Should the feet stay in one place, or move from place to place while you play?**

One end of the range of possibilities is that the feet never move, once planted in one place on the floor. At the other end of the range the feet adjust themselves frequently.

In many passages, or types of bow stroke, it is better to keep a solid, stable base. If you shift your balance from one foot to another, or make other postural changes, you can easily disturb your own playing and make mistakes that you would not have made if you had kept still.

Moving may also disturb the music: it is difficult to play long phrases or long musical lines if you adjust your posture every couple of notes or bars; or, say, continually nod the scroll up and down.

In other passages it may be more natural to alter the balance of the body before beginning a stroke, phrase or passage, and the feet should be allowed to adjust their position accordingly.

Swaying, rotating, shifting the balance

You may like to stay quite still when playing, or you may allow yourself to move more. If you basically keep still, the essential thing is not to be fixed in one position but to keep a feeling of balance and flow.

Either way, experiment with swaying and rotating in order to find a basis of freedom and naturalness:

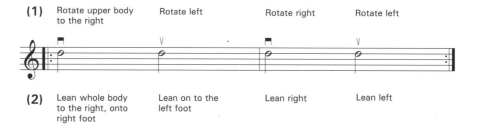

(1) Without moving your feet, turn your upper body almost 90° round to the right as you play the down-bow, and the same to the left as you play the up-bow.

Arrive at the point as you finish turning to the right; at the heel as you finish turning to the left.

Make sure you remain free and flexible at the costal arch.[1] Look for a feeling of smoothness and flow, and of 'going with the bow'.

Rotate 'all-of-a-piece', i.e. do not move the violin round with the left arm. The relationship of the bow to the violin, and the speed of the bow, should stay the same as when you remain still.

[1] See *Freeing the middle of the back and the costal arch*, page 176

(2) Instead of rotating, lean your whole body to the right during the down-bow, so that your left foot almost leaves the floor; lean on to the left foot during the up-bow.

Feel your whole body as one piece, with your weight going heavily into the floor through your feet.

(3) Combine **(1)** and **(2)** so that, while rotating, your whole body leans to the right during the down-bow and your left foot almost leaves the floor; rotate and lean on to the left foot during the up-bow.

Homeostasis: the 'wrong' things may be 'right'

Most living creatures are 'designed' or 'programmed' to seek balance, health and pleasure, and to flee from imbalance, disease and pain, simply in order to survive. As part of that process, if you begin to fall over you instinctively try to right yourself; when the outside temperature falls, the pores of your skin contract to keep you warm; when you run, your heart beats faster as you require more oxygen, and so on.

Maintaining balance is everything, and all functions like these are the body's attempts to maintain it whenever there is a change in circumstances. The attempt to maintain balance is called homeostasis.

Everything you do is 'right' even if it is 'wrong'

Your instinct to find balance and general well-being means that everything you do on the violin – how you hold the instrument and bow, how you move the fingers, the general posture you adopt – must be some sort of striving for balance and physical ease. It is impossible for you to do otherwise.

This means that when there is something 'wrong' in the way you hold the violin and bow, or in your technique, there must be some definite perception of an advantage to yourself in doing whatever it is, because otherwise you simply would not do it. Therefore everything you do is 'right'.

Q But there are many things I do, when I play the violin, that I know I should not do. For example, my left thumb grips the neck of the violin so much that my left hand seizes up. I wish I could stop doing it. I try to stop, but cannot. How can it be 'right' that I am squeezing my thumb?

Although pressing the thumb against the neck is not in itself a good thing to do, in some way it must be giving you something that you need (or that you think you need). The advantage seems to outweigh the disadvantages. The price seems to be worth paying.

Then it is difficult to stop gripping because the truth is that actually you want to grip. The answer is to get the advantages by some other means, so that you can release the thumb without feeling you are losing something vital to the functioning of your playing.

There must be a sense of benefit

Suppose your left elbow is always pulled in too far to the right, in front of your body.

The question is, what is this giving you? What is the benefit that you are gaining from doing this?

Suppose your neck and shoulders become sore with tension because you clamp the violin tightly between the shoulder and the chin. There must be a good, intelligent reason why you are doing it, i.e. something to do with finding balance or 'survival' of some sort.

If you place the violin too low on the shoulder at the top of the chest, it is natural and 'correct' to fold in with your shoulders;[1] if you press the fingers too hard into the strings, like playing a guitar, you are 'right' to counterpress with the thumb;[2] if you have a gap between the violin and your neck, you are 'right' to press hard into the chin rest;[3] if you place the pad of the finger on the string rather than the tip, the finger is 'right' to straighten; and so on. Examples can be found in every area of playing:

[1] See Fig. 15a, page 28

[2] See *Freeing the thumb*, page 53

[3] See *Mind the gap*, page 31

- Locking the left upper arm against the side of the chest

  The perceived benefit could be that this raises the left knuckles higher above the strings, as though this helps the finger action (which it doesn't); and a sense of stability when the upper arm uses the side of the chest as a support. The price to pay is that elbow steering becomes impossible, which forces the left wrist to twist unnaturally to play on the E string.[4]

  [4] See *Keeping the upper arm free*, page 142

  Another disadvantage is that resting the upper arm on the chest causes the scroll to point down instead of keeping the strings more or less level with the floor.

  The solution is first to experience the greater freedom of playing with lower knuckles; and to replace the apparent advantage of resting the arm on the side of the chest with a feeling of the violin supported by a 'cushion' of air, and with a sense of buoyancy in the instrument and in the arm.

  Suspend the arm in the air by finding a sense of natural balance rather than effort. Help maintain the feeling of buoyancy and balance by raising the chest and lengthening the back to keep the instrument up, rather than using only the arm.[5]

  [5] The Hungarian teacher Kató Havas suggests using the mental image of a length of cord tied to the scroll of the violin, stretching over your left shoulder and attached to a weight behind your shoulder blade. As the weight moves down, the scroll moves up with a feeling of effortlessness and balance.

- Pushing the left wrist outwards in low positions

  In middle to high positions the left wrist must curve outwards, but in low positions it should usually stay in a straight line with the forearm, or even at times give inwards. (However, there are plenty of double stops that feel more natural and more comfortable with the wrist curving out slightly.)

  The perceived benefit of pushing out may be that you can reach the strings more easily with the fingers. In fact, pushing out usually makes it more difficult – rather than less – to reach the strings, and the unwanted side-effect is tension in the wrist.

  The answer is to keep the advantage of having the wrist in a straight line or sometimes giving in, but to help the fingers reach the strings by widening at the base joints. Sometimes you can also help the fingers reach the string by using a small amount of extra clockwise forearm rotation.

- Too-low right elbow

  Playing with a 'low' elbow (i.e. below the level of the hand) is today mostly seen as old-fashioned and lacking in power.[6] The apparent benefit may be one of greater relaxation in the arm. The unwanted side-effect is that in order to lower the elbow you have to rotate the upper arm clockwise – away from the string – thereby making it less easy to lever the bow into the string.

  [6] The Hungarian violinist Joseph Szigeti, as recently as the early 1970s, was teaching his pupils to practise with a book held between their right upper arm and their side; and until the 1990s Shin'ichi Suzuki (who also held to the equally old-fashioned idea of drawing the left upper arm in to the centre as far as possible), was recommending tying elastic from elbow to elbow to help draw them in towards each other.

  A further knock-on effect is the extra effort you then have to use to make up for the lack of power coming from the arm, e.g. pressing the bow with the fingers or trying to use an unnatural amount of anticlockwise forearm rotation.

[1] See *Experiment without the bow*, page 127

Another disadvantage of the elbow remaining very low at the heel is that it breaks the speed connection between it and the frog.[1]

The solution is to keep the elbow higher, and at times above the level of the stick, but to have as much ease as a lower elbow gives you.

You can get this by suspending the arm in the air with a feeling of balance, rather than by muscular effort; by using the muscles in the back rather than in the arm; by finding a feeling of active 'muscle tone' rather than passive 'relaxation'; and by using the elbow (or anticlockwise upper arm rotation) to lever the bow into the string.[2]

[2] See *Upper half of the bow*, page 129

- Straight fingers in the bow hand

  Flexibility, give and springiness are essential elements of the bow hand, while straightening the fingers produces automatic rigidity and tightness.

  Few violinists intentionally hold the bow with straight fingers. Usually they do not know they straighten their fingers until it is pointed out to them.

  The fingers on the bow should curl around the bow and be spring-like and flexible, and responsive to all the tiny, subtle movements that are transmitted by the bow into the bow hand.

  Though unconscious, the perceived benefit of straight fingers may be that unless you hold the bow tightly and rigidly, it will 'have its own life' and 'go its own way'. Apart from the perception that you may drop the bow if you relax the hand and curve the fingers, there may be a sense that flexibility would take away real fineness of control of the bow.

  In fact the opposite is true. There is more chance of dropping the bow if you hold it rigidly than if the fingers are flexibly responding to every last 'message' from the bow.

Adapting to your physique

Something that is 'wrong' may be right for a particular player when there is an actual physical reason behind it. One student plays with apparently far too flat fingers, but it turns out that their finger tips are very flat; if they place the finger on the tip there is not enough contact with the string. Another has an apparently too-straight right thumb, but it turns out that their thumb is unusually bulbous at the end; it is unnatural for them to place it on its tip.

But it is not true that they are 'wrong'. They are right to do these things, and their natural, unconscious search for 'balance' leads them directly to such approaches or actions.

Localizing: the key to mastery

Streamlining your playing by not-doing

We often get too caught up in all the things we have to do, and forget about all the things we have to *not* do. For example, in both music and sport one of the most common things is for a performer to tighten just before performing an action.

The key to absolute mastery of the violin is in not allowing unwanted extra physical movements to occur as a knock-on effect, or by-product, of the actions that are actually necessary.

Every action must occur in isolation as a focused, economical, minimalised movement that uses the least energy or effort. It takes place only there, in that locale, without anything else in the surrounding areas reacting.

Suppose you want to drop a finger onto the string and then lift it off again. The only thing that must happen is that the finger moves down, and then moves up again:

- What you do not want to do is push your wrist out, straighten the other fingers, squeeze with the thumb, clench your left upper arm, grip the violin more tightly between the chin and the shoulder, make a face, tighten the right shoulder, press harder with the bow, hold your breath, and so on.

Naturally there are sympathetic movements that occur throughout the body, in reaction to every action, which are an essential part of balance and flow. The more we operate from a position of balance and mobility, and the more every action is localized, the more easily and naturally these sympathetic movements can occur.

Suppose you are going to play a *martelé* stroke.[1] There are two elements of the stroke that may encourage excess or unnecessary effort: (1) making the bite at the beginning of the stroke, and (2) the fast–slow and heavy–light speed and pressure pattern.

[1] See *The martelé lesson*, page 290

- To 'bite' the string before playing the stroke, while the bow is stationary on the string, the right hand must lever the bow down into the string so that the hair grips the string.

  During that moment of direct pressing, do not use a single muscle in your bow arm that is not required to push the wood down towards the hair, and to push the hair into the string. Grip the string with an imperceptible movement of the hand, forearm, and first and second finger.

  What you do not want to do, as you play the *martelé*, is to raise your upper arm; raise your shoulder; jerk your head; pull a face; tense your left arm; press the left finger harder; squeeze the neck of the violin between the thumb and finger, and so on.

- The same applies in the moment of the fast–slow and heavy–light *martelé* stroke itself, which is very energetic and powerful. There may well be a natural, sympathetic 'follow-through' motion elsewhere in the body which is desirable, but that is clearly a different matter. Basically, keep still and do only what you need to do to make the stroke.

When every action on the violin is performed in a localized way with minimum effort, everything becomes light and easy. These ideas are not modern. Here is Alexander Bloch writing in 1923:

> Relaxation, or, to speak more accurately, the localization of tension required for the effort of violin playing, is entirely a question of mental control. Thus, we can press thumb and finger together so that the entire arm tightens, or, by so willing it, confine the tension to a small radius. [Fig. 122] There are some who tighten so that merely to watch them gives one a crick in the back: the hand grasps the neck of the violin frantically, the chin clamps the fiddle in a death grip, the shifts in position are a series of spasmodic jerks, the bow arm seems as though cast in one piece. How to stop this? Simply by *willing* to relax. The muscles will obey the brain; and in practicing, when the tightening spasm comes on, stop, consciously relax, and begin again, until the control becomes automatic.[2]

[2] Martens, *String mastery: Talks with master violinists, viola players and violoncellists* (New York, 1923), 9

Fig. 122

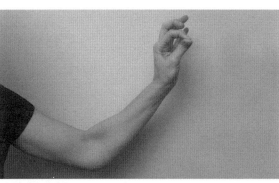

(a) Localized   (b) Unlocalized

You've got to stop before you start

Two key terms in Alexander Technique are 'inhibition' and 'direction'. Inhibition is like saying 'no', when you stop yourself from doing or acting in any particular way. Direction is like saying 'yes'.

Before you start, you've always got to stop. 'Stopping before you start' is the opposite of rushing into an action.

I often think of the first time I took my violin to my Alexander lesson with Walter Carrington. Having arrived in the room I put the violin case down on a chair while Walter stood and waited, watching me. I took the violin out of the case, put the shoulder rest on, took the bow out and tightened the screw, turned to Walter and put the violin up on to my shoulder, and began to tune.

He immediately stopped me. "That was a bit hurried!" he said.

"Suppose you want to take the violin up into playing position," he explained. "First, don't put the violin up into playing position. Just stop. Then, only when you're ready, raise the violin. Never rush!

"The stopping is a chance to find balance and a clear vision of exactly what you want, and what you don't want. Having become completely clear, and without any hurry – moving only when you want to, and not before – let the action complete itself naturally, on its own, without any effort or interference."

At first, practising stopping may be conscious and deliberate, and each stop may be measurable in seconds. Once you have formed the habit of stopping before you start, your playing (as well as your everyday life) becomes filled with millions of unnoticeable, undetectable moments of 'stopping'.

Suppose you want to shift from one position to another. First, don't shift; then, in the next instant, make the shift.

'Fast fingers', i.e. moving the left finger later and faster, is a feature of left-hand technique that is a natural application of 'stopping before you start'.[3] So is balancing the bow for an instant before placing it on the string.[4]

[3] See *Fast fingers: the key to a great left hand*, page 152

[4] See *Finding the moment of balance*, page 276

'Stopping before you start' in sport

In any short period of any game of football, tennis, or practically any other sport, there are always countless examples of 'stopping before you start', or of rushing into an action because of not 'stopping'.

A footballer finds the ball coming towards him. There is nobody in the way between him and the goal, and he suddenly has a chance to score.

If you watch closely you can plainly see that the successful player, on nearly every occasion, literally stops for an instant before going for the shot. There is the briefest moment when he is not yet acting on the impulse or desire to kick the ball. He is finding his balance, his aim and focus, all in an instant. Then he strikes, and the ball invariably goes in.

Similarly, it is plain to see how the unsuccessful shot is usually rushed at, without any stopping whatsoever before launching into the action.

Tennis offers endless clear examples of players being offered an easy point but then rushing at the ball and missing it completely.

Naturally there are all those occasions when there really isn't time and you simply have to move as a reflex action, and act instantly without preparation. Those situations are a different matter. However, the more balanced and generally un-rushed you are, the better you are able to react unconsciously at lightning speed when instant reactions are required.

Saying 'no' and 'yes'

Suppose you have a habit of raising your right shoulder during each up-bow in the lower half:

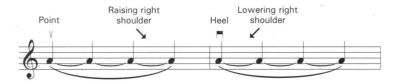

Having decided that this is not something you want to continue doing, the first thing is to say 'No!' to the shoulder going up as you bow towards the heel.

At the same time you have to be saying 'Yes!' to the shoulder staying down.

This is one reason why part of the art of teaching is in showing what *to* do, but part is in showing what to *not* do.

Directing individual actions

A child's fingers will typically move to the right as the fingers lift off the string. It can be enough simply to point out that in, say, a descending scale, after a finger lifts from the E string the next string it is needed on is the A string, i.e. to the left of the E string – and the same with the other fingers. So it makes no sense to move the fingers out to the right after lifting off, since that is the opposite direction.

Instead, it is a simple question of willpower to train the fingers to go in the right direction. Try actually moving to the left on lifting off:

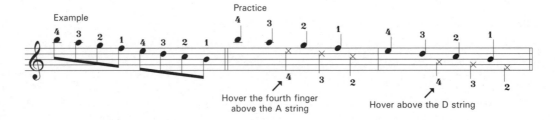

Carrying on until a new habit is formed

The important thing is to carry on correcting – and saying 'no' – long enough to form a new habit. Once or twice is rarely enough.

Suppose you often catch yourself in the middle of a frown. It is not enough simply to relax your forehead and then forget about it. If you put your attention back on to your forehead just a minute later – or a few seconds later – you may easily find that the frown is back there again.

Instead, you have to put your attention on to your forehead constantly until a new habit is formed.

Muscle tone and direction, not relaxation

Relaxing all the muscles, i.e. letting go and becoming floppy, is good for only one thing: going to sleep.

'Muscle tone' is the term used to describe the muscles in an alive, buoyant state, actively controlled and directed.

Traditional images to illustrate the finger movement at the heel are the flowing motion of your hand as you move your forearm backwards and forwards in water, or the movement of the bristles on a paintbrush when you change the direction of the stroke.

However, these images are misleading if they are taken as being only passive movements – you *let* the hand wave in the water, the movement of the bristles happens like a spring – rather than active movements that you control *while* you let them happen naturally.

Just as an artist may control precisely how the bristle behaves when he changes the direction of the stroke, you can stay in control of the fingers as you change from up-bow to down-bow at the heel, rather than passively 'letting go' of the muscles and relaxing.

Many players try to change bow with a sort of 'flick' of the hand, like a tiny amount of the same movement used to crack a whip. This has the opposite effect to creating a smooth bow change, since it suddenly increases the bow speed at the very moment that you want it to slow.

Everything must be directed. Placing the bow on the string, placing or lifting the left fingers, vibrato and everything else in violin playing requires this same controlled, active muscle tone, rather than 'letting go', 'relaxation' or floppiness.

True stories: James

James was a freshman (first year) music college student. He was a good musician who played with great energy but always with obvious over-effort: puffing and panting loudly, not listening, over-pressing the bow and playing out of tune, and banging every finger down on the fingerboard with a clearly audible thud of unnecessary impact.

When he played Kreutzer 37 there were a number of things he needed to stop doing.

Kreutzer: 42 Etudes ou caprices, no. 37, *b. 1*

He played the whole study through, from beginning to end, with the bow only on soundpoint 5.

Throughout, during each up-bow quaver (eighth-note) he moved his head from quite far to the left, to quite far to the right.

Then, on each down-bow, he threw his head back to the left again. At the same moment he made a large accent on the E string:

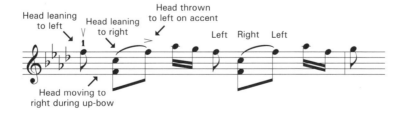

As well as this, the beginning of each down-bow was scratched. This was partly because the bow was crashing on to the string instead of being placed; partly because the left fingers were often not ready, causing the bow to play on half-stopped strings.

There were other factors that he could turn his attention to later, but these were the ones to start off with. The question was, how to cure all this?

He was not aware of what he was doing, and was playing the right notes but without any direction, i.e. control. Neither did he know what he could be aware of, and what he could actively direct. First he had to know what to do; and to know what to stop doing.

In this situation, one way to approach the study is to take it note by note:

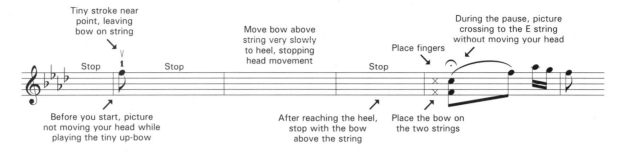

- Before you start, stop. Picture playing the up-bow, and your head not moving whatsoever.

  All you want to do is make the bow travel along the string a very short distance, and with enough weight into the string for the contact. Nothing else needs to be added.

- Play the F with a very small amount of bow near the point. Leave the bow on the string at the end of the stroke. Stop.

  Without actually doing it, picture moving the bow through the air with no part of your body moving except your arm.

  Think of the exact part of the bow-hair that will contact the string to begin the down-bow. At this moment it is far away from the violin, since the point of the bow is on the string.

  See where that bit of the bow-hair is now – under your hand out to the right of your body – and picture bringing it through the air to reach the place where you want it to be.

  This is the central issue, the only thing that is important – to bring that part of the bow-hair from where it is now, to where you want it to be.

- Move the bow very slowly, in the air just above the string, to the heel. Move only the bow, keeping the head and everything else still.

  Focus on bringing that bit of the bow-hair from where it is, out to the right and in front of you, through the air to its place above the string at the heel.

  Having arrived at the heel (the bow still not on the string), stop.

- Place the second finger on the F–C double stop, and place the bow on the string. Stop.

- Draw the bow slowly on the down-bow – a sort of sustaining while stopping – all the time visualising your head not moving when you cross to the E string.

  Then cross to the E string with only the bow moving and everything else remaining still.

One thing triggering another

One of the challenges facing any instrumentalist is that of doing one thing with one hand while doing something completely different with the other hand at the same time.

In the same way, you often have to do more than one thing at the same time with the fingers in one hand, without the actions of the fingers affecting each other.

You have to say 'no!' to certain things, and 'yes!' to others, at the same time. One thing often triggers another. Key examples:

Finger preparation

[1] See *Finger preparation: the secret of legato*, page 145

Simple finger preparation exercises often provide moments where you need to find how to stop yourself:[1]

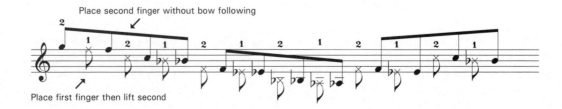

Many players find that the act of preparing the underneath finger causes an instant reflex action of lifting the finger that is on the string; or when they place it on the next-lower string, they cannot stop their bow from instantly following.

Instead there has to be a clear sense of 'no' to lifting the held-down finger, or moving the bow too early, and 'yes' to placing the prepared finger on its own, without anything else happening accidentally as a result.

Chords

The act of placing the bow on the string, to play a chord, should not be an automatic trigger to pull the bow to play the chord.[1]

Place the bow on the string, and the fingers on their notes, then stop. Then play the chord.

[1] See also *Exercise for placing*, page 275

Spiccato

One of the most frequent causes of unclean sound in *spiccato* is that the left finger does not stop the string sufficiently before the bow plays the stroke.

The problem is often caused by the finger-placement triggering the bow stroke. Invariably the bow gets there first; and then the earlier you place the finger, the earlier the bow gets there.

The answer is to gain a feeling of: place the finger – stop – play – stop – place – stop – play – stop.[2]

[2] See *Co-ordination: don't always blame the bow*, page 286

Left-hand *pizzicato*

Separate the different actions in left-hand *pizzicato* so that one thing does not trigger another:

Sarasate: Malagueña, op. 21 no. 1, *b. 55*

After playing the first *pizzicato* chord you have to place the third-finger A on the E string.

The action of placing the third-finger A should not be an automatic trigger for the bow to play the note. After placing the finger on the string, stop.

Then play the note, the short up-bow A. This bow stroke must not be an automatic trigger for the third finger to pluck the first-finger F♯ (the third note).

In the first two bars of the piece, practising stopping before each action could be represented as follows:

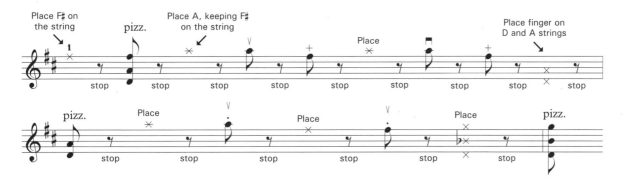

Place the first-finger F♯ on the string. Stop.

Play the first *pizzicato* chord (with the right hand). Stop. Keep the first finger down on the string.

Place the third-finger A. Stop.

Bow the A, leaving the finger on the string after the bow has lifted. Stop.

Pluck the F♯ (with the left third finger). Stop.

Place the third-finger A. Stop.

Revealing the posture

One reason why a student may be slow to change their posture can be that they simply do not realise what they are doing as soon as they are holding the instrument and are in the heat of playing.

¹ See *Looking at the angles objectively*, page 33

An answer can be to arrange with them to 'freeze' as described on page 33.[1]

- Take the violin away from them while they remain as still as if posing for a photograph (Fig. 123a).

- The student should hold that posture for 10 or 20 seconds, or for as long as they can stand it (Fig. 123b).

The posture shown in Fig. 123b may look exaggerated, but it is not unusual. Holding the position for as long as they can bear gives them the chance to discover exactly what they are doing, and quickly produces a great feeling of wanting to stop doing it.

Fig. 123

 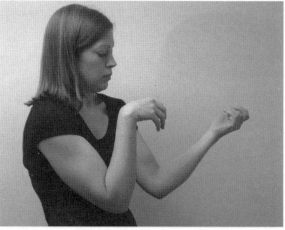

(a) Say 'freeze' when the student is in the middle of playing

(b) The student holds the posture while you take the instrument away

Background essentials 2

Understanding technical and musical timing

This subject is as important as the principles of tone production, intonation, or of how to hold the violin or bow. Yet compared to these it is a 'hidden' subject, often unrecognised, and the results of poor musical and technical timing can be heard even in the performances of otherwise high-level players.

Musical timing is when you want the note to sound; technical timing is often before the note sounds.

A clear example of technical and musical timing, away from the violin, is in keyboard-playing (see right).

The thumb moves under the second (index) and third (middle) fingers, towards the F, long before the moment when the thumb actually plays the F.

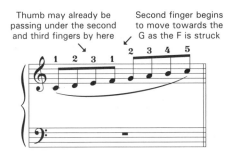

Thumb may already be passing under the second and third fingers by here

Second finger begins to move towards the G as the F is struck

Imagine if the technical and musical moment were to happen together: the thumb would continue to hover over the C until the last fraction of a second, and would then suddenly rush towards the F at the precise moment that it was already meant to be playing it.

Key examples where the technical and the musical timing are different from each other:

- Finger preparation – place each lower finger before lifting the upper finger
- Pivoting – start moving the bow towards the new string before you want it to sound
- *Martelé* 'click' – catch the string before beginning the stroke
- Shifting early – begin the shift before the moment that you want to arrive
- Thumb preparation in shifting – move the thumb before the hand
- Dropping fingers – begin to move before the moment that the finger lands on the string.

How can I stop my playing sounding all the same?

Contrast and tonal colour

In the painting on the front cover of this book, if two adjoining but separate and distinct shapes were exactly the same colour they would merge into one another. The two distinct shapes would disappear, and a new, larger shape would take their place.

This is so obvious it seems ridiculous to state it; yet playing consecutive phrases with one tonal colour, one vibrato colour, one level of sound and so on, is one of the greatest and commonest dangers that a musician must guard against.

The colour of the violin sound, the character, expression, emotion or atmosphere, should change not only passage by passage but phrase by phrase, and often note by note.

Q But if you make each phrase a different colour doesn't it break up the musical line into too many little bits? Don't you lose the longer line, the bigger structure?

- If you focus only on playing with highly varied, coloured, expressive phrasing, the performance may lose its way and sound fragmented.
- If you focus only on playing long lines, and go for a sense of large-scale structure, you may miss the little moments of beauty along the way.

- The best performance combines a sense of overall structure and moment-by-moment expressiveness and contrast.

If you look too closely you miss the big picture; if you stand too far back you miss the detail. There may be a danger of losing the longer line or structure if you play only this little bit, then this little phrase, then this group of notes, and so on. But if you keep an eye on the main framework, the overall structure and the long-range aiming-points, the larger design does not have to be lost.

The German flautist Johann Quantz wrote about the ever-changing emotions:

> …Each piece may have in it diverse mixtures of pathetic, flattering, gay, majestic, or jocular ideas. Hence you must, so to speak, adopt a different sentiment at each bar, so that you can imagine yourself now melancholy, now gay, now serious, etc. Such dissembling is most necessary in music. He who can truly fathom this art is not likely to be wanting in approval from his listeners, and his execution will always be *moving*.[1]

[1] Johann Joachim Quantz: *Essay of a Method for Playing the Transverse Flute* (Berlin 1752; trans. Edward R. Reilly, London, 1966), 126.

Mountains and deserts

Imagine a huge mountain on its own in the middle of a desert. You would be able to see it from hundreds of miles away. But a similar mountain in the middle of the Swiss Alps might not stand out at all.

In the same way, if you play everything with equal great intensity, many of the points you make are lost. In order to give more, first you have to give less.

The same applies to individual notes: to make more vibrato or more accent, there must be less in the notes before and after.

Making the design big enough

Dorothy DeLay used to say that you have to 'hit your audience over the head' with your musical ideas, otherwise the audience will simply never get them.

Crafting a musical phrase on the violin has to be done clearly or exaggeratedly enough for it to be like stage makeup – exaggerated lipstick, eye-shadow, mascara etc. – which looks ridiculous when seen from close up but correct from a distance; or the exaggerated timing and articulation of someone speaking to a large audience as opposed to speaking close up to one person.

Imagine that you are playing to an audience who have never heard the violin played before, and have never heard a note of classical music before either. Play with such clear dynamics, phrasing, type of stroke and vibrato, that even *they* understand what you are doing.

Or imagine that you are playing to someone who is writing down every note as a musical dictation. They have to write down every dynamic, nuance, phrasing and attack that they can, and you have to play in such a way that they do not miss anything.

Vibrato

If the vibrato is always the same (i.e. the same speed and width) the playing in general will sound all the same even if there is plenty of variety in other elements, e.g. type of stroke or accent.

In this typical passage from the Franck Sonata, almost every note or pair of notes needs a slightly different vibrato to help the bow make different colours. For example, the three A♯s in the first and second bars should each be played with a different vibrato – perhaps the first the slowest, the second faster, and the third the fastest.

As well as highlighting a note with a new vibrato, you can also bring out a group of notes. Make the bracketed passages stand out, and create a new expressive moment, by making the vibrato completely distinct from that of the first two bars:

Franck: Sonata in A, *mov. 2, b. 56*

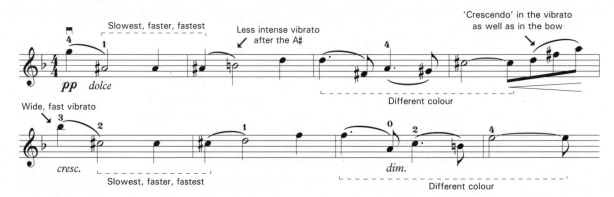

Varying the strokes

Mozart: Concerto no. 4 in D, K218, *mov. 1, b. 57*

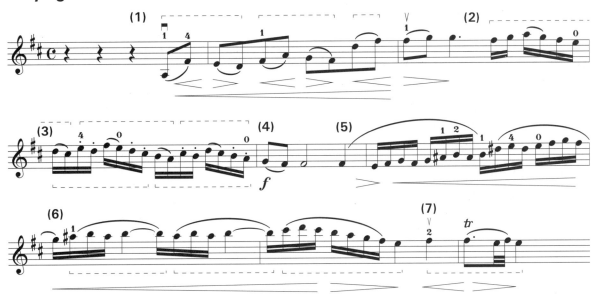

(1) The three steps (shown with brackets) are one long up-beat, each played with a different character: the first exploratory, the second more sure, the third finding the way; or the first more sure, the second less, and the third more; or however you see it.

The string-changes help change the colour but are not enough on their own. Use the pattern 'least, more, most' for the three stages: increase the vibrato, how accented the stroke is, how near the bow is to the bridge, and so on, to make each step distinctive.

In the second bar the first and third beats are each like a written-out appoggiatura. They could have been written as a quarter-note (crotchet) D and F♯, with the E and G written as appoggiaturas. An appoggiatura is a 'leaning' note, so is always played with a diminuendo.

Even if the bow makes a diminuendo over the two notes, this will not sound unless the vibrato is more on the first note and less on the second.

(2) The sixteenth-notes (semiquavers) must not be played with the same sound or colour as the previous dotted quarter-note (dotted crotchet) G.

Here, the first sixteenths do not have dots on them (this depends on the edition), so they are like an upbeat to a sequence beginning at **(3)**. Give the upbeat a different colour by playing with a more sustained stroke, and then let the separate bows come out of the string more at **(3)**.

(3) If **(2)** is played as an upbeat to **(3)**, this bar becomes a sequence with two steps, with the second step like an upbeat to **(4)**. Or you can see it as part of a three-step sequence beginning at **(2)**.

Either way, each group can have an up-and-down within it, i.e. crescendo on beats one and three, diminuendo on beats two and four. It is effective if the second group is less than the first, and takes away any risk of anticipating the subito *f* in **(4)**. Or you could crescendo into **(4)**.[1]

(4) The warmth of tone and vibrato (the bow deep in the string, near enough to the bridge, the vibrato wide enough and fast enough) should be a new colour entirely different from anything in, say **(1)**.

(5) After the half-note (minim) F♯, the quarter-note F♯ must be played with an entirely different bow stroke and vibrato (further from the bridge, the stroke lighter and faster, and the vibrato narrower).

(6) This passage, which again has three stages, is both an arrival point as well as something that builds and gathers towards the climax. Each stage must have a clearly different tonal colour (and volume).

Apply the patterns 'least, more, most', or 'more, less, most', to the three stages. Change the vibrato speed and width, the volume and amount of accent, the soundpoint, the bow speed, the amount of the hair, the articulation of the left fingers, the holding or pushing of the tempo, and so on.

(7) The last quarter-note in the bar (F♯) is an upbeat to the trill in the next bar. The quarter-note before it (E) is what Casals called a 'dual-function' note, i.e. it is the last note of the previous sixteenth-note scale, as well as being the first note of this quarter-note phrase at the end.

These two quarter-notes should be played with distinctly different tones – and with a crescendo over them so that the first is played less. This avoids a bump at the end of the preceding phrase.

[1] Raphael Bronstein said of bar 44 of this piece (shown on page 162) that you should play the first half of the bar well, and then play the second half even better!

The same approach could be taken to this bar too.

Apply this approach whenever you can throughout the repertoire, not only to individual bars but to any repeated phrases or passages.

How much is too much?

When playing anything on the violin, the question to ask is how much would be too much? Then do almost that much, but not quite that much. How loud would be too loud, how heavy would be too heavy, how light would be too light? How sharp would be too sharp, how wide or narrow a vibrato would be too wide or narrow, how accented would be too accented, how much *diminuendo* would be too much, and so on.

However much that would be, do almost that much. If it is not too much, it is not too much. Thinking in this way instantly brings extraordinary stature, power, variety and courage into the playing.

When you play *p*, or anything that involves restraint, approach the question from the other side: how little would be too little? Then do just a little more than that.

Playing to the limit

We spend all our time trying to make a beautiful tone, or trying not to make an ugly one. The last thing we want is for scratches or squeaks to be part of the sound. As a result it is easy to end up not playing 'to the limit', not giving your all or letting go, not chancing disaster by dancing right on the edge of the cliff; but always holding back and fearing to go anywhere near the edge.

Instead, practising is a matter of constant experiment to find the limits at both ends of the spectrum – loud, soft; hard, soft; more vibrato, less vibrato; and so on. If you do not risk over-stepping the boundaries it is impossible to know how far you can go.

Playing *piano* and projecting

In the theatre, the term 'stage whisper' means that you 'whisper' in such a way that it is really quite loud and projects so that the audience in the back row can hear you.

Playing music, it is easy to play softly but with nobody able to hear you at the back of the hall; it is easy to play loudly but without observing the dynamics or playing with dynamic contrast.

What you have to be able to do is project *piano*, and every other subtle colour, to the back of the hall.

Pablo Casals said that the range of *piano* extends all the way from quite soft to really quite loud, depending on the music; and that the range of *forte* extends all the way from loud to really quite soft.

The difference between volume and character

Dynamics are not indications of the decibel level of the playing. It is not the same as turning the volume up or down when you are listening to a recording. *Piano* does not mean 'soft'; *forte* does not mean 'loud'. What they mean is to create an expression, or atmosphere, or colour that is '*piano*' or '*forte*' – to give the impression of *piano* or *forte*.

In the following example, nobody would be able to hear the violin over the orchestra if the opening were truly played '*sotto voce*', i.e. 'under the voice' or *p*:

Wieniawski: Concerto no. 2 in D minor, op. 22, *mov. 1, b. 68*

espressivo ma sotte voce

Instead, you have to play a 'soloist's *p*', possibly quite near to the bridge and deep in the string.

Key point: So long as the strokes do not become accented, you can keep the character of *sotto voce* even while playing quite near the bridge and actually playing quite loudly. But the moment you play with accents, even if the volume is no louder than before, the character will be altered and begin to sound *f*:

Volume and distance

Another aspect of dynamics is the way they create a sense of space and distance. A sound appears to get softer if its origin moves away from you, even though its actual volume does not change. So by playing something more softly you can give an impression of its being further away.

There is a reduction of energy when something becomes quieter without moving away from you. But when something gets quieter because it is moving away, or louder because it is approaching, its level of energy can seem as much when it is quieter as when louder.

You have to use actual volume to create the illusion of distance, near or far. It is not the same as giving an impression of *piano* while actually playing quite loudly.

J. S. Bach: Sonata no. 1 in G minor, BWV1001, *mov. 4, b. 1*

The concert hall, the violin, and the soundpost

Here is an excellent way to approach playing in any situation, from a room to a large hall, so that even when you play *piano* you reach the back of the hall but still sound as though you are playing softly, while at the same time the *forte* or *fortissimo* is always just the right amount without ever forcing.

The violin is a resonating box.[1] We play the strings, and the bridge transmits the vibrations to the resonating chamber where they are amplified.

[1] See *Understanding resonance*, page 4

But instead of thinking of playing on the strings of the violin, which are amplified by the resonating box, imagine that the hall is the resonating box and the violin itself is the string. Then you can *play the hall* instead of playing the violin *in* the hall. 'Playing the hall' changes your entire approach to the instrument, and a completely different quality enters the playing.

Identifying waves

Pablo Casals often spoke about the way everything that has life or motion moves and functions in waves. If music is played in a 'straight line' without rising and falling, without ebb and flow or tension and release, it becomes dull and lifeless because it no longer reflects nature.

A wave-form is anything that grows and then diminishes; anything that gets more and then gets less – like the waves moving in and out on the sea shore, coming up the beach to the furthest point they reach, then retreating back into the sea, then coming in again.

Breathing in and out is a wave: you breathe in until the highest point, then breathe out until the lowest point. The change from night to day is a wave: the sun moves higher and higher in the sky until the day is at its brightest, and then moves lower and lower again until the day is at its darkest again; Spring–Summer–Autumn–Winter is a wave, and so on:

Franck: Sonata in A, *mov. 2, b. 48*

The Hungarian violinist and teacher Sándor Végh, friend and colleague of Casals, taught each year at Prussia Cove in Cornwall, England. The room in which he taught looked out on to the ocean. It was a feature of his teaching that he would frequently point out of the window to the waves rolling in against the rocky beach below, and remind the student to liken the music to waves and not to play 'straight'.

Two of the essential elements of western classical music are ebb-and-flow, tension-and-release. Both are wave-forms, represented below by crescendos and diminuendos:

J. S. Bach: Sonata no. 1 in G minor, BWV1001, *mov. 1, b. 1*

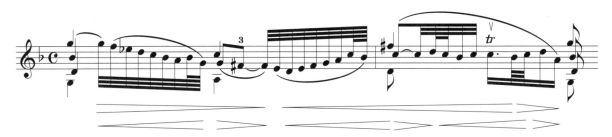

- Work through everything you play from the point of view of either getting more, or getting less, but never staying the same, i.e. never playing even two notes in a row with the same sound, the same volume, the same vibrato, unless you mean to.

Don't sustain

Casals would tell you that if you go up on top of the highest mountain you can find and shout out as loudly as you can, all you will be able to do is make a *diminuendo* – because it is impossible to sustain a shout. Only a machine can do that.

If you listen closely for just this one point – whether the student is sustaining any one note or phrase unremittingly – there are often many examples of notes that are being sustained but which should either be getting louder or getting softer, or sometimes one and then the other.

It is in the tapering of notes, in the natural relaxation or the 'ebb' part of notes or phrases, that most attention or sympathy seems to need to be given, perhaps because players become too concerned with 'generating sound' all the time. You've got to be able to let it go. This note from *Havanaise* is a typical example:

Saint-Saëns: Havanaise, Op. 83

The minim (half-note) B must not be sustained like a note on an organ but *diminuendo* like the natural dying away of a note on a piano. But unlike the piano, which is an instrument of diminuendo, we can also crescendo and the tapering marked in the example by the diminuendo is not the only musical view that can be taken. One might *diminuendo* the B sooner than marked and then crescendo into the new passage. The number of variations is uncountable and it should not be possible to play the note in exactly the same way twice. But the one thing is that something must change.

A simple principle of phrasing serves most situations well: if the notes rise, get louder; if they fall, get softer; but just as often when they rise get softer (as though weakening in the effort against gravity, or as though going off into the distance), and get louder as they fall (as though gathering energy with 'gravity'). It all depends on the harmonic tensions and relative musical intensity of the notes – but the one thing you can't do is play them all the same.

Imagining orchestration

One way to find the colour of a phrase is to imagine an orchestra playing it.

Example 1

Mozart: Sonata in B♭, K454, *mov. 1, b. 50*

The two up-beat C's come three times, each time with a slightly different character. If they are played on the string, starting in the upper half, they are played quite gently with slightly fast–slow bow speed and slightly heavy–light pressure.

Lead the bow from the left hand by playing a separate vibrato accent on each C, so that the vibrato speed is fast–slow and the width wide–narrow:

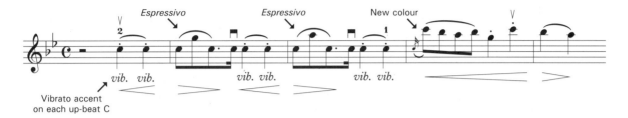

The pattern marked 'Espressivo' comes twice. The third pair of up-beat C's introduces a new phrase which must be a different colour from the two 'espressivo' phrases.

Should the new phrase be louder or softer, or played with a wider or narrower vibrato? Whatever it is, it must not be the same colour as the previous phrase. Imagine that the theme is played first by the violins, and then the violas join in, in octaves:

Example 2

Kreutzer: 42 Etudes ou caprices, no. 31, b. 20

The types of strokes in the first two beats of these bars, and those in the second two beats, are quite different; yet if you just 'play the notes' the phrase comes out sounding all the same:

The sixteenth-notes (semiquavers) in the first two beats are sustained strokes; the semiquavers in the second two beats are played either as short, on-the-string *martelé*-type strokes in the upper half, or off-the-string strokes (*spiccato*) in the lower half.

- Imagine the first two beats played by the violins, then the second two beats played by a flute:

- In the 'flute' phrase, the beginning of the note with the trill needs to be a different colour from the preceding sixteenth-note (semiquaver). The trill alone is not enough to make the contrast.

● As a general rule it is often good to begin a trill with extra bow speed to begin it with a 'kick'; and here the trill can receive a clear accent to give it its colour:

● Looking more closely, the separate-bow notes in the second beat are clearly a different character or colour from the over-lapping slurs of the first beat. Imagine the oboes, with rests both before and after, playing notes 6–9 in unison with the violins:

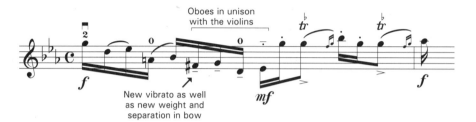

● Looking more closely still, bring out the syncopation – created by the slurs being off-the-beat – by 'leaning' on the second and fourth notes. Imagine the violas playing notes 2–5 an octave lower underneath the violins:

● The overall shape of the phrase needs direction and flow as well. For example:

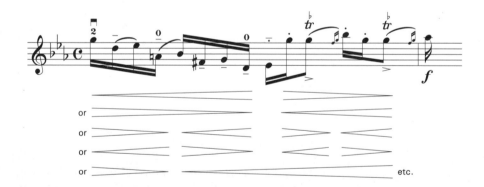

Changing the key or the notes

A simple method of finding or accentuating the character of a phrase is to play it in the major, if it is in the minor, and vice versa:

Sarasate: Playera, op. 23, no. 1, b. 4

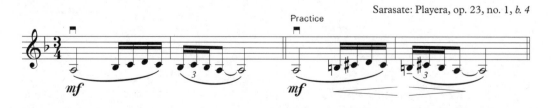

Afterwards, playing in the correct key, the character stands out clearly. There are endless possibilities for doing this, and it is a central practice method that can be used frequently throughout practising.

You can do a similar thing by experimenting with different notes: afterwards the tonality of the correct note seems easier to feel exactly:

Prokofiev: Sonata in D, op. 94, *mov. 1, b. 1*

About energy

Increasing or decreasing energy in violin playing was one of Dorothy DeLay's favourite themes. She said that she first began to think about energy when, as a student, she played the Mozart G major Concerto to her teacher:

Mozart: Concerto no. 3 in G, K216, *mov. 1, b. 78*

He suggested she play the ascending scale with 'more energy'. So she played it more loudly:

"No, no, not louder," he said; "just more energy." She played more lightly again, this time *spiccato*:

He stopped her. "No, no, not *spiccato* – just with more energy," he said. She played it again, but now with a more accented stroke:

"No, no, not accented – just with more energy," he said again. So she played it again, this time faster. "No, no," he said, "not faster – just with more energy."

And so it went on. So the question is, what gives more energy to the playing, and what gives less energy? The following is a partial list:

More energy	Less energy	More energy	Less energy
Faster tempo	Slower tempo	More leverage in the bow hold	Less leverage
Louder	Softer		
Heavier	Lighter	Right knuckles flatter	Knuckles more raised
Nearer bridge	Nearer fingerboard	Faster vibrato	Slower vibrato
Heavier bow weight	Lighter bow weight	Wider vibrato	Narrower vibrato
Faster bow speed	Slower bow speed	More percussive fingers	Less percussive fingers
More accented	Less accented	Sharper sharps, flatter flats	Tempered tuning
Longer strokes	Shorter strokes	Faster drop and lift-off	Slower drop and lift-off
More hair	Less hair	Faster shifts	Slower shifts

Sometimes the headings sit equally well in either column, depending on the music and the context.

For example, you could be playing longer strokes and increase energy by making them gradually shorter:

On the other hand, it could just as easily be that you are playing shorter strokes, and increase the energy by making them gradually longer:

It is not unusual to hear string players using all the factors, all at the same time, that give the least energy, i.e. playing an entire piece with the bow constantly too near the fingerboard, using little bow, without sufficient accent or emphasis, with slow fingers, playing the piece at a slow tempo, with a slow, wide vibrato, with too-low ♯'s and too-high ♭'s, and so on.

It is easy to change this. The moment you look at playing from the point of view of energy, it becomes a simple matter to raise it onto an entirely new level of excitement and interest.

It does not take more than a few minutes to explain the basic concept of adding or subtracting energy, and to go through the dozen or so main items on the list. Then, approached from that angle, low-energy playing like this can be changed quickly, i.e. within minutes rather than within months.

Combining high and low energy

When you play with high energy in one hand but with low energy in the other, it is like the classic game of trying to tap one hand on top of your head while rubbing the other hand in circles on your stomach.

- Playing quietly with a fast vibrato

Playing quietly with a fast vibrato produces a wide range of sensitive and delicate tonal colours. The 'trick' is to be able to combine the high-energy fast vibrato with the low-energy light bow:

Grieg: Sonata in C minor, op. 45, *mov. 1, b. 145*

Some players are able to do this easily from the beginning, while others can develop it – which you can easily do using simple speeding-up exercises.[1]

[1] See *Speeding up with the metronome*, page 111

- Speeding up/slowing down, in crescendo/decrescendo

Unintentionally speeding up during a crescendo, or slowing down during a decrescendo, is one of the most common faults found in everything from instrumental playing to singing and conducting.

Playing louder is an increase in energy; playing faster is an increase in energy; but doing one thing must not make you unconsciously do the other.

- Moving the bow faster near the bridge

Unintentionally moving the bow faster when the bow moves closer to the bridge, instead of slowing it, is often the reason for impure tone.

Playing nearer to the bridge is an increase in energy; so is moving the bow faster; but the two factors must remain separate so that the bow is slow enough near the bridge, and deep enough in the string, that the tone does not whistle or squeak.

- Pressing the left fingers too hard in f

Unintentionally pressing the left fingers harder, as the bow sinks more heavily into the string, is one of the commonest causes of left hand tension.

Playing more heavily with the bow is an increase in energy; so is pressing the fingers harder into the strings; but the principle of 'as heavy as necessary to stop the string cleanly, but as little as possible' applies whatever the dynamic.

- The faster and more vigorous the playing, the higher you lift your left hand fingers

Fast, separate bow strokes are high-energy, particularly if played f. But at the same time the left fingers need to stay close to the strings for speed. Lifting fingers higher and with more energy the faster the tempo of the passage, is a common reason for passages beginning to break down the faster they go.

- Tensing the left hand in fast shifts

Shifting faster is an increase in energy; so is pressing the strings harder; but it is essential that the faster you shift, the lighter and freer the shift is, in every part of the hand and finger.

Playing with more accent

It is common to see string players trying to increase energy by using volume alone.

This works only so far because although you can play more loudly and immediately gain more energy, and then play still louder and gain even more energy, soon you reach a ceiling of maximum volume where you simply cannot play any louder.

At that point, or before reaching that point, you have to do something else to increase the energy, and one of the first things to add is accent:

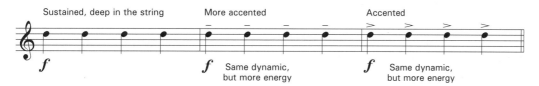

Example 1

Elgar: Sonata in E minor, op. 82, *mov. 1, b. 131*

To create the crescendo in the second line, the beginnings of the strokes have to become increasingly more accented:

Example 2

Tchaikovsky: Three pieces, op. 42, *Meditation, b. 34*

Although it ends up only at *mf*, this scale needs to be played with a big crescendo if it is to have enough stature. (Later on in the piece, at bar 69, there is a similar scale that rises up the E string; compared with the E-string brilliance of that one, it is difficult to play this earlier scale up the A string too loudly.)

At the bar marked '+' the strokes must not be too smooth. You cannot use increasing bow weight alone to make the crescendo and the climax:

Watch the great players

What is it about players like Maxim Vengerov or Leila Josefevitch that makes their playing so exciting? Of course there are an uncountable number of factors, but much of it comes down to the sheer energy with which they play.

What that means is that they put together all the things that give the playing more energy: more bow, deeper in the string, nearer the bridge, faster vibrato, greater left hand articulation, faster trills, and so on.

For students, playing with more accent – which generally means more bow – is usually the place to start when working on increasing the overall energy of their playing. Where the student uses 10 centimetres of bow during the fast part of a stroke, the virtuoso uses 20. It is often as if the student is playing the violin underwater, at the bottom of a swimming pool, where the resistance of the water slows everything down.

Here is a simple warm-up exercise:

Play a repeated accented stroke, each time using more and more bow during the fast part of the stroke. Each tied pair of notes represents one, unbroken accented note:

Start each stroke at the heel or the point. Move very quickly at the beginning of the stroke and then sustain at a later and later place in the bow. Join the 'kick' at the start of the note with the sustaining part so that it is one, seamless note that begins with a burst of energy. Repeat the same exercise playing only in the lower half, and in the upper half.

There are plenty of examples of slow-fast bow-speed strokes throughout the repertoire, but for every one of them there must be hundreds of fast-slow speeds, i.e. accented.

- Working through any music in your repertoire, whenever the bow speed is not even always ask the simple question: can I do this with more bow?

Using a model

Imagine a top-standard violinist sitting in the corner of your room all the time you are practising. Whenever you want to hear or see how something *could* be played, this person is always there and willing to demonstrate. Then, having heard them play it, you have a much better idea what to aim for.

Suppose you are playing something at the top of the G string. The sound is coarse and scratchy, the pitch wavering. How might your model virtuoso play it?

Brahms: Sonata no. 3 in D minor, op. 108, *mov. 2, b. 43*

Your model plays the phrase to you. The tone is rounded and pure, and at the same time full and deep; it sounds as good as you playing it in 1st position on the A string. So *that* is what it could sound like at the top of the G string.

Turn the process back to front and create the model yourself. Play the phrase on the A string with full expression; see what it sounds like; and then make the top of the G string sound as good as that:

In the end real technique is driven or created by the musical intention, not the other way round; so the purity and excellence of the sound-model in your mind is often enough to make you play the proper fingering immediately much better.

- Any passage that includes a shift may be helped by first hearing what it would sound like without shifting:

- Play the arpeggio across the strings in 1st position. Play strongly and evenly, without any hesitation from note to note:

Think to yourself: that is how it could sound played on one string by an international-standard violinist. Then keep that same result clearly in your mind as you play the correct fingering shifting up the string.

- Use models for vibrato, since different fingers may have a tendency towards one sort of a vibrato or another. The fourth finger vibrato may be narrower than the third; by hearing what the note sounds like with the third finger, and then holding that sound in your mind as you play the same note with the fourth finger, you may be able to bring an entirely new quality of vibrato immediately into the fourth finger.

- Use models for trills. Suppose you find that trilling with the third finger seems less agile than trilling the same notes with the second finger (or *vice versa*): find the sound with the second finger and then keep that sound in your mind as you trill with the third finger.

- Suppose you are playing a scale in thirds, and you have decided to practise by putting both fingers down as normal, but bowing only one string at a time:

(The x-notes indicate the fingers on their notes on the string, but unplayed by the bow.)

How well could this be played? Find out by playing the lower notes on their own but using a normal fingering in 1st position:

- Play with the bow solidly and evenly in the string, making each note sound with deep resonance and sonority.

- Then find the same evenness and quality of tone using the thirds fingering, playing only the lower string as before.

- Alternate between the two until there is no difference.

About rhythm

Looked at from one angle, you cannot say that any one of the three factors of playing – pitch, sound or rhythm – is more important than another. You cannot do without a high standard of any of them.

Looked at from another angle, rhythm is the most important.[1]

[1] 'Rhythm is an international language – not harmony, not melody, but rhythm.' Dave Brubeck, jazz musician

Rhythm gets your foot tapping

When you sit in the audience and listen to a concert, you do not even think about intonation unless the playing is out of tune. It might happen that a phrase, which you know to be particularly tricky, is played incredibly well in tune, and so for a moment you notice the good intonation; but most of the time you notice the tuning only when it disturbs you.

Similarly, you may notice a beautiful, dark, rich tone on the G string, or a sweetness on the E string, or whatever; but when you are really transported by the music you are not aware of *sound* as such. Music is something else, an experience created by the physicality of the performer, the instrument or the sound, but at the same time beyond it.

But it is rhythm that locks the audience on to the performer. Rhythm is the quality or factor that can actually get the audience's feet tapping. If you play in tune and with a good sound, but with poor rhythm, you cannot grip an audience the way you can if you play with many accidents of pitch or sound, but with infectious rhythmic vitality. You should play in tune and with a good sound as well – it goes without saying – but that is not the subject here.

Trying to play notes in tune with a good sound

Many string players, even if they have not been playing for long, will make a face if they play a note out of tune, or if they scratch or squeak; but if they play a little too long or too short they will often be unaware of it, even if they are quite an advanced player.

In other words, the focus is only on playing in tune, and with a good sound.

Feeling the pulse

Playing the printed rhythms is one thing, but playing them on top of a foundation of a regular rhythmic pulse is another. The underlying rhythmic pulse is the base on which you stand, without which you may constantly feel technically and musically unstable.

It is common for an otherwise advanced player not to realise that they play without a strong, underlying rhythmic pulse. Of course, where there is a quarter-note (crotchet) they play a quarter-tone; where there is a sixteenth-note (semiquaver) they play a sixteenth-note; but this does not come out or feel the same as playing with a strong underlying pulse.

Sub-dividing

One of the keys to feeling the pulse is to sub-divide everything you play into smaller units, except notes that are too fast. For example:

- Playing half-notes (minims), feel an underlying pulse of quarter-notes (crotchets) and eighth-notes (quavers). You may even feel a flow of sub-divided sixteenth-notes (semiquavers), depending on the tempo.

- Playing crotchets, feel an underlying pulse of quavers; playing quavers, feel semiquavers.

- Sub-divide dotted notes and triplets in the same way.

Good rhythm aids good co-ordination

Rhythm is the 'most important' of the three for another reason. The more precise the moment when two things must happen at the same time, the better the co-ordination. The stronger the underlying rhythmic pulse, and the more exact the timing of the note-values, the better the co-ordination is between the two hands as they perform all their finely-timed operations in playing the violin.

The mechanics of rhythm on a string instrument

There are six technical factors that affect when a note sounds:

1 In playing slurred notes on one string the rhythm is created only by the left fingers. The bow has nothing to do with it:

2 In playing separate bows on one note, all the rhythm is in the right hand and none in the left fingers:

3 In playing different notes with separate bows, the rhythm is in both hands:

A particular danger is that it is often much easier for the bow simply to stop, change direction, and go the other way, than it is for the left finger to find its place on the string. If the bow plays with more immediate rhythm than a slightly-delayed left finger, the result is the impure sound of bowing a half-stopped string.

The way to avoid this is by always leading the bow with the left hand, rather than the left hand following the bow.[1]

4 During string crossings, all the rhythm is in the bow:

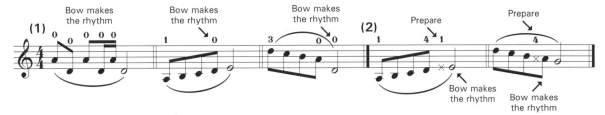

(1) All the rhythm is in the bow; none in the left fingers.

(2) There is a particular problem of co-ordination when you have to prepare a finger on the new string before touching that string with the bow. The rhythm is still all in the bow, but that is a matter of the *musical* timing.[2]

The *technical* timing is earlier than the moment when you want the new note to sound: the left finger must be ready on the string before the bow gets there; and the bow must start moving towards the new string before the moment when it must arrive there and sound the note.

Prepare the first or fourth finger on the string and then time the sounding of the note with the bow.

5 The timing of dropping a finger is different from that of lifting a finger off the string.

- When a new note is played by placing a finger during slurred ascending notes, the finger starts off in a place above the string; moves towards the string; and only when it arrives does the new note sound. The order is: 'move, new note'.

- When a new note is played by lifting a finger during slurred descending notes, the new note sounds the instant the finger begins to move; then the finger continues away from the string. The order is: 'new note, move':

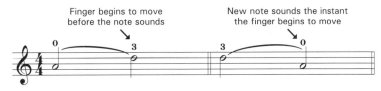

Notes played with bad rhythm due to fingers dropping too late are not so common; but fingers lifting too early, before the notes should be played, instead of lifting them at the precise moment that the new note should sound, is a frequently-heard cause of notes rushing.

Key point: The single thought to keep in mind is to lift *when* the note is to sound.

[1] See *How can I get my fingers and bow to work together better?*, page 144

[2] See *Understanding technical and musical timing*, page 205

1 See *Understanding timing*, page 243

6 Starting to shift at the precise moment that you actually want to arrive is a frequent cause of faulty rhythm. Timing a shift is like dropping a finger onto the string, where the finger must start the journey towards the string before you want it to arrive on the string. In the same way, the shift must begin before the moment when you want to arrive on the new, shifted-to note.[1]

Playing expressively in time

I often remember hearing the Romanian pianist Radu Lupu playing Beethoven Piano Concerto No. 1. His playing became a landmark reference point in my mind. He played with the apparent freedom of rubato that you would expect in a piece by Chopin; yet if a metronome had been switched on he would not have got out with it for a moment, because he was actually playing so in time.

It is relatively easy to play metronomically in time, but without musical expression; it is relatively easy to play expressively with lots of rubato, pulling the phrase about and disturbing the pulse and the rhythm. It is music-making on a much higher level when you can play in time and expressively.

The Russian pianist Artur Rubinstein was once asked if he was from the 'playing in time school of playing', or from the 'playing with feeling school'. He replied: 'Can't one feel the music in time?'

Rhythmic licence is the last thing to consider

In orchestral playing you cannot ever use time to be expressive on your own, or take time for technical reasons, since everyone in a section has to play together.

In solo playing, time is always the last thing to use to make musical expression or to make the musical point of a phrase. First, exhaust every other means by trying different textures and colours in the tone, different accentuation, different vibratos, or different tuning of individual notes. Then, when nothing else remains and you are still not satisfied, that may be the time to allow some freedom with the rhythm, i.e. placing a note, or moving forwards or holding back slightly.

This does not mean that you have to play 'straight' for a long time before you can allow some rubato. You may already know that a phrase demands flexibility after playing it 'straight' only once or twice. The principle is only that using time is never the first but the last thing you consider.

Making musical expression through rhythm

Harpsichordists and organists often use far more *rubato* than pianists, and will hurry and slow down within a simple phrase where a pianist would play rhythmically straight. This is because on the harpsichord or organ you cannot adjust the volume of individual notes, even though a master musician can give the impression of doing so. On these instruments you really have only pitch and rhythm to make your musical expression within a particular phrase, not tone.

As a string player, you command all the means of varying the expression or colour of an individual note that an organist or a harpsichordist lacks. Nevertheless, follow their example and, to an extent, do use rhythm to shape and give meaning to a phrase (in a solo piece) in the same way that you use sound, vibrato or intonation to create the expression.

However, except in the really 'big' or expressive moments, if anyone can too-easily notice you using time to make expression, it will probably already be too much.

Creating accents by playing early

Instead of using only bow weight to play an accent, which can make a note too heavy, it is often possible to replace some of the bow weight by playing the note slightly too early.

In pop music and jazz this is called a 'push', and the note is played noticeably early. In classical music the note should not be played so early that anyone would immediately notice or realise, but only the slightest degree too early.

Brahms: Sonata no. 3 in D minor, op. 108, *mov. 1, b. 29*

- To bring out the syncopation, play fractionally early at each of the places marked '+' rather than using accents – especially since the notes need to grow through to the next bar.

The blended sound of a brilliant orchestral section

When everyone in a section plays in tune, with a similar tone, and exactly together, a magical, silky sound quality appears that is completely different from that of, say, fourteen violins playing the same notes but where you can almost pick out individuals in the mix.

It is in the sound you make, that you are allowed the most variation without compromising the blended section sound. Your playing can be slightly stronger or weaker within a narrow range (and one that widens and narrows depending on the music you are playing), but the overall corporate section sound still remains blended and pure.

Almost no variation is allowable in intonation, but depending on the note or composer there can be extremely slight differences of opinion as to what exactly the pitch of a sharp or a flat should be, or a B, C or F, and yet the section can still play one together that blends and sounds unanimous.

It is in rhythm that no variation at all is possible. If just one person in a section plays slightly too early, or holds on slightly too long, or plays with the slightest lack of rhythmic control, the blended, corporate sound of the section is lost.

This is why excellent rhythm is so vital in anything to do with orchestral playing, and can determine the success of an audition – yet the player may be concentrating mainly or entirely on playing 'in-tune notes with a good sound'.

Practising musically

'Mechanics' and 'Technique'

Under the heading of 'mechanics' come the basic physical operations of holding the violin or bow – for example, moving the fingers up and down from the base joints, rather than partly from the hand; moving the bow parallel to the bridge; the basic setup of the vibrato or shift; subtle aspects of technique like finger preparation; and so on.

All the mechanics of playing are describable, and therefore teachable. Just about anybody can learn them if they want to.

'Technique' is the overall ability to play a phrase musically and expressively, in a flowing and natural way. This is of course helped by good mechanics; but it comes more from musical expression and instinctive 'singing through the instrument' than from conscious mental commands aimed at specific mechanics.

It is like a horse pulling a cart: the 'horse' is the musical expression – the emotion, character, colour, atmosphere, drama, and so on – the 'cart' is the technique that happens as a result of the musical expression.

It is not the other way round, i.e. a technical horse pulling a musical cart. Music does not come from technique, but technique comes from playing music. Mechanics, however, do not come from the music.

The first thing is to have musical imagination; then to play music rather than 'play the violin'; then to listen closely to the sound.

The inner super-computer

Suppose you are playing a long, slow, sustained down-bow, and you want the tone to change to a slightly darker, more expressive colour in the middle of it.

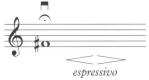

espressivo

Part of the colour will come from the left hand, perhaps making the vibrato slightly faster and narrower for a moment. Part of it will come from the right hand ever-so-slightly altering the weight and speed of the bow.

There is no doubt that you do need to be in control, make decisions, and 'send' certain commands to the fingers, hands and arms; but at the same time it is as – or more – important to concentrate on the overall tone and expressive quality that you want, and forget about the hands and fingers.

- If you try to create the subtle change of colour only by deliberately doing something – e.g. leaning the right hand more on to the first finger, or doing something with vibrato – you may send perhaps three or four commands to the fingers, arm or hand.

- Instead, if you let the bow arm do what it needs to do, your brain may send hundreds of thousands of commands, or thousands of millions, to the muscles in the arms, hands and fingers, in the same time that you would have been able to send only a few.

Nobody is 'clever' enough, using conscious control, to play a musical instrument as complex and subtle as the violin; but the brain is a super-computer that responds at faster-than-lightning speed to the musical images you hold in your mind. It produces a quickness, smoothness, and flow of muscular action that you cannot imitate using conscious control.

Whistling experiment

You can prove how incredibly clever your instinctive system is by means of a simple experiment.

● Whistle a note, and then sing exactly the same note; then the same a tone higher, and so on:

Most people can do this immediately, or at least without much practice. To be able to shape the lips so precisely, to within thousandths of a millimetre, so that the whistle is exactly the same pitch as the one produced by shaping the vocal chords to within thousandths of a millimetre, is a miraculous ability that we cannot take credit for, since we could not possibly do it using conscious control.

Q **But the bow is not going to play by itself. Surely, you have to control what you are doing somehow.**

The few instructions that you can send may not seem much, compared to the millions that your internal super-computer can send in the same period of time, but luckily they are all you need.

The player must concentrate on the music, and even if the way they hold the instrument and bow, and move their fingers and so on, is not text-book correct, the right physical responses will follow. Naturally, the best way often falls between the two extremes, with a constant mixture of making things happen and letting them happen.

Consider the held F at the beginning of this entry in Zigeunerweisen:

Sarasate: Zigeunerweisen, op. 20 no. 1, b. 7

You may want to diminuendo after the initial attack and then crescendo again; or sustain throughout; or crescendo throughout; and so on:

But whatever happens, the few instructions you might issue to yourself could be: 'Keep near to the bridge,' or 'keep the vibrato narrow,' 'keep the finger light,' 'don't kill the tone on such a note as this, halfway up the E string, where it needs much less weight,' and so on.

All you need to attend to are the basic issues of holding and using the instrument in a sensible way. Meanwhile, you feel the emotion, drama and character of the music, holding in your mind a clear artistic picture of what you want, listening closely to the sound and linking that sound with all the sensations in your bow and finger. Then it is as though your body takes care of everything else for you.

Staying out of the way

Not caring too much

While you must hold in your mind an image of the result you want (musical and/or physical), at the same time the important thing is not to care too much about the result.

Caring too much in the wrong way may mean that you brace yourself for failure; in the moment of bracing yourself for failure the muscles tighten; and then the sense of imminent failure turns out to have been a self-fulfilling prophecy, when the tight muscles directly cause the result that was feared in the first place.

Sports commentary on television is often fascinating because of the way the psychology of the players is considered and discussed as much as their technique. During a tennis match at Wimbledon, the British champion Tim Henman was having problems. He had been doing well in the previous matches and his tennis was full of neat, clever or daring shots that were consistently successful. In this match, he was still making those same shots but they were all played too long or wide. At one point the commentator remarked:

> Henman is trying too hard. When you are trying as hard as he is, all the playing goes on to a conscious level instead of remaining on a deep, instinctive level. He needs to forget himself. He should just run to the ball and hit it, and remember what it feels like to enjoy hitting the ball, without caring so much about the result.

Rephrasing that for playing the violin, when you try too hard all the playing goes on to a conscious level, instead of remaining on a deep, instinctive level. You need to forget yourself, and just put the bow on the string and move it; and remember what it feels like to enjoy playing the violin, without caring so much about the result.

It is through the not-trying that ease and artistry comes into violin playing. Getting in the way of themselves is one of the commonest problems that many performers often have to deal with.

Not interfering

Staying out of the way means not 'interfering', which means not trying to take control by performing actions yourself. The moment you turn on your conscious, thinking, directing mind, you turn your super-computer off.

For example, most people have experienced the difference between walking naturally, when you are not thinking about it, and what happens if you become self-conscious and try to place one foot in front of the other. Then the natural, instinctive action of walking becomes awkward, and you may even have a sensation of being on the verge of losing your balance and falling over.

The same interference happens if you try too consciously to move each finger and play each note: the more control you take, the less your body can 'play for you'.

Another clear example is the sort of wooden bowing you get if you 'hold' the bow and try to pull or push it 'yourself', rather than the smooth flow that comes when you feel a sense of momentum in the bow's movement, and *follow* it instead.[1]

[1] See *Feeling the momentum of the bow*, page 14

During the second world war fighter pilots making perilous landings at night on improvised airstrips were taught to look rapidly from side to side of the runway rather than to stare fixidly at it in their efforts to land. Otherwise they were liable to lose control and crash the aircraft. Similarly, avoid interfering in playing the violin by not 'staring' mentally, but 'look either side' of your playing.

True stories: Ann

A non-musician friend told me this story when I was a student, and ever since it has remained a favourite reference point concerning 'not getting in the way'.

> When Ann was 11 or 12 one of her favourite bicycle rides included a footpath that went down the side of a park. At one point, the footpath had iron bars across it, designed to get in the way of cyclists but leaving enough space open, right in the middle, for someone to be able to walk through.
>
> Ann used to cycle at speed along the footpath, approach the narrow gap in the iron bars without slowing down, and whiz through without thinking about it. One day she was out cycling with her friend Susan. They found themselves riding along the footpath by the park. Ann, who was in front, approached the iron bars at great speed and raced through them.
>
> Following behind, Susan slowed down almost to a halt; with wobbling handlebars, she managed to get through the iron bars and then accelerated again to catch up with Ann.
>
> When they next stopped, Susan asked: "How do you ride through those iron bars so quickly? It's so dangerous. There are only a few centimetres clear on either side. If you hit the bars you'd have a horrible accident."
>
> "It's easy," Ann said. "You just go through. I've never thought about it."
>
> But the next time she approached those bars, riding on her own again, she nervously slowed down to a wobble and then accelerated again only once she was through. Never again could she ride through at speed.

This is a vicious circle. She was right to worry since she had switched from 'autopilot' (her unconscious doing the measuring between the posts, sending a million corrective commands to her muscles while she simply enjoyed the ride) to 'manual control' (issuing the commands of 'more to the left; more to the right; more right; more left' herself with conscious mental control, and at an incredibly slow rate compared to the speed of the unconscious brain).

Then due to worrying she interfered even more. The same vicious circles happen during violin playing.

> *Q* **If you lave lost your confidence in a particular aspect of technique or area of playing, and then get in the way even more and make it worse, what is the solution?**

One easy way to regain trust in yourself, so that you forget about what or how you are doing and instead 'just play', is to practise individual elements of technique on their own in the form of exercises that isolate each technical detail.

By practising exercises for shifting, intonation, left finger action, tone, vibrato and so on, and continuing until they have become completely fluent and natural and 'in your fingers' – and thus sink into the unconscious – a new confidence inevitably enters your playing.

Picturing the perfect result

A big trap to avoid is that of being aware only of what you are doing, and the sound you are making, instead of keeping most of your attention on the inner picture of the perfect result you are after.

You do not want to be 99% aware of what is happening, and 1% aware of your artistic vision; instead, keep 99% of your consciousness on the inner vision, and only 1% on what is actually happening. You simply do not need much more than that to be aware of everything that is going on.[1]

[1] See also *Filling your mind with the perfect result*, page 324

Shifting

Suppose you want to practise this run from Lalo's 'Symphonie espagnole':

A simple method of practising shifts is to 'trill' the two notes of the shift:

Doing this shifting exercise, if you try to shift – if you try to control the second finger, then the first finger, then the second finger, then the first finger, and so on – it may feel difficult to play it fast.

Instead, if you hold in your mind a picture of the finished result – if you see yourself playing it fast, the notes beautifully in tune, the shifts light and fluid – then something extraordinary happens and you soon find that you really are playing the notes like that.

[2] See *Using a model*, page 216

- One way to help this process is to give yourself a model.[2] First play the repeated E–G's with a normal 2–4 fingering. Then make the 2–1 fingering sound exactly the same:

- While you are 'trilling' the shift, fill your mind with the image of the sound you made when you played 2–4. Concentrate so hard on the inner picture that you blot out everything else except the sound, which you listen to as though it is the only thing in the world.

Playing like this brings an extraordinary freedom and ability, compared with when you are 'trying', getting in the way and interfering.

Bowing smoothly

If you want to draw the bow smoothly and evenly, the one thing you must not do is try to hold the bow and pull it in such a way that it is smooth and even.

The moment you try to do it, you interfere and 'get in the way'. Instead, visualise the bow in a perfect, ideal state of moving smoothly and evenly. Keep all your attention on that inner picture of the bow in its perfect state. As you do so, that will become the result that begins to enter your actual bowing.

If there is any problem, or anything you do not like in the result, picture the absence of that problem, the opposite of it, the perfect result, even more clearly than what is actually happening.

Whatever happens, keep returning to visualising the perfect result.

Picturing the musical quality

Instead of trying to make the right physical movements and the right sound, in order to bring out the music, it always feels easier if you do it the other way round, i.e. first you go for a certain expression, and as a result of that, your muscles make the right movements and you find the right sound.

Vibrato and trills are clear examples:

What is vibrato?

The answer to this question is not: 'Vibrato is what happens when you wobble your finger backwards and forwards on the string'.

Vibrato is the quiver of emotion in the singing voice of the violin. The vibrato throb is like the sound and feeling of sobbing, which curiously is often identical to that of laughing.[1] This makes vibrato sometimes joyous, sometimes sorrowful. If you try to vibrate only as a physical action it is never the same as when you also picture its expressiveness or colour and let it happen by itself.

[1] See *Vibrato: the throb of pure emotion*, page 252

If you try to vibrate fast, the action may seem tiring. If instead you issue only one or two commands, such as to keep it narrow or relax the left upper arm, and meanwhile you picture it being physically exactly what you want, and picture its expressiveness or colour, you will find the vibrato 'playing itself' and working much better.

What is a trill?

The answer to this question is not: 'A trill is what happens when you move your finger up and down fast on the string'.

Pablo Casals would say that a trill is like putting a crown on a note. A trill gives a note a halo, a shine, a sparkle. Here are three plain, ordinary notes; then the same, but with one of them wearing a 'crown':

Suppose you want to play a fast trill. If you try to move your finger quickly, it may seem clumsy. This is because you are 'getting in the way' and trying to do it yourself.

Instead forget about the finger and focus on how the trill makes the note 'shine', and let your fingers play it for you. You will notice an immediate feeling of ease and greatly improved speed in the trill.

If it were in a piece I could play it, but as an exercise I can't

Ordinary technical exercises must be played with musicality as well, since this is what triggers all the lightning-fast technical responses, rather than with 'detached mental control':

Suppose you are practising these broken thirds with over-lapping bowing. Play with expression, perhaps as though it were an expressive passage in a piece:[2]

[2] Of course it may also be useful to practise an exercise like this without expression, looking at it simply as a question of pure mechanics. Which approach to take is similar to the question of whether or not you should use vibrato in scales.

One answer is that sometimes you should practise scales with vibrato, and sometimes without.

Similarly it may be useful to practise an exercise, scale, study or piece without expression; but often it is by playing with expression that we literally become more talented.

You can even approach finger tapping exercises 'musically'. Find a feeling or a perception of 'drawing the note out of the string' in an upward direction, as described on page 187, at the same time as making the mechanical, downward motion of tapping the finger onto the string.

When I was a student, and I practised Ševčík-type finger patterns – exercises where you repeat a group of notes several times, first as quarter-notes (crotchets), then eighth-notes (quavers), and then sixteenth-notes (semiquavers) – I used to find certain patterns confusing:

Beyond a moderate metronome speed I could rarely get to the end of playing these patterns – with four beats of 32nd-notes on the down-bow, and four beats of 32nds-notes on the up-bow – without my fingers getting in a muddle and tripping up.

At the time, I assumed that this was because some fingers were 'weaker' than others; or because some patterns are 'more difficult' than others.

It was only years later that I realised that when I found a pattern confusing, it was because I was trying to move my fingers in the right order. Instead, if you think more of the expressiveness of the pattern and approach it in a singing, musical way, and stop 'trying to move the fingers', it is extraordinary how much easier the patterns suddenly become. When you approach the patterns as 'music', the fingers 'play themselves'.

Playing from the inside out

Suppose you want to make a particular sound or play a particular bow stroke. First you must 'pre-hear' the musical and tonal result that you want, before you go to play it.

The next thing is to control what is happening at the point of contact of the hair of the bow with the string. A great way to form a sharp image of this is to ask the student to hold the hair against the string as shown in Fig. 124a and b.

Fig. 124

(a) Fixing the bow on the string with one finger of the left hand   (b) Focus attention here

As a result of what the hair does to the string, the right arm and hand make certain movements.

Then the right arm and hand seem 'clever'. This is playing from the 'inside out': you begin with the result you want, and a certain process automatically takes place to enable it without you 'doing it yourself'.

It does not work so well the other way round, i.e. if you make certain movements, with the right arm and hand, in order to end up with a result that happens where the hair meets the string.

That is playing from the 'outside in': using conscious control, you try to 'do' something in the arm and hand, in order to try to get a certain result in the actions and contact of the bow-hair with the string.

True stories: Jane

Even when you are playing a single-note tone-production exercise, it does not work so well if you try to 'play the violin'. If you 'hold' the bow and try to 'move' it in such a way that it 'makes the string vibrate', instead of feeling the note musically, it is as though you become less talented.

A clear example was provided by one of my first students – a freshman (first year) college student called Jane – who quickly became a reference point. I still always have her at the back of my mind when I work with anyone on tone production.

It was Jane's first lesson. She began by playing the Gavotte from the Bach E major Partita.

Although her tone was not bad, she clearly knew little about tone production or the use or feel of the bow. The bow was near to the fingerboard throughout, and in a hall her playing would have sounded small. The sound appeared to be coming from the violin, out into the room, rather than filling it, as described on page 7.

So I showed her how to divide the playing area into five soundpoints; touched briefly on the basic elements of tone production, i.e. the string being harder or softer at the different distances from the bridge, the string swinging to and fro under the bow, and so on; talked a little about proportions in general, and proportions of speed, pressure and soundpoint in particular; and then she began to play Exercise 1 (page 11) from the beginning, using whole bows on soundpoint 5:

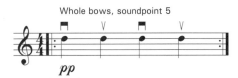

Players often find soundpoint 5 the most difficult when they do this exercise for the first time, and begin to find it easier as they move to soundpoint 4 and then to soundpoint 3.

Still, I was surprised at how difficult it was for her. The bow was not parallel to the bridge, and was sliding about between soundpoint 6 and soundpoint 4; and the bow pressure was far too heavy for playing near the fingerboard, where the strings are so soft.

As she played the repeated D's on soundpoint 5, I called out suggestions to make the bow lighter or heavier; faster or slower; to make the strokes more even, or to use more bow; to stay on soundpoint 5 without drifting over to 6 or 4; to keep the right elbow more on the same level as her right hand; not to raise the shoulder at the end of each up-bow; to 'float' the bow on the string, particularly at the heel; and so on.

After a while the stroke had finally begun to settle down. She moved to soundpoint 4 and started again. I expected her to find this easier, so I was surprised that again it seemed awkward or unnatural for her.

The strokes were uneven again and she was over-pressing. I began to wonder how she could have seemed so talented one moment, when she was playing the Bach, and so apparently untalented now, when she was playing one single note.

All at once the answer became obvious. When she was playing the Bach, she was playing musically, expressively, with inspiration. She was not aware of holding the bow or manipulating it in any way.

Now she was playing consciously and mechanically. She was holding the bow and trying to move it up and down along the string.

The only suggestion Jane needed was: "Imagine that these whole bow strokes, on one note, are a dolce, expressive moment in a piece, concerto, or string quartet."

Instantly, her bowing became smooth and even, the speed and pressure changed instinctively to just about exactly the right amount; you could see the blur of the strings as they vibrated widely and freely; and the instrument began to ring. When she then added vibrato, the dolce espressivo was beautiful.

The difference was extraordinary. She was instantly like a completely different player. I learnt my lesson, and realised the importance of stressing the musical approach from the beginning.

Key point: The question is not whether or not you should practise technique alone, or whether you should concentrate only on playing *music*. You can and should practise certain elements of technique separately from 'music'. But you should do so *musically*, even if you are repeating only one note over and over again.

True stories: Sarah

Sarah came to her lesson and played Sarasate's Zigeunerweisen. The piece is full of little technical challenges, and if you liken it to a hurdle race, Sarah fell over at every hurdle. There was a mishap in every technical passage, with something going wrong in every run, change of position or double stop.

In previous lessons the subject had often been that Sarah seemed to be 'holding the violin' and 'doing things to it' with the bow, using too much conscious, detached mental control, instead of 'losing herself in the music'.

So it was an obvious thing to suggest that perhaps she was regarding the piece as being 'all technique', and that if she approached it more as a piece of music, with every phrase having a musical intention first, rather than a technical one, she would find everything working more easily. In other words, to see that every technical challenge was a means to a musical end, rather than being an end in itself; also that the musical result creates the technical means by which it is achieved.[1]

"What do you mean!? – of course it is all 'technique!' – how can you look at it musically!? – it is Sarasate, not Beethoven!" she said half-jokingly – but only half.

We began to look at various phrases on their own. Each time there was a four-stage process: first Sarah played the phrase or passage, and each time there was some sort of difficulty; then I reminded her to think of it musically; then she protested that 'of course' it was an empty technical challenge without any musical importance; then she played it while concentrating more on the expression, and each time it was so much better, i.e. more accurate, that she was astonished.

[1] The principle of the physical action being led or created by the result you are after, rather than the other way round, applies to everything that we do. Consider digging with a spade. The spade, and the earth you are digging, dictates how you hold the spade at any given moment, the angle at which you hold it, the force with which you push the spade into the ground, and what you do with your back, your feet, your balance, and so on. The result dictates and creates the action.

And so it went on, each passage the same, until we arrived at the left-hand *pizzicato*:

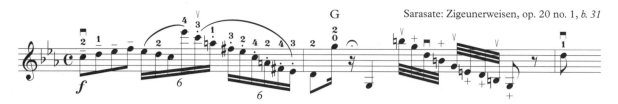

Sarasate: Zigeunerweisen, op. 20 no. 1, *b. 31*

Again her fingers fell over themselves as she tried to play the left-hand *pizzicato*. Again I suggested that it was 'not just technique' but music, and that she should approach it with a musical intention rather than 'trying to pluck the strings with her left fingers'.

"Play left-hand *pizzicato* musically?" Now she thought it was me who was joking. She thought it was impossible.

But she played it a few times without the *pizzicato*, bowing normally and looking for ways to make it expressive. The first note to bring out 'musically' is the E, since it is the one note that does not belong in the G major arpeggio. She played it a few more times, still with the bow instead of *pizzicato*, experimenting with different shapes and expression:

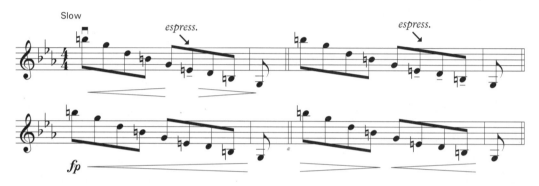

After a couple of minutes of playing the phrase with exaggerated expression, she played it again as written with left-hand *pizzicato*. It was so much better, and the left-hand *pizzicato* seemed to 'play itself' and felt so much easier, that the difference was extraordinary.

We moved on to the last two pages. Here, Sarah's fingers got in a tangle each time she tried to play the recurring scale up to the top A:

Sarasate: Zigeunerweisen, op. 20 no. 1, *b. 88*

Again, she was trying to play 'fast' and 'in tune' by 'trying' to 'put her fingers down' fast and in the right place.

To get a musical feeling for the phrase she played the scale slowly against a standard D minor scale chord-progression played on the piano:

Once more, when she then played the scale in context, and up to speed, it was amazing how her fingers seemed to move on their own, were much more relaxed and fluent, and were now in tune.

Belief: living the music

'Belief' is a term used in acting, and is to do with using genuine personal emotion to become one with the role an actor is playing.

When the music is happy, I am happy

My first encounter with this subject came when I would listen to the Bulgarian violinist Vanya Milanova playing in Yfrah Neaman's masterclasses at the Guildhall School of Music and Drama in London.

She was an incredibly good player, the sort who really could play pieces like Paganini's *I Palpiti* with complete ease, mastery and delight. Every note was in tune and clean, but at the same time played with grace and style and every conceivable colour and emotion.

I wondered what it felt like to be able to play the violin like her. One day I asked her: "What do you think about when you are playing?" Her English at the time was rudimentary but the support words were all she needed, and after thinking for a moment she replied: "When the music is happy, I am happy...when the music is sad, I am sad..."

She also said that sometimes she might see herself standing on top of a mountain, looking out at fabulous scenery stretching out for miles below, or whatever picture was appropriate to the music.

Stanislavsky: the father of modern theatre

Constantin Stanislavsky (1863–1938), is often regarded as the father of modern theatre. The basis of the Stanislavsky System (known as 'The Method'), is that the most important thing is for an actor to be believed rather than only recognized or understood. The same principles that exist in acting apply equally to playing an instrument, as we strive to get away from 'playing the violin' and lose ourselves in the music instead.

To get to this 'belief' Stanislavsky used 'emotional memory'. To act a role that involves happiness, the actor must remember a time when they felt happy; to act a role that involves fear, the actor must remember something frightening; and then live the role in the play using the emotional energy that they had once felt.

Stanislavsky divided acting into three categories: Mechanical Acting, Representative Acting, and Belief:

Mechanical acting

In mechanical acting you do not feel the character or the emotion of the drama at all. When you are playing Romeo, you remain yourself and merely say Romeo's words and try to make appropriate gestures and expressions.

There is a lot of acting like this in the original silent, black-and-white movies, where the characters replaced words by making all their actions and expressions larger-than-life: if they wanted to appear happy or sad, they made clown-size gestures.

In playing the violin, mechanical playing means that there is no emotional involvement. You hold the bow between your fingers and learn how to pull and push it in a straight line. You learn how to raise and drop the left fingers, or how to vibrate or change position, and so on. All the time, you remain 'in your head': the controlling 'you', which is somewhere behind your eyes and between your ears, issues commands to the hands and fingers.

You know that this note should be loud, so you play it loudly; you know that that note needs more vibrato so you vibrate wider and faster; and so on.

Representative acting

In representative acting you start off with a genuine feeling of the character or the drama.

Imagine that you are on your own rehearsing your lines. You are enjoying your work, and feel inspired by the character you are acting. You speak and act with feeling and conviction.

You notice that as you said a certain word you made a particular gesture with your hand, and at the same time made a particular expression in your face.

The gestures, and the expression, seem especially good and fitting. After all, they happened naturally and spontaneously. So you repeat the passage a few times, each time making the same gesture and facial expression, memorising how to do it. Then, the next day, when it comes to the performance, you reproduce again all the gestures and the expressions that you have rehearsed beforehand.

Although these expressions and gestures started in a moment when you had 'become the character', later on when they were mechanically reproduced they were no longer real. They may easily come out stiltedly and unnaturally because now they are being reproduced coldly and deliberately. But at least they were genuine at first.

We do the same thing practising the violin. You are enjoying playing, and notice, say, how the bow seemed to sink into the string on a particular expressive note, and how your vibrato widened and quickened, producing a warm expressive colour.

So you go over it several times, doing the same thing with the bow and the vibrato, memorising how to do it again so that you can reproduce, or represent, the 'expressive colour'.

Of course, by the time you are up on stage playing the piece, and playing bow strokes and vibratos that you have practised in order to represent what you had once felt in the past, the aliveness and spark in the playing is now lost.

Belief

When an expert actor is acting Romeo he does not remain himself, merely saying Romeo's words and trying to make Romeo's gestures: instead, he draws on his own emotional history and identifies with Romeo's situation so completely that he *becomes* Romeo, and thinks and feels as Romeo does.

Many musicians make the mistake of trying to express the *music*, instead of expressing *themselves* through the music, and try to remain 'out of the way' as they objectively control the ups and downs, and light and shade, of the playing.

Mesto: put yourself in a mood of sadness

This twentieth century idea of Belief in the theatre is identical to eighteenth century ideas about expression in music. In 1751 Geminiani wrote:

> I would besides advise, as well the Composer as the Performer, who is ambitious to inspire his Audience, to be first inspired himself; which he cannot fail to be if he chuses a Work of Genius, if he makes himself thoroughly acquainted with all its Beauties; and if while his Imagination is warm and glowing he pours the same exalted Spirit into his own Performance.[1]

In Leopold Mozart's Violin School, published in 1756, he includes a short dictionary of Common Italian Terms. Defining the word 'mesto', Leopold does not say only that it means 'sad':

> Mesto: sad. This word serves to remind us that we must imagine ourselves in a mood of sadness, in order to arouse in the listeners the melancholy which the composer has sought to express in the piece.

At the end of the section Leopold Mozart finishes by saying:

> From all these…terms is to be seen, as clear as sunlight, that every effort must be made to put the player in the mood which reigns in the piece itself; in order thereby to penetrate the souls of the listeners and to excite their emotions.[2]

In 1778, 22 years after Leopold Mozart's Violin School, C. P. E. Bach published a *Treatise on Keyboard Playing*. He included a section about performance:

> A musician cannot move others unless he too is moved. He must of necessity feel all of the affects that he hopes to arouse in his audience, for the revealing of his own humour will stimulate a like humour in the listener. In languishing, sad passages, the performer must languish and grow sad. Thus will the expression of the piece be more clearly perceived by the audience…Similarly, in lively, joyous passages, the executant must again put himself into the appropriate mood. And so, constantly varying the passions, he will barely quiet one before he rouses another.[3]

Playing with inspiration

I often think of a telephone conversation I had with Dorothy DeLay around the time when I had first discovered these quotes from C. P. E. Bach and Leopold Mozart. 'Becoming one with the music' was the big theme in all of my teaching and playing at that time, so over the phone I read to her the passages quoted above. I asked her what she thought of it all. Of course she liked it very much.

"But you know, everything you have said there is all in eighteenth-century language," she said. "Today, in the late twentieth century, the equivalent is to say of somebody that he or she plays 'with inspiration!'"

In fact, that was one of the words Leopold Mozart used himself.

First I've got to learn it

A common approach to practice is like this: 'First I have to learn how to play it; then I will put some feeling into it and lose myself in the music.'

This often does not work because the day rarely arrives when everything is so perfectly polished and reliable that you do then decide to 'put some feeling into it'. Most people find that there is always just one last little area that they feel they need to practise first. Then it may easily end up that you are standing on the stage the first time you really try to 'go for it'.

More often the opposite is true: it may seem that you cannot play musically, or play with feeling, until you can play it technically; but it is far more likely that until you play with inspiration you will not find the technique to play it.

Playing with inspiration is like becoming more talented. You do not have a fixed amount of 'talent' that you were born with. You can increase or decrease talent like opening or closing a tap, depending on how you go about doing things. It is only by playing with inspiration that we arrive at the stage where a passage is reliable in the first place.

[1] Francesco Geminiani: *The Art of Playing on the Violin* (London, 1751; Facsimile edition, David D. Boyden, London 1952), v.

[2] Leopold Mozart: *A Treatise On The Fundamental Principles Of Violin Playing* (Augsburg, 1756; Eng. Trans. Editha Knocker, Oxford, 1948), 51, 53.

[3] C. P. E. Bach: *Essay on the True Art of Playing Keyboard Instruments* (1778), 147, 152.

All about changing position

What is a position?

The term 'position' is an abbreviation for 'position of the hand'. The first finger is normally the marker of a position of the hand: on the A string, first-finger B (♭, ♮ or ♯) are all 1st position; first-finger C of any type is 2nd position; first-finger D of any type is 3rd position; and so on.

½ position on the A string gives first-finger A♯, second-finger B, third-finger C, fourth-finger D.

The frame

In each position of the hand, think of the fingers as basically covering a perfect-fourth range. Galamian called the perfect fourth between the first and the fourth finger the 'frame' of the hand on the violin.

In 1st position small hands are more likely to have a natural spread that is less than a perfect fourth, while large hands may have one that is wider; and the frame gets smaller the higher up the fingerboard you play; but still the perfect-fourth always serves as a natural reference-point.

- Strengthen the feeling of the frame in each position by practising octaves and major seconds:

Shifting

Thinking of positions as 'positions of the hand' affects the way you move from one position to another, since you want to avoid anything that weakens the clear feeling of the frame.

For example, when shifting upwards from third finger in 1st position to first finger in 4th, it may cause a momentary insecurity if, while playing the third finger, you extend the first finger up to a place just behind the third finger (Fig. 125a). Instead, keep the first finger on or near the string in its natural position (Fig. 125b).

During the shift the first finger may naturally extend forward a small amount before arriving on the E; but this is entirely different from any conscious, deliberate movement.

Fig. 125

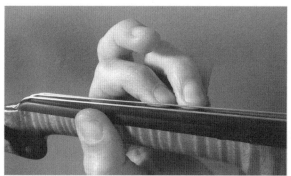

(a) Extending the first finger towards the third may weaken the clear feeling of the position

(b) Keeping the first finger on or above the string maintains the sense of position

Fingering

Good fingerings are often the ones that do not disturb the frame. There is a feeling of 'blocks' of fingers all working within the position, and a clear sense of the position of the hand without too much moving around from note to note or phrase to phrase (wherever possible or musically desirable).

Use extensions sparingly (i.e. reaching a finger higher or lower beyond the range of the normal notes in that position) so that they do not upset this secure feeling of the position.[1]

[1] Although extensions are an essential part of left-hand technique, if they are used in the wrong place or too many times in a short space of time, there is a danger of losing sense of what position you are actually playing in, which always leads to all kinds of intonation problems. See *Extending a finger away from its usual note*, page 162

There is no such thing as a shift

The most important thing about changing position is to forget altogether about 'shifting':

Example 1

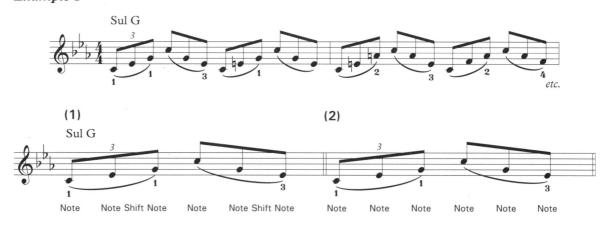

(1) The thing to avoid is that you play one note, then make a shift, then play the next note. This gives a feeling of 'note–SHIFT–note'.

(2) Instead, forget about the shift and play with a feeling of 'note–note'.

When you stop thinking about shifting, the immediate improvement in ease and accuracy is obvious. You can feel and hear the difference, and the correct timing occurs naturally and instinctively.

Example 2

In slower passages you can think about making the change of position if you want to, but the faster the passage the more you have to play 'without shifting':

(1) At speed you have no choice but to play simply note–note–note–note. Typical passages like these become 'bumpy' and without flow if you try to play note–note–SHIFT, note–note–SHIFT, etc.

(2) Always isolate the shifting-finger in a regular sequence like this. Play the notes purposefully but without thinking of the shifts. Afterwards keep the same feeling in the first finger as you add the other notes back in.

True Stories: Oscar

Oscar, aged 12, was playing this exercise for the first time. The exercise is played quite slowly:

Oscar repeated the first bar a few times. He missed each top A by as much as a semitone, sometimes too high, sometimes too low; the shifts were jerky, and the shifting finger was too heavy as it glided along the string. It was all hard work, with Oscar frowning and raising his right shoulder on each up-bow in his efforts to play it.

We worked on various ways to make it easier, such as listening to the 'ghost' sound of the finger sliding up the string, or lightening the shifting finger more, or slowing down into each top octave using a 'Slow Arrival Speed' shift.[1]

[1] See *Slow Arrival Speed: the end of fear in shifting*, page 245

We worked on moving the bow nearer to the bridge on the ascending shifts, and further away on descending; and how to use vibrato to help each top note sing.

We talked about 'not getting in the way' through over-trying. To force himself to 'disengage', he experimented with reciting his name, address and telephone number while playing the sequence.

He found how he could relax his left arm more easily if he did not clamp the violin between his left shoulder and chin; and he worked for a while on not raising his right shoulder on each up-bow.

Approaching the shifting exercise from many different angles in this way, we practised the first bar together for 10 minutes or so. The shifts gradually became more accurate and even; but still they did not seem easy, fluent or natural.

Something was missing. He was now playing it much more accurately than at first, but it could still be better. The fact that he had never before played such a sequence shifting up and down the G string, or that he was 'only 12', did not seem relevant or important.

At last I realised what he was doing. He was *trying* to move his finger along the string. He, Oscar, was trying to make 'his' finger (which he could see a short distance away, 'over there' on the G string), move along the string until he could hear that it was in the right place.

Instead, all he needed was to think of the exercise as *music*. We discussed it for a moment until he could imagine it as a grand, slow, stately passage in the middle of a huge symphony:[2]

[2] The is the equivalent for the left-hand of trying to do tone exercises purely with detached mental control of the right arm and hand. See *True stories: Jane*, page 226

At once the shifts became smooth, even, and accurate, and the entire use of the bow and the sonority of the tone were suddenly better.

Playing with inspiration and feeling unlocks your talent. Whenever you change from playing a phrase or passage with 'mental control', to playing with talent and inspiration, the results are always dramatic.

 But could he have achieved that result if he had not already done all the previous work that you did together on the shift?

In his case he probably could have gone straight to the end result, though everything that had been out of place (tension, raising the shoulder and so on) would still have been there; somebody else might first need all the work we did beforehand; but it is clear that without the musical feeling, no amount of instruction will finally bring you to the point of ease and musicianship.

Hearing notes in advance

Pre-hearing the note before you move to it – rather than thinking about the shift itself – is the first essential element of shifting.

A simple exercise quickly engrains the habit:

- Playing in an octave that suits the range of your voice, play a sequence of shifts and pause on the first note of each.

- During the pause sing the arrival-note of the shift – or pitch it clearly in your mind – and only then shift to it:

Fig. 126

Leading from the fingertip

According to the principle of 'The more delicate the action, the closer to the fingers; the bigger or the more powerful, the closer to the upper arm', you should 'lead' shifts from the fingertip.[1]

[1] See *The more delicate, the closer to the fingers*, page 48; *Leading from the fingertip*, page 144

Think of the action of the fingertip gliding up the string, looking for its new place of contact, as something subtle and intimate between the fingertip and the new place on the string. How can such a delicate and close operation be controlled or directed from such a far-off place as the part of the forearm near to the elbow?

The finger leads the hand and arm

Ask children to imagine a 'smiley' on their fingertip (Fig. 126). Explain that it is the fingertip that senses where to go, listening and looking closely up the string as it searches for its new place of arrival, and pulls the hand and arm along with it – rather than thinking of the arm pushing the hand which in turn pushes the fingertip.

Lightening the bow

Playing slurred shifts during a legato, sustained passage, you often have to create an illusion of sustaining during the shift while actually lightening – and slowing – the bow slightly:

> A certain complication arises when the fingering during a slur involves a substantial change of position…It involves a slight slowing down of the bow stroke and a gentle lifting of the pressure during the motion of the left hand. If this is done, it has to be carefully effected so that the gain in camouflaging the slide is not more than offset by a too audible disruption of the legato flow.[2]

[2] Ivan Galamian: *Principles of Violin Playing and Teaching* (New Jersey, 1962), 64.

You can make a little exercise on each shift by starting from an extreme of lightening and slowing, and then gradually reducing it:

Exercise 1

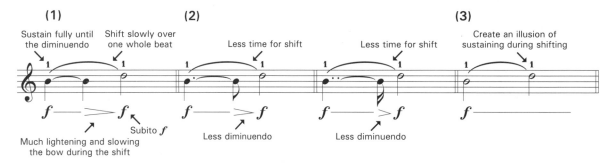

(1) In the first bar, sustain the first note solidly. Then, just before shifting to the D, and during the shift, greatly lighten and slow the bow.

Having arrived on the first-finger D, immediately play deeply into the string again like a subito *f*.

(2) Repeat several times, sustaining the first note longer each time. Lighten and slow the bow less, and later, before the shift.

(3) Finally, slow and lighten the bow so little that it is inaudible. Create an illusion of a perfect legato during the shift.

Exercise 2

Another helpful exercise or (practice method) approaches the question from the other extreme: while shifting the finger on one string, bow another (open) string and sustain the bow solidly.[3]

[3] See also *True-legato warm-up exercise*, page 261

Silently finger on the A string, bow the D string

- Do not allow the smooth, even, solid, sustained bow stroke to change in any way as the finger moves along the string.

Afterwards, playing and fingering normally on one string again, keep the same feeling of sustaining in the bow – even if you do instinctively lighten and slow the bow an infinitesimal degree during the shift.

Measuring: using intermediates

Intermediate notes are guide-notes that are played (or used as silent aiming points) between the two actual notes of a shift.

For example, two of the most common types of shift are 'Classical' and 'Romantic' shifts:

(1) Classical shift (or 'Beginning shift' – you shift on the finger you begin with).

> The note you are shifting to, third-finger F♯, is in 3rd position. Shift with the first finger to 3rd position. This note, D, is the intermediate note. Whether it is audible or not depends on the passage and the bowing.

> Having arrived there simply drop the third finger on F♯. Although the sound of the shift is a perfect fifth, the actual distance of the shift is a minor 3rd, B to D played first finger to first finger.

(2) Romantic shift (or 'End shift' – you move the hand on the finger that ends the shift).

> Having played the B with the first finger, place the third finger lightly on the string as if to play a harmonic. This is the intermediate note, though it should never be audible.

> Shift with this finger on the string, sliding the finger into the F♯ from below. Although the sound of the shift is again a perfect fifth, the actual distance of the shift is a minor 3rd, D♯ to F♯ played third finger to third finger.

Practice method

An obvious way to practise intermediate notes is simply to play them first as properly-sounding notes; then play them shorter and shorter until they disappear:

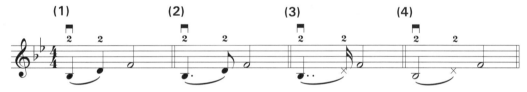

(1) Play the intermediate note

(2) Shorter intermediate note

(3) Intermediate note beginning to disappear

(4) No audible intermediate note

Finding the common denominator

In basic maths, adding fractions is easier when the lower numbers are the same, e.g. 2/6 + 3/6 = 5/6.

When you add fractions where the lower numbers are different, e.g. 1/2 + 1/4, you have to find a 'common denominator'. In this case, 1/2 is the same as 2/4, so 2/4 + 1/4 = 3/4.

Similarly, when a shift seems to be from one finger to another finger (1–2, 1–3, 2–4 etc), in many cases the actual shift is really 1–1, 2–2, 3–3 or 4–4.

When shifting up from, say, first finger to fourth finger, think of only one finger, not two:

- Is the first finger the 'common denominator', so that you move on the first finger as a 1–1 shift, and just drop the fourth, in tune, directly down on its note?

- Or is the fourth finger the common denominator, so that you move on the fourth as a 4–4 shift?

Single-finger scales and arpeggios

Since so many shifts use only one finger, i.e. 1–1, 2–2, 3–3, 4–4, a simple way to improve shifting in general is by playing broken intervals, scales and arpeggios using only one finger.

This also improves the accuracy of the silent intermediate notes that help measure the shift when it is played with different fingers, i.e. 1–4, 2–4 and so on.[1]

Practise single-finger scales and arpeggios at all speeds – slow, medium and fast.

[1] The first person I saw recommending single-finger scales was Yehudi Menuhin during a masterclass at the Guildhall School of Music. When he demonstrated them he played them extremely fast – shooting up the scale and down again, perfectly in tune and clearly articulated. He had a wonderful left hand.

Scales

Example 1

etc.

- Hear the next note clearly in your mind before shifting, and continue to hear it during the shift.
- Help to maintain a good hand position by keeping the fourth finger so close to the string that it is in danger of touching it. You can also keep it lightly and silently on the next higher string, as though practising the lower note of 4–1 octaves.

  Basically, keep the hand-shape the same as if you were playing an ordinary 1–2–3–4 fingering. If the fourth finger were to touch the string, the note it played would be in tune.

Example 2

- Stop each note with as light a finger as possible, without pressing down hard for each note.
- Lighten the finger even more during the shift.
- Help to maintain a good hand position by keeping the first finger near to the string or even lightly touching it. You can also keep it lightly and silently on the next lower string, as though practising the top note of 4–1 octaves.

Example 3

Example 4

- Play slowly at first, using the overlapping bowing shown in the first bar.

Single-finger scales and children

Use single-finger scales to teach children how to play in high positions. The earlier high positions are introduced the better, but this does not mean that children have to play pieces beyond their ability. If a child can sing a scale in tune (singing 'la', or doh–re–me) then they can play a scale in tune, using one finger, all the way up to the top of the string.

¹ Another way for less advanced players to get used to high positions, while still playing pieces only in the lower positions, is by practising the *Two essential intonation exercises*, page 73.

This means that at the same time as playing simple or elementary pieces in the lower positions, the pupil can also be practising single-finger scales right to the top of the string, i.e. the full two octaves. Then the high positions do not seem challenging when they are encountered in the future; and confidence increases greatly because a small shift from, say, first to 3rd position seems unremarkable after playing much higher shifts at the top of the fingerboard.[1]

Arpeggios and broken intervals

Example 1

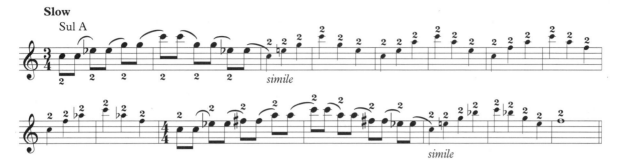

Example 2

Example 3

Timing and measuring the shift: filling in the interval

An extremely powerful and effective way to improve both the timing of a shift and the measuring of the distance, is to fill in the notes of the interval with semitones:

Example 1

Example 2

Five different types of shift

1 Classical   **2** Romantic   **3** Combination   **4** Substitution   **5** Exchange

There are always two notes to consider in a shift: the last note you play in the old position before shifting, and the first note in the new position after you have moved the hand.

The question is whether you move the hand on the finger that played the note before the shift, or on the finger that is going to play the new note you are shifting to.

The next question is which of the following possibilities the shift is:

- Ascending, shifting from a lower finger to a higher finger (i.e. 1–3): Classical, Romantic, Combination.

- Ascending, shifting from a higher finger to a lower finger (i.e. 3–1): Exchange.

- Shifting to the same note with a different finger (i.e. 3–1, 1–3): Substitution

- Descending, lower finger to higher (i.e. 1–3): Exchange

- Descending, higher finger to lower (i.e. 3–1): Classical, Combination

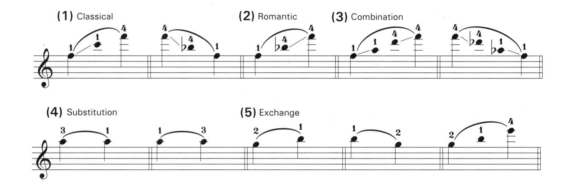

(1) Classical (so-called because when played in Baroque and Classical period music it sounds purer and less romantically expressive than a 'Romantic' shift) or 'Beginning' shift: move the hand up or down on the finger you are already playing. Then when you are in the right position simply place the new finger on its note.

(2) Romantic or 'End' shift: move the hand up on the finger you are going to play until you arrive on the correct note.

This shift is used only for ascending shifts, so although you can shift up or down with a Classical shift, if you shift up with a Romantic shift you have to shift back down again with a Classical.

While it is often desirable, in ascending shifts, to shift up to a place just below the arrival-note and then glide slowly up to it, it is almost never desirable in descending shifts to shift down to a place just above the arrival-note and then audibly glide down into it.

However, with the right timing or lightening the bow you can sometimes play a descending Romantic shift, leading with the finger you are going to play, as in a Combination shift – providing that there is no audible downward slide into the note.

(3) Combination shift: begin like a Classical shift, moving the hand up on the finger you are already playing, then finish like a Romantic shift.

Like Romantic shifts, Combination shifts are used mainly in ascending, but with the right timing or bowing can sometimes be used on descending shifts as well.

(4) Substitution shifts: a substitution is a change of position made by replacing a finger with a different finger on the same note. They are a very clean, 'shiftless' way of changing position.

(5) Exchange shifts are a type of Combination shift since you begin to move the hand on one finger and finish on the next. However, during the shift the fingers 'exchange' or swap with each other, e.g. ascending 2–1, or descending 1–2.

Exchange shifts are also used together with Classical shifts, as in the example in the third bar of **(5)** on the previous page, which shows a shift from the second finger to the fourth finger.

This shift could be played as a Classical shift, shifting up on the second finger to a B and then placing the E as an extension; or as a Romantic shift, sliding up on the fourth finger until reaching the E; or as an Exchange shift from the G to a first-finger B as shown, followed by placing the fourth-finger E.

Exercises

An obvious way to practise shifting is to play simple sequences of fingerings that cover every area of the violin.

Step-by-step sequential exercises expand and sharpen your knowledge of the geography of the fingerboard. The increased security that comes from constantly remembering the feel of every finger, on every note, is remarkable.

There are endless examples to choose from, but the following are typical useful sequences.

Classical

Exercises for Classical shifts focus on the intermediate note to find the exact position of the hand:

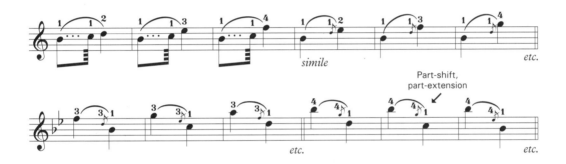

Romantic

Exercises for Romantic shifts focus on the 'slow arrival speed' of the shifted-to note:[1]

[1] See *Slow Arrival Speed: the end of fear in shifting*, page 245

- Another method is to use a short–long dotted pattern, aiming at the note one semitone lower than the arrival-note, to force the slow arrival:

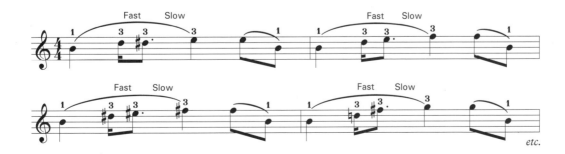

Combination

Combination-shift exercises use intermediate notes to gauge the exact distance of both fingers:

- Keep the first finger held down lightly on the string throughout.

Substitution

Substitution exercises have been recommended for centuries, for example this exercise from the Campagnoli violin school c1795:

Campagnoli: *New method for the violin, part 4, no. 236*

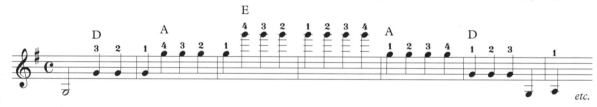

- Practice methods usually involve moving backwards and forwards between the two notes:

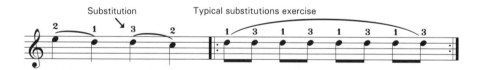

- Devise sequences including the combinations of 2–1, 3–1, 4–1, 3–2, 4–2, 4–3, and play them in every part of the fingerboard:

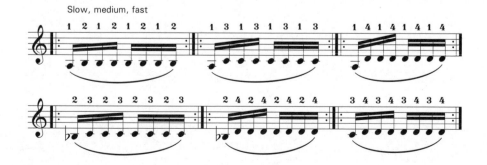

Exchange

Substitutions, as well as being a type of shift in their own right, can be used as a key part of exchange shifts:

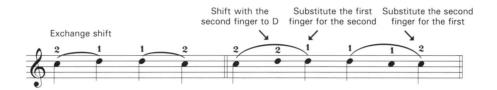

- Shift to the arrival-note (shown without a stem) with the finger that plays the beginning note of the shift (in this case the second finger).

- Then substitute the finger that plays the ending note of the shift (the first finger). Practise descending shifts in the same way.

In the beginning I learnt to shift as follows:

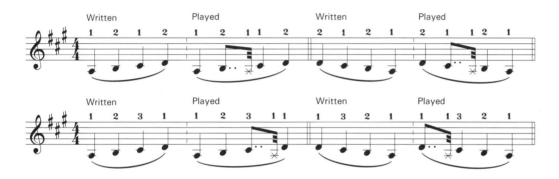

Clearly this unites the fingering so that the shift remains 1–1 instead of 2–1 or 3–1 (ascending), and 1–2 or 1–3 (descending). This establishes the 'from' and 'to' of the hand-position and gives you the sense of the hand based on the first finger (if desired).

Although it can be useful to practise with these intermediate notes and shift in this way, my playing seemed to become much easier, with less to practise, when I discovered that there was another way of doing it. You can make a far smoother and more flowing shift by using a substitution instead:

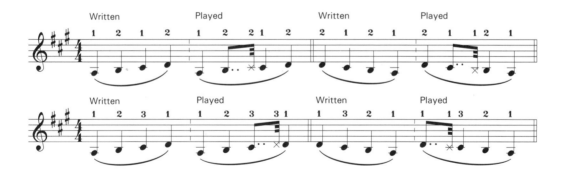

Shifting in this way makes the two notes of the shift seem closer together. There is also a greater feeling of flow because in the ascending shift you 'carry on in the same direction' rather than 'going back before going forward'.

In the descending shift there is a feeling of aiming directly on to the destination note, instead of going below it and then placing the new finger.

Example 3 Sarasate: Carmen Fantasy, op. 25, *Introduction, b. 65*

Two ways of making the changes of position (written out at half speed for clarity):

(1) Although it may be helpful to plot the first finger like this a few times at a slow tempo, if you try to shift like this at speed there may be a sense of too many 'stops' that make it hard to play the scales fast or evenly.

(2) After practising the scales at a slow tempo with substitutions as the guide notes, an extraordinary feeling of ease and fluency comes in to the scales when played up to tempo.

Exercise

(1) First play each section through as written (see example below). Play with an evenly sustained tone, and with a light left hand.

(2) Then repeat the section, playing the intermediate note quickly and softly (known as 'ghosting').

(3) Play without the intermediate at all, as simply one shift to another.

● Practise on different strings in different positions.

Listening and the feel of the violin

Fig. 127 Easy shifting depends upon two things: being sensitive to the feel of the hand and fingers contacting the instrument and the string; and close listening. Both provide 'feedback' so that the hand knows exactly where it is, and the finger can find its note accurately.

Experiment

See what it is like to find a note without any feedback at all: play a shift such as the one shown below in (1) and take the hand slightly away from the neck after playing the first note. Without

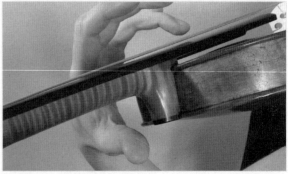

Lose all contact with the instrument

touching the violin at all, try to land the finger directly on to the B (Fig. 127).

It is difficult to find the note because there is no way of measuring where you are. Once the hand contacts the neck and touches the shoulder of the instrument, and the fingers can feel where they are in relation to each other, you can feel and hear your way to the note.

Listening to the shift

The most common accident is that the shift over-shoots and the finger has to come back down again to the arrival-note:

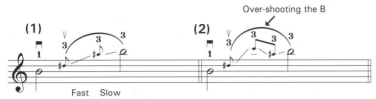

(1) Normal Romantic shift, the finger moving quickly up to a place somewhere below the arrival-note (not necessarily an A♯), and then moving slowly into the arrival-note.

(2) Over-shooting the B, so that the finger has to come down again – perhaps straight to the arrival-note or as shown: first too high, then too low.

The faint background sound of the finger gliding up the string, and slowing into the note, tells you instant-by-instant exactly where the finger is. So if you miss the note and continue shifting beyond it, it can only mean that you are not receiving the instant feedback that the sound provides, i.e. you are not listening.

Imagine watching a slow-motion, close-up film of the finger shifting up to the note and over-shooting it: you can see the finger nearing the note, getting closer and closer, reaching it, but then continuing on past. Yet the sound was there all the time telling you exactly where the finger was.

Therefore, not missing the note is not a question of learning 'better shifting technique', but simply of better listening and reacting split-second by split-second.

Listening to the shifting finger

Start off by listening to harmonics up and down the string. Children are always fascinated by the sound:

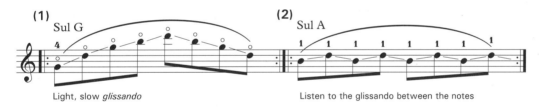

(1) Starting on the harmonic G, move all the way up to the top of the fingerboard, and down again, several times. You can also hear many other harmonics between the ones shown.

Move the finger in a steady, feather-light *glissando* rather than moving from harmonic to harmonic:

Also find the same harmonics by starting in the same place but moving the finger down the string.

(2) Then listen to the sound of the lightly-shifting finger in a normal shift, repeating several times.

Understanding timing

Stealing time from the note before the shift

The time for the shift must be taken from the note before the shift. Ivan Galamian seems to suggest the opposite:

> One of the commonest faults found in shifting is that of shortening the note preceding the move…Conscious attention to the rhythmic value and sound of the note preceding the shift is imperative until correct habits are formed.[1]

[1] Ivan Galamian: *Principles of Violin Playing and Teaching* (New Jersey, 1962), 26.

This must simply be a mistake in use of language, since one of the commonest faults heard in shifting is that of *not* shortening the note preceding the shift. Galamian must have meant that it must not *sound* as though the note before the shift has been shortened.

You can easily demonstrate that the time for the shift must be stolen from the note before the shift. Play a slurred arpeggio with a metronome click on each beat.

The tendency of many players is to begin to shift at the moment that the finger is actually meant to be arriving on the new note:

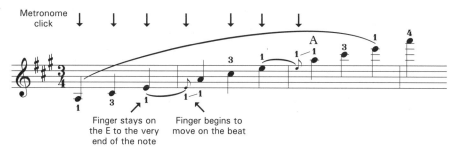

Instead, in order to arrive in time exactly on the beat you have to begin to shift during the previous note, not at the end of it:

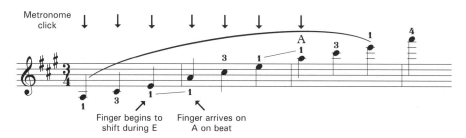

The only way that the note before the shift can sound as if it has been shortened is if you play the arrival-note too early.

As long as the arrival-note is exactly in time, it will not sound as though the note before the shift has been shortened, whatever you do. This is true even if the note before the shift is played very short, with the rest of the note's value taken up by the shift. This becomes even more true, the faster the passage.

- To practise a shift, cut the value of the note before the shift by half and use the remainder of the time to shift.

- Then gradually lengthen the note before the shift, and increase the speed of the shift, until it happens at exactly the right moment, i.e. a fraction of a second before the shifted-to note should sound.

Key point: The thing to focus on is the rhythm of the actual notes. In a scale or arpeggio, or whatever the group of notes that includes a shift, you need a rhythmic feeling of 'now, now, now, now' as you sound each note; not 'now, now, SHIFT...now, now'. If you concentrate on the musical rhythm, the timing of the shift will take care of itself.

Avoiding tension

When a shift is made too late, i.e. when the note before the shift is played full-length, each shift becomes a sort of emergency situation. You know you are already late before you have yet set out.

This can easily cause an unconscious, momentary tensing of the hand (and left arm), making each shift feel tight or heavy.

Instead, shifting early immediately produces a feeling of great ease in the hand. The sense of having 'plenty of time to get there' makes the hand relax and soften, and then the shift works lightly and easily.

Practice method

Example

- In the first bar begin to slide the first finger up the string the moment the E begins to sound.

- Slide at the regular, even speed that makes the finger arrive on the A exactly on the third beat.

- Gradually stay longer and longer on the E and shift later and later, and therefore faster and faster.

Missing out the note before the shift

An excellent way to find the correct or natural timing of the shift is to miss out the note before the shift.

- Pretend that this is how the music is actually written, and is how you are going to perform it.
- Play exactly in time.

When you put the missed-out note back in, you may be amazed at the new feeling of fluency and ease.

Example 1

Example 2

Example 3

Example 4   Grieg: Sonata in C minor, op. 45, *mov. 1, b. 254*

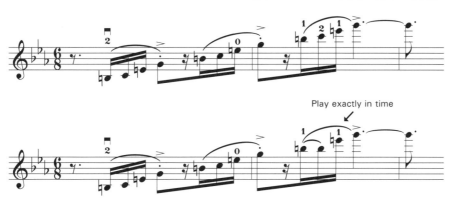

Slow Arrival Speed: the end of fear in shifting

By the time I had finished my undergraduate studies I already knew a lot about shifting. I had been fortunate enough to have had several teachers explain the basic mechanics to me over the years, each in their own way, and I knew the descriptions of shifting in Flesch and Galamian *et al.*

Yet still I sometimes felt insecure. In long shifts up the G string I would worry about missing the note or getting 'stuck' on the way up:

Sarasate: Carmen Fantasy, op. 25, *Introduction, b. 158*

Dorothy DeLay provided the answer that I had missed until then: Slow Arrival Speed. The speed of the shift is not constant. The finger travels very fast until it is just below the arrival-note, and then slides more slowly into the in-tune note:

This at last explained why shifts of mine before, of this type, had been good when they were good (when unknowingly I was slow-arriving into the shift); why they had ever felt unreliable; and what I had been improving when I had practised a shift until it did become reliable.

'Slow Arrival Speed' can be used on most shifts with the exception of Classical ('beginning–finger') shifts, although even in these there can be an element of slow arrival onto the intermediate note.

Parking Dorothy DeLay's car

Dorothy DeLay told how, when she was a student, she would always go to hear the concert of any touring virtuoso that happened to be playing in town. She would often wonder how they managed to hit all those long shifts, all those high notes, so in tune. How did they do it? How did they get there so easily and securely?

One day she finally worked it out, she said. In an ascending shift they never shifted to a pitch *above* the arrival-note and then moved back down to the in-tune note; they shifted quickly to *just below* the arrival-note and then moved slowly up into it. Like a singer often does.

One of her favourite ways to illustrate Slow Arrival Speed was to tell a story about parking her car. In American car parks ('parking lots') you often have to leave your car at the entrance, and an attendant gets into your car and parks it for you. When you come to collect the car, the attendant brings it back for you while you wait at the entrance, and then you get in and drive off.

DeLay told how she had bought a new car – her first car ever – and took it to a parking lot for the first time. The lot was crowded, and she watched nervously as the parking attendant drove off at breakneck speed and…slipped the car into a space without a bump or a scratch. How did he do it? Slow Arrival Speed! He drove quickly until the last moment, and then slowed down into the space.

 But does that mean you have to *glissando* every shift?

Slowing the finger into the arrival-note does not have to be audible to the listener. Slow Arrival Speed shifts can be done in three ways: completely clean and inaudible; faintly audible, mainly only to the player; and as a full *glissando*, audible to the listener.

It does not matter where you shift to

The only essential thing is that you never ever shift above the arrival-note and then come back down into it.[1] Then, one of the beauties of Slow Arrival Speed is that when you shift to 'somewhere below the arrival-note', it no longer matters where exactly you shift to: as long as you are below the arrival-note, whether you are slightly below it – or slightly more below it – does not make any difference.

[1] See *Listening to the shift*, page 243

If you feel worried about a shift, you must be looking at it like this:

I must shift to exactly the in-tune note. I must not be a millimetre too high or too low. There is one place where the finger will be in tune, and one place only. Anywhere else, and it will be wrong.

Instead, the need for precision and exactness – and thus any concern – is completely removed when you know that you can shift a little higher, or a little lower, and it makes no difference at all – so long as that place is slightly below the destination-note.

Once you know how to slow into the arrival-note, one effect is that the idea of 'practising' such shifts suddenly seems pointless. What is there to practise? The shifts become so reliable and accurate, and become so much more a matter of listening than of practising, that suddenly you find you have a lot of extra time in your practice – i.e. all the time that you used to spend practising long shifts.

There is no such thing as a long shift: there are only short shifts

Finally I discovered that you can take the idea of a 'fast–slow' shift much further. Rather than thinking of dividing the shift into fast and slow, forget about the fast part of the shift altogether.

Having played the lower note do not think of 'shifting'. Simply replace the hand somewhere higher up the string, i.e. somewhere just below the arrival-note, and then do a short, slow shift into the note.

In the Sarasate example above, you finish playing the lower note, the B, and then simply take your hand away and reposition it higher up on the G string somewhere a little below the arrival-note. Then do a short, slow shift into the D. Very simple.

Everywhere on the fingerboard is close

There is another thing to add to the approach of 'there is no such thing as a long shift, there are only short shifts' (see above), which makes things even easier.

A series of illusions can combine to give you a false impression that the violin string is much longer than it actually is. Shifting up an octave or more, on a single string, may then seem a scarily long way to go:

Once you have established that in fact the string or the fingerboard is not so long, even the longest shifts do not seem daunting.

A thousand notes on each string

There are about 50 notes you can play on the G string if you count all the enharmonics separately (counting G♯ and A♭ as two notes), and go up about two and a half octaves.

But these are only the correct, in-tune notes. What about all the out-of-tune notes between the in-tune ones? There are any number of 'notes' between G♯ and A that you can play too. They are all wrong notes in the sense that they are out of tune, but they are still there.

The feeling of a thousand notes on each string makes it seem much longer than it actually is.

Optical illusions

At Wells Cathedral School in Wells, Somerset, England, which dates from the 13th Century, part of the Music School backs on to an old, cobbled street called Vicar's Close, which is the oldest known continuously inhabited street in Europe (Fig. 128).

This short street serves as a good illustration for the students studying string instruments there, because it was designed so that one end of the street is much wider than the other. When you stand at one end, looking down the street, it looks longer than when you stand at the other end, looking up the street.

Fig. 128

The same optical illusion of greater distance occurs on the violin, because the strings are further apart at the bridge end and closer together at the nut. This increases the apparent length of the string.

Look at it the other way round. The fingerboard looks shorter, as it does for the cello and bass.

Vicar's Close, Wells, Somerset, UK

It's so much easier to miss and play out of tune

If you place a finger half a millimetre too high or too low in 1st position, the note will be a fraction sharp or flat; but at the top of the fingerboard, half a millimetre makes the note very out of tune.

This adds to the feeling that there is a long way between one end of the string, where the notes feel safe and easy to hit, and the other end of the string where the slightest mishap is a disaster, like a trapeze artist doing acrobatics high off the ground without a safety net.

The fingers get all cramped together at the top of the string

Playing in 1st position there is space between the fingers, and a feeling of freedom of movement. Even if you have large hands, when you play a semitone the two fingertips might not touch each other.

In high positions the fingers are all crowded together and on top of each other. Even if you have small hands you cannot play a semitone and leave the lower finger down on the string. Everything feels contracted and squeezed together.

This creates an illusion of great height because, like an object getting smaller as it disappears into the distance, the semitone at the top of the fingerboard seems tiny compared with the semitone at the bottom of the fingerboard. This makes the high positions seem high up, and the violin string seem long.

Precariousness of the bow

The higher up the string the finger stops a note, the shorter the portion of the string the bow is playing on. The shorter the string, the less weight it can take from the bow. Playing at the top of the string is the easiest place to bend the pitch of the note using bow pressure alone, without moving the finger.[1]

Every bow stroke in 1st position feels safer because the margin for error is so wide, compared with playing at the top of the string. In 1st position you can unintentionally give a lot more weight on a note without causing it to break or bend in pitch. In 10th position, every note is 'low-percentage' because the slightest misjudgement could spoil it.[2]

This further adds to the feeling of great height when you are at the top of the string, 'looking down' to the safer regions of the lower positions. Again this increases the apparent length of the string.

[1] See *Getting more for less: speed not pressure*, page 2

[2] See *Understanding percentage shots*, page 107

Look at it from a different angle

One way to get rid of any illusion that the violin string is very long, is simply to measure the distance of a shift and then look at it from a new angle.

Coming back to the octave shift on page 247, the distance of the shift is not an octave anyway, but a perfect fifth at the most:

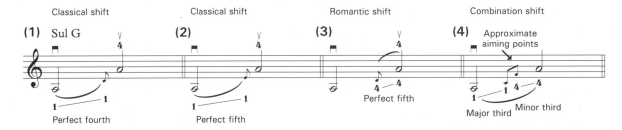

Fig. 129 You can move on the lower finger as a Classical shift from A to D **(1)** or A to E **(2)**; or on the upper finger as a Romantic shift from D to A **(3)**; or as a Combination shift, sharing the shifting distance between the lower and the upper finger **(4)**.

Suppose you choose **(3)**, the Romantic shift. Put the violin on your lap and measure the shift with your fingers as shown in Fig. 129.

The distance between the two notes now seems little. From this angle it is clear that your previous picture (of moving a great distance), was more the one you might have if you played the same octave shift on a cello.

The two notes of the shift seem close together when seen from this angle

The vibrato lesson

String players have used vibrato since the earliest times. In 1756 Leopold Mozart's instructions for playing his first 'division' of the bow included to use vibrato:[1]

> For if we strike a slack string or a bell sharply, we hear after the stroke a certain wave-like undulation (*ondeggiamento*) of the struck note. And this trembling after-sound is called tremolo…Take pains to imitate this natural quivering on the violin, when the finger is pressed strongly down on the string, and one makes a small movement with the whole hand; which however must not move sideways but forwards toward the bridge and backward towards the scroll.

The German violinist Louis Spohr (1784–1859), speaking about vibrato in his Violin School (1831), does not mention changing the width of vibrato, which 'should only be slight, in order that the deviation from purity of tone [intonation] may scarcely be observed by the ear'.

But he lists four chief speeds of '*tremolo*': 'The quick *tremolo* is indicated 〰, the slow 〰, the gradually accelerating 〰, and the gradually slackening 〰.' Spohr used vibrato only on selected long or important notes, and marked these symbols over the notes in the music.

A picture of the general use of vibrato in 1908 was given by the Scottish violinist and teacher James Winram.

> There should be no close shake [vibrato] in exercises or scales, other than melodic exercises, and it should be judiciously used at all times, as it is quite possible to have too much of a good thing. Beethoven's music will sound lovely with very little close shake, or if preferred with none at all; whereas Wagner's will gain rather than lose by its introduction. The character of the music must be taken into consideration, and good taste will surely be a sufficient guide. There are many who contend that the close shake should never be used, but when we consider that the world's greatest violinists all use it more or less, it surely must have some virtue.[2]

What should vibrato sound like?

Speed and width

The two main factors of vibrato are speed and width. By varying only these, without doing anything else, you can already produce a great variety of different colours.

Then, once you add different degrees of finger pressure, different areas of the fingertip or pad, or different degrees of speed within the vibrato (the forward movement of the vibrato is faster than the backward movement, i.e. you stay on the principal note longer) an infinite range of colour contrast opens up.

Q **How wide should it be? How fast should it be?**

You cannot say exactly how vibrato should sound, since no two are the same.[3] However, we can hear in the vibrato of the great players that what they have in common is the ability to play a vibrato that is 1) very narrow, and 2) very fast. Of course this is not always musically required, and it is no good if the vibrato sounds 'nervous' or neurotic; but still, even the basic, middle-of-the-road vibrato of top players, before they add intensity, is never slow.

A good model to aim for in vibrato is *sautillé*, where the same pitch is repeated rapidly, rather than thinking of vibrato as being like a very narrow trill:

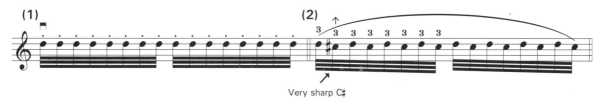

Very sharp C♯

(1) '*Sautillé*-like' vibrato sounding like DDDDDDDD

(2) 'Trill-like' vibrato sounding like D, then the note a quarter tone or so below, then D again. The note 'wobbles'. Some players call this vibrato 'wobblato'.

---

[1] Leopold Mozart: *A Treatise On The Fundamental Principles Of Violin Playing* (Augsburg, 1756; Eng Trans. Editha Knocker, Oxford, 1948), 98.

[2] James Winram: *Violin Playing and Violin Adjustment* (Edinburgh and London, 1908), 34.

[3] Carl Flesch used to point out that if any two famous violinists stand behind a screen, and take it in turns to play the same phrase on the same violin – without vibrato – you would never be able to tell who was playing.

But the moment they play the phrase with vibrato, you know immediately when it is one player and when it is the other. Vibrato is something unique, like a fingerprint. It is one of the most distinctive elements of your playing.

Four basic groups

There are four basic groups of vibrato. Elements of all the groups can be found in each player, of course, since nobody has only one vibrato that they use whatever the composer, the phrase, the notes, or the particular finger; but dividing into these groups serves as a useful starting-point for understanding vibrato.

Each of the following examples represents one legato whole-note (semibreve); the note-values represent the movement of the finger as it rocks backwards and forwards on the string in vibrato.

Group 1

This is a vibrato that you can rarely use because it makes it sound as though you are playing out of tune.

In this vibrato, the finger moves around the principal note, above and below it, i.e. moving between a pitch fractionally sharper and one fractionally flatter than the principal note:

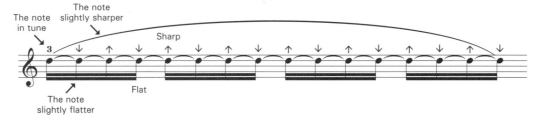

The problem with this vibrato is that the audience's ear catches the upper pitch of a vibrato rather than the lower pitch, and thinks that it is the principal note. So playing, say, D♮, which should ordinarily be in tune with the open D, it comes out sounding as though you are playing sharp, even if the finger actually stopping the note is exactly in tune.

Therefore, the rocking movement of the finger should not go above the pitch of the principal note. To an extent you can get away with the sharpening effect of this vibrato when playing sharps or flats because there is often a range of tunings for these notes, sharper or flatter, which are all still in tune.

The test that proved the wrong result

It is often believed that vibrato takes the finger both above and below the pitch of the principal note. There is a story, perhaps apocryphal, that one reason for the myth continuing to flourish is because of a test done in the early 1960s.

Apparently, an experiment was set up using an oscilloscope – a scientific device that looks a bit like a small television screen. When a sound is played into the machine, patterns and sequences of moving lines form on the screen representing that sound.

This experiment satisfactorily proved that the pitch of the vibrato did indeed go above and below the principal note. The only trouble was that they used an operatic bass singer for the test – not a violinist or other string player – and this singer had a vibrato that was about a major second wide. The actual note was somewhere in the middle of it.

This myth persists to the present day. In a recent book on violin technique (1998) the author states the incorrect perception clearly and says: "The width of a vibrato movement should be the same below and above the basic notes."

Yet there is no doubt that if you vibrate sharp of the note, it will sound as though you are playing sharp. You only have to stop and listen to an in-tune note played without vibrato, and then with vibrato, to know that the vibrato cannot go above the principal note.

Group 2

In this vibrato, the finger rocks between the principal note, and the same note fractionally flattened:

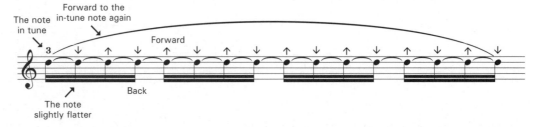

While clearly better than the too-sharp intonation that the previous vibrato causes, this is still not a vibrato that you can use often. It may sound too 'wobbly', because the lower pitch of the rocking movement is as audible as the pitch of the principal note. This is because the rhythm of the forwards and backwards vibrato movement is even, not a dotted movement – see Group 3.

There is another reason why this 'even' vibrato may cause problems: if the rocking movement is equal up and down, it may be difficult to play a fast vibrato. Clapping provides a perfect model:

The clapping experiment

- With your hands staying quite close together, clap lightly and quickly. The movement is 'in–in–in–in'. It is easy to do this extremely fast.

- Again keeping your hands quite close together, move the hands away from each other in a sort of 'anti-clapping' movement. The movement is 'out–out–out–out', which again is easy to do fast.

- However, it is difficult to make both an active movement in, and an active movement out, i.e. 'in–out–in–out', fast.

In the same way, the feeling of the movement of vibrato is one of 'forward–forward–forward–forward', not one of 'forward–back–forward–back'. You get this with the dotted motion illustrated in the next group.

Group 3

In this vibrato, there is a dotted rhythm between the principal note, and the same note fractionally flattened. You can still hear the lower pitch clearly, but the emphasis is now on the upper pitch:

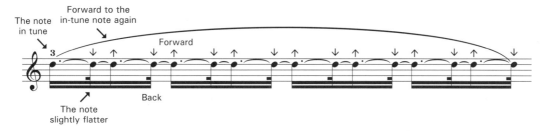

This type of vibrato 'throbs'. It 'pulses' clearly, and this gives it a lot of energy. However, you do not always want to hear these 'pings' in the vibrato. There are many vibrato shades of colour where all you want to hear is a general sweetness, rather than a quality of 'ping–ping–ping–ping'.

Because of the audible, lower pitch of the vibrato, this type of throbbing, dotted-rhythm vibrato may sometimes sound too thick, or too wide.

Group 4

In this vibrato, which is often the ideal, there is also a dotted movement, but now the lower pitch is almost (or completely) inaudible, and is represented here by an x-note:

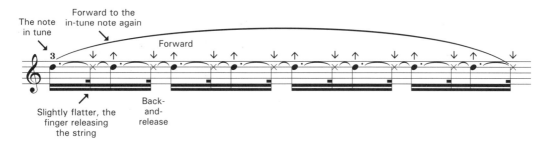

Apart from the inner dotted rhythm of the vibrato, the way to get rid of the sound of the lower pitch is to release the string slightly on the backward movement.[1]

This ends up sounding like D–D–D–D, rather than the 'quarter tone trill' illustrated on page 249.

[1] See *Speeding up with the metronome*, page 111; *Finger vibrato*, page 255.

Listening to your vibrato at half-speed

You can discover a lot about your vibrato by recording yourself and playing it back at half speed. The first thing you may notice is that the vibrato is too wide, or goes above the true pitch of the note, and spoils the intonation of the note in a way that you had not realised before. Another thing you may notice is that on many notes the vibrato actually consists only of one movement backwards and one movement forwards. In other words, it is so slow that there wasn't time to get more vibrato oscillations in before the note was over.

The perfect analogy for the speed of vibrato is the speed of trills. The more brilliant you want a trill to sound, the more notes there must be in it; and the more notes – within the same time-period – the faster the notes have to be.

- In your recording find those notes or fingers where you are doing only one or two 'wobbles' of vibrato per note, and see if you can make the vibrato faster. (So first make it narrower.) Then record yourself again and see if you can count more 'vibratos' in each note.

Vibrato: the throb of pure emotion

The quivers of vibrato, and of human emotion, closely resemble each other. When you laugh or cry you make similar physical motions in your breathing and in the muscles in your chest, solar plexus, and so on.

Joy and sorrow are so closely related that sometimes we 'weep with joy' or 'laugh with horror'. Sometimes you cannot tell if someone who has become hysterical is laughing or crying; and in fact, one moment they may be doing one, and in the next moment the other.

You may suffer an ice burn; or, lying in a hot bath, if you put your foot under the cold tap the cold water may feel as though it is scalding you; often, at a moment of the greatest joy or happiness, there may be a certain sense of pain or sorrow contained somewhere within it; equally, in pain there can be a feeling of pleasure.

In all music, from Baroque to film and popular music, there are often melodies which, being in a major key, may at first seem 'happy', bright, positive and so on – as opposed to having the 'sad' qualities of the minor – and yet you cannot really tell if they are one or the other. A certain turn of phrase may seem happy and in another moment sad; or it may contain elements of both at the same time. In the same way, the throb of vibrato on a string instrument is like pure emotion; but is it joy or sorrow?

True stories: Gabriel

I often think of a discussion I once had with a professional orchestral cellist about vibrato. I showed her how to make a pulsing, throbbing sound by rocking the finger in a dotted rhythm, and then hearing that pulsing in the fast, normal vibrato like this:

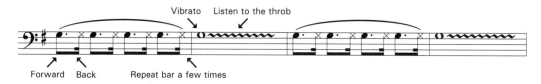

She did this a few times, and then sat back in her chair and said:

> "I've just realised something: I have been playing the cello for twenty years, and before this moment I have never actually listened to the throb of the vibrato. I've always thought that if this was happening" – she made a vibrato movement with her left hand in the air – "then vibrato was ok, vibrato was taken care of. I would think about something else, perhaps what the bow was doing, or the intonation, or whatever. So long as the hand was shaking I gave it no further thought. Never before have I stopped and listened to, and actually heard, the pulsing in the vibrato."

It sounds extreme, expressed like that, but actually this is not so unusual. The moment you make a connection between the vibrato 'throb' and emotion, and you listen to your vibrato, it takes on a new emotional quality as it moves from merely mechanical to truly expressive.

How to develop vibrato

There are two basic types of vibrato: arm vibrato and hand vibrato. There is a third type, finger vibrato, but this is usually only a part of hand or arm vibrato, rather than a vibrato in its own right.

The development of vibrato is entirely simple and natural. The first step is always to concentrate not on vibrato itself, but on the general balance and lightness of the hand.

Then, take an all-round approach by using not one or two exercises, but every possible one you can find. Whatever your basic type of vibrato – arm or hand – any vibrato is a combination of many different tiny or imperceptible movements.

Practise vibrato from every angle – arm, hand, finger, the rotation of the forearm, the individual movements of the three parts of the finger, the different areas of the fingertip, every possible combination of width and speed, finger vibrato, and so on. Sooner or later the vibrato that is distinctively 'your vibrato', with all its variations, then emerges and takes shape naturally.

Change your vibrato

Many players have a thought, perhaps unknown at the back of their mind, that in the end vibrato is so much determined by the shape of your fingertip, and by the size and shape of your hand, that you simply have to accept what you were born with. This is the quality of your vibrato, and this is basically how it will always be.

Yet it is the desire for a particular sound that makes the vibrato, much more than the actual physique. Suppose someone else could suddenly inhabit your body, take control of it, and play the violin with your hands and fingers instead of you. An interesting question is whether their vibrato would sound the same as yours, given that they are using the same fingertip.

Vibrato is something that constantly changes and evolves. It is easy to prove this by comparing performances of any artist who has made recordings over many decades.

During Nathan Milstein's 50-year recording career his vibrato is said to have changed every six or seven years, with a clearly different vibrato in each period. When he was young he had an extraordinarily fast vibrato, perhaps faster than anybody before or since; but this had slowed considerably by the time he was midway through his recording career.

When Fritz Kreisler was young his vibrato was very fast, and had very clear 'pings'. In the recording of the *Meditation* by Massenet, made in his twenties, the number of vibrato pings often fits the rhythmic value of the notes exactly, coming out something like this:

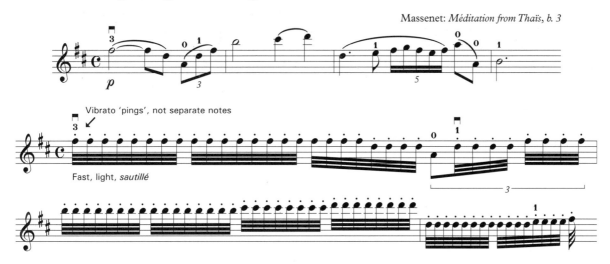

Doubtless this was not on purpose, and the speed of vibrato and the tempo of the piece just happened to coincide so that some notes had a mathematically correct number of pings.

But Kreisler's vibrato had so changed in later years that you cannot 'count the pings'. In his recording of *Liebesleid* made thirty years later, the vibrato has a quality that is impossible to describe except in abstract terms of 'warmth' or 'humanity', and so on. The earlier and the later vibratos are equally beautiful and natural, yet entirely different.

Changing the elements

Change is easy to achieve since everything about vibrato comes from only a few factors. An adjustment in any one of them changes the overall quality of vibrato entirely:

- Which part of the fingertip – change between more on the tip and more on the pad

- The width of the movement – change between wider and narrower

- The speed of the movement – change between faster and slower

- The heaviness of the finger in the string – change between releasing more, or releasing less, during the backward movement

- The direction of the movement – change between more dotted (pulsing to the upper pitch of the vibrato) to a more even rhythm in the vibrato movement.

Which part of the fingertip?

You can tell almost any student violinist – even before you have heard them play – that there is something they need to reconsider in their vibrato. You can say: 'Although I have not heard you play, I can tell you there is something you do not think about in your vibrato. It never occurs to you.'

When you then tell them what it is – that they do not constantly change the exact part of the fingertip that contacts the string, in order to create different vibrato colours – most will agree that yes, it is true: they never ever think of varying it.

You could not say the same about the width or speed of vibrato. At least half would protest and say no, they do often change the width or speed. But in nearly every case it will be true about changing the area of the fingertip. This is something that most players forget to do most of the time.

Changing the anatomy of your fingertip

If you think that your particular vibrato on each finger is the result, to a large extent, of the shape of your fingertip – and you cannot change what you were born with – this is all the more reason to vary which part of the fingertip contacts the string.

After all, if you put the finger down in an infinitesimally different position, it is like having a slightly different physical build to your fingertip. Then, if again you change the amount of pad touching the string, you have another different fingertip, and so on.

Which is better: hand or arm vibrato?

It has often been suggested that one type of vibrato is better than another. The question is similar to another question: are big hands better for playing the violin, or are smaller hands better?

A simple answer is that some of the greatest violinists have had small hands, and some have had large hands. Therefore how good you are as a violinist cannot be a question of the size of your hands.

Equally, some of the best players have had a hand vibrato, and some have had an arm vibrato. Some have been able to do both; and anyway, a good arm vibrato contains elements of hand vibrato.

 If you have the 'wrong' vibrato, is it possible to change from one type of vibrato to another?

Most players use only one type of vibrato, though there is always the occasional player who can use an arm vibrato for one passage, and a hand vibrato for another.

It is usually better not to change from whichever vibrato is the most natural for you. It is not uncommon to see intermediate-level players with an awkward-looking vibrato, and for it to turn out that they used to have an arm vibrato but a previous teacher changed it to a hand vibrato, or *vice versa*.

The fastest improvement can often be gained by immediately switching back to the vibrato they had originally. Then a previously awkward-looking hand vibrato may quickly – or sometimes instantly – become an excellent arm vibrato, or a clumsy arm vibrato become an excellent hand vibrato.

Forcing a student to use a particular vibrato can be like forcing a left-handed child to write with their right hand. It is often better to develop writing with the left hand in such a way that it works perfectly for the child, rather than force something on them which may be too unnatural to succeed.

 What is the main difference between hand and arm vibrato?

The difference between hand and arm vibrato used to be described (wrongly) as follows. In hand vibrato the forearm remains entirely motionless, the hand moving at the wrist to perform the rapid backwards-and-forwards vibrato motion; in arm vibrato there is no movement whatsoever at the wrist, all the vibrato coming instead from a rapid backwards-and-forwards motion of the forearm.

However, if you make an arm vibrato like that, by 'swinging' the forearm from the elbow and with no movement at the wrist, the movement is too wide and slow because the lever used to produce the movement – the forearm and hand combined – is too large. Imagine splints on either side of the wrist. Use two pencils (Fig. 130a).

A more practical arm vibrato uses the forearm to create a sympathetic shaking in the hand, so that there is indeed a movement of the hand at the wrist in arm vibrato. The 'motor' remains in the forearm and upper arm – there is no active movement by the hand – but there is a visible passive movement of the hand at the wrist.

Exactly the same principle can be seen in the right arm. A small amount of hand movement, during string crossing, saves a much larger amount of arm movement.

Experiment in trying to prevent an arm vibrato

Whilst vibrating with a fast, relaxed, free arm vibrato, it is possible for someone to grip your arm just below the wrist (at the watch-strap), without the vibrato stopping:

Student

Get ready to play, say, third-finger D on the A string.

Teacher or assistant

Place your fingers lightly around the student's forearm just below the wrist (Fig. 130b). At first, let the student play the D with arm vibrato. Then hold their forearm more tightly and try to prevent them from vibrating.

Fig. 130

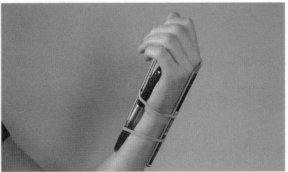

(a) Imagining 'splints' that prevent any movement of the hand during arm vibrato – this is the way *not* to vibrate

(b) It is still possible to vibrate, using an arm vibrato, with someone trying to stop you

If the mechanism of the student's arm vibrato is correct, you will not be able to prevent the vibrato. Although the vibrato has an impulse coming from somewhere just above the elbow, the movement of the forearm is slight or imperceptible, while leading to a larger, passive, 'swinging' in the hand.

Finger vibrato

In finger vibrato the fingertip presses and releases the string. This is rarely done on its own because it is unnatural or difficult to do it fast enough without the hand joining in, in some way, in the movement. But as a part of arm or hand vibrato, a degree of it adds to the clarity and purity of the vibrato and is a key element in creating a Group 4-type 'D, D, D, D' vibrato.[1]

[1] See *Group 4, page 251*

Feeling the buoyancy of the string

Press the string down towards the fingerboard and release it back up again in different rhythms and at different speeds. Use the entire exercise *Speeding up with the metronome* (page 256) but do a finger vibrato on each written note instead of a movement that comes from the hand or arm:

- Begin with the finger resting on the surface of the string as if to play a harmonic. Feel the buoyancy of the string, its give and resistance.

- Gently push the string down all the way to the fingerboard (remembering that normally the finger pressure should not be this much) and release again. The essential thing is to feel a slight degree of rolling into the string rather than pressing it vertically downwards.[2]

[2] See *Rolling the finger into the string*, page 190

- As you roll forwards into the string, feel the left thumb rotating clockwise slightly; feel it rotate the other way when you release the string.[3]

[3] See *Thumb rotation*, page 182

- For the purposes of the exercise press the string with the finger alone rather than partly using the hand or arm to help the finger push the string down. Do not actively do this in normal vibrato. Just let traces of it naturally come in to your playing through doing the exercise.

Releasing to a harmonic

- Alternate between playing a harmonic on the pad of the finger, and rolling forward to stop the string.

- Begin with the finger resting on the string rather straight, and on its pad rather than the finger tip.

- Roll forwards so that the finger stops the string (resulting in an out-of-tune note); roll back and release to the harmonic again.

- Do this in a dotted rhythm with the metronome: start at ♩ = 60 and gradually speed up from there.

Play harmonic with pad of finger

Roll forward to a very sharp E, more on the tip of the finger and with the finger more curved

- Use the same perfect fifth harmonic on each string.

By its nature this exercise forces you to vibrate the wrong way round, i.e. from in-tune to above the in-tune note. Remember to return afterwards to normal, and vibrate up to the in-tune note, not above it.

How to play a fast vibrato without tension

Start from nothing

The first thing that many children do when they first try to vibrate (or even just put a finger down on the string) is to tighten the hand.

To counter this, start in an exaggerated state of relaxation and work up from there, gradually introducing more muscle tone until there is just the right amount:

- Place a finger on the surface of the string, as though playing a harmonic.

- Make your hand go limp and soft. Let go of every muscle in the hand and fingers so that there is no muscular activity at all. Let go of the muscles in the wrist, forearm, upper arm and shoulder.

- Keeping the hand feeling limp and 'jelly-like', begin to vibrate the finger on the string.

- At first, allow the finger to be far too loose and wobbly. It does not matter if the fingertip slips on the surface of the string and the pitch of the note keeps changing.

- Begin to allow the muscles in the hands and fingers to work more, so that gradually the vibrato becomes more stable and focused – but strive at the same time to keep the floppy, loose feeling in the hand and fingers.

- Finally arrive at a point where the finger stops the string properly, and the vibrato is narrow and focused, but the entire hand is beautifully relaxed and free.

Make it narrower

Fig. 131

The faster the vibrato, the narrower it needs to be. It is easy to illustrate this by using a bow as a pendulum (Fig. 131).

Clearly, the wider the movement the longer it takes to travel from one side to the other. To move it quickly you have to keep the movement narrow, as little as a few centimetres.

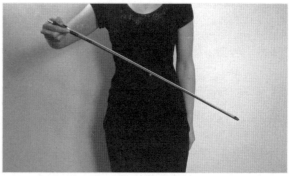

The wider the movement, the longer it takes to travel from one end to the other

Wide and slow, or fast and narrow, are natural combinations of speed and width; but at times you can also use a slow, narrow vibrato (less energy) or a wider, faster vibrato (more energy), as well as all the different degrees in between.

If you have any difficulty speeding up your vibrato, the width is the first area to consider. It is nearly always possible to make it narrower.

Staying free in the upper arm

Fig. 132

[1] See *Widening at the shoulders: releasing the minor pectoral*, page 174

A key area to keep free, especially in arm vibrato, is the minor pectoral muscle[1] in the lower shoulder (Fig. 132). The common problem is one of pulling the left upper arm inwards and clenching this muscle at the same time.

Constantly remain aware of keeping an open space between the left upper arm and the side of the body, and always look for a sensation of lengthening and widening the pectoral muscle.

Stay free and open in the area of the upper arm and the minor pectoral

Speeding up with the metronome

Speeding vibrato up with the metronome is a straightforward way to get it faster. This exercise is also excellent for developing one of the key elements of a fine vibrato: the slight release of the string during the backward movement of the finger.

- Begin at 60 (one, two and four vibrato 'pings' on each beat), and then 63, 66, 72 etc. up to 120.

- With each increase in speed make sure that you make the vibrato correspondingly narrower.

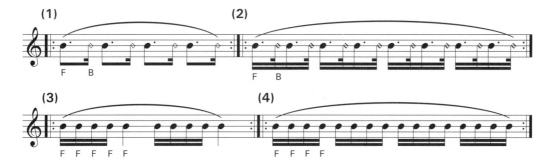

(1) Vibrate forward to the in-tune note on each beat.

The notes shown as harmonics represent rolling the finger backwards, flattening the note and slightly releasing the string (so that the note no longer sounds pure), before coming back up into the note on the next beat.

Play four beats on the down-bow, and four beats on the up-bow.

(2) Vibrate forward to the in-tune note twice on each beat.

Continue in the same pattern of four beats on the down-bow, four on the up-bow.

(3) Each sixteenth-note (semiquaver) represents one vibrato 'throb'. The quarter-notes (crotchets) represent the note played without vibrato.

Play forward–forward–forward–forward, then forward-and-stop on the in-tune note, i.e. play throb–throb–throb–throb–throb, throb–throb–throb–throb–throb, etc.

Play four beats on the down-bow, and four beats on the up-bow.

(4) Play continuous vibrato without stopping.

Play 'throb–throb–throb–throb' on each beat without stopping.

Maintain the symmetry of playing four beats on the down-bow, four beats on the up-bow.

As an extra stage before you play **(4)**, or as a separate exercise, try making up various rhythms in the vibrato before playing the regular groups of four without stopping:

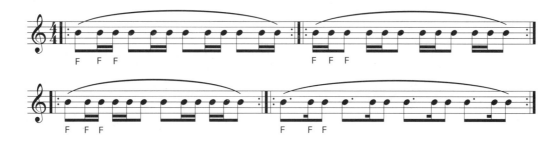

When doing the exercise for the first few times

When they practise this exercise for the first time, many players find that they can do it without any difficulty only at certain speeds. For example, they may be able to do each stage easily in the 60–75 range; find it difficult to control the final stages in the 75–90 range; then be able to do the final stages in the 90–105 range but with a lot of effort; and then not be able to do it any faster than that.

But if players practise the exercise for just one or two minutes as part of the daily warm-up, it usually does not take long before they are able to control the exercise at every speed.

Sub-dividing the larger unit

There is an analogy between vibrato and *spiccato*.

When you play slow *spiccato* strokes, you can play each one as an active, controlled, bow stroke. As you play faster, you quickly reach a speed limit where it is natural to begin to play in pairs of notes, then groups of fours and even eight notes.[1]

¹ See *Groups*, page 109

Approach vibrato in the same way. If you want a faster vibrato, it feels effortful if you try to make each individual cycle of the vibrato faster.

Instead, feel the vibrato in groups of 8 'forwards to the in-tune note'. This is another example of always dealing with larger units that you then sub-divide, rather than making each sub-division and trying to put it all together afterwards.

The same applies to the bow arm: rather than having many little movements that you try to make individually, and try to join together into one larger stroke, think instead of the whole stroke, and let the individual components look after themselves.[1]

[1] See *Building the bow arm*, page 122

Using the vibrato trill as an exercise

Vibrato trills are played by positioning the tip of the upper finger of the trill close to the string. The rocking movement of the vibrato makes the finger touch and leave the string and produces an extremely fast, brilliant effect, without you actually moving the trilling finger up and down at all.

Trilling like this is normally done only in semitone trills, and even then only in high positions; but it is useful in 1st position as an exercise.

- Do not think about the movement of the arm, hand, or finger. Simply use the sound of the trill to speed up the vibrato:

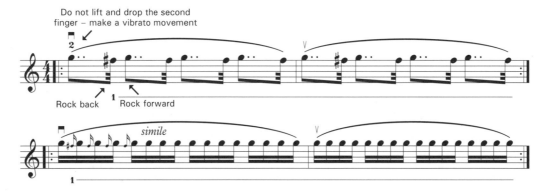

- Do the same with the other fingers:

- Begin at ♩ = 60, and repeat at 70, 80, 90 and 100.

Tapping with the middle joint of the thumb

It is often easier to control a tapping movement, and to speed it up, than it is to control an actual vibrato. Afterwards, the vibrato feels easier too.

Fig. 133

- Begin with the hand in 3rd or 4th position, so that the palm of the hand is close to the end of the neck (Fig. 133).

- Moving the forearm from the elbow, tap the middle joint of the thumb against the neck block – i.e. where the neck attaches to the body of the violin – and then return to the starting position.

Also tap by keeping the forearm still and moving only the hand.

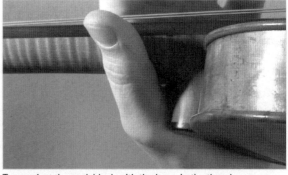

Tap against the neck block with the bone in the thumb

- With the metronome set at 60, tap once on each beat, then 2, 3, 4, 6 and 8 times.

- Then move the metronome up to 65 or 70 and repeat.

- Continue increasing the metronome until you simply cannot tap any faster; then continue to push against that limit.

- As the speed gets faster and faster, remember to make every action smaller and smaller. Keep the left upper arm and shoulder free.

One of the secrets of artistry: leading accents from the vibrato

Leading bow accents with vibrato accents is one of the great keys to both technical and musical artistry.

A vibrato accent is made by suddenly giving a single note extra width or speed, or both at the same time, to make it stand out from the notes around it. You can also play a series of consecutive notes with an individual vibrato accent on each.

There is a good feeling of the hands working together when playing vibrato accents. The bow moves fast–slow and heavy–light. The vibrato pattern is fast–slow and wide–narrow.

Instead of making an accent with the bow, and giving that note vibrato, don't think so much about the bow. Make a vibrato accent, and let the bow look after itself.

Of course you have to give different degrees of attack in the bow as well; but when you lead the bow accent from the vibrato you can have a sense of there being only one action, not two: instead of moving the bow and at the same time vibrating, it feels as though the vibrato is the trigger that sets off the bow:

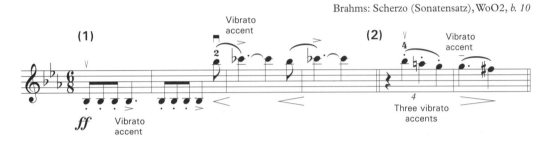

Brahms: Scherzo (Sonatensatz), WoO2, b. 10

(1) In the first two bars the triplet eighth-notes (quavers) are played *spiccato* in the lower half. Lead each bow accent with a vibrato accent. In the second two bars play the up-beat quavers with very little bow, then make the accent with the vibrato.

(2) The quarter-notes (crotchets) are played along the string in the upper half, each with a slightly fast–slow and heavy–light stroke. Lead them from the left hand with a vibrato accent on each. In the second bar the notes are like a written-out appoggiatura, so the G is played with a 'lean' and a diminuendo to the F♯. Instead of playing a heavy–light stroke coloured by vibrato, lead the stroke (and the expression) with a vibrato accent.

Playing accents in the air

To get more of the feeling of leading accents from the vibrato, practise by 'playing' a phrase with the bow in the air just above the string:

- Mime the bow strokes, with the same fast–slow bow speed for each accent, and at the same time make an exaggeratedly wide–narrow and fast–slow vibrato accent in the left hand.

- Feel the 'trigger' for the movement of the right arm in the vibrato.

Make sure there is no feeling of doing two things at the same time, i.e. making a fast–slow movement in the air with your right arm, while at the same time making a sudden, violent vibrato movement in the other.

Instead, feel the two actions as one thing. Focus only on the vibrato and let the right arm move by itself.

Continuous vibrato

The modern approach to vibrato is that every note in a phrase should be vibrated, each note melting seamlessly into the next, unless the phrase or passage is too fast for this to be practical.

Continuous vibrato is one of the most important qualities to develop as part of your general tone. It produces a unique and classy quality of expressive singing, and whenever you urge a student to play a phrase with continuous vibrato where before they did not, the difference is always dramatic.

Continuous vibrato means two things. First, so long as the passage is not too fast each note in a melodic phrase is vibrated, without some notes unintentionally and unknowingly played 'bare'. Second, the vibrato must begin at the absolute beginning of the note, without any momentary delay, and continue to the end of the note.

Yfrah Neaman, pupil of Carl Flesch and Max Rostal, suggested that it should feel as though the hand itself is vibrating continuously, so that the fingers are already 'vibrating' as they drop and touch the string, and do not stop vibrating as they lift off.

Of course, like anything else continuous vibrato must be used judiciously. There are plenty of occasions – especially in passages that are more than moderate in tempo – where a 'cleaner' sound without vibrato would be desirable anyway, or where vibrato would make an otherwise-simple passages more difficult.

However, until a group of notes is obviously too fast for any vibrato at all, you can often use a 'background vibrato' - minimal width and speed of movement, but just enough vibrato to colour the notes slightly and give them life.

There is much debate about the use of vibrato in earlier centuries. Some are convinced that before Fritz Kreisler, in the early twentieth century, vibrato was used only sparingly, on certain long or important notes, and in most cases used like an ornament.

Others argue that the natural phenomenon of vibrato – and not just the occasional use of it – has been around for as long as people have been playing string instruments.

In Geminiani's instructions for vibrato in his 1751 *Art of Playing on the Violin*, ('You must press the Finger strongly upon the String of the Instrument, and move the Wrist in and out slowly and equally'), he suggests the various qualities that vibrato may lend to long notes (Majesty, Dignity, Affliction, Fear). However, then he goes on to say:

> '...when it is made on short Notes, it only contributes to make their Sound more agreable [sic] and for this Reason it should be made use of as often as possible.'[1]

[1] Francesco Geminiani: *The Art of Playing on the Violin* (London, 1751; Facsimile edition, David D. Boyden, London 1952), viii

So perhaps some type of continuous vibrato was practised in former times. Given that the earliest violinists played with no shoulder rest or chin rest, often without the chin on the instrument, continuous vibrato in the modern sense seems hardly likely. Yet at least by Mozart's time there must have been enough vibrato going on for Leopold Mozart to complain, 'Performers there are who tremble consistently on each note as if they had the palsy.'

Continuous vibrato has its opponents. Continuous vibrato at the wrong time may cause moments of left hand insecurity in intonation, shifting, evenness of finger action and so on.

Another point is that when heard in context (and especially from a slight distance) notes played without vibrato often sound perfectly natural and acceptable.

Another argument against too much vibrato is that if you do something all the time you cease to notice it; and that the best way to bring out a note with vibrato is to lessen (or stop altogether) the vibrato before and after the note in question.

However, assuming it is not exaggerated, there are two aspects to continuous vibrato:

1 Every note in a phrase should be vibrated, unless it is too fast or you have chosen not to vibrate. Non-continuous vibrato, the vibrato stopping at random on odd notes for no reason, could be represented like this:

Bruch: Concerto no. 1 in G minor, op.26, *mov. 1, b. 37*

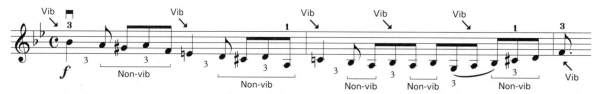

Instead, every note in such a passage should receive vibrato – some notes more, some less, some faster, some slower, some wider, some narrower – unless a deliberate musical effect or expression is desired.

2 The vibrato must not be late starting at the beginning of each note, or stop at the end of each note.

Even if there is vibrato on every note, and it is continuous in that sense, if the vibrato starts and stops on a note it is not the same as a truly continuous vibrato which continues between notes.

Improving key bow strokes

True-*legato* warm-up exercise

One of the first things a beginner has to tackle is how to do one thing with one hand while doing something completely different with the other. The issue does not disappear as you become more advanced, but continues to be a factor right up into the most advanced playing.

Two problems are 1) keeping the left fingers light when the bow is playing heavily into the string, and 2) keeping the horizontal bow stroke even and sustained as the left fingers move vertically up and down.

This simple exercise, which covers all possibilities of playing from one finger to another, produces instant results. Use it not only for warming up, but as a regular part of practice as you apply it to strokes and phrases in pieces:

(Silent fingering on the A string, bow the D string)

- Play on the D string, sustaining the bow solidly and evenly; finger on the A string.

- Concentrate on the evenness of the bow stroke, completely unaffected by the fingers lifting and dropping on the other string.

- More advanced players can also use the Ševčík scale and arpeggio sequence:

(Silent fingering on the A string, bow the D string)

Another way to warm up quickly is to forget about exact intonation and simply move the fingers up and down in a variety of patterns using all combinations of fingers – all while bowing on another string:

- Make up different random finger patterns, trills, double stops, and so on. Move the fingers quickly and lightly without worrying whether they are exactly in tune or not.

It is remarkable how just a few moments of practising like this produces a wonderful feeling of silky smoothness when you then play normally again; and an entirely new, special quality enters the tone. You can do the same thing in pieces by missing out notes, and sustaining and expressing through the bow as you will in the piece:

Schubert: Sonatina in G minor, op. posth. 137, no. 3, *mov. 4, b. 1*

Son filé

Son filé means long, slow bow strokes lasting sixty seconds or more. This used to be seen as one of the most important practice techniques for developing tone production and bow control. In 1756, Leopold Mozart described practising long, slow bows in his Violin School:

> …a very useful experiment may be made. Namely, to endeavour to produce a perfectly even tone with a slow stroke. Draw the bow from one end to the other whilst sustaining throughout an even strength of tone. But hold the bow well back, for the longer and more even the stroke can be made, the more you will become master of your bow, which is highly necessary for the proper performance of a slow piece.[1]

In 1924, Carl Flesch mentioned them in *The Art of Violin Playing*:

> [son filé]…are among the oldest, best-known, most popular and also most appropriate of tone and bow exercises…Their simplicity and usefulness…give them a place of honor in the arsenal of bowing and tonal exercises."[2]

Holding one note for a whole minute may seem an impossibly boring proposition. Even Flesch added that *son filé* "may be regarded as the most tiresome item in the whole field of violin technique."

However, the results of only a little work on *son filé* are both extraordinary and immediate – even if the sound scratches or disappears from time to time because of the bow speed being so excessively slow. Afterwards, all the bow strokes feel marvellously smooth and even.

There can be nothing simpler than practising *son filé*. If all you do is sustain one single note for as long as possible, you will already begin to feel the benefit.

- Begin with the longest stroke that is comfortable – say, 20 seconds down-bow, 20 seconds up-bow.

- Then increase to 30 seconds, 40, 50, 60, and so on as far as you can go.

- When the bow is excessively slow it does not matter if the tone ends up as only a half-audible scraping noise. Just keep the bow moving as evenly as you can.

Afterwards, playing any strokes at all (not necessarily long bows), you may be amazed at the smoothness and ease that is instantly there in your bow arm.

Adding dynamics: Leopold's 'divisions'

- To go further with *son filé*, add dynamics. For example, during one, long down-bow you can crescendo from *pp* to *ff*, then on the up-bow diminuendo from *ff* to *pp*:

Leopold Mozart divided the various dynamic patterns in *son filé* into several 'divisions'. Division 1 was Soft–Strong–Soft, Soft–Strong–Soft:

> Begin the down stroke or up stroke with a pleasant softness; increase the tone by means of an imperceptible increase of pressure; let the greatest volume of tone occur in the middle of the bow, after which, moderate it by degrees by relaxing the pressure of the bow until at the end of the bow the tone dies completely away.[3]

Leopold's Division 2 was the pattern 'Strong–Decrease–Weak, Strong–Decrease–Weak', and Division 3 was Weak–Increase–Strong, Weak–Increase–Strong:

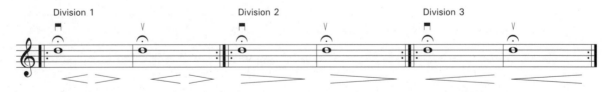

- Another way to practise *son filé* is to keep the dynamic of individual bow strokes the same throughout, but to change the dynamic from note to note:

[1] Leopold Mozart: *A Treatise On The Fundamental Principles Of Violin Playing* (Augsburg, 1756; Eng. Trans. Editha Knocker, Oxford, 1948), 99.

[2] Carl Flesch: *The Art of Violin Playing* (New York, 1924), Vol. 1, 98.

[3] Leopold Mozart: *A Treatise On The Fundamental Principles Of Violin Playing* (Augsburg, 1756; Eng. Trans. Editha Knocker, Oxford, 1948), 97.

- Going further still, add string crossings and position changes:

The American violinist Thelma Given (1896–1977), a pupil of Leopold Auer, spoke in 1923 about practising *son filé*:

> Then there is bow control. There the difficulty is to secure absolute poise and balance in the control of long bows. I always practice half an hour daily on long bows, and, before giving a concert, I devote an hour to them for the space of a month: half an hour in the morning and half an hour in the afternoon. It is very monotonous to play them up the scale and down at the slowest possible tempo; but it is very rewarding. Zimbalist always did a good deal of long bow practice; and aside from bow control I found it helped me to gain that equalized quality of tone which a good violinist must have. It is a wonderful refining process for tone, but must be kept up.[1]

[1] Frederick H. Martens: *Violin Mastery: Talks with Master Violinists and Teachers* (New York 1919), 53.

Just how do you change bow smoothly at the heel?

There is no such thing as an inaudible bow change. You can give an impression of a seamless join if you change note at the same time as changing the direction of the movement of the bow, but when playing up and down on one note alone it is impossible to disguise the joins.

You can see the proof of this if you look closely at the vibrating string as you draw the bow up and down. Playing, say, an open string, look at the place on the string that is in the middle between the nut and the bridge, i.e. the place where the string vibrates the widest.

During the course of each down-bow and up-bow the string swings widely from side to side, pulled or pushed by the bow-hair. At the exact moment that the bow changes direction, the bow stops moving entirely – like a playground swing stationary at its furthest dègree of movement – and then the bow starts pulling the string instead of pushing it (or *vice versa*). During the stopping of the bow, and its changing direction, the string must stop vibrating for an instant, and you can see it stop.

Active finger movement at the heel

When I was a child I was occasionally taken to classical orchestral concerts by my parents or my school. I would watch the violinists who made visible flexing movements with their fingers on the bow, as they changed from up to down at the heel, and I would think: 'Those are the best players. Moving the fingers like that is what really good, professional players do – they make that classy-looking curving movement with their fingers at the heel.'

But later on, as a student, having learnt how to flex and straighten my fingers in the way that I had thought was the ideal when I was a child, I discovered that the finger action actually made things more difficult at the heel.

The problem is that unless you are careful, a too-active movement of the fingers at the bow change increases the speed of bow just at the moment when you want it to slow down.

 Why do you want the bow speed to slow down?

One of the keys to a smooth bow-change is in the bow slowing just before changing direction. It needs to move slower, slower, slower, and then stop, all in the space of the last centimetre or half-centimetre.

 How does a movement in the fingers add to the bow speed?

If the bow is already travelling along the string – transported by the arm – and the fingers and hand begin to add new movement to the already-moving bow, the combined speed must be greater.

Imagine walking up the carriage of a train that is moving at 100 miles an hour. If you walk at three miles an hour in the direction in which the train is going, it means you are actually travelling at 103 miles an hour in relation to someone standing beside the track watching the train go by.

One answer to this problem of increased bow speed, is to slow the arm movement by the exact amount that the fingers increase the speed. Described in words, that seems like a difficult thing to gauge and co-ordinate; but of course if you do it naturally and with instinct, and forget about it, it can work.

Sometimes it feels suitable to allow the finger-movement, or deliberately to create it, and sometimes it does not feel suitable. The important thing is to understand the factors involved, and then to play one way or the other as you wish.[1]

Using the 'fist bow hold'

The smooth, seamless bow change at the heel (or at the point) is a wonderful illustration of the principle that in the end real technical control comes as a result of a clear musical desire rather than from sheer mechanics.

Fig. 134

It is easy to prove this. Hold the bow tightly in your fist (Fig. 134) and perform a perfect, smooth, seamless bow change anywhere in the bow. You will instinctively slow down in the last fraction of a centimetre before you change direction, and at the same time allow the tiniest amount of circular movement around the string.[2]

[2] See *Pivoting*, page 294

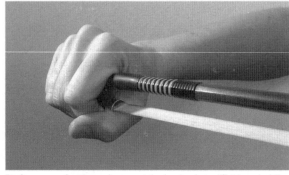

Perform a perfect bow change at the heel using a 'fist bow hold'

Then the question is: how much 'technique' do you need to perform a perfect bow change? The answer has to be 'none' – you need only the wish for the change to be smooth, and the instinct to do all the right things comes from that.

Once you have made a perfectly smooth change holding the bow like that, it feels very easy to do it with a proper bow hold – without active finger movements, but with a natural give and springiness in the fingers.[3]

[3] Many students play all kinds of things better using a 'fist bow hold' than they do using a 'good' bow hold, e.g. deep-in-the-string tone, lifted strokes such as *spiccato* or *ricochet*, or chords.

This happens if the student is getting in their own way by trying to do the 'correct' thing instead of following their instinct. The moment they hold the bow in their fist they immediately stop thinking and play only by instinct and natural feel. Then a miraculous new ability immediately appears.

Flesch himself didn't like the finger movement

I thought for a long time that an active finger movement at the change of bow at the heel, which I had found unhelpful, was one of the hallmarks of the Carl Flesch bow arm. Flesch divided the movements of the right arm into six fundamental types, and the finger movement is No. 6:

1 Vertical movement of the upper arm

4 Forearm rotation

2 Horizontal movement of the upper arm

5 Vertical movement of the hand at the wrist

3 Opening and closing of the forearm at the elbow

6 Finger movement (flexing and straightening)

I realised my mistake when I discovered that Carl Flesch himself did not approve of too much finger movement, saying that 'if the change of bow is seen, it will also be heard.'

Imagine some of the violinists that went to Flesch for lessons. They were not all on the level of Ginette Neveu, Henryk Szeryng or Joseph Hassid, and certainly not when Flesch was yet an unknown teacher. In his time he would have given lessons to amateur players, to beginners, to ungifted students.

You can easily imagine players coming to him with awkward, stiff bow holds, with straight fingers, white knuckles and so on, and you can imagine Flesch experimenting to find ways to loosen them up. It makes sense, if someone has stiff fingers, to give them exercises like this one which I was first shown by Yfrah Neaman (himself a pupil of Flesch):

Very slow at the heel and point

Straighten the fingers to move the bow down   Flex the fingers to move the bow up

Kreutzer: 42 Etudes ou caprices, no. 13, *b. 1*

The idea is to play very slowly, using only the fingers to make the stroke, without using the arm or hand at all. Straighten the fingers to move the bow down, flex to move up. The best thing is to practise it at both the extreme heel and the extreme point, and to play f.

This is very good to do and to be able to do; yet afterwards all you want is flexibility, not active movements. (However, whenever an active movement of the fingers feels natural and desirable, there can be no harm in allowing it or deliberately making it.)

It is especially useful in certain string crossings, because a little flexing of the fingers can take the place of a much larger movement of the hand or arm. This works in exactly the same way as in larger string crossings, where a small movement of the hand can take the place of a much larger movement of the upper arm.

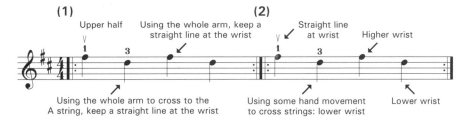

(1) Feel the over-large movement of the upper arm if you use the whole arm to cross between the A and E strings.

(2) Using some hand movement to cross strings, feel how the upper arm now has far less distance to travel.

Use finger movement in the same way to streamline your playing and to avoid working harder than you need to.

The tilt of the bow

Lower half

In the lower half, it is often easier to play sweetly if you do not use all the hair, but turn the bow so that you play slightly more on the outer edge. You can always use more hair for more powerful playing.

In the lower part of the bow, playing more on the outer edge of the hair fits in very well with the bow arm: the slight arching of the wrist turns the bow towards the outer edge anyway.[1]

[1] See *Wrist*, page 129

If you keep the hair completely flat, on the up-bow, all the way to the heel, the hand and forearm naturally want to stay flatter, and this may lead to a cramped feeling in the bow arm.

When the bow comes down from the air on to the string near the heel, it is often essential, for a soft-edged landing without scratch, to impact the string on the outer edge of the hair rather than all the hair.

The power and projection of modern playing is far greater than in earlier centuries, so the question of how much hair is perhaps different today. But these are still the essential principles:

> The stick of the Bow should be inclined towards the fingerboard. The whole breadth of the hairs should not be used but only the edge of the hairs. This is imperative for the production of *mezza-voce* and *piano*. The reason is not far to seek: In employing the whole breadth of hair the friction is not the same at all its points of contact with the string. But produced with a few hairs only, the vibrations of the strings will have a greater carrying power. The tone is duller when produced with the whole breadth of hair than when produced with a few hairs only. The latter method allows the string to vibrate more freely, the tone is clearer and more beautiful…Of course, in *forte*, crescendo, and in certain springing bowings the use of the whole breadth of hair cannot be dispensed with. But as a rule, only a medium loudness is required. Professor Joseph Joachim used to play in this style. The great violin-master J.B. Viotti and his celebrated pupil P. Rode are also known to have employed the described bowing.[2]

[2] E. Kross, H. Leonard, *La Gymnastische Übungen auf der violine* (Mainz, 1911), 5

High positions

It is especially important to consider how much hair you use when playing notes high up on the fingerboard. There, the hair is proportionately much wider because the string length is so short. Playing full hair on a very high note is like playing an open string with hair five centimetres wide.

Playing with full hair

Few violinists need to be encouraged to tilt the bow. The problem is in remembering to use flatter hair when playing powerfully.

A good example of an aural 'blind spot' is that many players do not notice the scraping sounds of the wood of the bow touching the string.[3] This happens when the bow is tilted over too far when playing *f*, which causes any downward pressure to result in the wood 'bowing' the string alongside the hair.

[3] See *Aural blind spots*, page xix

Check the wood of the bow, underneath at the middle, to see if it is covered in scratches from contact with the string. It is a sobering thought when you consider that at the time of their creation, each of these marks made a scraping sound which was an unnoticed part of the tone.

- In the same way that you might spend a portion of practice working only on intonation or vibrato through a piece, also work through considering and questioning only the tilt of the bow. In particular, check that you are using enough hair in the *f* passages.

Choreography of the bow

Choreographing the bow can be likened to choreographing movements on stage in acting or dancing:

Stage right	heel of the bow	**Front of the stage**	near the bridge
Stage left	point	**Back of the stage**	near the fingerboard

Just as stage choreography is planned in minute detail, with nothing left to approximation or chance, all the actions of the bow can be designed.

- Where in the bow does the note begin?

- Where in the bow does the note end?

- How far is the bow from the bridge? Does it stay the same distance from the beginning of the note to the end, or does it move closer to or further from the bridge?

- What is the bow speed and pressure? Do they remain even, or increase or decrease?

Everything is completely planned and mapped-out in advance. This is how artists such as Heifetz could play the same piece or even a concerto two or three times in a row and give exactly the same performance each time (sometimes earning criticism rather than praise as a result).

However, far from causing a performance to lack spontaneity, having a structure to what you are doing brings greater freedom, since only once you know the boundaries can you play 'to the limit'.

Designing the strokes

Example 1

- Plan the division of the bow precisely:

Franck: Sonata in A, *mov. 2, b. 168*

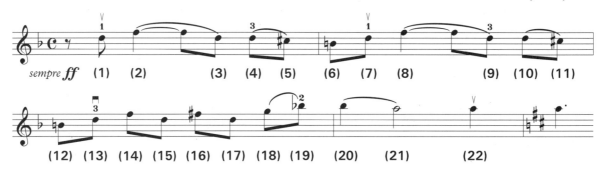

(1)   For a large-scale, *ff* approach, use the whole bow beginning near the point on soundpoint 3.

(2)   Begin at the heel and play closer to the bridge since this is a slower, more sustained stroke than the preceding up-bow. Rather than letting the energy ebb during the tie, crescendo or fully sustain through the F, leaving the last third of the bow for the next note **(3)**.

(3)   Sustain with the same intensity as the preceding F.

(4)   **(5)** If these two eighth-notes (quavers) begin at the point and take the bow back to the heel, with half a bow each, the D receives too much 'kick' from the bow speed, creating an unwanted accent.

Also, the change of finger on the D must not cause the bow to make an accent. Even if you manage not to accent the D, too much bow takes you too far to play the next note **(6)** without an accent.

Instead, play the two notes together within half the bow length. Give slightly more bow to the D than to the C♯ because they are part of a falling phrase with a slight diminuendo.

(6)   This B should not be accented. It is the end of the phrase following on from the previous two notes. Begin at or slightly past the middle of the bow, using little bow length.

(7)   This D, which begins between the middle and the point, is like **(1)** and must be as strong despite having less bow. Play nearer to the bridge and deeper in the string than **(1)**, and with a more intense vibrato.

(8) Sustain as before but with a more intense vibrato (since it is the second time), in particular keeping the intensity during the 3–3 shift.

(9) **(10)** **(11)** As before.

(12) Take particular care not to use too much bow, since this must be saved for the next note **(13)**.

(13) **(15)** **(17)** The three repeated D's, played on the A string, are all up-beats to **(14)** **(16)** **(18)** played on the E string. Each up-beat needs to be played with less power than its following note. In part this contrast comes ready-made because of the different colours of the A and E strings. Go further by sustaining both notes solidly, but playing the down-bows on the A string more evenly and the up-bows on the E string with more accent.

(18) **(19)** These two up-beat eighth-notes take the bow all the way back to the heel. Since they crescendo into the climax note **(20)**, the second note needs more bow than the first, and to be played slightly nearer to the bridge. Save bow on the first note.

(20) Play deeply in the string close to the bridge, with quite a slow bow and the fastest, widest vibrato of the passage. Since this and **(21)** are like a written-out appoggiatura, and therefore need to diminuendo slightly, lighten the bow into and during the A, and diminish the vibrato.

(22) Using a lighter stroke and different vibrato, and bowing slightly further from the bridge, play a whole bow to the heel as an upbeat to the next melody.

Example 2

- Plan the soundpoints:

Mozart: Concerto no. 5 in A, K219, *mov. 1, b. 40*

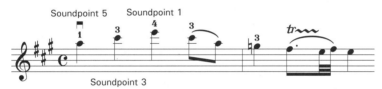

The first two notes are like an up-beat to the third, which is where the orchestra begins. Save the vibrato in the beginning so that it develops through the three notes in a least–more–most pattern.

The soundpoint indications are naturally only approximate, since everything depends on the responsiveness of the instrument and the type of string, as well as who you are playing with and where.

Example 3

- Plan speed and pressure:

Saint-Saëns: Concerto no. 3 in B minor, op. 61, *mov. 1, b. 20*

The two half-notes (minims), marked '+', are a strong up-beat to the following accented F♯. Begin with little bow at the start of the E, and use the narrowest vibrato. The E♯ needs more bow, and to be played closer to the bridge, than the E.

Speed–pressure–soundpoint–vibrato during the two-note crescendo:

- Bow speed: slow getting faster

- Bow pressure: light getting heavier

- Soundpoint: further from the bridge, moving closer

- Vibrato: least at the beginning and increasing

The patterns on the climax note F♯:

- Bow speed: fastest at the beginning then getting slower

- Bow pressure: heaviest then getting lighter

- Soundpoint: nearest the bridge then moving away

- Vibrato: fastest and widest to begin, then lessening

Using enough bow

The two factors of speed of bow, and length of bow, are so closely related that often they are the same thing. If you alter the speed of bow but keep the duration of the stroke the same, you must alter the length, and *vice versa*.

To play with enough speed of bow means that you have to use enough length; and using more length is something that most players can always benefit from. Thinking that you are using the entire length of the bow, when actually you are not doing so at all, is a common mistake.

Unintentionally, many players always stop well short of the point at the end of the down-bow, and stop at the place where their fingers 'begin' at the end of the up-bow (see Fig. 135a). Instead, you can play 'under the fingers' at the extreme heel (Fig. 135b).

Fig. 135

(a) Starting the down-bow, or ending the up-bow, 'where the fingers begin'

(b) Playing 'under the fingers'

(c) Hitting against a barrier nearing the end of the down-bow

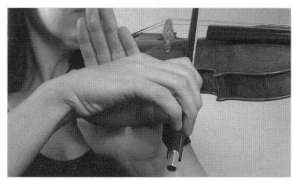

(d) Hitting against a barrier nearing the end of the up-bow

(e) Imagine that you can play beyond the end of the down-bow

(f) Imagining playing beyond the end of the up-bow

Imagine that you hit against some sort of barrier near the end of an up-bow (Fig. 135c) and near the end of the down-bow (Fig. 135d).

Instead you can have a perception that the entire range of the stroke extends way beyond the end of the down-bow (Fig. 135e) or up-bow (Fig. 135f).

Proportions

When you are used to bowing only between those two points (stopping a few centimetres before the end of each bow), and then you add that little extra bow at each end, the bow speed can seem disproportionately much faster.

- The total playing-length of the hair, leaving out a little space at each end, is about 64 centimetres.

- If you add the 7 centimetres that you miss out at the heel, to the 7 centimetres you miss out at the point, you get a total of 14 unused centimetres.

- Therefore, the amount of bow you are not using is actually just a little less than a quarter of the bow. So an increase of about 25% in bow speed, playing whole bows, is not disproportionate at all.

Whether playing exercises like the shifting studies in Ševčík Op. 8, or playing a concerto, using all the bow (where appropriate) raises the stature of the playing to an entirely new level.

In both of the following examples every down-bow can begin a couple of centimetres from the heel; every up-bow can begin a couple of centimetres from the point:

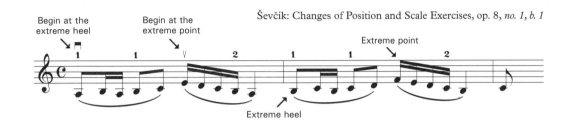

Ševčík: Changes of Position and Scale Exercises, op. 8, *no. 1, b. 1*

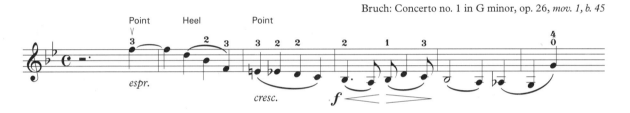

Bruch: Concerto no. 1 in G minor, op. 26, *mov. 1, b. 45*

Accents

Accents are as much a part of musical language as consonants are an essential part of speech. They range from a simple stress, or leaning on to a note, to the most powerful attack.

If there is one simple way to transform either your own playing, or someone else's, it is to make sure that in the places where you are not wanting to play legato the accentuation really is all there, with no unintentional lack of articulation; and that the accent is enough. Most student string-players could double the power of their general accentuation – and especially the really sharp or big accents – and then double the power again, and it still would not be too much.

To play a perfectly even stroke, the factors that make up the stroke must be even, so the speed and pressure, and the distance of the bow from the bridge, must remain constant throughout the stroke.

To play an accent, the pressure pattern is 'heavier–lighter', and the speed pattern 'faster–slower'.

As a quick warm-up exercise, play repeated strokes on one note while changing between smooth and accented strokes.

- Begin very smoothly, with perfectly even speed and pressure.

- Gradually make the strokes more accented (gradually more heavy–light, fast–slow) until they are heavily accented.

- Then gradually make them smoother until they are perfectly even again.

Repeat several times

Experiment on each string in low, middle and high positions. Use different lengths of bow at the heel, middle, and point.

Avoiding bulges

Bulges are made by unintentionally creeping into the beginning of a note, so that the bow has already moved a few centimetres before you start to make the actual sound you want.

The problem is made worse if the sound, having developed late, then begins to fade again, which creates the pattern soft–loud–soft, which is often known as a 'bulge note' or 'banana note'.

Bulges are caused by three things:

1 Bow speed: slow–fast, or slow–fast–slow

2 Pressure: light–heavy, or light–heavy–light

3 Vibrato: a delay in beginning the vibrato at the start of the note, so that the note is not fully vibrating until a moment after it has begun.

¹ They are not always easy to get rid of, either. I often think of a colleague lamenting once about her constant habit of playing banana notes. She was a quartet-player, and described how she would practise her bow strokes to make them perfectly even; she would practise her quartet part and eliminate every single banana note; but then she would go to the next rehearsal, and within ten seconds of beginning to play, she would find herself bulging again, playing banana notes at every expressive moment. This is not uncommon, but not impossible to defeat in the end.

Bulge notes are so widespread in the string-playing world that it is sometimes surprising to hear someone play without bulging.¹ Of course there is nothing wrong with shaping a note like that if it is played intentionally. What you have to guard against is unintentional, unconscious bulging.

Q **How can you make sure that you do not bulge?**

- The way not to bulge is firstly to be conscious of drawing the bow absolutely evenly at the start of the note, without any hint of slow–fast or light–heavy.

- Secondly, by making the vibrato already part of the sound at the very beginning of the note. The bow must not move several centimetres before the vibrato starts (unless deliberately).

- Keep the thought at the front of your mind, as you go to begin any note, that unless you want to creep in to it, or begin it with an accent, the note should 'begin as you mean to continue': the tone and vibrato at the very beginning of the note is exactly the same as the sound a little later on.²

- The most important thing is to be aware in advance of the type of note where you are likely to bulge. Then, always thinking ahead, make sure that you do not bulge when you get there.

Upbeats in particular may suffer from bulges, but other strokes may be prone to bulges as well:

Bulge notes often stem from worry about intonation, which leads to the habit of 'testing' the note for a fraction of a second before confirming it:

It is particularly tempting to test double stops before committing yourself to playing them:

Paganini: 24 Caprices, op. 1, no. 15, *b. 15*

Bulge notes are often caused by good musical intentions, e.g. feeling a musical emphasis or large expression, or an agogic accent, but unintentionally letting it translate into 'creeping in' to the note before fully playing it:

Tchaikovsky: Concerto in D, op. 35, *mov. 3, b. 416*

Beethoven: Sonata in E♭, op. 12 no. 3, *mov. 1, b. 5*

Lead with the vibrato

One way of making sure that banana notes do not happen is to 'lead' the bow from the vibrato, rather than 'adding vibrato to the note'.

This is just the same as in accented strokes like *martelé*, where there is a perception of the vibrato triggering the bow rather than the other way round.[1]

Avoid bulge notes by beginning the note with the vibrato, but without making any accent in the bow.

[1] See also *One of the secrets of artistry: leading accents from the vibrato*, page 259

Working out the proportions

Creating a bow stroke is quite simple if you consider the factors that make up the stroke – speed, pressure and soundpoint – one by one.

Suppose you are playing Kreutzer 8:

Kreutzer: 42 Etudes ou caprices, no. 8, *b. 1*

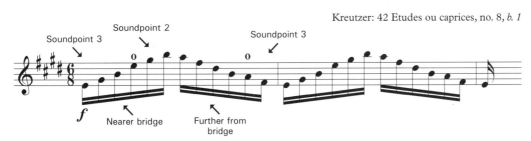

Suppose you have decided to play a broad *détaché* in the upper half.

Speed of bow: Once you have decided where the strokes are going to begin and end, and once you know the tempo you are going to play at, you therefore know the bow speed.

Soundpoint: Decide which soundpoint, or range of soundpoints, you will use. In this case, suppose you decide that on the D string you will play around soundpoint 3, on the A string a little nearer to soundpoint 2, and on the E string around soundpoint 2.

Pressure: The only question left is how much weight. Therefore simply sit on one note and try more pressure, less pressure – while staying on that one soundpoint, and keeping the same length of bow and tempo that you have decided on – until you are certain that the string is vibrating to its maximum:

Speed:	Decided by length, 10 centimetres upper half
Pressure:	Experiment until string is vibrating at its widest

Speed:	Decided by length, 15 centimetres
Pressure:	Experiment

Then find the same stroke-designs in the context of the whole phrase.

Approach each question from different angles at the same time:

- If you know where to begin and end the stroke, you know how fast the bow speed will be given the tempo of the passage.

  This tells you how close to the bridge, and therefore how much weight to use.

- Or if you decide first that you wish to play the phrase deeply in the string near to the bridge, or lightly near the fingerboard, this will dictate the speed of bow, and therefore where to begin and end the stroke.

How much bow weight? Watch the great players

Look at a movie of, say, David Oistrakh playing the Sibelius concerto. Watch his bow in a passage like the following:

Sibelius: Concerto in D minor, op. 47, *mov. 1, b. 20*

Leaving aside vibrato, the question is what are the exact amounts of speed, pressure, and distance from the bridge, that Oistrakh is using to get the fabulous sound he makes?

You can see and hear how he is playing, but you cannot immediately tell, just by looking, how heavily he is playing into the string. But you can work it out.

There are only three main factors to consider in tone production. Every sound is the result of a certain combination of speed, pressure, and distance from the bridge.

- You can see that he is using whole bows on every note; and you can hear and see the tempo of the passage. Therefore the exact bow speed is an entirely measurable and known factor.

- You can see that the bow (on this occasion) is exactly one centimetre from the bridge, so the precise soundpoint is also an entirely known factor.

- Therefore you can easily work out how much weight he must be using.

Try it for yourself and see: play whole bows on soundpoint 2 at the tempo of the Sibelius:

(1) Simply keep the bow on soundpoint 2, and keep playing whole bows.

Then, all you have to do is adjust the weight until you sound like Oistrakh.

At that point, add vibrato.

(2) You can also add the rhythm of the passage. Afterwards, when you play the actual notes of the passage, make sure the speed/pressure/soundpoint design is the same as when you played on one note.

It is impossible to scratch if the bow keeps moving

If the bow keeps moving sufficiently, it is impossible to scratch through using too much pressure or weight. The understanding of this gives a player confidence to sink the bow more deeply into the string since many of the reasons for holding back, through fear of making an ugly sound, vanish.

Example 1

Try this simple experiment: play the following chord as heavily as you can:

- Begin by resting the bow on the middle of the three strings (the A string), quite near to the heel.

  Keep the bow at around the mid-point between the bridge and the fingerboard (soundpoint 3).

- Push the middle string down with the bow-hair until you can see the hair touching the outer strings.

- Without releasing, now simply move the bow at a medium speed and play the chord.

It is easy to scratch the tone if the bow speed is too slow. But try to scratch while keeping the bow moving. However hard you press the bow down into the string – and really do try to 'press' the bow in all the bad senses of 'pressing' as opposed to 'sinking the weight of the bow into the string' – you will find that it is still impossible to produce a scratch.

If you think you can produce a scratch, it can only mean that the bow speed is too slow.

Find how to play the heaviest but still the cleanest chord. Moving closer to the bridge, play to the absolute edge of the instrument's range of power but at the same time without a hint of scratching or forcing.

It may seem easy to play Example 1 without scratching, even though playing it at its absolute maximum volume, since it is a three-string chord. But what about playing one note on its own?

Example 2

The same applies to one note as to three notes together: as long as the bow keeps moving – as long as the bow speed is sufficient and the bow is near enough to the bridge – it is impossible to scratch, no matter how heavy the weight or the sharpness of the attack into the string.

Try attacking a note like 3rd finger A on the E string. No matter how hard you 'hit' the string, it is impossible to scratch so long as you are not too far from the bridge, and so long as the bow keeps moving.

One of the most important factors is the angle of the attack. If it is too steep, scratch is almost certain, like an aircraft approaching the runway at too steep an angle and crashing. Maintain the correct smooth curve into the string, close enough to the bridge, and however heavily you contact the string the tone will not break.

Yfrah Neaman suggested imagining that the violin has an open B string, a fifth string after the E. To attack the E string, position the bow on the level of the imaginary B string, and move from there to attack the E string.

Example 3

It is impossible to over-play a fortissimo, double stop, up-bow attack in the upper half:

Bruch: Concerto in G minor, op. 26, *mov. 1, b. 16*

Try playing the attack more and more loudly. Starting with the bow just above the strings (Fig. 136), bring the bow down with a great impact into the string. Repeat, trying to attack more and more heavily each time as you try to find the limit, the breaking point:

Fig. 136

So long as you remain near the bridge and gauge the speed of bow correctly, you cannot scratch or over-play the attack.

Attacking like this, at the heel or point, there is not much further to go once you are playing *ff*. Playing *ffff* is much the same.

.[1] See *About energy*, page 213

You quickly reach a limit beyond which you cannot go.[1] It is like driving a car with the accelerator pressed down to the floor. You are going at full throttle. The car cannot go any faster. Yet even playing at this maximum volume that the bow and violin can produce, it is still possible to play without any scratch whatsoever.

Attack the double stop from here as strongly as when beginning at the heel

I never know how to start a note

Being sympathetic to the string

When you stroke a cat it is not enough that you wish to stroke the cat, or that you enjoy stroking it; you must understand what it feels like to be the cat being stroked by you.

When you apply the bow to the string, you must understand what it feels like to be the string being played by you.

Instead of 'playing the violin' the way you think best, look at it more from the violin's point of view: how would it like to be played? Consider any attacks like the following on the E string or G string:

When a pupil brings the bow down towards the string to play notes like these, it often seems as though they are not considering what the string itself might like. The gesture they make with the bow is what they think they should do, or what they have been taught to do.

But if you look at the event – the moment the hair of the bow impacts onto the string – from the string's point of view, you use the bow differently as you consider different questions: what sort of impact might the string prefer? At what angle might the string wish the hair to meet it (more rounded or more vertical); how weak or strong is the string at the point of impact; how far from, or close to, the bridge might the string prefer the contact, the impact?

Picture the moment that the hair lands on the string as though through a strong magnifying glass. See it very close up and with every detail enlarged enormously. Picture it in slow motion, as though you are watching the action-replay of a moment in a sports event on television.

Imagine the vast bow moving through the air and landing with a tremendous impact on the string. How exactly would that event appear magnified? How would the hair and the string behave at the moment of contact? How would the string most like to be approached and landed on by the bow?

What is the difference between what the E string might like, and what the G string might like? The taut, thin, highly-strung metal E string feels happiest with a stroke that is quite different from the one which the slacker, thicker G string would most like. What is the difference at the moment of impact, seen from close up and in slow motion?

Starting from the air or from the string

Starting from the string

There are three ways to begin a note:

1 You can 'creep in' to the beginning of the note from nothing, creating a properly audible sound only after a couple of millimetres.

2 You can begin with an accent of some sort, ranging from a slight stress at the start of the note, to an actual 'click' where the bow bites the string.[1]

[1] See *Gripping the string to make the bite*, page 291

3 You can 'begin as you mean to continue'. The sound at the very beginning of the stroke, and the sound after the stroke has begun, are exactly the same.

Exercise for placing

If starting from the string, how soon after placing the bow do you move?

Placing the bow on the string is one thing; deciding to move it is another. Placing it should not be the trigger for moving it. Separate the two factors:

- Playing exactly in time (using a metronome is helpful) practise placing the bow on the string, then waiting, then playing the note.

- Wait less and less time before playing the note, measuring the rests exactly.

- Repeat using all up-bows in different parts of the bow.

Starting from the air

If the bow starts from above the string, the important thing is the angle of attack.

- Experiment with all the different possibilities of attacking more steeply or more smoothly:

- First, the moment that the bow touches the string is shown as an eighth-note (quaver): curve into the string flatly.

- As the bars progress, the moment is shown as a shorter and shorter note as the 'moment of impact' takes less and less bow. The approach to the string becomes less and less curved.

- By the fourth bar, the attack is almost vertical. The initial impact onto the string uses almost no bow at all, before the stroke continues evenly along the string.

- Repeat using all up-bows.

Practise beginning notes

Practise beginning notes in every position on each string:

- Begin notes in the lower half, middle, and upper half, starting up-bow as well as down-bow

- Start from above the string, and from on the string

- Practise creeping in, accenting, and 'beginning as you mean to continue'

- Practise in low, middle, and high positions on each string.

Finding the moment of balance

¹ See *You've got to stop before you start*, page 199

In the fraction of a second before beginning a stroke – whether before attacking the string from the air, or before placing the bow on the string – there must be a moment of complete balance. This is similar to the principle of 'stopping before you start'.¹

Example 1

As part of the up-beat gesture to begin the first note, bring the bow to within a couple of centimetres of the string, and then stop. For an instant, find a feeling of balance (the bow in the hand, the weight of the bow balanced by the little finger; the feeling of the arm suspended in the air with only the minimum effort to stay there, and a feeling of floating) and then place the bow on the string to begin the G:

Bruch: Concerto no. 1 in G minor, op. 26, *mov. 1, b. 6*

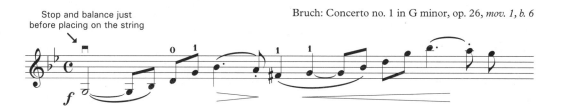

To begin the second entry on the E♭, where you might attack from the air, again stop just before reaching the string – find the feeling of balance – and then continue:

Bruch: Concerto no. 1 in G minor, op. 26, *mov. 1, b. 10*

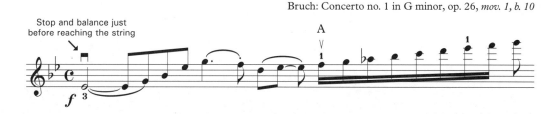

Example 2

Tchaikovsky: Concerto in D, op. 35, *mov. 1, cadenza*

Here, the bow must move from the A–E strings at the end of the chord, to the G string level. During the 'stop' make sure that the bow is on exactly the right plane to play the first-finger A. Feel the weight of the bow balanced on the fouth finger.

Example 3

Sarasate: Carmen Fantasy, op. 25, *Introduction, b. 137*

Stop just above the string,
balance, before playing

It is essential not to rush into playing the harmonic. Find exactly the right plane for the bow before placing it on the string.

How to feel confident beginning up-bow at the point

Placing the bow on the string at the point is something that many players readily admit to sometimes finding difficult or nerve-racking, particularly in a *pianissimo* passage where you have to 'creep in' from nothing, and where the slightest juddering of the bow on the string might easily be heard.

- One answer is simply not to think about it. Instead, concentrate on the music and do not 'get in the way'. Then the technical action of placing the bow on the string takes care of itself.

- Another approach is nearly the exact opposite: visualise the action of placing the bow on the string at the point perfectly, in exquisite detail.

Sitting with a good, balanced posture, freeing the shoulders, or making sure that you are not holding your breath, may be all that is necessary to ensure a smooth beginning to a note. However, here are a few other simple ways of increasing the feeling of safety in placing the bow on the string.

Experimenting with leverage

One of the things that may make it feel precarious to place the bow on the string at the point, is the fact that you are holding the bow so far away at the frog.

If you hold a pencil the same way that you hold a bow, there is a feeling of great control because the end of the pencil is so near to the fingers. You can get a similar feeling of extra control if you hold the bow in the middle.

Fig. 137

Work down to the frog from here

Exercise 1

- Play repeated up-bows at the point, beginning *pianissimo*:

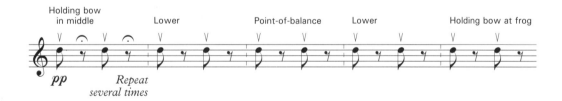

- Begin with your hand in the middle of the bow (Fig. 137). Feel how you can control the placement of the bow on the string precisely.

- Place your hand lower down on the bow, and find the same degree of control that you had before.

- Gradually work your way down the bow until holding it normally at the frog – with the same comfort in placing the bow on the string at the point as you had when holding it in the middle.

Exercise 2

Using a normal bow hold at the frog, play repeated up-bows from the air. Begin at the middle of the bow and gradually move up towards the point:

One action, not two

[1] See *Rolling the finger into the string*, page 190

Rather than first stopping the string with the left finger, and then concentrating on bringing the hair of the bow to the string (i.e. two separate actions), find how to merge the two actions into one. This is similar to rolling fingers into the string.[1]

- Get ready to play by placing the finger on the surface of the string without stopping the note, as though to play a harmonic (see the x-note in the example below).

  At the same time position the bow just a fraction of a centimetre above the string.

- To play the note, lean the finger gently into the string almost at the precise moment that you want the note to start. Concentrate on the left finger and *let* the bow find the string and begin the note.

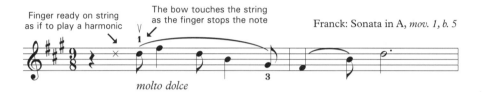

Pretend it is the action of the left finger itself that lowers the bow perfectly. Then there is a feeling of the hands working together as one, rather than the feeling of trying to co-ordinate two separate actions that have nothing to do with each other but which need to happen at the same time.

Moving the string towards the bow-hair

Rather than holding the instrument so that it is absolutely still and fixed in one position – and then trying to get the hair of the bow down on to the unmoving string without the bow bouncing on impact – find a feeling of flow in the body and the violin so that there is a very slight movement towards the bow as it approaches the string. This is a good moment to make sure that you are not holding your breath.

The amount that you move may be so slight as to be imperceptible, but even so this can help remove any chance of becoming 'locked', and again help to create a feeling of 'one action, not two'.

Releasing the thumb

Control may be lost if the bow is gripped tightly instead of being balanced by the fingers. One important area to watch is the thumb, which should not press up unnecessarily hard into the bow.

The natural principles of leverage dictate that when playing at the heel the thumb can be light on the bow even in the heaviest *forte*; but playing heavily into the string at the point does require counter-pressure from the thumb.

- Experiment by sitting the bow on the string near the heel. Without moving along the string, press the bow down quite hard into the string.

- Feel how relaxed the thumb is, despite the extreme downward pressure of the hair into the string.

- Repeat at the point, feeling how the thumb now naturally exerts counterpressure.

A common error is to counterpress at the point even though playing softly, when the thumb can be as light on the bow as it is at the heel. Similarly, when suspending the hair just above the string ready to begin a stroke at the point, there should be no upward pressure into the bow from the thumb whatsoever.

Placing the bow on the string at the point, *pianissimo*, concentrate on balancing all the weight of the bow with the little finger, rather than 'holding' the bow, and keep the thumb light and uninvolved.

Leading with the vibrato

When you play any sort of accent with the bow, it is usually desirable to make a vibrato accent at the same time; and to feel the start of the vibrato as an impulse that launches the bow.[1]

Then there is a feeling of the two hands working together as one. You forget about the bow and focus only on the vibrato, and the bow stroke takes care of itself.

In the same way, you can feel the placing of the bow on the string at the point, and the beginning of the vibrato, as if they are one thing.

[1] See *One of the secrets of artistry: leading accents from the vibrato*, page 259

- Get ready to start by hovering the point of the bow half a centimetre above the string.

- Forget about placing the bow on the string and focus only on beginning the vibrato, and allow the bow to take care of itself and place itself on the string perfectly.

Practising it

- Add a couple of minutes of 'up-bows at the point' to your warm-up. Cover a wide range of different notes, positions and strings:

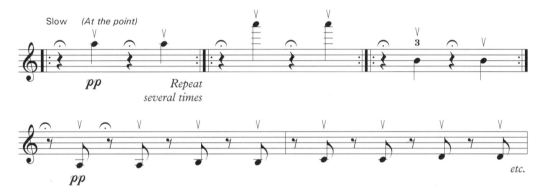

- Remember to experiment with different amounts of hair, from beginning on the outside edge of the hair (bow tilted towards the fingerboard) to beginning with full hair.

How can I improve lifted strokes like *spiccato*?

There is often confusion about what lifted strokes actually are, partly because different terms are used to describe the same strokes: 'lifted', 'springing', 'bounced', 'off-the-string', are often used interchangeably, as are (incorrectly) the words '*spiccato*' and 'staccato'.

- Playing 'on the string' means that the bow-hair remains on the string at the end of a stroke as the bow begins to move in the opposite direction to begin the next stroke.

- Playing 'off the string' means that the bow-hair lifts above the string at the end of one stroke, before landing on the string again to play the next stroke.

- However, although when you play 'on' the string the bow-hair never leaves the string, when you play 'off' the string the hair does not always leave the string.

While it may *sound* as though the bow-hair is bouncing off the string, actually it may not be. There is a type of brushed *spiccato* in orchestral playing called 'onff', (a combination of 'on' and 'off') where the hair does not leave the string. Playing *sautillé*, the hair may leave the string or it may not.

The hair clearly leaves the string during shorter *spiccato*, *ricochet*, and flying staccato. It stays on the string during solid staccato.

The bow wants to bounce

Bounced strokes are more natural than sustained strokes

Many players have a thought at the back of their mind that bounced strokes like *spiccato* are more difficult or complicated than playing on (along) the string.

This idea may go all the way back to their first experiences of playing the violin at an elementary level. At that time, playing on the string seems straightforward:

For the beginner, playing the same notes *spiccato* may seem more difficult to control:

Sautillé seems an advanced, difficult stroke:

Ricochet may seem impossibly advanced:

Paganini: Concerto no. 1 in D, op. 6, *mov. 3, b. 2*

Yet actually the most important aspect of these bowings is that the bow *wants* to bounce. If Paganini had written *legato* instead of *ricochet*, the passage would actually have been more 'difficult' – despite the appearance of virtuosic brilliance that the *ricochet* gives – because if you play it *legato* you would have to 'do' something to keep the bow solidly in the string:

You can easily demonstrate the natural bounce of the bow:

● Feel the springiness of the wood (Fig. 138a), the hair (Fig. 138b) and the string (Fig. 138c). When any of the three are stretched, all they want to do is spring back into their state of least tension.

Fig. 138

(a) Feel the springiness of the stick

(b) Feel the springiness of the hair

(c) Feel the springiness of the string

Experimenting with the spring of the bow

- Push the wood of the bow down to touch the hair, and then suddenly let go (Fig. 139a). The bow does not remain sitting on the string as a dead weight, but springs back up out of the string. (Don't prevent it from springing back up with the right index finger. Try holding the bow as shown in Fig. 139b.)

- See how the bow naturally wants to bounce by holding the bow with only the thumb and the second finger and playing a few continuous down- and up-bow *spiccato* strokes.

Fig. 139

(a) When you release the bow, it springs up out of the string and bounces

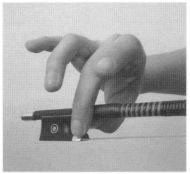

(b) Held like this, the bow naturally bounces as you move it up and down along the string

(c) Practising *ricochet* without the first finger

Start with a proper bow hold but as soon as the hair has touched the string for the first note, take the first, third and fourth fingers off the bow so that you continue with only the thumb and second finger (Fig. 139b). Move the bow up and down without trying to make it bounce. Let it bounce by itself:

After the first note, take 1st, 3rd and 4th fingers off the bow

Continue with only thumb and 2nd finger on the bow

- Experiment to find the exact part of the bow where you can do this – it may not work if you do it too high in the bow or too low.

Since all that the bow wants is to bounce out of the string, lifted strokes are easier than on-the-string *legato* because you do not have to do anything. If you let them, they play by themselves. What you have to do is allow the bow to bounce.

Experimenting without the first finger

A simple way to practise springing bowings is simply to take the first finger off the bow, since it is the player getting in the way of the natural bounce that is often the reason for the stroke not working.

Try playing *spiccato* or *ricochet* without the first finger on the bow (Fig. 139c). Then find the same 'give' when holding the bow normally.

Finding the sweet spot in *sautillé*

You have to find the right place in the bow to play *sautillé*. Where it is depends on the length of the arm, and the qualities and balance of the individual bow.

The sweet spot, where the least effort produces the most natural and 'willing' bounce, will be somewhere around or just above the middle of the bow. Slightly too far above or below this point may mean than the bow refuses to settle into a regular, natural and easy stroke.

- Playing *sautillé* on one note, begin slightly below or at the middle of the bow. Without stopping, gradually make your way higher up the bow until the *sautillé* really begins to work; try going too high in the bow until the stroke no longer works, and then come back down again to the sweet spot.

Spiccato

Raising the elbow

One way to approach *spiccato* is to play it with almost the same bow-arm as ordinary *detaché*. There is a little downward curve in the line of the stroke and the hair contacts the string at the bottom of the curve, but apart from that you just move the bow down-bow and up-bow the same as for on-the-string strokes.

The elbow is on a level with the stick and moves to the right on the down-bows, and to the left on the up-bows. The elbow moves at the same speed as the bow, giving a feeling of great control:

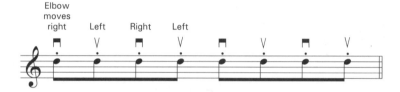

However, moving the whole arm like that can be quite a large action, and often a cumbersome way of going about it – particularly if the *spiccato* is a delicate one.

The alternative way of doing it is to play with a higher elbow, rather like the exaggerated position shown in Fig. 62b, page 126. Then it is possible to play the same *spiccato* stroke with the elbow hardly changing its position in the air.

Fig. 140 Get the feeling of it by resting your elbow against the wall (Fig. 140). Feel how the apparent opening-and-closing forearm movement (that moves the bow down-bow and up-bow) is actually coming from upper-arm rotation.

The final, unexaggerated stroke will probably be a combination of both approaches, though it is often desirable to play very much one way or the other, depending on the passage.

The same high elbow and upper-arm rotation is also a great help in *ricochet*. Try playing the *ricochet*

You can keep the elbow in one place while moving the forearm

in the Paganini example (page 280) with a low elbow, and only by opening your arm at the elbow; then try it again with a slightly raised elbow, and with a feeling of the upper arm rotating anticlockwise (infinitesimally) as the bow plays the *ricochet*. The higher elbow, and the upper arm turning into the string, adds so much more energy to the stroke that it practically plays itself.

Fig. 141 ### The bow hold does not matter

Changing what you do with the fingers on the bow may affect the *spiccato* stroke in some way or other; but the bow-hand and fingers should not be the first thing you think about.

Do you need to be taught how to bounce a ball? Of course not. If you throw a ball at a wall, do you know the angle at which it is going to bounce off it? Of course. In the same way, you already know how to bounce a bow on the string. Prove it by playing *spiccato* while holding the bow in your fist.

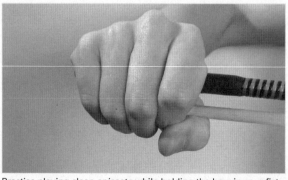

Practise playing clean *spiccato* while holding the bow in your fist

- Holding the bow in your fist (Fig. 141), play *spiccato* in various parts of the bow.

- Experiment with longer and shorter strokes; faster and slower; higher and lower bounce; higher and lower in the bow.

- At each place in the bow play a perfectly good, clean *spiccato* simply by moving the bow with your arm and guiding the bouncing of the hair on the string with natural instinct.

Once it is clear that even when holding the bow in your fist you can play a perfect *spiccato*, playing it with a normal bow hold seems easy.

Experimenting with a 'fist bow hold' is often a solution if a student gets a mental block about playing *spiccato*. If nothing seems to help, and they still find the stroke awkward however they hold or move the bow, using a ridiculous bow hold can solve the problem entirely.[1]

[1] See also *Using the 'fist bow hold'*, page 264

True stories: the virtuoso who could not play *spiccato*

Sandra Kim was fourteen and already had a very good left hand. It was not only that she could play fast, tricky passages accurately and easily, but she did so with a natural virtuosity that made her playing stand out. However, she often stumbled over *spiccato* passages. The notes were not always pure and even, and her right arm lacked the naturalness and ease of her left hand.

We decided to spend an entire lesson on *spiccato*. I showed her every approach and exercise I could think of; but still her *spiccato* seemed slightly wooden, and the purity of the sound was unreliable.

Finally I realised that it was her trying to do the 'correct' thing that was getting in her way. I suggested she hold the bow in her fist. Her first attempts to play *spiccato* like that were 'splashy' and uncontrolled; but within seconds she began to approach it naturally and instinctively, as you do when bouncing a ball or skipping a stone on a pond, and the strokes immediately began to work.

From there it was a short step to get the same result while holding the bow normally. In many cases this should be the first approach to teaching *spiccato*, not the last.

Up not down: playing *spiccato* like a pianist

Playing *spiccato*, the feeling is one of the bow coming up out of the string, not a feeling of it going down into the string.

Watch a pianist playing short, staccato notes, the equivalent of *spiccato* on the violin. They do not appear to make a downward movement of the finger into the key to play each note, but more an upward movement away from the key. There is a sudden acceleration at the bottom of the movement. This creates an illusion that the key has been struck by the finger coming up, not going down.

Then, in a passage like the following, there is a feeling of playing 'up–up–up–up', not 'down–down–down–down':

Playing *spiccato* with the bow is the same:

Example 1   Mozart: Concerto no. 4 in D, K218, *mov. 1, b. 42*

The feeling is one of pulling the *spiccato* out of the string, like a *pizzicato*, rather than of moving the bow down into the string:

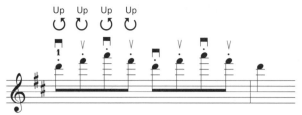

Example 2

The *spiccato* in Example 1 can be played short and almost like a *collé*, so the feeling of 'up–up–up–up' is clear; but there is the same feeling of going 'up', not 'down', in a passage of more running *spiccato*:

Mozart: Sonata in B♭, K454, *mov. 1, b. 14*

Playing around the string, not hitting

Every bow stroke curves around the string in some way, and in *spiccato* there is a fraction of a second of playing *around* the string rather than merely 'hitting' it and bouncing off again.

If you find that there is always a scratch or whistle in *spiccato*, or particular notes always scratch, try exaggerating the curve by playing a short stroke around the string:

Schnittke: Suite in the Old Style, *Ballet, b. 9*

Written at half speed for the sake of clarity:

- After playing the double stops, repeat the same exaggerated curved movement but without playing the open strings – almost touch them, but not quite.

Afterwards, find a fraction of the same rounded quality of stroke in the normal *spiccato* in the passage.

Understanding proportions in *spiccato*

Spiccato is a good stroke to use as an example of proportions. There are two main elements in *spiccato* and it is easy to demonstrate how changes of proportions produce different results in the stroke:

- How high is the bounce off the string

- How long is the stroke

The amounts of these factors change according to:	All of these are further affected by:
• How near to the bridge	• The thickness of the string (G thickest, E thinnest)
• Where in the bow	
• The tempo of the notes	• How much hair

When the amounts of these factors add up correctly, you can play a clean *spiccato* anywhere on the fingerboard at almost any distance from the bridge.

Height and length

The first thing to consider in *spiccato* is the combination of height and length. Carl Flesch approached training *spiccato* starting with height of bounce:

- Begin by bouncing the bow like a drum stick, slightly below the middle of the bow, as a purely vertical, bouncing stroke. Use forearm rotation to do it.

- This will make no proper sound whatsoever. Gradually add length (so that the stroke is still not pure for some time), beginning with only the slightest amount and continuing until the stroke is rounded and pure:

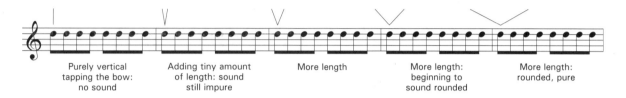

The Greek violinist Demetrious Dounis approached *spiccato* the other way round from Flesch. He described it as being like a very short *détaché*, and with exactly the same arm movement as *détaché*:

- Begin by playing solid, on-the-string *détaché* slightly below the middle of the bow, as a purely horizontal stroke.

- Gradually add height, beginning with only the slightest amount and continuing until the *spiccato* is rounded and pure:

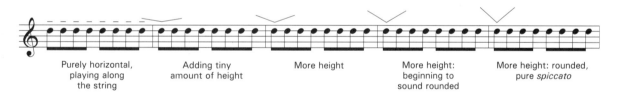

Where in the bow

You can play a very short *spiccato* where the hair barely touches the string; you can play a very long *spiccato* where the hair travels along the string for a centimetre or more.

Find the right place in the bow for the type of *spiccato* required:

- Playing on one note, begin near the middle of the bow with faster, lighter, lower, shorter *spiccato*, and gradually work your way down towards the heel (slower, heavier, higher, longer) and back up again to the middle:

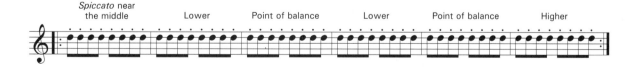

Thickness of string

On the E string, the *spiccato* stroke is much lighter and shorter than the equivalent stroke on the G string, where it is likely to be longer and heavier.

The feeling of *spiccato* on the D string, which is the weakest, most fragile string on the violin, is quite different from the feeling of *spiccato* on the tighter A string.

- Experiment with the different proportions of height and length needed by each string:

- On each string experiment with light, short *spiccato* just below the middle; heavier longer *spiccato* at the point of balance; and heavy, long *spiccato* near the heel.

Soundpoint

- Practise *spiccato* on different soundpoints, moving from one to another without stopping:

Tilt of the bow

- Experiment with the tilt of the bow on each soundpoint:

- Play through from most tilted, to least tilted, to most tilted, all on soundpoint 5.
- Repeat all on soundpoint 4; soundpoint 3; and soundpoint 2.

Experimenting with flexibility

- Experiment with different degrees of flexibility in the fingers and thumb:

Co-ordination: don't always blame the bow

One of the most important elements in any lifted stroke is actually nothing to do with the bow itself. The bow often takes the blame for a scratchy *spiccato* when it was really the left finger not being ready that was at fault.

There are two points to good co-ordination:

- The left finger must stop the string enough for the *spiccato* stroke to make the note ring. If the finger does not make a solid-enough stop, the *spiccato* may sound dead or impure.

- The left finger must stop the string early enough before the bow plays the *spiccato*. If the finger is still in the process of stopping the string when the bow plays it, there may be the sound of bowing a half-stopped string.

These sounds are similar to scratches caused by the bow. The faster the passage of *spiccato*, the more careful you have to be to stop the string sufficiently before the bow plays the note.

Even in a passage of slower *spiccato*, it often sounds as though there is not enough length of bow in the *spiccato* when actually the proportions in the bow stroke are correct – and the blame rests entirely with the fingers not stopping the string sufficiently:

Mozart: Concerto no. 4 in D, K218, *mov. 3, b. 23*

Practising better co-ordination in *spiccato* is simple: play very slowly and make a great point of placing each finger before the bow.

- Feel a syncopation in the rhythm, i.e. place–play, place–play, place–play:

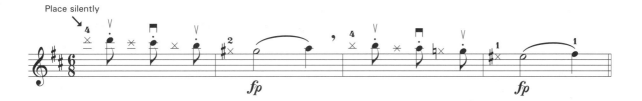

Exercise for placing the fingers early

Co-ordination problems are unlikely to occur in the first place if your basic approach to playing is that you never do anything with the bow until you have first felt the contact of the fingertip with the string.[1]

However, it is often helpful to make a practice exercise out of placing the fingers early:

- Place the fingers gradually later and later.

The exercise is written as quarter-notes (crotchets) for clarity, but you can do the same thing with any value *spiccato* note:

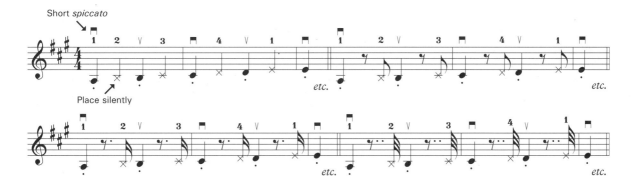

[1] See *Leading from the fingertip*, page 144

Pizzicato

Co-ordination in *spiccato* is improved in an immediate and extraordinary way just by playing a passage *pizzicato* instead of with the bow. Play the whole passage *pizzicato* and with a strong tone, to force the left fingers to stop the string fully and in time before the bow. Notice how the fingers instinctively and naturally stop the string before you pluck with the right hand. Afterwards, playing the passage *spiccato* again, you will notice that the co-ordination is immediately much better.

Staccato

Up- or down-bow staccato is a unique and individual stroke, and so long as it works it does not matter how you do it. It is a curious fact that there are many cases of violinists who are not particularly fine in any other respect of their playing, except that they can unleash the most fantastic staccato. On the other hand, there have been many famous violinists who could never master it.[2]

There is a type of on-the-string staccato played by making the arm go into a sort of spasm which produces an uncontrollably fast (and often rather scratchy) stroke. The most desirable staccato is light and *spiccato*-like, played with a free and relaxed right arm and controllable at any speed.

[2] David Oistrakh often played staccato runs using ordinary *spiccato* (though his staccato in the last movement of the Sibelius Concerto was exemplary). The great Polish violinist Ida Haendel, in her autobiography *Woman with violin*, described how, at the age of twelve, she had a busy solo performing career but could not play staccato. Finally she was put in touch with a local violinist who was not a good player, but had a fine staccato. Ida Haendel spent an entire day working on her staccato with him, and at the end of it was at last able to do it herself.

Working from the inside out

As in the other lifted or bouncing strokes, the fact that the bow wants to bounce is again the most important element of staccato. The first thing is to go with the hair's natural inclination to bounce, rather than try to do something specific with the arm or hand.

Any movement of the right arm, hand or fingers then responds to that natural bounce of the hair out of the string. Encourage the bow, give life to it, but do not get in the way of it.[1]

[1] See *Understanding what the bow does to the string*, page 1

Little dipping movement of the point

Like every other stroke on the violin, the basic movement of each individual note in a staccato run is curved, and in this case causes the tip of the bow to make little dipping movements.

Look at the point during staccato: it should not be going along–along–along the string (Fig. 142a), but up–up–up as the bow goes along the string (Fig. 142b).

The up motion, at the end of the tiny curve, causes the hair to impact the string at an angle that brings it out of the string. Obviously, an along-the-string stroke will produce no impact into the string and therefore no bounce out of it.

Fig. 142

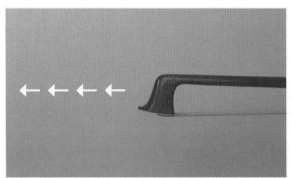

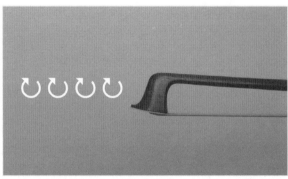

(a) The bow does not go along the string in staccato

(b) The point of the bow makes little dipping movements during staccato

Direction of bow

- In up-bow staccato, play on the outer edge of the hair, and angle the bow 'in' (heel closer to bridge than point).

- In down-bow staccato, play on the inner edge of the hair, and angle the bow 'out'.

Finger movement

There is often a particular movement of the fingers that is behind the most spectacular staccatos, the fingers moving the bow up–up–up with a tiny flex–flex–flex movement. In other words, the fingers go from slightly straighter and higher knuckles (Fig. 143a) to more flexed and lower knuckles (Fig. 143b). The photos exaggerate the movement, which may be very slight.

This finger movement is passive rather than active, and happens in response to the movement of the hand and arm (though an active finger movement might work for some – nothing can be ruled out when it comes to staccato).

Fig. 143

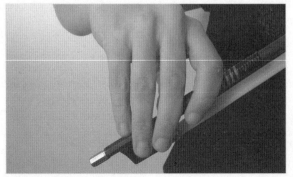

(a) Fingers ready to flex slightly

(b) Fingers ready to straighten slightly

- While practising a run of staccato at a slow tempo, use an active, deliberate finger movement to build the motion into the stroke. Afterwards, let the action happen rather than making it happen.

- Give a little extra bow pressure just before each flexing, so that the movement becomes press–flex–straighten; press–flex–straighten, etc.

Three stages of the arm in staccato

1 In the upper half, the chief movement of the right arm in a staccato run is the forearm moving at the elbow. Go 'up–up–up' with the forearm.

2 As the bow travels up-bow towards the middle of the bow, the forearm movement decreases and the upper arm takes over. The feeling is one of 'push–push–push' with the elbow, which moves at the same speed as the bow.[1]

3 As the bow continues up-bow past the middle and into the lower half, the stroke turns into a fast *spiccato* in the last few notes of the run.

[1] See *Experiment without the bow*, page 127

Paganini: 24 Caprices, op. 1, no. 15, *b. 19*

Rocking the hand

An element in many successful staccatos is a sort of fast rocking of the hand (i.e. back and forth between upright and leaning) made by a very fast forearm rotation (as though turning a door handle back and forth).

- Practise with the arm in position in the air without the bow: keeping the fingers completely relaxed and floppy, shake the hand so fast that the hand and fingers become a blur (Fig. 144a).

- Then find an element of this motion during the staccato.

It is to allow this forearm rotation to happen that Galamian (and others) suggest taking the second and fourth fingers off the bow, and slightly turning the hand away from the first finger (slightly more on to the fourth) so that the hand is more supinated (Fig. 144b).

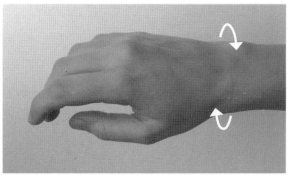

Fig. 144

(a) Rotate the hand in a tiny, tremor-like movement

(b) Typical bow hold for staccato

Soundpoint practice

In learning how to play staccato it is very helpful to practise a run on soundpoints 5–2. The bow jumps more readily at the fingerboard because the strings are so soft, and without needing so much downward force into the string. Remember to 'go with' the bow, and let it jump by itself. It wants to bounce.

- Starting up-bow, begin each group somewhere a little below the point and finish before you get to the middle (M). Starting down-bow, begin around the middle of the bow.

- As you repeat nearer and nearer to the bridge, you can feel how you have to direct the bow more and more down into, or towards, the string:

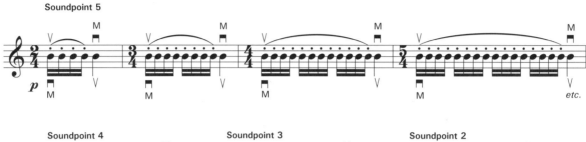

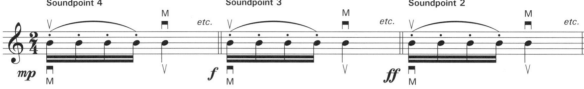

Also experiment on the other strings. Afterwards add fingers to the patterns. For example:

The *martelé* lesson

Separating the elements

One way to describe *martelé* is to think of it as a composite stroke. 'Composite' means made up of separate components. A composite violin is one that has been put together out of parts taken from other violins – one where the front was made by, say, Stradivarius, the scroll also made by Stradivarius but taken from a different violin, the back made by Amati, the ribs unknown, and so on.

Martelé is made up of the following distinct components:

- **Bow speed**

  Fast–slow. The stroke begins very quickly and then slows.

- **Bow pressure**

  Heavy–light. The stroke begins very heavily and then lightens.

- **'Bite'**

  Before the stroke begins, the hair momentarily grips the string extra-hard, causing a 'click' at the beginning of the stroke. This click is an extra component in addition to the heavy–light bow pressure, i.e. the pressure pattern is: click–heavy–light.

- **Space**

  There is a silence at the end of each *martelé*, ranging from a large gap between the strokes to the smallest. It is during the space between strokes that the bow bites the string ready for the next stroke.

Before playing the complete stroke, first try each separate component on its own:

Gripping the string to make the bite

The most common mistake made in playing *martelé* is in not separating the moment of gripping the string from the moment of moving the bow. The difference is between 'technical' and 'musical' timing.[1]

[1] See *Understanding technical and musical timing*, page 205

- To get the feel of the bite, press the bow down heavily into the string, without moving the bow along the string, to grip the string with the hair.

- Then, without allowing the hair to lose its grip or to move along the string, pull and push the string sideways.

  You can move the string only a small distance, but go as far as you can before the build-up of tension makes the string spring back. So long as the hair does not lose its grip, this is entirely silent.

- Having moved the string from side to side a few times, stop the bow on the string without releasing the pressure. Then play one *martelé* stroke.

- The most important thing is to try it on different soundpoints, since the different tensions of the string determine how you make the click:

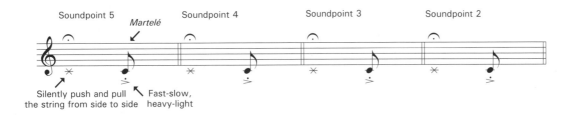

Many players experience difficulty in the tiny silence between *martelé* strokes, since the bow often makes a little scratch there.

This can happen only if you let the bow move along the string horizontally. If the bow sits on the string in one place, it is impossible for it to make any sound at all, however hard the downward pressure.

Fast-slow speed-pattern alone

- Rest the bow on the string in the upper half.

- Using no bow weight at all, so that the hair skims across the surface of the string without making a proper tone, make one down-bow and stop. At the end of the stroke, leave the bow on the string.

  The 'swishing' sound that this makes is represented by x-notes, below.

- After the fast beginning to the stroke, slow down:

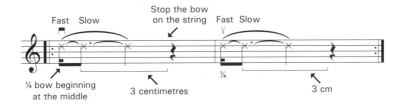

Heavy–light pressure–pattern alone

There is little point in isolating the heavy–light pressure–pattern from the fast–slow bow speed. Without extra speed during the heavy part of the stroke, the tone simply becomes crushed.

However, it may be useful to isolate the heavy–light pattern from the click at the beginning of the stroke.

● Alternate between playing the heavy–light pattern with, and without, a click at the beginning of the stroke:

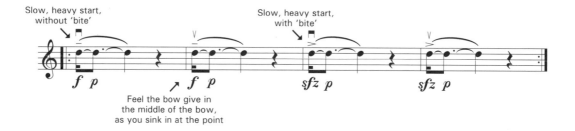

[1] See *The give of the wood and the hair*, page 15

● Playing the heavy beginning to the up-bow at the point, feel the wood giving (in the middle of the bow) as you push down heavily into the string with the part of the hair that is near the point.[1]

Finger movement alone

A tiny amount of finger movement adds a great amount of extra energy to the beginning of a *martelé*.

The fingers move in the same direction as the bow. On the down-bow the fingers straighten slightly (Fig. 145a); on the up-bow they flex slightly (Fig. 145b).

Fig. 145

(a) Fingers ready to flex slightly during the up-bow

(b) Fingers ready to straighten slightly during the down-bow

This straightening and flexing movement is natural, like straightening the fingers as you reach out to grasp an object and closing your fingers around it to bring it towards you. You do not close your fingers into a fist as you reach out, and stretch your fingers out again as you bring your hand back.

The finger movement creates bow speed (the bow would move a few centimetres even if the arm remained motionless), which is geared up by the arm movement. This is what creates such a feeling of extra energy from such a seemingly insignificant amount of finger movement.

● Try the finger action on its own:

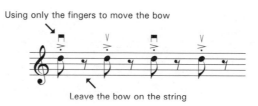

● Do not move the arm at all. Move only the fingers.

● Make sure the thumb moves as well. The thumb and the fourth finger work together. When the fourth flexes, the thumb flexes; when the fourth straightens, the thumb straightens.

● Then add the arm movement to the finger movement.

Adjusting the bow hold for power

Because *martelé* is a powerful stroke, adjust the bow hold so that you get maximum leverage: move the first finger a little further up the bow away from the thumb; possibly move the second up a little as well; lower the knuckles; pronate the hand a little more than usual (lean the hand on to the first and second).

(a) Normal bow hold

(b) Fingers spread for more leverage in *martelé*

Fig. 146

See the contrast between an ordinary, 'neutral' bow hold (Fig. 146a) and a *martelé* bow hold (Fig. 146b). The difference in appearance is only slight; yet because of the way numbers grow so quickly when you continue to double them, i.e. 1, 2, 4, 8, 16, 32, 64 etc., there is a big difference in the feeling of leverage into the bow.

There is little difference between pressing the bow 30 centimetres from the thumb, or pressing it 29 centimetres away (a small percentage difference); but a tiny adjustment of the first finger, to move it further away from the thumb, can easily be a difference of as much as 50%.[1]

[1] See *Experiment in leverage*, page 40

There is always a clear difference between the feel of a bow hold where the first finger is just slightly too close to the thumb, and another bow hold where the first finger has moved slightly further up the bow away from the thumb – even though there is little visible difference.

String crossing

In order to understand string crossing – or rather, its central element, pivoting – it is helpful to look also at the other ways the bow can move relative to the string.

Five ways to move in relation to the string

There are five ways that the bow can move in relation to the string during normal playing. None of them are normally ever used on their own but always in combination with at least one of the others:

1 **Vertical** (tapping the string without making a sound)

   This movement makes no sound, but added to the horizontal, it creates bounced bowings like *spiccato*.

2 **Horizontal** (moving along the string as a down- or up-bow)

   Any apparently horizontal movement along the string contains a hidden curved element which comes from a tiny amount of pivoting (the movement around the string). Even one, long bow on one string is curved.

3 **Forward and back** (moving closer to or further from the bridge while keeping the bow straight)

   The forward and back movement (the bow parallel to the bridge) produces no sound; but combined with the horizontal (and/or the sideways) allows the bow to steer towards, or away from, the bridge.

4 **Sideways** (moving the frog so that one end of the bow is nearer the bridge than the other

   The sideways movement (making the bow crooked to the bridge) again produces no sound; but combined with the horizontal (and/or the forward-and-back) allows the bow to steer towards, or away from, the bridge.

5 Around (pivoting)

Combined with the horizontal movement along the string, pivoting makes it possible to travel to a new string-level while playing the note before the string crossing.

It may be easier to understand pivoting if first you look at it away from the violin. Bow on a pencil (Fig. 147a). With nothing on either side of the pencil to stop it, the bow could pivot full-circle around it.

Take another pencil and hold it parallel to the first one (Fig. 147b). You can move the bow along one pencil, while at the same time pivoting over to the next pencil.

Fig. 147

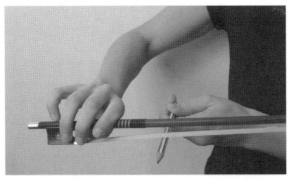

(a) The bow can turn around the pencil 360°

(b) The bow can move along one pencil while pivoting over to the other

Smooth string crossing was described beautifully by Ivan Galamian:

> If the crossing is made gradually enough, a double stop will sound momentarily between the two notes. This double stop should form so subtly that it is not possible to distinguish either the exact moment of its beginning or the instant of its termination. A very slight pressure of the bow, just as the crossing is made, will help further in binding the tones smoothly together.[1]

[1] Ivan Galamian: *Principles of Violin Playing and Teaching* (New Jersey, 1962), 65.

An obvious way to practise this is to begin with a longer double stop that you can hear clearly. Then gradually make it shorter and shorter until it ends up as Galamian describes, i.e. a double stop where you can hear neither when it begins nor when it ends:

Start to move towards the new string during the dot

Smooth string crossing

The art of smooth string crossing lies partly in beginning to move towards the new string earlier rather than later, but in particular in staying close to the new string before crossing to it.

There are seven basic levels of the bow:

Level 1 G   **Level 5** A

Level 2 GD (double stop)   **Level 6** AE

Level 3 D   **Level 7** E

Level 4 DA

It is natural to suppose, then, that in any piece that has no double-stops the bow will play only on levels 1, 3, 5 and 7. But this approach leads to jerky, last-minute string crossings. In order to play smoothly, half the time you have to play almost on levels 2, 4 and 6.

A simple way to approach this is to add two new levels to each of the single strings. For example, when playing on the A string the bow does not have to be on a plane exactly midway between the D and the E strings (Level 5). The hair can be almost touching the D string (Level 5-), or almost touching the E string (Level 5+).

The same applies to the outer strings: when attacking the G string from the air, the hair may be further from the D string than normal (Level 1-); attacking on the E string the bow may be further from the A string than normal (Level 7+).

When practising to make a passage more *legato*, consciously direct the bow closer to one string or another:

Kayser: Etudes, op. 20 no. 1

Practise this by playing the notes before and after the string crossing as a double stop. Use this as a central method that you return to constantly in many different types of passage:

Gaining or losing bow on the string crossing

When you change bow on one string, without crossing to another, the exact place on the hair is the same at the end of one stroke and the beginning of the next.

In crossing from one string to another, the exact place on the hair where you finish one stroke is not the same place on the hair where you begin the next.

Play a stroke on the G string, stopping the bow on the string at the end of the stroke.

Note the exact place on the hair that the bow stops (Fig. 148a).

- Pivot silently over to the next string without moving the bow along the string.

Note the new place on the hair, about a centimetre lower (in the direction of the frog) where the bow will begin the stroke on the D string (Fig. 148b).

- Repeat the same pattern beginning on an up-bow.

- Feel the different contact-points of the bow-hair with the string in a repeated string-crossing passage:

Fig. 148

(a) Note the exact place on the bow-hair that is contacting the string

(b) The contact-point is now one centimetre lower

(c) The contact-point is now three centimetres lower

Following the curve of the bridge

'Following the curve of the bridge' produces a wonderful feeling of 'gluing' the bow to the string, and of solid control.

Not following the curve of the bridge on the down-bow means that you use too much bow at the beginning of the stroke; and your hand moves out too horizontally to the right, instead of curving down to the E string level.

Examples   Beethoven: Sonata in G, op. 30 no. 3, *mov. 1, b. 51*

Kreutzer: 42 Etudes ou caprices, no. 30, *b. 11*

Mendelssohn: Concerto in E minor, op. 64, *mov. 1, b. 85*

Tremolo

Where is tremolo powered from in the arm?

There are two ways of playing a tremolo: with the hand alone, or with a combination of arm and hand. A third way is to use the arm alone as a solid unit, with no visible movement at the wrist and almost none at the elbow, but except for short bursts of tremolo this may easily be too tiring.[1] Looking around an orchestra you can usually see all three methods being used.

Tremolo can be likened to vibrato, where the two main types are hand and arm vibrato. It often seems that players who use a hand vibrato play tremolo with a hand movement, and those that use an arm vibrato use the forearm to perform tremolo.

In arm vibrato the movement of the forearm causes a passive, sympathetic shaking of the hand moving at the wrist; and the laws of leverage dictate that a tiny amount of forearm movement creates a larger amount of hand movement. Similarly, in tremolo the tiny sympathetic movements of the hand (if you make the tremolo from the forearm), take the place of a lot of movement in the forearm.

The movement of the hand in tremolo

It is difficult to make a fast, sideways hand-movement (the hand moving at the wrist). The apparent fast motion of the hand in tremolo is actually an up-and-down movement, not a sideways movement. You get this by slightly turning the forearm anticlockwise so that you alter the angle of the fingers on the bow. A slight lifting of the right elbow helps to get the correct angle as well.

The hand movement does not happen on its own, but together with an imperceptible degree of forearm rotation.[2]

Many players find that these movements of the hand, and the slight forearm rotation, happen automatically if they tilt the bow towards the bridge and play on the side of the hair nearest to them. It is also helpful to take some of the fingers off the bow. It is common to see a tremolo played without the third or fourth fingers, and even without the second finger as well.

[1] Many orchestral players dread a long passage of tremolo, as they know that their arm will be burning with pain, or seizing up entirely, before they get to the end of it.

[2] See *Forearm rotation*, page 122

Speed of tremolo

The tremolo should be extremely fast, the movement of the fingers and the movement of the point of the bow becoming completely blurred. A slow tremolo may occasionally be required as a special effect, but often it is seen as poor and a mark of technical deficiency.[1]

- One way to build the tremolo is to use a metronome, starting slowly and gradually speeding up:

♩ = 60, 65, 70, 75, 80, 85, 90, 95

At the extreme point

Remember to speed up by using smaller movements, not by increasing effort or muscular tension.

- Alternatively, begin at, say, 60, and play eighth-notes (quavers), sixteenth-notes (semiquavers), and demisemiquavers (32nd notes) before moving on to the next metronome speed:

At the extreme point

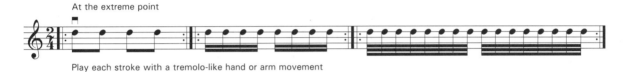

Play each stroke with a tremolo-like hand or arm movement

- Practise a simple study such as Kreutzer No. 2 using 16, 8 and 4 tremolo strokes to each note:

Experiment with more or less hair, and different effects: atmospheric, 'impressionist' tremolo, near the fingerboard; stronger, more articulated strokes a little lower in the bow and nearer the bridge.

Chords

Seven common misconceptions about playing chords

1 'Chords must be played near the fingerboard'

The advice to play chords near to the fingerboard stems from the fact that the strings are flatter nearer the fingerboard, and more curved nearer the bridge, and the strings have less tension there.

While there are plenty of occasions when the quality of sound that you would get at the fingerboard, with a fast stroke, would be exactly right, equally there are as many occasions when thicker, fatter, more powerful chords require to be played nearer to the bridge.

Because the weight of the bow is spread between two or more strings, you simply need a large amount of weight when you play a chord on soundpoint 3 or 2.[2]

- Experiment with different soundpoints in the same way as you do any other note or phrase:

Soundpoint 5	Soundpoint 4	Soundpoint 3	Soundpoint 2	Soundpoint 3	Soundpoint 4

[1] Make sure you tremolo fast, since although somebody may not be able to hear you, a slow-moving tremolo can be clearly visible from a long way away, and make you stand out as a low-energy contributor to the section.

Other visible factors like this are: not using enough bow in general; not using enough bow at the beginning of accents; playing too far from the bridge; using too slow and wide a vibrato.

[2] See *Standing on two weighing machines*, page 307

2 'Chords must be played with a fast bow'

This is linked to the idea that chords should be played near the fingerboard. There, a faster, lighter bow may be necessary; but as you play nearer and nearer to the bridge, you can play with a slower and slower, and more and more sustained bow, until finally you can sustain three strings at the same time for several seconds.

- In each of the following bars, sustain all three strings for the full length of the chord:

3 'Chords must be hit from above the string, not starting from on the string'

[1] See *Starting from the string*, page 275

Just as you can begin a single note 'as you mean to continue', i.e. the sound at the beginning is exactly the same as the sound a little further on into the note, you can do the same with three-string chords.[1]

First press down on the middle of the three strings until you can see the hair touching the two outer strings. As Carl Flesch put it, 'first you have to satisfy the eye'. Then, without changing the pressure or the soundpoint, and making sure that you keep contact with each outer string, simply pull the bow.

The crucial thing is not to alter the level of the bow as you move it, since too far one way or the other loses the upper or the lower string.

4 'Chords must be played with long bows'

Sometimes chords do require a lot of bow, but often they can be played with little bow. You can even play chords with a heavy *spiccato* stroke.

Play the *spiccato* at the point-of-balance, or lower, using large, slow, heavy curves that aim for the middle string of each three-string chord:

Bruch: Concerto no. 1 in G minor, op. 26, *mov. 1, b. 34*

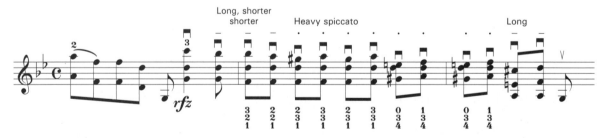

Here, one way to approach the chords is to begin slower, and to slow down at the end, but to play faster in the middle; and to play the slower chords longer, and the faster chords with a heavy *spiccato*.

5 'Chords cannot sound pure and sweet unless played *p* or arpeggiated'

It is not true that if you play chords with any force, scratch is inevitable and an acceptable part of chord playing. Chords can be played with a ringing, rounded, pure tone at every volume:

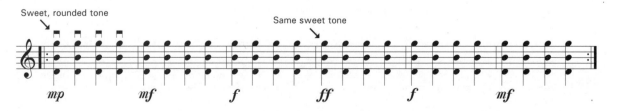

- Experiment by beginning gently with a sweet, rounded tone, and then gradually increase the volume – and gradually play nearer to the bridge – while keeping the same purity of tone, and then diminish again back to the starting place.

6 'The left fingers must press the strings harder'

It is easy to fall into the trap of over-pressing the left fingers when you play double stops. Then the hand becomes tense, and intonation difficult.[1]

[1] See *Light left hand in double stops*, page 307

- Practise chord sequences on the back of your hand, with a 'tickle-light' touch.[2] Then keep that sensation as you place them on their notes and bow heavily into the strings.

[2] See *Experiment on the back of your hand*, page 172

7 'You cannot vibrate chords'

Sometimes a chord may feel awkward to vibrate; but generally, if the fingers remain as light in the string as when playing single stops, a little vibrato is often possible in a chord when desired.

- Experiment with more and less vibrato on the same chord:

Silent placing exercise

This exercise is a good test of 'command–response'.[3] When a finger seems to take a long time to get to its note, it vividly illustrates the need to speed up the response part of the command–response unit.

[3] See *Command–response*, page 105

- Without the bow, practise placing all four fingers at the same time in a particular formation, and then moving them instantly to a new formation. Move quickly between one placing and the other.

- Start with either the 'natural' setting, or the 'reverse' setting (the 'Geminiani chord', page 140) and move from there to one of the following chords:

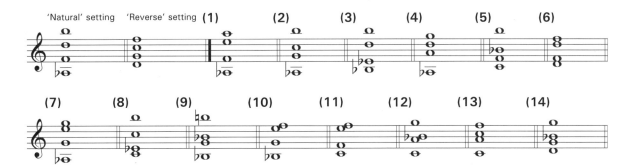

These chords include every possibility of different finger-placements of the original two basic chords.

Example

- Alternate between one chord and the other, placing the fingers decisively:

Reducing effort in three-string chords

Triple-stops are often much easier than they may at first appear because usually they are a matter of creating an *illusion* of fully sustaining three strings at the same time.

(1) As written.

(2) Split. So in fact the triple-stop is actually two double-stops.

(3) This is the most usual way to approach the chord when you want it to sound like one played on the piano. To the listener this *sounds* like a triple-stop, but actually the bow plays all three strings together for only a few centimetres, and the rest of the chord is only a double-stop.

(4) It is often desirable to end up only on the top note, so although the audience hears it as a three-string chord you actually play three strings for only a few centimetres, then a double-stop for a few more, and then only one note on its own.

So in the short moment that you play three strings at once, you use no more than a few centimetres of bow. This is very easy, since the principle of 'the less bow, the less weight' works in your favour.

Localizing

Sit down and lean against the back of the chair. Rest the violin against the top of your chest, completely away from your chin, and with the scroll very low so that the violin is pointing down. Put on an act of being completely relaxed, nonchalant and indifferent. Perhaps cross your legs.

Place the bow on the middle of the three strings, somewhere around soundpoint 3 and near the heel. Push the middle of the three strings down until you can see the hair touching the outer strings.

Make sure that the pushing-down is entirely localized: maintain your relaxed and easy posture, and indifference, in every part of your body except the few muscles necessary to push the bow down.

Having contacted the outer strings, simply pull the bow a very short distance and stop – either stopping on the string or lifting it into the air. Make sure there is no reaction or knock-on effect anywhere else – just move the bow.

This should feel remarkably easy, and the three strings should sound pure.

Then see if you can recapture exactly the same ease while standing up and holding the violin properly.

Background essentials 3

Scales and arpeggios

Why practise scales?

Putting off practising scales as a student

It took me a long time to realise how beneficial it is to be able to play scales and arpeggios as well as if they were part of a concert performance of a concerto, sonata or concert piece. Like most students I always used to put off practising them. Whereas you cannot get away with missing something like your school homework, if you have not practised your scales it is undetectable, especially if you are rarely asked to play them in the violin lesson. So it was all-too-easy to put off practising scales, and of course weeks soon turn into months, which then quickly turn into years.

There were scales in the regular examinations, but like many students I would always leave practising them until the last minute, until I no longer had any choice and simply had to. The scale practice would peak on the day of the exam, and then stop until the next time when again there would no longer be any choice. Then once you have finished studying, nobody ever asks you to play a scale again.

My first ten years of playing and teaching

After I had stopped studying I continued all the work on basic mechanics I had done as a student, i.e. exercises for tone production, shifting, string crossing, intonation, and so on. As part of that work, once or twice a year I would go through a brief phase of practising scales. Each time I was pleased to see that they had improved a lot since the last time, without having practised them at all in-between.

I would find I could play a scale in thirds more in tune, faster, and with a more relaxed hand, than ever before; but all I had done was practise exercises in thirds. Four-octave scales would be far easier than before, but only because I had practised shifting exercises and finger patterns at the top of the G string.

As a teacher at that time I would rarely ask a student to play a scale either. I reasoned that since the scale was made up of specific elements, e.g. moving the fingers freely, changing position lightly and inaudibly, smooth string-crossing, and so on, it made more sense to work on those things directly rather than in a scale – after all, if the student had problems shifting, or had stiff fingers or did not play with a singing tone, how could they play a scale well if it was itself made up of those elements?

So I would work with them on basic technique and only work on scales around the time of their scale exams. Again, I was always pleased with their progress and would marvel at how their scale-playing would improve. The scales always got better on their own. Later, I was delighted to discover that Dounis had had exactly the same approach, and also preferred working on the elements of the scales rather than on the scales themselves.

Getting the best of both worlds

Another support for this approach to scales was that although some players or teachers saw scales as the cornerstone of technique, others doubted whether there was any point in playing them at all.[1] So by not practising them, but by improving them anyway, I thought that I was getting the best of both worlds.

There was also the point that even great violinists would not necessarily be excellent at playing scales. In a famous story about Henryk Szeryng going to play to Jascha Heifetz, he turned up to the lesson ready to play a selection of big concertos. But Heifetz was not interested in hearing any of them. First he wanted to hear a three-octave scale. That was the real test.

When I was a student, a friend who had recently won an international competition said to me, 'If you ask me to play the Brahms Concerto to you I would be perfectly happy; if you asked me to play a three-octave scale in C major I would fall flat on my face!' She is an excellent violinist, I reasoned; so if I don't practise my scales it does not mean my career need suffer either.

[1] I once asked the Austrian pianist Alfred Brendel, having just heard him play a late Schubert piano sonata at the age of 78 with superb technical control, how he kept his technique in such excellent condition. Did he practise scales and exercises? No, he said, he had never played scales or exercises in his whole life. He practised everything from the point of view of musical control, trying to find how to make the music sound as he wanted it to, and all the technique came from that.

The Israeli pianist Daniel Barenboim says that practising scales is positively bad for you since when you come to a scale in a piece you might play just a scale rather than music.

(But scales are full of inner musical tensions and resolutions. I'd bet the same people who play a "scale" instead of "music" would probably play in the same unmusical way, even if they did not practise scales!)

Exercises–scales–studies–pieces

Finally I began to realise how good it is to practise scales and arpeggios themselves. After all the building work of practising the elements – shifting, intonation, string crossing and so on – the next step is to practise scales and connect everything into a streamlined whole. There is simply nothing to replace what regular scale-practice brings.

All the previous ideas about saving time by practising the elements separately are obviously correct, but what I had not fully realised was the benefit that comes into the whole of your playing when you do practise scales regularly. Practising scales in the same key as the piece you are playing is also one of the best ways to improve overall intonation in the piece, and the evenness of all the playing quickly increases.[1]

How is a scale when it is played well?

While part of the art of scale-playing is to play them musically, at the same time the most important goal is machine-like evenness and regularity. When a scale is played well the three main pillars of music – pitch, sound and rhythm – are all completely even:

- The intonation is even, the same note-names not sharper or flatter in different octaves. The notes are evenly spaced, e.g. in the major scale the whole tone from the first note to the second is not wider (aurally) than from the second note to the third.

- The sound is even. No note is louder or softer than its neighbour, and remains even in tone for however long each note lasts.

- The rhythm is even.

Be extra careful to maintain evenness of tone and rhythm at three crucial places:

1 Before or after a change of bow

2 Before or after a change of string

3 Before or after a change of position.

The top of the E string, where the string becomes short and the bow has to sit close to the bridge (though not too heavily), requires great evenness of bowing.

Extra factors that make rhythm uneven are fingers not being ready for the new string,[2] and fingers lifting off too soon when descending.[3]

Yfrah Neaman used to say that the ideal in melodic playing would be to play on one string, in one position, with one finger, and with one long bow that never comes to an end. Then playing the violin would be like singing, where all that the singer has to do to create a long, seamless line is one thing: exhale.

Playing the same long, seamless line on the violin is more difficult because the line is so easily broken up into little, unmusical bits by all the constant changes that happen – changes of string, position, finger and bow direction.

Practising the elements of the scale

Holding down the first and fourth fingers

- Keep the first finger down on the string all the way up to the top of the scale and back down again to the end. The only time you need to lift the first finger is to place it on the next string.

- Ascending, hold down the fourth finger while playing the first finger on the new string.

x-note = first finger ready on string

[1] One of David Oistrakh's last concerts in London was a performance of the Beethoven concerto in the Royal Albert Hall. The rehearsal finished at 1.00, but Oistrakh remained on stage for the entire afternoon practising slow, three-octave scales and arpeggios. He wanted to play the concerto in tune, which is not necessarily easy even if you are a player on his level.

[2] See *Finger preparation: the secret of legato*, page 145

[3] See *No. 5*, page 219

Holding down the fourth is called overlapping. As well as helping to bind the string crossing together smoothly and seamlessly, holding down the fourth also helps in keeping the fingers above and close to the strings, curing any habit of raising them too high or too far away from the neck.

Double stopping string crossing is good for both hands

Make scales both feel and sound very smooth by double stopping the string crossings. This forces the left fingers to prepare, and the bow to move early to the next string – instead of it moving too suddenly and 'bumping' on to the string:

Double stopping the string crossings in arpeggios is helpful for the same reasons. However, it may cause intonation problems if you make the resulting intervals in tune as double stops: the tuning of a note played on its own is often different from how it would be tuned if played as part of a double stop.[1]

[1] See *The difference between single-stop and double-stop tuning*, page 90

- Tune the notes the same as you would in the normal arpeggio:

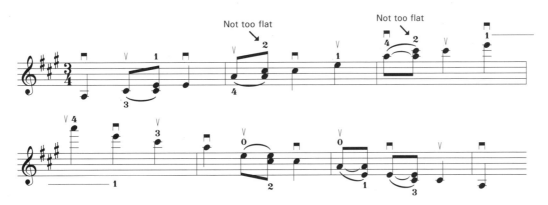

In this example none of the double stops are a possible problem except the ones marked in the first line. If the 'third tones' of these major thirds were to be in tune, the C♯'s would have to be played very low; but that same low pitch for the C♯, played on its own in the arpeggio, would sound much too flat and the arpeggios would seem dull and lacking brilliance.

Half of forty-eight is twenty-four: the mumble strategy

The educational reformer John Holt used to show how children use all kinds of tricks and strategies, in the classroom, in their efforts to please their teachers or to stay out of trouble if they do not know something. In *How Children Fail* he tells a story about Emily, aged nine:

> The question arose the other day, 'What is half of forty-eight?' In the tiniest whisper she said, 'Twenty-four'. I asked her to repeat it. She said, loudly, 'I said,' then whispered 'twenty-four'. I asked her to repeat it again, because many couldn't hear her. Her face showing tension, she said, very loudly, 'I said that one-half of forty-eight is...' and then, very softly, 'twenty-four.' Still, not many of the students heard. She said, indignantly, 'O.K., I'll shout.' I said that that would be fine. She shouted, in a self-righteous tone, 'The question is, what is half of forty-eight. Right?' I agreed. And once again, in a voice scarcely above a whisper, she said, 'Twenty-four.' I could not convince her that she had shouted the question but not the answer.

> Of course, this is a strategy that often pays off. A teacher who asks a question is tuned to the right answer, ready to hear it, eager to hear it, since it will tell him that his teaching is good and that he can go on to the next topic. He will assume that anything that sounds close to the right answer is meant to be the right answer. So, for a student who is not sure of the answer, a mumble may be his best bet. If he's not sure whether something is spelled with an a or o, he writes a letter that could be either one of them.

> The mumble strategy is particularly effective in language classes...[2]

[2] John Holt: *How Children Fail*, (1964)

Exactly the same thing is happening when you hear scales or arpeggios played like this:

Example 1

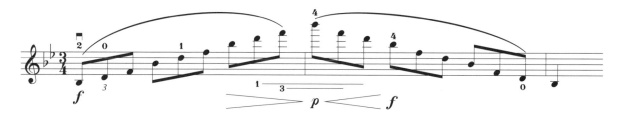

Playing in safe, familiar, secure, 1st position is like saying 'Half of forty-eight is'; playing at the top of the E string, where you might easily play out of tune or make a scratch in the sound, is like having to state the answer.

● Do the opposite to correct this. Practise exaggerating the arrival to the top:

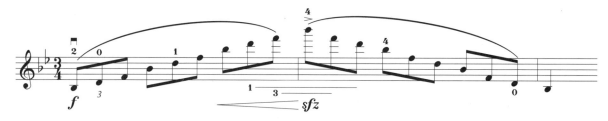

[1] See *True-legato warm-up exercise*, page 261

Another way to practise this is to finger on one string while bowing on another.[1] Take the last part of the scale and finger it while bowing smoothly and evenly on the A string.

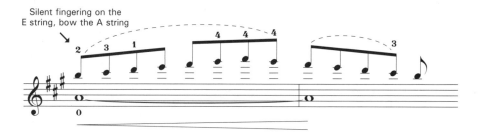

You can also do it the other way round, bowing on the E string while fingering on a lower string. Bowing on another string has as good an effect as bowing on the one that you will actually play after doing the exercise.

Example 2

There may be certain chords more difficult than the others, and caution may make a passage come out as follows:

J. S. Bach: Sonata no. 1 in G minor, BWV1001, *Fuga, b. 4*

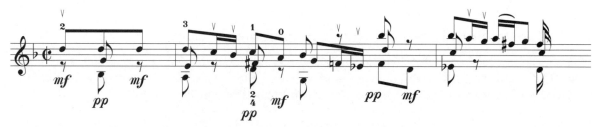

● Practise by doing the opposite. Play the rest of the passage normally, or a little more gently than usual, while playing the avoided chords extra loud and extra long:

Chromatic scales

Slow and fast fingering

While there are many ways of fingering the chromatic scale up or down the E string, in 1st position there are two fingerings: the sliding fingering 1–1, 2–2, 3, 4, and the shifting fingering 1, 2, 1, 2, 3, 4:

While the sliding fingering is sometimes seen as old-fashioned and the shifting fingering modern, it may be better to call them the slow and the fast fingering. 1–1, 2–2 is more melodic and expressive, and 1, 2, 1, 2 more mechanical and functional.

Example 1

If played prestissimo, passages like this feel awkward with the slow fingering.

Example 2

Tchaikovsky: Concerto in D, op. 35, *mov. 1, b. 40*

Even a passage as fast as this may be played with the slow fingering, which offers an alternative range of expression to the more straightforward, functional (though equally effective) 1–2–1–2 fingering.

Keeping the thumb in one place

In the fingering 1–2–1–2 the thumb should not change its position on the neck of the violin. Playing the first-finger G♯ and second-finger A, the hand is in half position; playing first-finger B♭ the hand is now in 2nd position; playing second-finger B♮ the hand is in 1st position again. Keep the thumb in one place so that the hand stays in 1st position throughout. Otherwise the hand can lose its orientation and intonation suffers.

Practice method: missing out the second finger

The two most common fingerings for playing the chromatic scale up the E string are 12, 12, 12 and 123, 123, 123.

Coming down, the usual fingering is 321, 321, 321.

Many players find this 123 or 321 fingering uncomfortable because of the way the hand has to contract. After playing two semitones with this fingering, the first and third fingers are a tone apart in spacing. The usual feel in the fingers is of a minor or major third between the first and third fingers.

The following exercise is a way to gain a new feeling of control and ease in the hand when playing chromatics.

Keep the first finger on the string

Fig. 149

- Miss out all the second fingers, playing only 13, 13, 13 (ascending) or 31, 31, 31 (descending).

- Shift a semitone after each third finger (ascending), and after each first finger (descending).

- To enhance the sensation of there being only a tone between the first and third fingers, pull the second finger up out of the way (Fig. 149).

- Keep the first finger down on the string both ascending and descending.

Pull the second finger exaggeratedly out of the way

Knowing what notes you are playing

It is easy to get lost in a three-octave chromatic scale, so that by the time you are halfway up the E string you do not know where you are, or when to stop and come back down again. This is easily cured by two simple things: play in groups, and know the names of the notes in the high positions.

Playing in groups

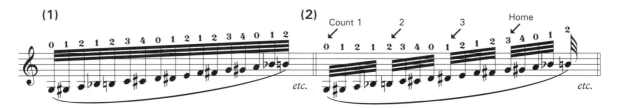

Rather than having a mental picture of the scale as shown in **(1)**, i.e. a non-stop stream of semitones, divide them into groups of four, so that after three beats there is a feeling of 'arriving home' on the tonic **(2)**. Or if you prefer you can play in groups of three, arriving home on the tonic after four beats.

Naming the notes

It is often a feature of musical talent, rather than the lack of it, when a player does not know the names of the notes in the high positions, and relies solely on the ear to know where they are in the scale. Nevertheless, it is extremely helpful to be able to use the name of the note as a 'hook' on which to hang the sound of the note.

- Play slowly, saying out loud (or thinking) the names of the notes. State each note emphatically:

Scale practice chart

When you are organised and systematic, and know exactly which scales you have played, it is much easier to keep up regular scale-practice, and practising scales becomes much more enjoyable.

Create a practice chart along the following lines, adding other items as desired, e.g. scales and arpeggios in one, two, three or four octaves, scales in broken thirds, double stops in broken thirds and sixths etc.

You may decide to have one chart for scales played with any sort of slurred bowings, and another chart for scales played with separate bows; another chart for rhythm practice; and so on.

	Scales				Arpeggios				3rds			6ths			8ths			Fingered 8ths			10ths		
	Maj	*Har*	*Mel*	*Chr*	*Maj*	*Har*	*V⁷*	*Dim*	*Maj*	*Har*	*Mel*	*Maj*	*Har*	*Mel*	*Maj*	*Har*	*Mel*	*Maj*	*Har*	*Mel*	*Maj*	*Har*	*Mel*
G																							
A♭/G♯																							
A																							
B♭																							
B																							
C																							
D♭/C♯																							
D																							
E♭																							
E																							
F																							
G♭/F♯																							

Maj = major   *Har* = harmonic minor   *Mel* = melodic minor   *Chr* = chromatic   *V⁷* = dominant 7th   *Dim* = diminished 7th

Some different ways to use the chart

- Put a tick in each box when you have practised it. A tick does not have to mean 'perfect' – simply that you have worked at it and made some progress.

- Do not repeat a key until the whole chart has been covered.

- Or do repeat keys before finishing the chart, using numbers instead of a tick. Write '1' the first time you practise a box, change this to '2' the next time you practise it, and so on.

- Instead of a tick or a number, mark the date, e.g. 11/07. If you choose to repeat a box rather than doing an empty one, you can rub out the old date and write in the new one.

- Instead of a tick, number or date, write in the metronome mark at which you played it, e.g. ♩ = 70. The next time you play it you can choose a faster or slower speed based on what you did last time.

Double stops

Light left hand in double stops

Standing on two weighing machines

Suppose you weigh 150 pounds, and you stand on two weighing machines, one foot on each. What would each machine register? They would each indicate 75 pounds, not 150 pounds, because your weight is divided equally between them.

Therefore, if you want to play a double stop at the same volume as a single stop, you have to use double the bow weight because it is divided between two strings. If you play three strings at the same time, you need three times the amount of weight.[1]

A simple experiment easily proves the principle. Sustain one note down-bow and up-bow. Play *forte* and look at the distance between the wood of the bow (in the middle of the bow) and the hair. Play at such a volume that you push the wood of the bow down about halfway towards the hair, and do not allow that distance to change as you move the bow up and down.

[1] Of course, describing it like this is only to illustrate the principle: with the left fingers causing the strings all to be different lengths, and with the different qualities of the strings, the weight will rarely be divided exactly equally between them.

Then without stopping, and keeping the bow-length and volume of the first note absolutely the same, add another note and continue as a double stop. Note how you are now pushing the wood of the bow nearly all the way down to the hair – and yet the first note will not have changed volume at all because the extra weight is divided between the two strings.

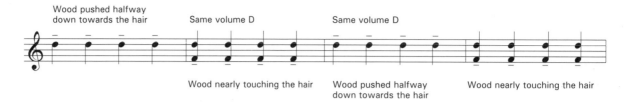

Try doing it the other way round: begin with the double stop, with the wood nearly touching the hair, and then keep everything the same as you play the single stop. You will get pure scratch.

But the amount of weight that the left fingers have to give, in order to stop the string sufficiently for a clean note, is the same whether you stop one note in the left hand or four notes.

Key point: Excess pressure stopping the strings, as an unconscious reaction to the extra weight in the bow, is one of the most common causes of left hand tension.

Excessive pressing in the left hand can be a reaction to holding down chords even when the bow is not playing heavily:

Example

Tartini-Kreisler: Variations on a theme by Corelli, *var. 1, b. 1*

As played in the left hand:

This passage can seem impossibly difficult to play in tune if the left fingers over-press. Instead, when the fingers remain almost as light as when playing harmonics, the passage immediately feels much easier because then the fingers can move quickly to each new position.

- Practise on the back of your hand, fingering the notes so lightly that the fingers tickle your skin rather than press.[1]

[1] See *Experiment on the back of your hand,* page 172

- Then find the same lightness when playing the passage.

Thirds

Thinking in intervals and tone-semitone patterns

There are three different tone-semitone patterns to think about with each third:

1 Is the third major or minor?

In the C major scale example above, the first third is major, the next is minor. The important thing to know is that when playing a major third as a double stop, the fingers are a minor third apart in spacing; playing a minor third as a double stop, the fingers are a major third apart in spacing.

Therefore a major third is a small distance or a narrow third; a minor third is a large distance or a wide third.

While playing one third, always be thinking ahead to identify the next third.

Shifting from 1–3 playing E–C to 1–3 playing G–E, the first finger shifts a minor third while the third finger shifts a major third, i.e. a shift from a small third to a large third:

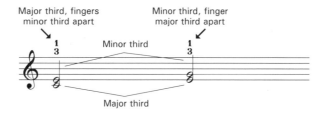

Think only of the finger that moves the bigger distance, and let the other finger 'look after itself'.

2 Moving from one third to another, is the distance between the fingers the same or not?

In the example above, in the first pair of thirds there is a semitone between the first finger and the second finger, but a tone between the third and fourth.

In the second pair the intervals are the other way round: a tone from 1–2 and semitone from 3–4. If the F were an F♯, the intervals would be equidistant, i.e. a tone from 1–2 and from 3–4.

3 What is the tone-semitone pattern of the four fingers together after playing 1–3, 2–4?

In the example above, if the fingers in the first pair of thirds were placed on the same string they would form the pattern semitone–tone–tone.

The second pair of thirds would form the pattern tone–tone–semitone.

Reaching back from the upper fingers

The most important thing about playing thirds and fingered octaves is that the hand be balanced on the third or fourth fingers, with the first and second fingers reaching back to their notes, rather than being based on the lower finger and having to stretch up to the third or fourth finger.

- Place the third finger on its own, without the first finger. Balance the hand to favour the third finger, so that it is naturally curved, relaxed and comfortable.

- Without altering the balance of the hand, or the shape of the third finger, reach back with the first finger and play the major or minor third.

- Playing 4–2, place the fourth finger on its own. Balance the hand to favour the fourth finger, so that it is curved, relaxed and comfortable. Then reach back with the second finger without affecting the balance of the hand, or the shape of the fourth finger (or affecting it as little as possible).

Practising the elements separately

Carl Flesch suggested that a simple approach to building good scale-playing in thirds is to take each of the three elements of thirds separately, and practise them on their own for one month each.

The three elements:

- Ascending, playing 1–3 then 2–4 (vertical dropping motion), or descending 2–4 then 1–3 (lifting motion)

- Shifting up on one string from 2–4 to 1–3 (or down from 1–3 to 2–4)

- Shifting from one pair of strings to another.

However, rather than practising only one element for a whole month, apply the same principle of separating the three elements but practise them all within one individual practice session:

- First practise finger-drops and lift-offs:

- Then practise shifts without string crossings:

- Practise string crossing shifts:

- Practise the three elements of fingered octaves in the same way.

Flow

There is a momentum in walking which provides a good image for playing a scale in double stops. There is no feeling of 'stop...stop...' as you place each foot. Instead, as each foot touches the ground you continue on, with a feeling of smooth flow and momentum, contact the ground with the next foot and continue on in the same flow.

In the same way, during a scale of thirds there needs to be a sense of carrying on moving towards the next third while the fingers are on the third that you are currently playing, rather than a feeling of getting 'stuck' on each.

Exercise

- Exaggerate the feeling of flowing into the next third by playing in a dotted rhythm.

- At the same time, release the string during the dotted note as though playing a harmonic (written as an x-note):

Mobility exercises

The essential thing in playing double stops is to keep the hand as soft and free as it is when playing the simplest single notes, i.e. as free as they are when you are not playing the violin.

Mobility exercises are good for discovering how to give and release, in the hand and fingers, while maintaining enough muscle-tone to play.

Exercise 1

Playing any double or triple stop, move the hand around while keeping the fingers in tune on the notes.

Even if there seems to be little movement possible, see how you can 'give' just a fraction more in each joint. Even the slightest extra freedom you gain feels enormous when you return to normal playing.

- Push the knuckles out, away from the neck of the violin, so that the fingers lengthen slightly, all the time keeping the notes in tune – or as in tune as possible.

- Pull the knuckles in, as though trying to make them touch the neck of the violin.

- Push the hand back, as though to flatten the notes, but keeping the fingers in tune.

- Pull the hand forward, as though to sharpen the notes, but keeping the fingers in tune.

- Move the hand in circles, clockwise and anticlockwise, giving in every joint and allowing every possible movement, however slight it is.

Exercise 2

- To gain more feeling of lightness and instantaneous adjustability, move the fingers above and below the correct tuning.

Play the first and third double stops in each bar in tune (as shown by the tick). The arrows represent moving the finger a quarter tone lower or higher. Where there is no arrow, play the double stop in tune:

When the arrow is above the stave, the lower finger does not move, and *vice versa*. When there are two arrows, move both fingers at the same time.

Fourths

Few violinists practise perfect fourths, perhaps because few scale books include them; yet they are a powerful tool for shaping the intonation of the entire hand.

Perfect fourths appear frequently in chord-playing, so the more used you are to playing them the less there is to practise when you play, say, unaccompanied Bach.

Once you get exercises in fourths well in tune, or play them in scales and broken thirds, they improve not only your feel for other double stops, but for ordinary single notes as well:

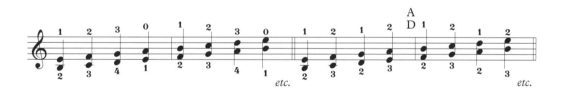

Broken fourths are particularly helpful in training the hand position so that the fingers do not lift too high but stay near the string; and in learning all the different tone-semitone patterns of the four fingers:

Perfect fifths

Perfect fifths are another double stop that are rarely included in scale books. It is helpful to practise them because individual fifths occur frequently in every kind of piece; they are a normal part of many three-string or four-string chords; and the fingers frequently stop perfect fifths during the normal course of playing.

Tuning the fifth

● Practise simple scales in low positions:

Key point: To tune a single stop note, you move the finger higher or lower on the string; to tune a perfect fifth you lean the finger more on to one string or more on to the other.

Leaning the finger more towards a string sharpens the note; leaning away from the string flattens it:

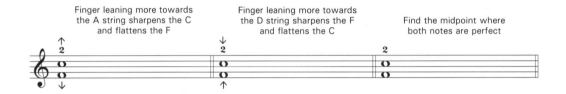

If, when the fifth is out of tune, you move the finger higher or lower instead of leaning it sideways one way or the other, both notes change by the same amount and the fifth remains out of tune.

Placing the fifth for single notes

Placing the fingers on the fifth, when playing single notes, requires a slightly different technique from playing them as a double stop.

Although the notes of these silent fifths are placed as a double stop, the hand (or finger) leans more towards one string and then more towards the other, as each note is played on its own.

If, while leaning the finger one way or the other, you were to play both strings as a double stop, the partially-stopped string would not sound properly.

Still, practising fifths as evenly-sustained, in-tune double stops improves this ability too.

Sixths

There are two chief problems in playing sixths:

1 Tuning major sixths

If you tune major sixths so that the third tone is in tune, in most cases they come out too narrow (either the lower note too sharp or the upper note too flat). Most of the time you have to play them deliberately 'out of tune'.[1]

[1] See *Ignoring the third tone*, page 92

2 Fingering consecutive sixths

There is no problem when you play sixths with separate bows. With good co-ordination – timing the exact end of one stroke, when the fingers can swiftly move to the next sixth, before the bow moves the other way – you can give an illusion of smooth connections in a run of separate-bow sixths.

The problem is in ascending, when a finger has to move across to the next string:

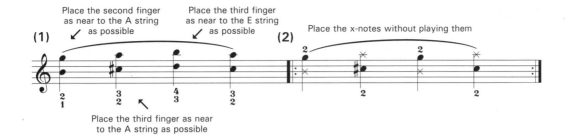

(1) Place the upper finger closer than normal to the lower string so that there is not so far to go.

Descending, place the third-finger D as close to the E string as possible.

(2) To practise, place all the fingers but play only the second finger and go backwards and forwards between the two notes.

Make the crossing from E string to A string, and back again, as smooth and seamless as possible.

The problem of moving the fingers across to the next string is naturally worse the higher up the string you play, as the strings get further apart. In most scale books the problem is solved, in the last octave of a scale of sixths, by playing consecutive 4–3 or 3–2, so that the fingers stay on the same string.

Octaves

Relaxing the hand rather than measuring

The fingers playing an octave are closer together the higher up the fingerboard you play; but playing octaves in tune is not a matter of somehow memorizing the exact distance between the fingers of one octave, and then memorizing the different distance between the fingers of the next octave, and so on.

What you have to do is simply keep the left hand and fingers entirely relaxed. If the hand is relaxed, it finds exactly the right distance between the notes automatically. Worry, and conscious trying, makes the hand tense, even if only imperceptibly, and then octaves can seem impossible to get right.

Remind yourself of the sensation of automatic self-correction by un-tuning the strings and seeing how the octaves feel then. Often they come out more in tune than when the strings are tuned properly, yet you have practised the passage on in-tune strings, and never before on out-of-tune strings.

Example   Wieniawski: Polonaise brillante, op. 21, b. 78

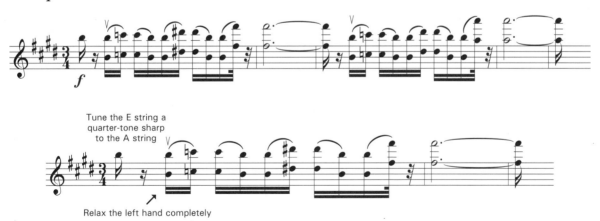

- Tune the E string a quarter tone (or so) sharp to the A string. Play the passage of octaves in your piece, or play an ordinary scale and arpeggio up the strings in octaves.

- Having found the first octave, make sure the hand and fingers are soft and relaxed and simply move from octave to octave. Hear in your mind the octave you are about to play, but consciously control the fingers as little as possible. Release the hand and let the fingers go to the exact, in-tune octave.

- Tune the E string a quarter tone or so flat to the A string, and repeat.

Having done this, you may be amazed at how well you play the octaves when the strings are tuned properly. Simply relax your hand, let the fingers find the notes, hear the octaves in tune in your mind before playing them, and listen. The octaves will seem to play themselves.

Experiment in the air

Another reason for simply letting the fingers find the octaves on their own is that as you go higher up the fingerboard the fingers naturally come closer together anyway:

- Without the violin, hold your left arm in playing position with your hand near your face. Relax the fingers so that they are naturally quite close together or touching.

- Stretch your arm out almost straight (as if going to first position on a very large viola). At the same time spread your fingers wide, as though playing octaves or ninths.

- Bring the hand back to near your face, and at the same time release the hand so that the fingers are close together again.

- Repeat several times.

- Then try doing it the other way round: see how unnatural it feels if you widen the hand and fingers as you come towards your face, and release them to a closed position as you extend.

Remembering to release, lengthen and widen

- Keep the fingers playing octaves light on the strings. The danger is that playing two strings, you press twice as hard. Keep a feeling of springiness in the strings by making sure you do not press them down to the fingerboard.[1]

- Release the left upper arm. The tendency of pulling it in slightly towards the body, and holding it there in a fixed and immoveable position, makes it difficult to have a soft and free left hand.

- When you come to a passage of octaves, feel your back getting longer, your chest widening and the violin flattening before you begin them.

[1] See *Light left hand in double stops*, page 307

Improving instantaneous adjustment

Improve instantaneous adjustment of intonation by practising flexibility or mobility exercises, which encourage the fingers to let go and respond more quickly.

The following example makes the fingers move along the string in contrary motion:

- This exercise is good for fingered octaves too, so practise three different fingerings: 4–1, 3–1, 4–2:

- Make sure the fingers are light on the string. Feel the springiness of the string, rather than pressing it hard into the fingerboard.

- Repeat the whole sequence on the D–A, and A–E strings.

- Repeat using quarter tones instead of semitones; then eighth tones.

Octaves: traditional practice method

- Play first one string on its own and then the other, with both fingers down throughout (as usual when practising double stops).

- Listen carefully to each note and repeat them separately as many times as necessary to be sure they are exactly the same.

Playing the lower note more loudly

There are several reasons why playing the lower note of an octave more loudly than the upper note is a helpful thing to do. First of all, if an octave is not perfectly in tune it sounds better the less audible the upper note. Even top international soloists can be heard almost to abandon the upper note altogether if a passage of octaves (particularly fingered octaves) does not come off well in performance.

Secondly, playing the lower note more loudly creates a particular colour consisting of a body of sound with a sheen on top. It is the same as when there is a passage in octaves in the orchestra – either between, say, first violins and second violins, or octaves divided at each stand between inside and outside players – when it is usual for those playing the lower note to play more loudly.

Thirdly, since the upper string in an octave is considerably shorter, played with the fourth finger, than the lower string played by the first finger, it cannot receive as much weight as the lower string anyway.[1]

[1] See *Bow-pressure and pitch*, page 84

Using scales and arpeggios

- As well as practising the actual notes of a specific passage, increase your overall skills in playing octaves by practising scales and arpeggios based on the notes of the passage.

   This can improve the passage much more than if you were to spend the same amount of time on the passage itself.

Example   Paganini: 24 Caprices, op. 1, no. 19, *b. 1*

- Practise a scale and arpeggio sequence beginning on B♭:

• Begin also on E♭:

• Practise the chromatic scale:

• Practise from the bottom up and from the top down:

• Repeat an octave lower on the G and D strings for the second two bars, using the fingering 1–3.

Fingered octaves

There are two issues that most players have to tackle in learning how to play fingered octaves:

1 Intonation

In fingered octaves, you have to play two extensions at the same time, i.e. the third and fourth fingers both reach up one note above their normal positions.

While the lower fingers try to pull these extended fingers down flat, they in turn try to pull the lower fingers up sharp.

2 Freedom of the hand

Flexibility and softness of the hand is the most important thing. In many players' minds, a tense and rigid left hand is inevitable if you try to play fingered octaves. Yet the muscular actions that expand the hand are one thing, and the actions to contract it (i.e. tense it) are another.[1]

[1] See *Expecting tension produces it*, page 172

Contracting the hand, while trying to expand it, is like trying to go forwards and backwards at the same time. Yet you can do one without the other. Your hand can remain as free and soft when playing fingered octaves as they are when you play single notes.

Exercises

Simple, gentle exercises help to increase the range of the hand:

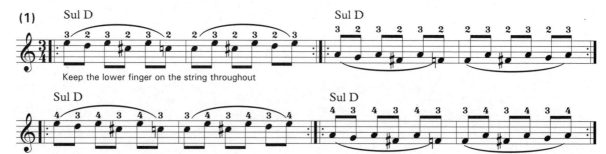

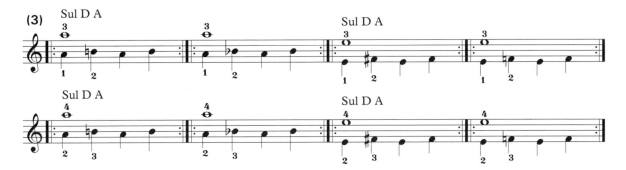

- In each bar keep the upper finger as upright as possible, i.e. vertical rather than leaning too much towards the scroll. At times it will lean towards the scroll whatever you do, and this will be natural and 'correct'. Simply try to keep it as upright as possible.

The part of the fingertip that contacts the string decides the angle of the finger. For the purposes of the exercise, try to position the upper finger as much on the right side of the fingertip as possible (looked at from the player's viewpoint), and the lower finger on the left side of the fingertip.[1]

[1] See *Fingertip placement: left, middle, right,* page 135

- It does not matter if you cannot stretch far enough for the wider distances. Never force. In exercises like these the benefits come from the trying – not from whatever the actual result is.

- Continually check that you are not over-pressing the strings. Keep the fingers as light as possible, so that a fraction less finger pressure would cause the sound to break.

- Also continually check that you are not contracting (tensing) the muscles of the hands and fingers, causing the them to feel tight and hard to the touch.

- If a bar such as the fourth of **(2)** seems difficult, try a few moments of freeing your wrist as described in *Manipulating the wrist* (page 184). You may be surprised at how much more easily you reach the notes.

To gain the feeling of lightness and freedom, practise the exercises using the back of your hand instead of the violin, with your fingers one side and the thumb the other. Make sure you do not press the thumb or the fingers hard into your left hand. Aim for a 'tickle-light' touch.[2]

[2] See *Experiment on the back of your hand,* page 172

Afterwards, playing the exercises on the violin, recapture the same feeling of lightness and ease.

- Practise the same patterns on each string.

Fingered seconds and harmonics

Fingered seconds or harmonics are an interesting alternative way to practise fingered octaves.

- Make sure you base the hand position on the upper finger, and reach back with the lower finger:

- Normally, the upper finger in harmonics may be quite straight; but for the purposes of the exercise, try playing with the sort of curved finger that you would have in fingered octaves:

etc.

Thinking in finger-spacing intervals

- As well as thinking of the aural distance of an interval, think of the two fingers as the same intervals they would be if both were playing single stops on one string:

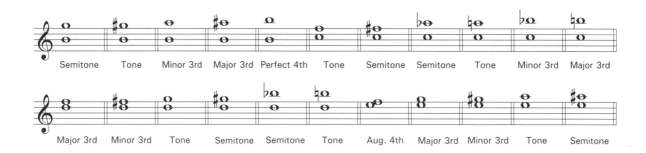

| Semitone | Tone | Minor 3rd | Major 3rd | Perfect 4th | Tone | Semitone | Semitone | Tone | Minor 3rd | Major 3rd |

| Major 3rd | Minor 3rd | Tone | Semitone | Semitone | Tone | Aug. 4th | Major 3rd | Minor 3rd | Tone | Semitone |

Notice the different balances in the bow depending on how close the fingers are to each other. The strings are the same length in a perfect fifth. In a minor sixth or augmented fourth, where the fingers are a semitone apart, the strings are almost the same length.

There is the most difference in octaves and tenths, where you have to play the shorter, upper string more gently than the lower string because it is much shorter.[1]

[1] See *Bow-pressure and pitch*, page 84

Tenths

For most players tenths in low positions – along with fingered octaves – are one of the big challenges in violin playing. It just seems impossible either to reach the upper note, or to play a tenth without the hand and fingers becoming rigid – especially if the hands are not wide across the knuckles.[2]

[2] The width of the hand across the knuckles is far more important than the size of the hand or the length of the fingers. You can easily have a 'large' hand with long fingers, but be narrow across the knuckles. This is a far less ideal hand for reaching notes and extending, and generally getting around the fingerboard, than a much smaller hand with shorter fingers, but which is wide across the knuckle joints.

You have more reach than you think

I have never known a single case of a student where, having established the apparent maximum distance the fourth finger seems to be able to reach in trying to play a tenth, I have not been able to coax another centimetre out of the finger and hand – usually to the player's surprise.

It is easy to do. The student should place their hand in third position:

- First, the student must relax their hand entirely. Go through the check-list: the thumb not too far back, and not squeezing at the base joint of the first finger; soft across the knuckle joints, soft in the palm of the hand; 'giving' at the wrist, free in the upper arm; not squeezing the violin between the chin and the shoulder.

- Then hold the fourth finger down on, say, C♯ on the D string (Fig. 150a). Make sure the finger is quite upright and curved. Gently keeping the fourth finger in place, slowly and gently move the first finger back to, say, an A on the G string (Fig. 150b). The student should take part in this, with you gently helping the fingers reach back rather than forcing them. Never force at any time.

Fig. 150

(a) Gently hold the fourth finger in position

(b) Gently encourage the fingers to reach back

- Then – very, very slowly – take your guiding fingers away. As you do so, the student can gradually take over fully, and see if they can keep the fingers in place on their own.

Reaching back

One of the keys to playing tenths is to position the hand to favour the fourth finger, and then to reach back with the first finger. Then the first finger naturally opens at the base joint, and there is no danger of clenching it together with the second finger.

Once you know the feeling of letting go between the first and second finger, you can just as easily extend forwards to a tenth.

Sliding exercise

It is easy to devise simple sliding-and-stretching exercises for tenths. For example:

Pizzicato

Pizzicato is usually the first thing you do as a beginner, but even professional players may find themselves uncomfortable in *pizzicato* passages. It is common for an otherwise fine professional orchestra suddenly to sound scrappy in a first rehearsal of the *pizzicato* movement of Benjamin Britten's *Simple Symphony*:

Britten: Simple Symphony, *mov. 2, b. 1*

Perhaps this is because we think of *pizzicato* as being easy, since it is something beginners can do, and therefore never practise it again once we have moved on to using the bow. Or perhaps the reason is that playing *pizzicato* can quickly make your fingers sore, so plucking is always kept to 'as little as possible'.

Trusting yourself to find the string

Fast *pizzicato*, rather like placing the bow on the string at the point to begin *p*, is an interesting test of your mental state. If you do not 'get in the way', and you simply let the plucking finger find the correct string by itself, the *pizzicato* is easy to play at the fastest speed:

If instead you get in the way and 'interfere', and try to find the right string to pluck, and try to pluck the right notes yourself, *pizzicato* can become impossible to do cleanly at great speed.

Should your right thumb rest on the fingerboard?

- Playing *pizzicato* at a slow to moderate tempo, the thumb can rest against the side edge or the corner of the fingerboard to support the hand.

  Playing individual *pizzicato* notes, with plenty of time between them, the thumb rests against the side of the fingerboard only before the *pizzicato*, and then leaves it as the note is plucked.

- In fast *pizzicato* it is often better to take your thumb off the corner of the fingerboard entirely, and pluck 'from the air'.

- Many players do not rest on the thumb, but pluck freely from above the string whatever the tempo. Some of the plucking movement then comes from the arm. In fast passages this can be much less tiring, since if the hand is stabilized on the thumb the finger has to do all the work on its own.

- The faster the tempo the closer the right finger must remain to the string, and this closeness must be maintained carefully. Bad ensemble in the *Simple Symphony* can often be cured by this alone, i.e. everybody keeping the plucking finger close to the string.

- Playing chords, the thumb is rarely used to support the hand, the hand making a guitar-like, sweeping movement. As Carl Flesch said, 'Such a movement not only produces well sounding vibrations, but also gives an impression of gracefulness.'[1]

[1] Carl Flesch: *The Art of Violin Playing* (New York, 1924), Vol. 1, 49.

What is the correct way to pluck the strings?

- Playing chords, the finger often plucks the strings diagonally, i.e. from left to right and forwards.

- For more power and less sweetness at the top of the chord, pluck more in the direction of straight across. For more power still, angle the pluck diagonally back in the direction of the bridge.

- Plucking more on the pad of the finger produces softer tones; more on the tip, harder tones.

- Playing single notes the direction need not be diagonal but is usually still from left to right, and never upward from below to avoid the string hitting the fingerboard. (Lifting the string so that it touches the fingerboard on the rebound is a special effect known as a 'Bartok' *pizzicato*.)

- Near the bridge, the string-tension is too hard to pluck (and you get rosin on your finger), and too far over the fingerboard the string is too weak.

- Find the right sound and feel of the pluck, by experimenting at different distances from the bridge like a soundpoint exercise:

How to practise *pizzicato*

- Practise *pizzicato* in the same ways you practise everything else, i.e. in groups, using rhythms and accents, speeding up with the metronome, plucking at different distances from the bridge, etc.

- Practise scales or arpeggios using *pizzicato*

- Practise studies like Kreutzer 2 or 8 using *pizzicato*.

- As a regular practice method, pluck a phrase or passage that is normally bowed. This makes the left finger clearer and firmer, and improves co-ordination. And frequent ten-second bursts of practising like this means you end up playing *pizzicato* far more often than you otherwise might.

[2] Why does an open string ring so much, compared with a stopped note? It is only because the open string is stopped perfectly at each end by the nut and by the bridge, but imperfectly by the finger.

With the violin on your lap, and while being careful not to damage the string (perhaps wait until just before putting a new string on anyway), try stopping the string with the side of a pencil or other hard object. See how any note then rings like an open string.

The one time you need to press the left fingers hard

Pizzicato is one of the few times when the harder the left fingers press the string, the better.[2]

Normally, playing with the bow, too much finger pressure can make the tone sound hard and brittle, and also causes tension in the left hand. The best amount of finger pressure is usually as little as possible – just enough to stop the note cleanly.

Playing *pizzicato*, the finger needs to stop the string hard so that each note rings on like an open string. Suzuki called this ring 'the true sound of the string'. Of course, when the *pizzicato* needs to be quiet, or dry, the left finger can release the string a little to prevent the note from ringing or to create a different colour.

● Experiment with different finger-pressures:

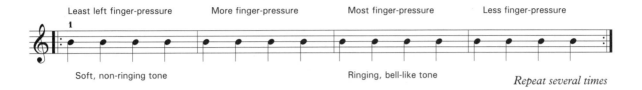

Placing the left fingers in time before plucking

It is easy for the right-hand finger to play a *pizzicato* chord, but the left fingers may need time to find their places on the string. They must be placed quickly enough to be ready before the finger plucks.

One of the most important things is to think ahead: it is often impossible to place the fingers in time unless you are thinking about the next chord while playing the previous chord.

Think of placing the fingers for the next chord as the final action of playing the previous chord:

● Play the first chord – instantly place the fingers ready for the next chord. (Play–place.)

Instead of: Place the fingers – play. Place the next fingers – play, and so on. (Place–play.)

Example 1

Sarasate: Zigeunerweisen, op. 20 no. 1, *b. 98*

● Practising by exaggeration, prepare both hands for the next chord earlier than necessary:

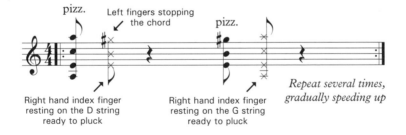

The x-notes show the left fingers on the strings, with the right hand ready to pluck the chord.

● Play strictly in time, placing the second chord on the string exactly on the second quaver beat.

● Begin slowly, and gradually speed up to the correct tempo for the passage.

Example 2

Brahms: Sonata no. 2 in A, op. 100, *mov. 2, b. 162*

- Practise with a feeling of syncopation, beginning at a slow tempo and gradually speeding up to as fast a tempo as possible:

Coming back for the next chord as part of the last

When you play a group of *pizzicato* chords (or notes), at the end of each pluck the right hand should finish up where it started: the hand continues in a circular movement, in the air, back to the heel:

- Play the first chord and in the same motion return in the air to the starting place. Wait.

- Play the next chord and return, and so on. (Play–return – wait – play–return – wait.)

- Instead of: Play the first chord. Wait. Return to the starting place and play the next chord. (Play – wait – return–and–play – wait.)

Miming

To exaggerate the timing, practise the plucking motion in the air without actually touching the strings:

(1) Get ready with your finger above the strings, as if about to play a chord.

(2) Make a sudden, fast movement away from the strings (in exactly the same direction and shape as you will move when you play the chord) and then move back again to the starting place.

Feel the movement away from the strings, and back again, as one movement: away-and-back, not away and then back.

Try to move so fast that if someone blinked at that moment they would miss it: your finger is hovering above the strings, there is a flash of movement, and the finger is back where it started.

Vibrato

It is easy to forget to vibrate *pizzicato*, yet the difference it makes can be extraordinary – especially when an ensemble plays large, ringing chords, or in a melodic solo line:

Brahms: Sonata no. 2 in A, op. 100, *mov. 2, b. 162*

An outline of mental rehearsal

Performers in a wide range of different occupations use deliberate, conscious, mental rehearsal. The following is an outline of some of the important principles.

There are four major areas where mental rehearsal can be extraordinarily powerful:

- Building technique
- Curing nerves
- Discovering deeper musicality
- Finding greater physical freedom

Mental rehearsal uses exactly the same simple mental picturing that we all do naturally from moment to moment in normal daily life, but in mental rehearsal you do it deliberately and consciously. You construct complex and detailed inner pictures, methodically building, crafting and shaping them as precisely as if you were building something brick by brick in the material world. It is just like going off into a day-dream, but one where you are entirely in control of the images: you build pictures of the perfect result, the perfect outcome, in minute detail, including and excluding whatever you like.

Mental rehearsal is not simply a matter of thinking positively. Suppose I have a performance to give tomorrow for which I am not sufficiently prepared. There are many passages that I am not completely sure of, or that I can play well only once or twice out of every ten attempts; I do not know the score well; many notes remain out of tune; my memory is not reliable, and so on.

'Positive thinking' means saying to myself again and again: 'It is going to go well, it is going to go well…' Unfortunately it may not go well at all. Instead, mental rehearsal means to picture yourself playing note by note, finger by finger, bow stroke by bow stroke. Golf champion Jack Nicklaus described how he uses mental rehearsal:

> I never hit a shot, even in practice, without having a very sharp, in-focus picture of it in my head. It's like a color movie. First I 'see' the ball where I want it to finish, nice and white and sitting up high on the bright green grass. Then the scene quickly changes, and I 'see' the ball going there: its path, trajectory, and shape, even its behavior on landing. Then there's a sort of fade-out, and the next scene shows me making the kind of swing that will turn the previous images into reality. Only at the end of this short, private Hollywood spectacular do I select a club and step up to the ball.

In the beginning of visualising playing something, you may keep getting stuck. You may be able to play, mentally, only a few notes at a time, before hesitating, or before finding a phrase – or a bowing or fingering – that is completely blank in your mind.

This is the quickest way to discover the areas you need to strengthen the most. Once you can visualise an entire piece note by note, without hesitation, you never worry about your memory any more when playing the piece. It is in the places where you hesitate in your mental rehearsal, wondering what the next notes, bowings or fingerings are, where you are most likely to have memory slips in your actual playing.

Mental rehearsal corrects problems which have consistently occurred each time you put bow to string in the past. It is striking how, when you visualise playing a note that typically feels tense whenever you play it, your finger or hand tenses up in exactly the same way when you picture it without the violin.

The benefits of visualising yourself playing that note with a relaxed hand or finger are obvious, since when you are mentally picturing yourself playing you are accessing the same 'data-bank' or 'program' that drives your playing when the actual violin is under your chin.

Changing the 'program' through mental rehearsal is exactly the same as changing it through practising. When you are practising you run a series of pictures through your mind as you play, and it is the changing of those pictures that changes the way you play; but accessing the 'inner operating system' through mental rehearsal goes straight to the heart of the matter with the most amazing ease and speed compared with the experience of actually playing.

You quickly discover, in trying to visualise the emotional or dramatic content of each phrase, the places where you have not yet got far in really understanding the music, or really and truly knowing what – and how exactly – you want to play.

When you return to practising with the actual instrument, you may be astonished at how improved it is. You feel as warmed-up and technically secure as if you had already been playing all day, even if you have not touched the instrument. Your memory will be infinitely more secure. Where you had visualised your hand feeling freer, it will feel freer when you now play the phrase on the violin.

Once players have discovered the power, ease and effectiveness of mental rehearsal, they may start to spend every available free moment running their piece through their mind, when working up towards a performance. Their available 'practice time' each day therefore suddenly increases by many hours.

Conquering nerves

One of the greatest applications of mental rehearsal is in eliminating stage-fright. The German violinist Anne-Sophie Mutter has said that she has never experienced stage-fright. She knows what it is because she has seen it in others or heard about it – but she has never ever felt it herself.

What this must mean is that she holds no images in her mind of self-doubt or fear of any sort at all, and therefore her autonomic nervous system does not produce the symptoms of 'flight or fight'. Her mind must be broadcasting non-stop images of the desired result in all respects of the performance. There is no room left in her mind for negative, distracting and energy-consuming thoughts that then detract from the playing, or spoil it.

If you do suffer from stage-fright, or from the fear of suffering from it, mental rehearsal is the water that can quickly put the flames out.

Suppose in everyday playing your bow is always smooth and even, and you are worried that it may shake in performance: picture yourself in the performance situation and see the bow being absolutely steady, smooth and comfortable; picture the shoulder and arm balanced and free of tension or obstruction, and so on.

If you build these pictures in enough detail, and for long enough, until you are able to summon them up all in one go and can have all the detail in your mind in an instant – and if you fill your mind with these pictures to the extent that you crowd out all other thoughts – then these results will be the ones you get.

You already rehearse mentally

It is not a question of beginning to rehearse mentally: you are doing it all the time anyway. Every time you think of an approaching performance – that concert, examination or audition coming up – you hold a picture of it in your mind. For an instant, or for several seconds at a time, but on many occasions over and over again, you imagine yourself in performance.

The question is: what are the images that you are returning to over and over again? Are they images of an outcome you want, or images of what you do not want?

When you think of yourself being anxious, or worry about losing your memory, or worry about the audience's reaction, or think of that shift you might miss at the bottom of the second page, or of that place near the end of the piece where your hand feels so tight, you hold a picture of each of these things in your mind.

It is easy to gain control of each of these moments of natural mental rehearsal. You simply say 'no' to the images that you do not want, and you do not allow them into your mind. At the same time you construct better ones – of freedom, enjoyment, flow, ease and confidence.

Filling your mind with the perfect result

When something is not working, or there is something you want to improve, the trap to avoid is that you fill most of your consciousness with what is actually happening – i.e. you fill your mind with pictures of the problem or difficulty – but give only a fraction of your consciousness to the picture of the better result that you would like.

It should be the other way round, so that you focus most of your attention on the inner picture of the perfect musical (or technical) result you are after. You do not need much of your available consciousness left over to be keenly aware of everything that is actually happening.

I made an important discovery one day when I was practising up-bow staccato, a stroke I had never played well. I was playing the run from the Wieniawski *A major Polonaise* over and over again:

Wieniawski: Polonaise brillante, op. 21, *b. 23*

None of the attempts was really successful, as on countless other occasions of my practising staccato over the years.

Then I suddenly realised that although I was concentrating and aware of every detail of what was happening in the bow, bow-hair, and left fingers, at the same time I didn't actually know what I really wanted. It was as though 95% of my attention was taken up with being conscious of what was actually happening in the bow and the fingers, with only 5% given to picturing the exact result I was wanting. My picture of what I wanted was actually rather blurred, fuzzy, and indistinct.

I shifted the balance from 95/5 to 5/95 – i.e. filled my mind almost entirely with clear images of what I actually wanted, in the precise detail of the bow-hair dancing along the string. The instantaneous improvement, from the run being rarely successful to it working well nearly every time, was astounding.

Key point: If you are reacting to what is already happening, it must mean that you reacting after the event. If instead most of your attention is given to picturing what you want, you are working before the event.

Seeing what you want

Without the violin, imagine playing fourth-finger D on the G string, and holding it down while playing first-finger E on the D string.

Then imagine the same, but this time an E♭:

There is a slight degree of pulling the first finger back to play the E♭, compared with playing the E♮.

● Wait! In your picture of pulling the first finger back to play the E♭, did you picture the finger feeling tense in the base joint?

● Stop! Replace the picture of the tense finger with a picture of it being utterly free and effortless in the base joint.

You may be amazed at how much freer it feels when you next come to play it.

Exactly the same applies to vibrato, trilling, shifting, tone production, and anything else you can think of in violin playing. Whatever result you are getting in your playing is always matched by a mental picture of it. Think about your playing, and that picture is the one you will see. Change that picture, and the result changes with it.[1]

Therefore 'practice' does not have to include putting the bow on the string. If you mentally rehearse in a focused and constructive way for one hour while sitting in the park, and actually practise the violin for three hours, you can tell yourself afterwards that you have done four hours' work.

Understanding the effect your mind has on your body

One key aspect of Mental Rehearsal is the powerful effect the conscious mind has on the body.

Your conscious mind can assess, reason and make decisions; your subconscious mind, or your autonomic nervous system, cannot. The subconscious can say only 'yes' to anything held in the conscious mind.

Your subconscious mind cannot tell the difference between something that you vividly imagine – such as a goal, a hope or a dream – and a real experience.

Imagine you are in the kitchen. You take a fresh lemon from the fruit bowl. It is cool in your hand. The yellow, dimpled skin feels smooth and waxy. It comes to a small, green, conical point at either end. The lemon is firm and quite heavy for its size as you look at it in the palm of your hand.

You raise the lemon to your nose. It gives off such a characteristic, unmistakable citrus smell, doesn't it?

You take a sharp knife and cut the lemon in half. The two halves fall apart, the white pulpy outer skin contrasting with the drops of pale, lemon-coloured juice that gently ooze out. You raise the lemon towards your mouth. The lemon smell is now slightly stronger.

Now you bite deeply into the lemon and let the juice swirl around your mouth. That sharp, sour lemon flavour is unmistakable.

Stop a minute! Is your mouth watering? Almost everyone's does. And yet the extraordinary thing is that if we had simply instructed you to "make your mouth water," you couldn't have done it.

The "imagery" worked because your emotional middle brain does not distinguish between experiences that actually occur out there in the "real" world, and experiences you imagine vividly in your head.

You can use this fact to "program" your emotional brain to believe very strongly in your success. It is important to do this programming – because it is frightening how quickly and unnecessarily we create self-doubts and self-limits.[2]

Present tense, personal, positive

Because the unconscious can say only 'yes' to whatever pictures are held (with belief) in the conscious mind, the only 'language' that the unconscious can understand is made of phrases couched in the present tense, in the personal, and in the positive.

If you say to yourself, 'I must relax,' or 'I must not be tense,' it has little or no effect on your state. If instead you say to yourself, 'I am relaxed, I feel terrific, I find everything easy' – and if you hold these thoughts in your mind clearly, and with emotion and belief – the results come almost immediately.

It makes no difference if, when your left hand feels as though it could be softer, freer and more relaxed, you say to yourself, 'It should be relaxed.'

Instead, if you picture your hand being in its most perfect state and proceed as if it is already true, you will find that the change happens by itself and your hand immediately feels better.

The same applies to improving almost anything. Suppose you want to improve your focus and concentration. If you say to yourself, 'I must try harder to concentrate,' it does not help. If instead you say, 'I am very good at concentrating, I concentrate well,' the concentration immediately comes.

[1] See *What is vibrato?*, page 225; *What is a trill?*, page 225

[2] Colin Rose: *Accelerated learning* (Topaz Publishing Ltd., 1985), 75.

Notes about practice

Moving up one level at a time

It is said that whoever you are and whatever you do, whether you are a musician or something else, there will always be four levels to your work: you will always be excellent in some aspects of your work, good at some aspects, mediocre at some and poor at some.

The same applies to your overall technique, or your playing of a particular piece. When you want to improve individual elements of your technique, or phrases or passages of a piece, it may sometimes seem difficult or daunting if you try to make all the poor areas excellent.

But it is often easy enough to improve the good areas until they are excellent; not too difficult to get the mediocre areas better until they are good; and quite easy to improve the areas that are downright poor until they are at least mediocre.

This approach, of concentrating only on moving each component of technique up just one level, is one of the fastest and most comfortable ways to improve playing.

What to practise

The main categories of daily practice are exercises, scales, studies and pieces.

Exercises

During a television interview Steve Cram, an Olympic Gold Medal-winning British running champion, was asked to describe the sort of training he regularly underwent in preparing for races.

He explained that a typical day might be spent first at the gym, lifting weights and using leg-strengthening machines and other mechanical aids, and doing push-ups and other strenuous work-outs. Then he might go to a forty-floor office block and run up the fire escape to the top of the building, down again, up again, and so on for a few hours. Then he might go out for a thirty-mile run. And all that in one day. He might repeat a day like that many times each week, and for months on end, just to prepare for one important race. That was not quite what he said, but it was something like that.

Then the interviewer asked him: "But now that you are winning gold medals and setting new records – now that you are so good – doesn't this mean you can ease up a little on this extraordinarily difficult and demanding training schedule?"

'No, of course not,' answered Cram, 'I have to carry on doing whatever I did that brought me to this level, in order to stay at this level!'

Many players avoid exercises because all they want to do is to play music. An athlete wants to run races, not run up and down the fire stairs of an office block. Yet the benefits are dramatic and obvious.

Building technique: finding new sensations of playing

Another word that could be used in place of 'practice' is 'experiment'. When we are practising we are experimenting to find the exact musical result that we are after; and at the same time instinctively looking for the easiest, most comfortable and least effortful way of getting it.[1]

[1] See *Homeostasis: the 'wrong' things may be 'right'*, page 196

When we are practising exercises we discover new sensations in the hands and fingers, new ways of reaching for a note or of widening the hand; new tonal colours, vibratos, new satisfying sensations in the bow and in the bow hand, and so on.

Afterwards, when playing music, you have to forget (almost) about all these things and 'just play'. Otherwise, too much conscious technical control gets in the way of actually making music.

 But what is the point of getting things right in the technical practice, and then getting them all wrong again the moment you start playing pieces? Isn't that two steps forward and two steps back?

Because of the instinctive search for ease and comfort, there is no need to worry about losing, during the musical playing, whatever you have gained in the technical work. The new sensations gradually 'seep' into your playing without you having to think about them.

In the technical work you discover more choices about how you can go about things, and it is only natural that over time you begin unknowingly to select these new physical sensations whenever they are called for. It takes only a short time for them to become part of your playing.

So the beauty of practising Basics-type exercises is that you can forget about them after doing them, and simply concentrate on the music, and the new or refined techniques will begin to appear by themselves in your playing.

Investing your time

Technical exercises save infinitely more time than they take to practise. Just a few short sessions each week, on a regular basis, brings fast results which improves all of your playing.

Like money, time can be 'spent' as an investment so that in the end you gain much more than you spent in the first place. A small investment of time in, say, one of the *Two essential intonation exercises* (page 73), saves much more time later on: when the exercise is 'in your fingers' it feels as if your whole hand is in tune and you can play anything with good intonation without first having to practise it.

If, say, you regularly spend a little time playing shifting, intonation or tone exercises, all of your playing gains in security and confidence, and it then takes far less time to master any particular passage.[1]

Varying the material

Build a library of technical books by a variety of composers, teachers and players, sometimes using one, sometimes another.

You never have to practise these books in order from cover to cover, front to back. Choose whatever looks relevant or interesting at the time. All that matters is that you keep a record of everything you practise. Tick every section, line or bar you work on. A tick does not have to mean that it is 'perfect'; only that you have looked at it and taken a few steps forward.

Unless you mark what you have practised, you cannot skip around out of sequence without losing track of what you have already done. The feeling that 'there is so much of this …I know I've done odd bits of it before, but I cannot remember what…I'll have to start from the beginning again' is discouraging.

Using ticks, you can start and finish wherever you like, and can leave it for weeks or months and still come back to it knowing exactly where you were. It is also a real motivation-builder to watch your ticks building up over a period of time.

Scales and studies

Practise scales with all sorts of different fingerings, on single strings, across the strings in one position starting on each finger, using the whole range of octaves, and in different bowing and rhythm patterns.

Studies offer a simple, step-by-step, ordered way to build technique, often by concentrating on one aspect of playing at a time. The 42 Kreutzer *Etudes* and 24 Rode *Caprices* remain as much the basis of modern violin technique as they were when they were first written.

Logical order of study

Progress through the studies over the years in a logical order of increasing difficulty. For example:

1	Hans Sitt	**6**	Fiorillo	**11**	Gavinies
2	Wohlfahrt	**7**	Dont op. 37	**12**	Wieniawski, L'Ecole moderne op.10
3	Kayser	**8**	Kreutzer	**13**	Paganini *Caprices*
4	Dancla	**9**	Rode		
5	Mazas	**10**	Dont op. 35		

There cannot be any one 'correct' order. Some of the Dont op. 37, which are meant to be preliminary to the Kreutzer etudes, are more demanding than the Kreutzer themselves; some of the Kreutzer are more demanding than some of the Dont op. 35; some of the Paganini are simpler than some of the Wieniawski. Use variations of this ladder as a general background, and at the same time 'skip around' from book to book and select different studies to suit the needs of the moment.

It is usually best not to try to get to the top of the technique ladder by taking large jumps. Many students play only a few Kreutzer etudes over the years, a couple of Rode caprices, one or two from Dont op. 35; and then try to play Paganini.

Instead, climb the ladder rung by rung. The best plan is to learn all the Kreutzer (following all the work that leads up to them), and then all the Rode. After that, once you are halfway through the Dont op. 35, and the Gavinies and Wieniawski, you will already be very high up the ladder and can go from there to anywhere.

Return to them frequently over the years. Working afresh on studies you have learnt before is another useful part of the week's work, and you can gain more and more from them each time.

[1] These, or the *Five essential tone-production exercises (page 11)*, or *Basics* exercises for vibrato, substitutions, string crossing and all the rest, can be likened to depositing money in a bank at an interest rate of 100%.

Most people, if they knew of a bank account that paid that amount of interest, would search for every last penny they could find to deposit. Once a player experiences the instant rewards of these exercises, they often begin to search for every last extra minute that they can find to practise them

Some other ways of spending time as an investment include attending concerts; reading about music, violinists, teachers and technique; watching videos and listening to recordings; attending masterclasses and taking lessons; and doing something else altogether, i.e. sport, yoga, Tai Chi, archery and so on, from which you can draw parallels to violin playing and learn in entirely new ways and from new points of view.

Relearning elementary studies

From time to time, more-advanced players should relearn simple studies by Wohlfahrt or Kayser, and set themselves the challenge of playing them perfectly.

At first glance you might think that a little 1st-position study in G major, with elementary bowing patterns, is too easy for you. But can you score a perfect 10-out-of-10 in each of the headings of pitch, sound, rhythm, and ease?

If you had studied with Pierre de Sales Baillot in France in the early 1800s, he would have told you to perform the following check, after tuning and before beginning to play:

1	The feet	**5**	The arms and elbows
2	The body	**6**	The hands and fingers
3	The violin	**7**	The head
4	The bow	**8**	The whole posture without stiffness

Can you keep all of these 'perfect' throughout playing an elementary study – as well as playing every note in tune, every note singing and without blemish, and with perfect rhythm? Not every violinist who can play advanced, technically-demanding pieces can answer yes to this, which means that the elementary study is not actually 'too easy' for them.[1]

[1] See also Starting from the point of complete security, page 105

The benefits you will find when you then return to your usual repertoire will be striking. Working like this is also extremely confidence-building, since you always know at the back of your mind that the foundations of your playing are not only solid but constantly being maintained.

Pieces

Ivan Galamian divided practising pieces into three parts:

- Building-time
- Interpreting-time
- Performing-time

Building-time is all the work of taking passages apart, playing slowly, playing in rhythms, gradually speeding a passage up with the metronome, and so on.

Interpreting-time is the work on structure, phrasing, dynamics, shaping, expression, and so on.

Performing-time is when you play through as if in a concert.

Playing through old repertoire

When I was a student I used to envy the way pianists so often seemed to spend so much time actually playing music – in contrast to being a violinist, where it seemed that you had to spend most of your practice learning how to play whatever single piece you were studying at the time; and little time actually just playing.

You would practise individual notes and rhythms, shifts, bow strokes and so on, up to a performance, with most of the actual playing-through and rehearsing usually close to the performance date; and after the performance date that would be the end of it, unless some other chance to play the piece arose.

Pianists, on the other hand, always seemed to be *playing*, with much less time spent doing the equivalent of practising shifts, intonation, bow strokes, and so on. Of course they do concentrated, over-and-over-again work too, and may spend hours mastering individual phrases or passages; and two pianists playing the same notes on the same piano may easily sound completely different from one another; but the difference between the violin and the piano remains – i.e. on the piano the notes are almost already there for you, but on a string instrument the notes have to be created 'out of nothing'.

It took me some years before I realised that relearning old repertoire is another important part of daily practice, and that by doing it we end up enjoying the same advantages as a pianist. We just *play*.

- At the same time as learning your current new repertoire, continually relearn all your previous pieces on a rotating basis, i.e. piece number one in week number one, piece number two in week number two, and so on until covering everything you have ever played. Then go back to the first piece and cycle through again.

- Practise one or two passages for a few minutes if you like, but basically just play through, enjoy the music and enjoy playing, and get the feel of it. Do this with concertos, sonatas, short pieces, everything important that you have learnt.

The feeling of being at home with a whole repertoire, instead of just one piece at a time, gives you confidence; and regular practice of already-familiar music greatly improves your overall command as a musician and instrumentalist.

When you have finished learning your current piece you can add it to the rotation list; and then move on and focus on your next new piece.

One hour like this each week soon adds up, and over just a couple of months you may be able to rotate your repertoire several times.

- Suppose you have learnt 10 concertos, 10 sonatas and 10 short pieces. (This would be a small repertoire for a professional soloist, but a much larger one than most players command.)

- Suppose the concertos and sonatas averaged 30 minutes each, and the short pieces 10 minutes each.

- The total running time of all the pieces together is just under 11 hours.

- So if you spent one hour each week on old repertoire it would take only 11 weeks to play all of it, and you could do this four times a year.

So with a much smaller total repertoire than that, it is even easier to rotate all of it in quite a short time.

Listening to recordings

Listening to recordings is sometimes seen as an unimaginative or untalented way to get to know a piece of music.

It is always interesting to learn a new piece uninfluenced by any previous encounter with it, having never heard it at a concert or on a recording, and to be able to approach it with a completely fresh mind. Even if you are going to listen to somebody else play it eventually, it is often best to wait and see what you make of the piece yourself first.

However, in principle there is no difference between listening to a recording and listening to a live concert, or listening to a teacher demonstrating in a lesson. Either way you are taking in someone else's ideas; and that can only expand your horizons, not narrow them.

Go to concerts and then do it yourself

I often remember Dorothy DeLay asking me if I had been to a recent Itzhak Perlman recital at Carnegie Hall. No, I said, I hadn't even known about it. When was it, I asked.

She was not impressed. Urging me to go to more concerts, she explained that the model to follow was a fabulous Russian student of hers who would always go to hear 'everybody who was anybody'.

Apparently, if he heard a single colour that he knew was not part of his normal tonal range – or a particular quality of vibrato that he knew was not part of his vibrato 'palette'; or a particular way of playing, say, a passage of chords, or other musical or violinistic effect, that he knew he had never tried – he would go straight home after the concert, pick up the violin, and not stop working at it until he too could make that sound, or vibrato, or whatever the quality was that he had heard.

You can approach recordings in exactly the same way. You hear a tone, or an expressive vibrato, that you know is outside your current range. Practise until you can do it too.

The criticism of this is that it is 'just copying'. Yet it is interesting how, whatever you do, it 'comes out' like you even if you do try to 'copy'. Some time later you hear the recording again and realise that you are nowhere near playing the phrase in the same way. Playing the same as someone else is not such an easy thing to do.

When Yehudi Menuhin was 17 or 18 he set himself the challenge of trying to copy Kreisler's own recording of *Caprice Viennois*:

Kreisler: Caprice Viennois, op. 2, b. 21

dolce con vibrato

He wanted to see if he could learn to play it exactly the same as Kreisler, sound for sound and phrase for phrase. He put the needle down on the record and listened to a phrase, then played it on the violin, then listened again, played it again, and so on, over and over again.

Improving listening

Listening carefully to recordings stimulates your musical imagination and improves your listening. Listen to the same phrase or passage many times, as Menuhin did:

- Listen only to the vibrato. Focus only on the width of the vibrato, then listen again only for the speed of vibrato.

- Play the same phrase again and listen only for evenness of tone.

- Play the same phrase again and listen only for intonation: focus only on the ♯'s and ♭'s, seeing how expressively high or low they are; then listen only for the musical phrasing or colouring; then listen only to the bow changes; and so on

Timing and planning

Practice which is planned in advance can be much more productive than practising at random.

- Before starting, decide how long you are going to practise in total.

- Then decide how many minutes you will give each part of your practice – exercises, scales, studies and pieces.

- Then plan what you will do in each category.

- Planning your practice of a piece, think of all the key areas you want to improve (an area can be one or two notes, a phrase or a whole passage).

  Is the improvement to be made in the left hand or the right? Is it a question of pitch, of sound, of rhythm, or of physical freedom? Do you want to work on co-ordination, or a particular type of stroke, or type of vibrato?.

- Decide how you want to practise to make the improvement, e.g. 'top of page 2, rhythm practice, fifteen minutes'.

You can do all this without pen and paper. But if you plan your practice on paper just once, it helps you to become systematic and organised, whether afterwards you do it on paper or not.

Structuring the practice

Begin by playing through the piece from beginning to end.

1 Make a list of every important group, phrase, or passage that you want to practise.

2 Divide the list into A, B and C:

    A   The passages that need most practice (worst)

    B   Medium

    C   The passages that need least practice (best).

3 Then take all the items from the 'A' list and divide them into A1, A2, A3.

    A1   Passages that are least fluent (worst of the worst)

    A2   Medium

    A3   Passages that are most playable (best of the worst)

4 Then take the first item from A1 and make a list of the details you want to improve, i.e. intonation, tone, rhythm, co-ordination, shifting, clarity, speed, ease of playing, memory, and so on.

At times of urgent practice, work on A1 areas before anything else. At other times, you can alternate working on A1 areas with work on B or C areas.

Again, writing this down on paper may be something to do only once and never again. But afterwards your approach to any practice session will be naturally more organised.

Concentrating on one thing at a time

At certain stages of practice, you can work on many different aspects of technique and interpretation all at the same time; at other times it may be best to concentrate on only one aspect at one time.

When a student of the Russian violin teacher Yuri Yankelevich was playing an important concert or competition, close to the event Yankelevich would stop teaching everyone else and give that particular student all-day lessons for a few days.

On the first day Yankelevich would say, "Today is day-of-intonation. Of course you play well in tune; but every note *could* be out of tune – so we must check each one. If anything else comes up, such as bowing or fingering or phrasing etc., we can look at it; but the main focus will be on intonation."

On the next day: "Today is day-of-sound. Of course everything you play is beautiful, expressive and correct, but any bow stroke *could* need to be improved, so we must check each one. If anything else comes up, we can look at it, but the main subject is sound."

And so it would continue with day-of-vibrato, day-of-rhythm, day-of-shifting, and so on.

Apply this approach to ordinary practice. You can work all the way through an entire piece concentrating only on intonation, or working only on sound, and so on. Some typical headings:

- Intonation: checking every GDAE with the open string; every ♯ and ♭ relative to the natural above or below, etc.

- Sound: choosing certain types of notes to practise (e.g. long notes in high positions; or fast, separate bow passages; or certain slow bows or double stops), and working on them one at a time – in each place that they occur throughout the piece – by experimenting with the proportions of speed–pressure–soundpoint.

- Rhythm: practising sometimes with a metronome to check or tighten rhythm. Return to musical rhythm afterwards but with the metronomic rhythm as a basis.

- Smooth bowing: practising every passage by bowing on one string while fingering on another[1]

- Bow tilt: checking that the amount of hair is suitable for the dynamic

- Left hand position: checking every phrase to see that the hand is neither too low nor too high

- Relaxation of the left thumb and minimum finger-pressure

- When to keep fingers down on the strings and when to lift them

- The speed of the finger movement (as opposed to the speed of the passage)

- Co-ordination

- Finger preparation

- Speed and width of vibrato, and which part of the fingertip

- Dynamics

- Phrasing

- Holding the violin up so that the strings are level with the floor

[1] See *True-legato warm-up exercise*, page 261

First study, second study, third study

'First study' means the first time you learn a piece, 'second study' the second time, and so on. Whenever possible, any important performance should be of pieces that are at least third or fourth study.

It often happens that students learn a new piece up to the date of the concert, audition or examination, and then walk on stage and perform it. Then afterwards, they say that they cannot understand why it all felt so difficult, when everything had seemed okay the day before.

Often, the simple reason why they were not so comfortable is that they had not got their playing to the stage where they did not have to think about it. They had got it only to the stage where, by concentrating hard, and remembering all the things they had to do to get round each phrase or passage, they could get through the piece well enough.

But when we are under pressure it is often difficult to think fast, or sometimes even to think at all. The remembering and self-instructing – that the performance depended on – completely stops. Then the player feels out of control because the piece is not at the stage where the hands carry on playing by themselves.

This type of preparation is similar to the way many stores order the goods they sell. Anything perishable needs to be obtained and supplied just before the customer wants it, and this is called 'just-in-time-delivery'.

Vintage wine

Instead, suppose you learn a piece (first study), play it in a lesson or two, and then leave it for some weeks or months. Then you relearn it (second study), perhaps now playing it with the piano.

Already you notice that all kinds of passages that tripped you up, or you never managed to play to your satisfaction, now feel easy and natural, and you no longer have to think about them. Now they 'play themselves'. Then you stop working on the piece again.

Some weeks or months later you relearn it again (third study), rehearse with the piano, play it in a lesson, and then perhaps perform it in an informal concert in front of half-a-dozen people.

Then you perform it in your important concert. This is like wine maturing in the cellar, as opposed to just-in-time-delivery.

When the shoe fits

When you have only recently finished learning a piece and play it through for the first few times, you may be too aware of everything you are doing – rather like, when you buy a new pair of shoes and first walk down the street in them, you are conscious of them with every step.

Once you have reached the stage of third or fourth study, playing a piece is like putting on well-worn shoes that have become part of you, and you are not conscious of wearing them at all. When you really know a piece well, you put the bow on the string and just play, without being aware of everything you are doing and without any feeling of having to make everything happen deliberately.

The Russian violinist David Oistrakh often had to give first performances because many composers wrote pieces specially for him. When he was rehearsing one day for a recital, one of the pieces was a new composition and this was the first time he had played it. Oistrakh had some difficulties with it, and at one point during the rehearsal he turned to the pianist and said, 'Sometimes I wish I could skip performances 1-9 and begin with the 10th!'

Often you simply have to learn something quite quickly and then immediately perform it. What can you do to make sure you are secure anyway?

One of the best things is to play through many times with the piano as a complete performance. Playing through as a serious performance to an audience – even if there are only one or two people listening – is of course the most helpful.

Another essential part of preparation is to practise performing the music rather than to 'practise practising'. In other words, while you may wish to continue doing building work (slow practice, practising in rhythms and so on) until close to the performance, it is essential to reduce this work if you can – the nearer to the performance you get – and replace it with playing 'as if in the heat of performance'. You do not have to wait until you are playing with the piano to do this.

Then, when you walk on to the stage to play, the performance feels like a continuation of what you were doing before. If the first time you play 'with heat and heart' is when you are in front of the audience, everything may feel so different that you are perpetually distracted.[1]

Not setting an ultimate deadline

Many people unconsciously give themselves a time limit within which they feel they must be able to master a piece. Then, when the deadline passes or they reach a certain age or stage – and still they cannot play it, or still cannot play that type of piece – they decide that it is not for them.

A classic analogy illustrates the importance of always carrying on and never giving up: in a game of baseball the bowler throws the ball at you, after three strikes you are out, and you are called out by the umpire; but in any field of learning like playing the violin you are the bowler, the batsman, and the umpire all at the same time. You can bowl yourself as many balls as you like, and try to hit them as many times as you like, and the only person who can call you out is yourself.

Setting a deadline and then giving up is like calling yourself out. It is like saying to yourself: 'You've had your chance, you didn't make it, so now forget it.'

The Russian violinist Vadim Brodsky tells of how he won a special commendation at the Tchaikovsky Competition for his performance of Paganini *Caprice* no. 1:

> No matter how much natural ability one may have, technical mastery can only be achieved through very hard work. I remember at the Tchaikovsky Competition I was commended for my performance of the Caprice No. 1 by Paganini, which involves coordinating *ricochet*-bowings with complex movements of the left hand. At one time this was a great problem for me, but I was the only one who knew I had been working on it for 13 years. After all, nobody really cares how long a violinist has worked on a piece. The only thing that is important is whether or not the piece had been mastered!"[2]

1 Similarly, when you first play a piece with the piano it is sensible to play from the music even if you already know the violin part from memory. Playing with the piano can easily be distracting at first, and there may be many places that you discover you now have to play differently. Then once you are used to playing with the piano from the music, rehearse with the piano from memory.

2 Samuel Applebaum and Henry Roth: *The way they play*, Vol. 10 (New Jersey 1981), 114.

Daily record

Everybody should work in whatever way suits them best. You can be the type who does all their practice more or less non-stop, i.e. it may take you only five hours to practise for four hours; or you may be more like Nathan Milstein, who said that you should do a little bit of practice in the morning, a little bit in the afternoon, a little bit in the evening, and a little bit before you go to bed.[1]

One way to motivate yourself to keep up regular practise is to keep a daily record of the times you practise. Enter these times in your day-to-day diary, or keep a separate practice-diary. For example:

3.55 – twenty minutes   7.00 – one hour

4.30 – thirty minutes   9.00 – fifty-five minutes

Use a stop-watch. Stop the timer when you stop playing to answer the telephone or make a cup of tea. Start it only just before you put the bow back on the string and actually begin to play again. Of course, if you stop playing and spend time looking at the music, working out structure, or whatever, this is as much 'practice' as bow-on-the-string work, so you do not have to turn the stop-watch off for that.

The importance of making mistakes

There is a famous story about the great inventor Thomas Edison, who carried out over twelve thousand experiments before he succeeded in creating the first electric light bulb.

After about five thousand experiments Edison was interviewed by a journalist who said, 'Mr Edison, everyone else seems to think that electric light cannot work, and you have failed 5,000 times. When are you going to admit it and give up?'

Apparently Edison answered: 'You don't know how the world works, young man. I haven't 'failed' five thousand times. I have successfully identified five thousand ways in which it does not work, so I am five thousand steps closer to finding out how it does work.'

Next time you play a note out of tune, or miss a shift, or realise that your playing lacks expression or that your vibrato is too slow, do not despair. Instead, rejoice that you have found yet another way not to do it.

The crucial thing is not to repeat something that actually you already know does not work. Thomas Edison would never have got anywhere if he had simply repeated the same experiment over and over again, hoping for a different result each time.[2]

Paying the price

I often remember a telephone call I had with Dorothy DeLay in which I mentioned that I say to my students, and tell myself, that you can aim as high as you like – that there is no limit to how well you can aim to play in the end, or how ambitious you are in your musical career plans – but that you must be prepared to pay the price, i.e. all the hard work, sacrifice, tears and frustration that it takes to get to that high point that you set yourself to achieve; and that the higher you aim, the higher the price.

She agreed, and said, "When a student says that a passage or a piece is 'difficult', I often say to them: 'It's not 'difficult' – it's time-consuming!'"

[1] Studies in concentration skills show that concentration is at a peak at the beginning of a learning session, and again just before the end, with a dip in the middle.

This means that if you practise for one hour without a break, you have two periods of peak concentration. If you divide that hour into two half-hours, with a short break in between, you will have four periods of peak concentration.

[2] See the margin note on page xvii.

General index

Index *of musical examples*

341

Basics

by Simon Fischer

The most comprehensive training compendium available to today's violinist. As well as presenting a wealth of original material, *Basics* also features ideas and principles traditionally associated with the great violinists, many of which have never before been written down.

Basics is a collection of practice methods and exercises, and belongs on the music stand, not on the bookshelf. It can be used by players of all standards, from concert violinists to students. Much of the material is also suitable for teaching elementary players.

Each exercise is designed to achieve the maximum possible result in the least possible time. Some are very short and need to be done only once or twice to explore a particular aspect of technique, whilst others can be returned to regularly.

Basics is not a book to play through from cover to cover (though, for easy reference, the exercises are numbered sequentially throughout). Everybody's needs are different, and there is little point in practising anything that does not need to be practised.

The book is invaluable, however, in its presentation of the most effective technical work in a single volume, making it possible to work directly on any aspect of technique that needs attention. By focusing on a single element at a time, each exercise is designed to achieve an immediately tangible and sustainable result in the shortest possible time.

As Simon Fischer himself says: "The same basic technical exercises can be used by players at all levels because most of the technical issues remain the same." – *Basics* is intended to be the violinist's companion for life: from the early stages right up to professional concert standard.

Available from all good music shops and *editionpeters.com*

Practice

by Simon Fischer

250 step-by-step practice methods for the violin

This essential follow-up guide extends the principles presented in *Basics* and applies them more fully to the violin repertoire. *Practice* offers an integrated resource which provides problem-solving guidance for the most awkward passages a violinist is likely to encounter.

The music examples in *Practice*, drawn from the standard solo violin repertoire, illustrate typical musical and technical demands that arise during the normal course of playing. By learning how to practise one passage, you learn how to practise other passages of the same type.

With more than 750 music examples (chosen from over 100 works) and over 100 photographs, *Practice* is packed with ideas and information to help you get the very most out of every minute that you practise.

- Some of the practice methods are ways of solving problems.

- Some are ways of finding out what the problems actually are. So often we know that something is not quite right, but we do not know why.

- Some are ways of trying to cause yourself problems, so that afterwards what you actually have to do feels easier.

- Some practice methods build and improve technique at the same time as making a specific passage easier to play. Then all other passages of that type take less time to learn because they feel easier to play in the first place.

Practice is intended just as much for the teacher as for the player. It offers a wide range of answers to the musical and technical problems that students typically present, and adds to any teacher's 'library' of practice methods that they pass on to their students.

Available from all good music shops and *editionpeters.com*

Scales

by Simon Fischer

Scales and
scale studies
for the violin

At last a book that provides not only a complete set of scales and arpeggios across two, three and four octaves in many variations – but also the necessary tools to master them. *Scales* is a novel and instructive publication that is destined to set the standard for years to come.

This is a scale book of unprecedented scope. Simon Fischer has developed an entirely new method in which, using the traditional ways of practising scales only as a point of departure, he focuses on numerous often-neglected aspects of the violinist's technique. For every element there are exercises that sensitise the ear, stimulate the mind and build the playing apparatus of the violinist.

The many outstanding features of this book include:

- how to structure intonation around perfect intervals and leading notes
- a new approach to learning how to time shifts
- extensive notation for preparing and holding down fingers
- two-octave scales and arpeggios on one string
- new sequences for single-finger scales
- one-, two-, three- and four-octave scales and arpeggios

Many well-known Fischer classics are incorporated, including practice methods for intonation, smooth bowing, string crossing, fast fingers, fourth-finger extensions and placing fingers in blocks. The innovative and wide-ranging material in *Scales* keeps the player turning the pages, discovering yet more exciting ways to approach scales. The wealth of thought-provoking exercises encourages violinists to re-evaluate their practice – developing the playing skills of violinists at all levels from intermediate to professional.

Available from all good music shops and *editionpeters.com*